LEFT HOOKS, RIGHT CROSSES

A DECADE OF

☆ POLITICAL WRITING ☆

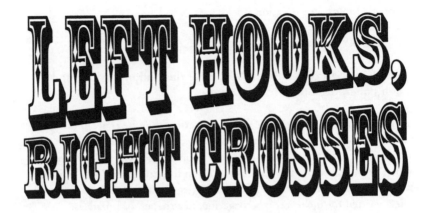

LEFT HOOKS, RIGHT CROSSES

A DECADE OF ☆ POLITICAL WRITING ☆

EDITED BY

CHRISTOPHER
CALDWELL

CHRISTOPHER
HITCHENS

Thunder's Mouth Press / Nation Books
New York

Published by
Thunder's Mouth Press/Nation Books
161 William St., 16th Floor
New York, NY 10038

Nation Books is a co-publishing venture of the Nation Institute and
Avalon Publishing Group Incorporated.

Library of Congress Cataloging-in-Publication Data

Left hooks, right crosses: a decade of political writing / edited by Christopher
Hitchens and Christopher Caldwell.
    p. cm.
  ISBN 1-56025-409-2
    1. United States—Politics and government—1889–1993. 2. United
States—Politics and government—1993–2001. I. Hitchens, Christopher. II.
Caldwell, Christopher.

E881 .L437 2002
973.929—dc21   2002071982

9 8 7 6 5 4 3 2 1

Book design by Paul Paddock

Printed in the United States of America
Distributed by Publishers Group West

★ LEFT HOOKS ★

★ RIGHT CROSSES ★

Christopher Hitchens:

For the late I.F. Stone, and in memory of his spirited attempt at "Jeffersonian Marxism."

Christopher Caldwell:

To the writers and editors of the American Spectator *who, until they answered Bill Clinton's hubris with their own, put out the best monthly magazine in the United States.*

LEFT HOOKS, RIGHT CROSSES

A DECADE OF

☆ POLITICAL WRITING ☆

LEFT HOOKS

★ INTRODUCTION ★

Christopher Caldwell

In some places, the terms "left" and "right" have retained all their Cold War meaning. An evangelical drill sergeant in Texas who votes Republican and a gay social worker in San Francisco who votes Green can fairly be said to occupy opposite ideological poles. But since September 11, 2001, the two of them should also realize that they are interchangeable American archetypes in the eyes of all their country's enemies, and many of its friends.

Among polemicists, if we may apply that word to those who write about politics in a non-boring way, the meaning of "left" and "right" has been in flux for over a decade. The "left-wing" editor of this collection (Christopher Hitchens) favored the bombing of Serbia and the removal of President Clinton while the "right-wing" editor (me) did not. A few of the writers I've chosen for the right-wing half of this book (Kenneth Anderson, Charles Paul Freund, Mark Lilla, and Jonathan Rauch, in particular) might be shocked, even embarrassed, to be so labeled. Maybe some of Mr. Hitchens's lefties are similarly mortified.

Yet we all know the left-right distinction remains meaningful, even when attempts to pin it down are marked by partisanship and self-justification. Just after the Berlin Wall fell, the Italian philosopher Norberto Bobbio wrote that the left was alive, kicking, and distinguished from the right by its hunger for equality. Bobbio neglected to credit the right with any positive political ideals of its own, but his model gets us halfway there. A good working definition might be this: Rightism is the belief that liberté, leftism that égalité, forms the basis for fraternité most in harmony with human nature. To the extent that the left believes in human nature.

The United States is probably the place of maximum confusion about the meaning of right and left just now. That's due not only to the September 11 attacks but also to the politics on which discussions of left and right get overlaid. The Democratic party—the party of the white social elite and of Sun King centralism—persists in calling itself a "left." The Republican party—which stands for razing time-honored institutions, from the Wal-Mart-threatened corner shop to the public school system—calls itself a "right."

The arrival of Bill Clinton further discomfited writers on both sides. What looked like the hot style of right-wing polemic at the start of the 1990s—a wowie-kazowie reporting modeled on Tom Wolfe and aimed at the Guy on the Shuttle, with his rictus of simulated amusement and his metronomic nod—lost standing as the Baby Boom left changed from a picturesque subculture into a Ruling Class. "Those crazy kids!" was a fine way to describe Altamont. It was inadequate for describing a clique that sought early on (starting with the reinstallation of a left-wing dictatorship in Haiti) to use the world's mightiest military for recreational and self-expressive ends.

The left's problems, though, have been graver. Even as they snuggle up to authority and spawn regulation, the most privileged leftist writers continue to howl that they're being ripped off by their betters. They won't take yes for an answer. When Democrats held the presidency, both houses of Congress, Hollywood, the entire print media, every nook and cranny of academia, and much of the corporate hierarchy, they posed as tribunes of the disempowered. As they were spearheading political correctness, they accused the other side of McCarthyism. As Bill Clinton was carrying 13 of the 17 richest congressional districts in the country, they stoked fears of a Republican plutocracy. To feel threatened, however irrationally, is to lack both humor and tolerance. These twin failings may help explain why Democrats no longer hold the presidency, both houses of Congress, or the entire print media.

There are, however, people on the left who maintain either a sense of humor or a sense of proportion, or (as rarely as in any walk of life) both. I'm grateful to Mr. Hitchens for flushing them out. The best of the pieces he has chosen (and I don't think this is my conservatism talking) tend to be those that police the left, whether against its excesses or its timidity.

We can distrust the Bobbio-esque oversimplifications in Philip Green's defense of liberalism (liberals are believers in democracy, Green claims, while conservatives are its opponents). But we should admire his willingness to inform the left that, while the state may be a bastard, it's their bastard. In "Martyrs and False Populists" Adolph Reed Jr. worries about an embourgeoise left that can reconcile its countercultural self-image with its privileged class position only by spouting anti-establishment cant. (I simplify.) He urges his comrades not to smash the state, "but to seize it and direct it to democratic and egalitarian purposes."

Reed's review of Murray and Herrnstein's *The Bell Curve*, also reprinted here, is an example of what the left can still accomplish when it acts like a left. Most leftists stalwartly refused to address the book's arguments even as it climbed the bestseller lists, contenting themselves with solipsistic protestations of moral purity. In this, they looked not principled but cowardly. Reed was one of only two writers with the guts to assail the book rigorously on the left's grounds. (The other was Charles Lane, himself not a leftist, in a masterpiece of scholarly delving in the *New York Review of Books*.)

Benjamin DeMott's attack on the newest communitarian canard is a treasure. For DeMott, "new scams of civility" are a way of refocusing attention from top-dog malfeasance to bottom-dog etiquette. In the Clinton era, such tactics got used more against the right than against the left. But every thinking person ought to heed DeMott's central warning—that in a propagandistic age, the easiest way to strip a country of its rights may be to embarrass its citizens into renouncing them voluntarily.

That "smoke-free environment" of yours is going to cost you a steep price in liberty.

Of all writers on the left today, Thomas Frank may be the one least duped by the kind of emotive hocus-pocus DeMott describes. Frank and his fellow contributors to the Chicago-based *Baffler* magazine came up with the most viable new left-wing politics of the Clinton era, a kind of Prairie populism flexible enough to address power relations in the global economy. Its major achievement thus far has been its unmasking of the liberal Yuppie, its insistence that you don't get a bye from the class war just because you don't wear a tie to work.

Marshall Berman's primer on *The Communist Manifesto* attempts to rescue Marx wholesale, not piecemeal. Berman, of course, understands that the game was hardly worth the Gulag. He nonetheless gives the first convincing account I've ever read of how an early reading of Marx could (and perhaps should) inflect a man's thinking on everything for the rest of his days. Since no description can do it justice, let me just say I'm glad I didn't read Berman's essay at fifteen. They might have had me.

Arundhati Roy's essay on India's nuclear bomb is marked by a glorious prose style (less inevitable than one might think when novelists write about public matters), deployed to ends both descriptive ("carrying the cancerous carcasses of our children in our arms") and polemical ("Coke is Western culture, but the nuclear bomb is an old Indian tradition?"). It amply compensates the reader for Roy's too-frequent focus on her own travails, and a good thing, too, for looming over such petty quotidian vanities as nuclear annihilation is always the cosmic enormity of Ms. Roy's recently won Booker Prize.

I also liked the reporting here. Leaving aside a disastrous Republican sally in the Clinton years, "investigative" reporting has been so much a province of the left that the left-wing exposé has become an establishment genre. If you were to strew a few diamond-brooch and mink-stole ads through the text of Anne-Marie Cusac's report on prison technology or Ruth Conniff's on Colombian death squads, you could think you were reading the *New York Times Magazine*. Non-leftists might disagree with Conniff's piece but their blood would hardly boil over it nowadays.

That points to a waning conviction—on left and right—that Third World peasants ought to be awarded the role of Egg in the global ideological omelet.

Who can rue the change? The terms left and right are unlikely to lose their descriptive force, in the coming years. But if they grow a little bit less useful, we'll probably be lucky.

★ HURT FEELINGS AND ★ FREE SPEECH

Nat Hentoff

FROM *THE PROGRESSIVE*, FEBRUARY 1992

The saddest I have ever seen Mario Cuomo was during his first run for governor of New York. In the Democratic primary, he was way behind Ed Koch, the swaggering mayor of the city of New York. I asked Cuomo one morning what he would do if he lost.

There was a long pause, a long sigh, and he said, "I'll tell you one thing I don't want to do, and that's go back to practicing the kind of law that makes rich people get richer."

He had to support a family, but maybe he could do that, he speculated, in some form of public-interest law. Instead, as every television viewer knows, Cuomo has stayed in public office.

The dream of a career in public-interest law is shared by many young lawyers and would-be lawyers, but most wind up in law-for-fees firms, large and small, and maybe do a touch of *pro bono* work every year. Justice William Brennan has told me a number of times how disappointed he is when bright young lawyers choose careers that will be of no relevance to the millions of marginal Americans who can't pay doctors' bills, let alone afford a lawyer.

So, it seemed four years ago, when a new law school opened in Washington, D.C., that Brennan and Cuomo might have been greatly pleased, for this was a place whose reason for being was public-interest law. The District of Columbia School of Law is the only publicly funded law school in the nation's capital, and among its priorities is encouraging more members of minority groups—and more women—to take up the law. It also enrolls older students and the poor; in its clinical programs, the school and its students represent people without resources who need help.

In a letter to prospective applicants, the school declares: "We at DCSL believe that public service is the best and highest use of educated minds."

Among the faculty, two professors are models of how to practice public-interest law. Bob Catz has worked with the Migrant Legal Action Program and the Legal Aid Society of Omaha and does appellate work in the Federal courts, including the Supreme Court. In 1990, he deinstitutionalized patients at the Forest Haven Facility for the Mentally Ill in Laurel, Maryland.

Tom Mack has worked in legal-service offices in Chicago and San Francisco and for the Office of Economic Opportunity. In 1990, he represented ten inmates at Lorton Reformatory who charged they had been severely beaten by guards. This kind of case is exceedingly difficult to win—the word of guards against the word of convicted criminals. Mack won a $175,000 judgment.

Yet Bob Catz and Tom Mack have become charged at their own law school with disloyalty, insensitivity, political incorrectness, and behavior unfit for a faculty member at a public-interest school. Their dean, William Robinson, told me that Catz and Mack must somehow redeem themselves if they are ever again to have the trust of the majority of the faculty and the student body.

What crime, what breach of ethics, did Catz and Mack commit? They chose to defend a very unpopular client on the grounds that he had the First Amendment right to publish his ideas—although both of them disagreed with what he wrote.

The client was Tim Maguire, then a senior at another school, the

Georgetown Law Center, who had written an article for the student-run *Georgetown Law Weekly*. Titled "Admissions Apartheid," the article asserted that "in every area and at every level of post-secondary education, the achievements of black applicants to *this* law school (and those accepted) are far inferior to those of whites." In college, Maguire wrote, black students had lower grade-point averages, and their Law School Admissions Test scores were much lower than those of whites applying to the law school.

Maguire got his information during the three months he had worked as a file clerk in the admissions office.

Black students at the Georgetown Law Center demanded that his degree—Maguire was a senior—be withdrawn. And the Black Law Students Association brought formal charges against him for violating confidentiality rules. That trial could have resulted in his being denied his degree.

Most of the black law students—and a good many whites—at the school did not want to argue with the accuracy of Maguire's findings. They insisted that it was a racist attack and that anyone defending it must be against affirmative action and must thereby be a racist.

For legal help, Maguire went to the Center for Individual Rights, a conservative group. No one on its small staff was sufficiently versed in the rules of legal evidence that apply to this kind of proceeding. So the Center asked various lawyers around the city to take on Maguire's case. As defense lawyers know, an unpopular client's attorney is usually associated—adversely—with that client's views. Nobody wanted to take Maguire's case.

Except Mack and Catz. They saw Maguire as a whistleblower (whether one agreed with the tune he was whistling or not) who was being penalized for exercising his First Amendment rights.

When word got out at the District of Columbia School of Law that two of their own professors were defending the guy who wrote that attack on affirmative action at the Georgetown Law Center, a majority of the faculty and students were outraged.

Mack and Catz were told they ought to drop this pariah of a client or they, too, would become pariahs. Moreover, they were accused of violating the D.C. Law School's mission to bring more racial and ethnic minorities into the practice of law. How could they defend an opponent of affirmative action while pretending to champion the admission of more minorities to their own school?

In an open letter, a student confronted the two professors with the almost capital crime of "making a politically incorrect statement."

Tom Mack told him and the other students that "the First Amendment and the rule of law" include "everything, not just what is politically correct."

In all of his public-interest work, Bob Catz told me, "This was the first time that I've had to worry about attacks from people around me."

The attacks continued. One student angrily told the two professors that the First Amendment they so prized "drove my family out of Alabama" because the Klu Klux Klan had had the First Amendment right to speak and demonstrate. He had never learned at the D.C. Law School that if the First Amendment had not been available to black protesters in the South, the demonstrations and marches that brought about the Civil Rights Act would have been crushed.

At an open meeting in the law school, a black professor walked out, and a black student said, "I don't question either of your right [sic] to go out and defend this man but when you stand in front of a classroom of 50 per cent black and minority students, I think that maybe you have to be sensitive about how that is going to impact that group of people. A professor at a place like DCLS had to be different."

There was an enthusiastic round of applause.

Catz and Mack kept trying to make the students—and, indeed, the faculty—understand that no law professor worth his students' attention can be so "different" that he checks the First Amendment at the door of any law school at which he works.

"There is great danger to us," Mack said at the open meeting, "when you don't defend the right to express views that are unpopular. The danger is to us, not to the Maguires of the world."

Also, the professors emphasized, if Georgetown succeeded in punishing

Maguire—while refusing to openly discuss its admissions policies, thereby shutting off debate on affirmative action—the rights of minorities throughout the country would suffer. People would ask what Georgetown was trying to hide. "Georgetown's reaction to this is all wrong," Mack said. "Ordinarily, what you do with dissent is you answer it, you don't punish it."

The professors also asked the students to reverse the facts. What if a student at another school had discovered—through access to the admissions records—that his or her law school had been discriminating against blacks? The very D.C. Law School students who were furious at Mack and Catz for their "disloyalty" would have vigorously supported a decision by Mack and Catz to defend *that* student.

As I followed the turmoil at the D.C. Law School, it was clear to me that something had been missing in the legal education of these future public-interest lawyers. Why didn't they understand the indivisibility of the First Amendment—that if it is not an effective defense for people and ideas they hate, they themselves will find it weakened when they need it.

I decided to talk to the dean of the law school. And there I found my answer to the hole in the soul of the D.C. School of Law. William Robinson, a graduate of Columbia University Law School, has a particularly distinguished record in civil rights law. A former director of the National Lawyers' Committee for Civil Rights Under Law, he was associate general counsel for the Equal Employment Opportunity Commission and first assistant counsel for the NAACP Legal Defense and Education Fund. In these roles, he has been involved in pivotal civil-rights legislation. And at the American Bar Association, Robinson has been chair of the influential Section on Individual Rights and Responsibilities. He is currently a member of the ABA Standing Committee on Lawyers' Public Service Responsibility.

Mack and Catz, Dean Robinson told me, are on "a kind of probation with some segments of the student body and with some faculty. Their relations with those people, I'd say, are damaged. It is not a formal probation, but I think it may take their doing some outstanding public-service legal work before they may, grudgingly, get back their standing here."

But, I said to Robinson, they were defending Maguire's First Amendment rights.

Well, he told me, "Civil liberties, while being within the pale, are not the focus here. Faculty members must keep in mind the hurt their actions will do to the community of the law school."

Hurt. Hurt feelings are to be a determining factor in how people learn to be lawyers in this school. Increasingly, at colleges and universities, students are being taught to see themselves as fragile.

At Stanford, when Alan Keyes, a black conservative, was debating Stanford law professor Tom Grey, architect of that university's code punishing offensive speech, Keyes said: "These codes punishing verbal harassment are patronizing and paternalistic. The 'protection' they promise is incapacitating. . . . The imputation is that there is some inherent genetic weakness—a black genetic weakness on my part. And that's why codes of conduct are needed to protect me. That is the most insulting, the most racist statement of all."

And at the D.C. Law School, students are encouraged to attack professors who have hurt their feelings by using the First Amendment that the students are not learning to use.

As for Tim Maguire, he received a reprimand for disclosing information he'd found in the admissions office, but the reprimand will not appear in his official transcript. And he did get his degree. He had two very good lawyers arranging the settlement.

★ COLOMBIA'S DIRTY ★ WAR, WASHINGTON'S DIRTY HANDS

Ruth Conniff

FROM *THE PROGRESSIVE*, MAY 1992

In a January 28 opinion piece in the *New York Times*, "COLOMBIAN BLOOD, U.S. GUNS," Jorge Gómez Lizarazo wrote that the United States is helping to finance a political war in Colombia and looking the other way while the Colombian military tortures and murders innocent civilians. On January 29, the author's secretary was dead.

At 6:30 p.m., hours after Colombian national radio broadcast Gómez's statements to the *Times*, Blanca Cecilia Valero de Durán stepped out of her office at the Committee on Human Rights in Barrancabermeja, Colombia, where she had worked for the past twelve years. As Valero walked to the curb to hail a taxi, a man who had been waiting outside the building jumped out and shot her in the side of the face.

The woman dropped to the ground, and the gunman approached to finish her off, firing another bullet into her head. Valero did not survive the short trip to the hospital. Witnesses saw the murderer run thirty or forty meters—past the local police station—to a motorcycle, and fumble with the ignition for a few moments before driving away. The police officers who usually patrol the area were nowhere to be found.

Valero was the third member of the human-rights office assassinated in the past year, and one in a long line of casualties of Colombia's "dirty war."

Shortly after Valero's murder, the army commander of Barrancaber-meja's Fifth Brigade told reporters that the human-rights office was a front for "subversives" engaged in a "tricky scheme" to discredit the military.

All over Colombia, the army, the police, and paramilitary soldiers trained and supported by the state are killing peasants, union leaders, progressive politicians, and people who speak out about the abuse of human rights. Amnesty International and human rights workers like Gómez and Valero have documented military involvement in thousands of murders.

Meanwhile, the United States Government has increased military funding to Colombia to $282 million over the next four years. In 1990, Colombia surpassed El Salvador as the hemisphere's top recipient of U.S. military aid.

U.S. officials say they must fund the Colombian military in order to fight the "war on drugs." But Colombians are not nearly so interested in narcotics. The Colombian Defense Ministry has made combating "insurgents" its first priority. In 1990, Colombian military officers stated flatly to a Congressional subcommittee that millions of dollars in U.S. "counter-narcotics" aid was, in fact, helping to fight political insurgency.

As a wave of violence engulfs the civilian population of Colombia, some members of Congress are increasingly worried that the U.S. Government shares responsibility for the slaughter.

One week after Valero's death, a small group of U.S. citizens traveled to Colombia on a good-will mission. A lawyer, a minister, an expert in co-ops and credit unions, a university student, and a journalist, we were by no means an official investigative team. What we saw and heard is readily evident to any observer.

On our trip we talked with some of the people who had been directly affected by the violence—former guerrillas, peasants, workers, and local politicians. They told us a story that has very little to do with narcotics or insurgency. Rather, it is the story of an economic war—a war that places the United States squarely in the camp of a profoundly anti-democratic elite, a corrupt military, and, ironically, the drug lords themselves.

On the losing end is the vast majority of Colombians, the poor workers and peasants, who are struggling for basic survival and who have suffered through a terrible repression. They told us their stories in the frank hope that the rest of the world would act to stop the violence.

We got off the plane in Apartadó, dazed for a moment by the Caribbean sun. Miles of green banana plantations surrounded the airport. The mayor of Apartadó walked onto the runway to meet us, applauding, the bright light glinting off his sunglasses. Behind him, a group of men in shirtsleeves followed, carrying machine guns.

Everywhere you look in Colombia there are guns. Soldiers stand by the side of the road, keeping an eye on the homeless squatters camped all over the countryside. Policemen and members of DAS, the Colombian secret service, patrol the streets with heavy combat weapons; armored police vehicles roll through downtown Bogotá. Murder is the leading cause of death here. Counting massacres, homicides, tortures, and forced disappearances, Colombia is the most violent nation on Earth.

One year ago, the former mayor of Apartadó was killed by her own bodyguards. Like the current mayor, she was a member of the Patriotic Union, or UP, a popular third party, whose leaders have been assassinated in localities throughout Colombia. The current mayor has added a few people he knows to the state-supplied protective service that follows him everywhere, to diminish the chances that he will be shot in the back.

Like other areas of Colombia where violence has reached epidemic proportions, the Urabá region around Apartaó contains a wealth of natural resources alongside extreme poverty and neglect. Urabá is the major banana-producing region of Colombia (narcotics do not grow in this humid, coastal climate), but it is nearly impossible to come by a banana in Apartadó. A few wealthy landlords, most of whom live in Miami, own the vast plantations. They send their bananas abroad—primarily to the United States.

We drove down the main street of Apartadó—a dirt road along a strip of tin-roofed buildings. Most local inhabitants do without electricity, running water, and other basic resources. In this atmosphere of deprivation, peasant cooperatives and labor unions have formed to try to improve the generally miserable living conditions of the people.

The national government has responded to local protests and organizing efforts by declaring the region a hotbed of subversion and sending in troops. In 1988, military and paramilitary soldiers massacred twenty-two union leaders on a banana plantation nearby.

We stayed in the guest house of a cardboard-box factory in Apartadó. Outside, under a roof of palm fronds, the mayor and other local leaders talked to us about the town, while the omnipresent bodyguards sat inside, watching soccer on TV.

"I came to Apartadó five years ago, a militant member of the Patriotic Union," said Mayor José Antonio López. "I thought that in Apartadó there were many things that needed to be done. I wanted to be mayor. I fought for that. It cost me a lot. For example, the only brother I had was killed during the electoral campaign, without being a militant of any political party. He didn't even live in this region. He came to visit one day. He got here in the morning and they killed him that night, while he was sitting in a tavern, waiting for me."

The mayor's voice broke and tears came into his eyes as he spoke; he stopped to recover his composure and went on. "But the moment arrives when you cannot turn back. Although there are things that try to stop you . . . for instance my family, my mother, my father, who have reached a certain age, and who don't have another son. But the moment comes when you are not capable of going backwards, and you continue on."

Today, the violence continues. Peasant co-op leaders told us about being pulled out of their homes in the early morning by uniformed men who had disguised themselves by painting their faces black. Some people were shot. Others disappeared. A few days before we came, a military plane strafed a rural school building, locals said, killing a three-year-old girl. "What they said in the papers, and the information that the rest of the country received, was that they bombed a place where the guerrillas were meeting," said a farmer, who witnessed the bombing from a nearby field. "But it was just us, the peasants. There were no guerrillas. We are just simple farmers."

Guerrillas have gained a foothold in Urabá, and over the years, skirmishes between the guerrillas and the military have claimed hundreds of lives. The people who pay most dearly for this are civilians, caught in the middle of a war zone.

Apartadó is lucky. Its government has worked out a cease-fire between the guerrillas in the area and the military. The mayor and the bishop of Apartadó worked together to achieve this official peace. "We went into the mountains to talk to the guerrillas, and we offered them jobs on the banana plantations," Bishop Isaias Duarte explains. "The social injustices that gave rise to the guerrilla movement have improved. Today there is more social justice. The difference that this mayor's administration has made is very positive."

But Apartadó's problems are far from over. More guerrillas have been assassinated during the cease-fire than died in combat before the official peace, the mayor says. And the number of civilians killed outside of battle has always dwarfed the number killed as a result of outright fighting between the guerrillas and the military.

"This is a very critical moment," says Harrison Martinez, a former guerrilla who had his hand blown off by a grenade during the years of armed conflict. "The peace process must be accepted as a necessity for the country as a whole, not for us, the guerrillas. We were part of the violence here. But there are other factors in the violence that will not be resolved over a table—social factors. Transforming the struggle is not easy. I believe that the social problems are worse than ever."

Bouncing over unpaved roads in a jeep, through enormous potholes and small rivers of mud, past rows of tin and plywood shacks, we toured the region around Apartadó. Everywhere, groups of peasants camped on the outskirts of banana plantations, with platoons of machine-gun-toting soldiers watching nearby. The squatters, with the help of the local government, hope to negotiate to buy a piece of property from the plantation owners. If they win, they'll build their shacks and set up a town.

Our jeep stopped on the outskirts of Apartadó, where members of a successful squatters' settlement had built a school. Rows of shacks and a few new cement buildings dotted what was recently a field. Under a large red tent, with the Coca-Cola logo scrawled across it in familiar white letters, schoolchildren in uniforms were standing in line, waiting to greet us. We were late, and they must have been there for more than an hour. They presented us with an elaborate fruit-and-flower arrangement, and then we listened to speeches from members of the community. Two representatives from the Coca-Cola Company spoke last, looking incongruous in their suits and ties against the background of dust and squalor. (They were invited, someone from the town explained later, on account of the tent, which Coke provides free on special occasions.)

"We used to think that the government should take care of our problems," one Coke man said. "We were waiting for someone else to come and give us everything. But now we realize that through privatization and the work of the people of this community, we can provide for ourselves."

Privatization for people in this area meant building their own sewer system. Government-regulated services like electricity, paved roads, and basic sanitation are virtually unheard of around Apartadó and other areas distant from the capital. So here the people showed us how they had learned to mix cement and cast the cylindrical pipes which lay beside the Coca-Cola tent.

It was a startling illustration of a policy promoted by the Reagan and Bush Administrations all over the developing world. Under President Cesar Gaviria, Colombia is pursuing "economic openness"—encouraging foreign investment and, at the behest of the United States and the World Bank, reducing Government spending on the country's infrastructure. Thus, for the rural poor, the situation promises to get worse.

Despite the dogged optimism of the people, there is little chance that the efforts of the peasant co-ops and community-action groups can make up for a missing infrastructure. Cooperatives are continually running out of capital to complete their projects. The community we visited, for instance, may or may not ever get its sewer pipes into the ground. Much depends on banks, which consider such projects a poor investment risk. Meanwhile, at the new school, 1,000 students have already signed up for spaces at the 100 desks.

The face Colombia presents to the outside world is quite different from the one apparent to natives, and to anyone who takes the time to travel through the countryside.

"The economic situation is not that desperate here," said one U.S. official who declined to be named. "The guerrillas' ideology is more political than economic. They've never been able to mount an economically based uprising."

But in fact, although the State Department and the World Bank issue cheerful reports about Colombia's growing economy and relatively high gross national product, 40 percent of Colombia's thirty-three million citizens live in "absolute poverty" and 18 percent in "absolute misery," according to the National Administrative Bureau of Statistics. The top 3 percent of Colombia's landed elite own 71.3 percent of arable land, while 57 percent of the poorest farmers subsist on 2.8 percent, the Washington Office on Latin America reports.

Double-speak about the political and economic situation in Colombia abounds. "Economic reforms" and the transition to a "freer" economy mean more abandonment and deprivation for the poor. By the same token, constitutional reform has accompanied more repression.

As far as the State Department is concerned, Colombia has a "strong, decades-old democratic system." A new, reform-minded constitution represents great progress in the protection of human rights, says a State Department report dated March 1992.

Colombians disagree. "In reality, the first three chapters of our constitution exactly describe human rights, the rights of the individual, and of the family," says Alfredo Vasquez Carrizosa, a member of the constituent assembly that drew up the new constitution. "All of this is beautiful—it is a symphony of human rights. But none of it applies."

A system of military impunity—expanded under the new constitution to include police officers—protects state security forces from retribution for human-rights abuses.

"The new constitution has not stopped the official repression, massacres, and official violence," says the Reverend Javier Giraldo, director of *Justicia y Paz*, a Christian human-rights group. "Repression has become more clandestine. What is happening now is that the government simply avoids responsibility."

One way the government avoids responsibility for military violence, says Father Giraldo, is to blame it on paramilitary forces—private armies operated by wealthy landowners and drug lords. But evidence collected by *Justicia y Paz* and other human-rights groups indicates that the army and the paramilitaries operate together.

"In this way," says Father Giraldo, "a democratic discourse accompanies a bloodbath."

Shortly after Blanca Valero's murder, on February 16, members of the Comando Ariel Otero paramilitary group distributed leaflets to the human-rights office and around town declaring: "We denounce and demand of the office of the attorney general of the nation that it initiate an investigation of the office of human rights and the office of the attorney general in Barrancabermeja, since they are run by members of the [guerrilla group] E.L.N. If this investigation is not undertaken, we will exterminate those guerrillas and we will take justice into our own hands."

Within days, Fifth Brigade Commander Roberto Emilio Cifuentes told the newspaper *Vanguardia Liberal*, "The office of human rights, naively or perhaps some of its members with ill intentions, has been used by the subversives to carry out some of their forms of struggle that are based on slander. I state this because it is all a setup that has no support. Some of those people are heedlessly echoing a tricky scheme in an effort to discredit the [military] institution."

Members of the army brigade do not openly acknowledge any

association with the paramilitary. But the two groups have cooperated in several attacks on peasants and oil workers in Barrancabermeja, according to investigations by the human-rights office. These attacks, says Gómez, together with government repression, protect the economic interests of wealthy landowners.

A recent increase in violence in Barrancabermeja coincides with the discovery of a vast new oil field in the area. Alynne Romo, a member of the steering committee of the Colombian Human Rights Network in the United States, believes that the United States, too, has a particular interest in ignoring human-rights abuses and supporting repression in Barrancabermeja: "You don't want the largest oil field in the Western Hemisphere in the hands of leftists," says Romo. "The economic question is the most important thing. It's not that we want to send the military down to Colombia and establish a military hegemony. It's an economic hegemony."

There is ample evidence that U.S. military aid earmarked for the war on drugs is in fact going to support a different sort of war in Colombia.

One particularly embarrassing example of this appears in a 1990 report by the House Government Operations Committee. Colombian Army Chief-of-Staff General Luis Eduardo Roca and Army General José Nelson Mejia, thanking members of Congress for $40.3 million in U.S. anti-narcotics aid, reported that $38.5 million of the aid would be used in "Operation Tri-Color," a program aimed at fighting guerrillas in the northeast part of the country, where narcotics are not grown or processed.

"When asked by the subcommittee staff to explain how a major military operation in an area not known for its narcotics production could advance the anti-narcotics goals of either country, the military representatives stated that *if processing facilities were located* during the operation, they would be destroyed," the report said [emphasis added].

It would not occur to the Colombian military officials that such a transparent alibi might bother subcommittee members. Colombians have never pretended to be serious about the war on drugs. After all, the

United States has continued to pour millions into that war despite the fact that, by all available measures, the effort has failed. Narcotics production in South America actually increased by 28 per cent in 1990, after the drug war reached a peak. And U.S. officials have never been sticklers about how anti-narcotics aid is used. In fiscal 1990, the Colombian Air Force received the largest share of U.S. military aid, much of it for eight Cessna A-37B "Dragonfly" airplanes, according to the Washington Office on Latin America. "The A-37B is known in armaments literature as a 'Counter-insurgency (COIN) aircraft,' " WOLA reports. "And one SouthCom [*sic*] official told WOLA that the Dragonfly is 'not a counter-narcotics capable aircraft.' " Colombian human-rights groups report that the Dragonfly has, on several occasions, bombed civilians.

Nor has the United States officially condemned the Colombian military's attacks on civilians. Despite denunciations by such groups as Amnesty International and numerous church and human-rights groups within Colombia, diplomats and embassy officials deny the military has been heavily involved in human-rights abuses.

"The military is not a bad institution," said one U.S. official who declined to be named. "It has a few bad apples, but overall it is a democratic institution."

To justify Washington's support for political violence in Latin America, U.S. officials have developed what is known as the "narco-guerrilla theory." They claim that killing guerrillas is a necessary part of the "war on drugs" because the guerrillas are in league with the drug traffickers.

"You've got a full-scale insurgency going on here," said Bob Danze, press attache at the U.S. embassy in Bogotá. "And a lot of these guerrillas are heavily involved in the narcotics trade."

In Colombia, this theory is particularly weak. The drug lords, who own vast tracts of land in rural Colombia, have long been affiliated with the political Right. The cartels run paramilitary death squads, which attack peasants struggling for land reform, and conduct "social cleansing" campaigns, killing prostitutes, homosexuals, and street children.

After the massacre of twenty-two union leaders in Apartadó, the attorney general's office discovered that the army major who commanded the region's military-intelligence squad had hired the Medellin cartel's paramilitary soldiers to make the hit. The case was one of the first official investigations to begin to unravel the complicity between the Colombian military, the paramilitary squads, and the drug lords.

"I can testify to the existence of alliances between members of the armed forces and industry and narcotics traffickers to construct and finance groups called 'black hand' or 'death squads,' " ex-intelligence officer Ricardo Gómez Mazuera declared to the assistant attorney general of Colombia. Officer Gómez reported that police officers and army personnel made up a group which, in 1986, carried out a nocturnal massacre of homosexuals in Tulua and threw the bodies in the Cauca River.

To finance the operations of the "black hand," a police major named Suárez received money from industrialists and drug traffickers in the valley, Gómez said. "One day in June or July of 1987, I myself accompanied him, in a white Toyota, to the company 'Green Taxis' in Bogotá . . . and there he received twenty-five million from the hands of Mr. Gustavo Gaviria Riveros, a narcotics trafficker in league with Pablo Escobar."

Bodies thrown in the Cauca River, which flows through southwest Colombia, have transformed the waterway into an open grave, human-rights workers say.

"I don't know how many bodies I saw float down the river during the [year] I helped retrieve them," a witness told *Justicia y Paz*. "But I could estimate the number at about seventy."

Fishermen and residents of the Cauca River Valley are afraid to pull out the corpses that float by, since to do so is to invite persecution and assassination. So the bodies—usually mutilated beyond ready recognition—slide downstream, occasionally washing ashore to lie untouched by anyone but the official investigators who may come through every few months.

One of the corpses dragged from the river was the Reverend Tiberio Fernández Mafla, who disappeared in the region called Trujillo, in the southwest corner of Colombia, on April 17, 1990. Photographs taken when the body was found a week later show a human form missing its head and forearms, lying in the mud at the feet of an investigator.

Father Fernández had helped organize several cooperatives, declaring that part of the mission of his parish was to raise the standard of living of its people. In 1990, he participated in a large protest march, intended to draw the government's attention to the extreme neglect of its rural population.

The government responded to the protest in Trujillo by sending in troops. There followed a series of disappearances, murders, and tortures, terrorizing the peasants in the area.

Father Fernandez denounced the murders from his pulpit and called for the return of the disappeared. The local military commander announced that the priest was a dangerous subversive and a guerrilla sympathizer. Shortly thereafter, Father Fernandez disappeared.

On Monday, April 23, 1990, a fisherman dragged the priest's body out of the Cauca River. A few days later the man who recovered the body was also assassinated. Headless, sliced open lengthwise, and castrated, Father Fernandez was identified by members of his family with the aid of x-rays which showed bone fractures he had suffered in a car accident earlier in his life.

Witnesses who testified before human-rights groups and the attorney general have no doubt that the military was responsible for Father Fernández's murder. Daniel Arcila was one such witness. He took part in the tortures and assassinations carried out by military personnel in the area around Trujillo, he said.

Arcila helped round up a group of peasants and brought them to "La Granja," a farm belonging to a drug trafficker in the area, he testified. There, Army Major Aliro Antonio Urueña Jaramillo and a paramilitary officer called "el tío" had breakfast together and then tortured the victims:

"The Army major sprayed them in the face with pressurized water from a hose," Arcila testified. "He pried off their fingernails with a pocketknife, he cut off pieces of the bottoms of their feet with a nail clipper, he poured salt in their cuts, then, with a gasoline flame-thrower he burned them on different parts of their bodies and their flesh cracked and the skin peeled off; he pointed the flame thrower at the genital area, he cut off their penises and testicles and put them in their mouths, and finally quartered them with a chainsaw.

"I transported the bodies of the people that were tortured and killed. . . . I had to do it because otherwise I was a dead man. . . . They got a truck to take the eleven corpses to the river."

The attorney general opened an investigation of the crimes committed in Trujillo, and brought five suspects before a judge in a court of public order—two paramilitaries, two narcotics traffickers on whose properties the tortures and murders took place, and Major Alirio Antonio Urueña Jaramillo.

The judge threw out Arcila's testimony, on grounds that he was mentally incompetent, over the objections of expert medical testimony called by the attorney general. Then the DAS guards assigned to protect Arcila left him to his own devices. On May 5, 1991, while Arcila was visiting his family in Trujillo, he was captured by local police and disappeared.

Today, no one has been convicted of the crimes in Trujillo. Major Urueña received a promotion to lieutenant colonel. Stories continue to circulate about hideous tortures and murders in Trujillo, and on the Cauca River, bodies continue to drift by.

At 8:30 a.m., on one of our last days in Bogotá, two peasants from the area near Barrancabermeja came to our hotel. We had arranged to meet them through the Foundation for Displaced Persons—a charitable organization that helps some of the thousands of internal refugees who pour into Bogotá each year.

We almost missed the two men sitting quietly, hands folded, on the high-backed chairs in the lobby—an old man with a straw hat, and the younger man beside him. They never approached the desk to say they had arrived. The younger man explained, after lingering awkwardly for awhile at the edge of the room, that he was waiting for our assistance, as he wasn't sure how to use the elevator.

Manuel Gallero and his nephew fled Santander one year ago, they told us. The whole family abandoned the small farm on the coast where Gallero had lived for forty years. As a farmer, Gallero had helped form a cooperative association and worked on the municipal council. As a member of the Patriotic Union, he was also elected to the regional council.

"All of this brought me the political persecution which forced me to abandon the region with my family," he said. Gallero's son was killed by assassins in the city of Barrancabermeja, and two of his nephews were murdered.

"I understand that this persecution is in part political and in part because I, as a representative of popular organizations, had a duty to denounce all of the persecution and assassinations of my companions, the other peasants, all of the arbitrary abuses of the same Colombian army," said Gallero. "On various occasions I had to denounce them, in front of the national and regional attorneys general in Barrancabermeja and in Santander, and in Bogotá, before the secretary of human rights for the government."

Gallero told us about numerous abuses by the military, which he had reported to the attorney general and the office of human rights. On January 25, 1989, he said, his own farm was strafed by military helicopters.

"They fired from helicopters at the house. That was the twenty-fifth. On the twenty-sixth, they brought not only guns and helicopters, but they began to bomb. And it was on the twenty-eighth that they killed my two nephews, the two brothers of my nephew here." He pointed at the young man sitting next to him. "And they decapitated them. They killed the two, and the witnesses who were there they had at gunpoint on the ground. All of this came out in the denunciation. A car came by, and they made the passengers get out. They made them walk over the two boys. No one said anything if they recognized the boys—because of fear.

"As for the boys, one of them—they cut off his ears, and mutilated him beyond recognition. The other, when they found him, was completely rotten. They had decapitated him, and they found his head a

28

month later. The body they had dressed in a military uniform, so it looked like he was a guerrilla. He was a boy who liked to play ball."

What about the guerrillas, we asked Gallero. Isn't it true that the army is fighting them?

"Yes. We certainly can't deny that there are guerrillas in our country. This is no secret from anyone. But we find that, clearly, the ones who pay the consequences are the civilian people. When a guerrilla comes into your house and asks you for a lemonade or a meal, you must give it to him. And when the army passes through it is the same thing. Whatever armed person comes in and asks for something, you give it to him. The army demands that we tell them where the guerrillas are. If you don't know, they say you are a sympathizer. So that is the pretext for assassinating us. Those of us who are in the middle are the ones who suffer."

Gallero himself was shot and crippled in an assassination attempt not long before he fled to Bogotá. He showed us his useless right arm, massaging it as he spoke.

"In Colombia we must denounce all of the violations and abuses committed by any member of the government, and by any person. Because otherwise these deeds can never be brought to light. But the truth of the matter is, one only denounces these things on pain of death," he said. "We believe—I believe—that it was necessary to do this, to denounce everything—the army, the paramilitary groups. For this reason, I had to give up my land, which I loved, everything we had achieved, all of the work of forty years with my family, and all, all that has happened. And now we find ourselves here. And I am going to say, *a la buena volutad.* . . I believe that we had to do it."

How can you go on speaking out, I asked Gallero at the end of our interview, in the face of such horrible persecution?

"It's very simple," he said. "One way or another, we are going to die. If we speak, they kill us for speaking. If we say nothing, they kill us anyway. But so much the worse if we die without having spoken the truth."

In the last days of our trip, we went to the U.S. Embassy in Bogotá, to find out what officials there had to say about the situation in Colombia. We passed through a series of heavy gates and had to surrender our cameras and tape recorders "for security reasons" before we were allowed to enter.

The U.S. officials we met spoke mostly off the record, as did the people at the State Department back in Washington. Of everyone interviewed for this article, including victims of political persecution, only representatives of the United States Government refused to be identified.

Bob Danze, the press attaché, came out to greet us after we announced ourselves at the embassy. He shook our hands jovially and led us through some serpentine hallways into what looked like a movie theater—all dark except for some dim lighting up on stage—where he sat with his feet dangling over the edge and answered our questions.

"There was a letter in the *New York Times* about two weeks ago, and the author's comment was something to the effect that American bullets are killing Colombians," said Danze. "What I found fascinating— since I am former military, so I happen to be familiar with this—is that they don't use American weapons here at all. They use *balas*, Brazilian weapons, so there is no way American weapons are going to kill Colombians."

Another embassy official, who joined us late, interrupted Danze at this point: "Well, there could be some argument on that point. . . . What's important is that the United States is supplying only *antinarcotics* aid."

Danze then admitted that the U.S. supplies military aid to Colombia, but assured us that it was all going to the war on drugs. Asked about human-rights violations, he summed up the detachment expressed by many of the U.S. officials with whom we spoke:

"I attribute it to the difference between the Northern European and a Latin culture. It comes partly from the Spanish—what you see in the Spanish is a bastardization of Islamic law—not a respect for law, but for who you know. You can see it, for instance, in the driving out in the streets here. People feel they can cut in, and commit all kinds of violations. If you see a red light, that's for the other guy, not for me. I have more important things to do. I guess you can say people are more self-centered."

The first thing U.S. officials say about Colombia is that the situation here is "very complex." So many different factors contribute to the violence—drug lords, paramilitary armies, common criminals, and so on. It is true that violence has permeated Colombian society to a frightening degree. But this does not mask the truth Gallero spoke about. Even to a group of naive North Americans, traveling to Colombia for the first time, the reality beneath the rhetoric about national security and "narco-terrorism" is unbearably clear.

As in other parts of Latin America, the political and economic injustices in Colombia are appalling. The stark contrast between rich and poor—the desperate struggle for economic necessities and social justice by the side that is labeled "subversive" against the rich and powerful—that is the real war. And it is clear which side the United States is on.

Despite this grim picture, our delegation flew home from Colombia with a feeling of hope. We were inspired by the courage of witnesses like Gallero, and by the dedication of the Jesuit priests at Colombia's internationally renowned human-rights research centers—tirelessly cranking out statistics, precisely documenting the name of every person murdered, the date of each disappearance, collecting these details in the faith that this sheer volume of data must eventually overwhelm the wall of impunity and cynical rhetoric that allows the abuse to go on.

And, they told us, there is reason for hope.

"The biggest problem we have in our international work is that the discourse of the government has been convincing to other governments and international groups," said Father Giraldo of *Justicia y Paz*.

International pressure, and particularly letters to Congress in the United States, can make a life-and-death difference for people in Colombia—people like Jorge Gómez, who recently received the Letelier-Moffit Human Rights Award in Washington, D.C. When international eyes are focused on an individual in Colombia, that person tends to live longer. Delegations from such groups as Witness for Peace, which visit people in areas afflicted by violence, also make a difference. Most of all, unabating pressure on the U.S. Government to stop the abuses and to hold the Colombian military and government accountable can make a difference.

Shortly after we returned from Colombia, the *New York Times* reported that the Government had shifted $75 million in antinarcotics aid from the Colombian army to the police. According to the State Department, the *Times* grossly exaggerated the figure. In fact, only a small portion of total military aid—about $20 million—will change its destination. And since all military aid goes into the same pool, to be received by the Ministry of Defense, the shift will be difficult to monitor. But at least the United States was forced to recognize that the Colombian army has not used antinarcotics aid to fight drugs.

Like Colombia, the United States has two faces, explained Cecilia Zarate Laun, a Colombian citizen who lives in the United States and helped arrange our trip. There is the imperialist face that most of Latin America sees. And then there is the democratic face, the face of the people who believe in human rights and who care what happens to the citizens of towns like Apartadó. That is the philosophy behind the sister-city program, the philosophy of people-to-people diplomacy. We all felt grateful to her for saying it. We wanted it to be true.

★ A FEW KIND WORDS ★ FOR LIBERALISM

Philip Green

FROM *THE NATION*, SEPTEMBER 28, 1992

Toward the beginning of the Reagan Administration James Watt, Secretary of the Interior, remarked that though he used to think there were two kinds of Americans, Republicans and Democrats, he'd now become convinced that we were divided into Americans and liberals. Just a few short years after that neofascist invocation, Mike Dukakis fled from the "L word" as though he had been accused of card-carrying Communism; and now Bill Clinton is doing the same. Liberal-baiting has replaced red-baiting as the favorite pastime of venomous conservatives.

How has it come about, this curious phenomenon of liberalism on the defensive in a cultural milieu that Louis Hartz famously described, in his *The Liberal Tradition in America*, as wholly and uniquely liberal? More curiously, why does liberalism seem to have, at least in the United States, such a self-annihilating history?

As Hartz pointed out, liberalism is an import from Britain, where it developed on the historical stage as a doctrine of individual property right (John Locke); unencumbered business enterprise (Adam Smith); utilitarian social reform to increase the general happiness (Jeremy Bentham); and equal civil liberty for all, individuals as well as collectivities, minorities as well as majorities (John Stuart Mill). In the United States it reached its modern apotheosis in the New Deal, but its direction can be seen as early as 1848, in Mill's *Principles of Political Economy*, in which, after countless encomiums to the "free market," he concludes with a discussion of "the grounds and limits of the laisser-faire or non-interference principle" that virtually lays out a complete theory of the contemporary welfare state.

Although it's sometimes said that the reformism and egalitarianism of Bentham and Mill have displaced the private-property, free-market orientation of Locke and Smith, what has always remained central to liberalism is the notion of a social order in which individual liberty will be able to flourish equally for all to the limit of their capacities, regardless of anyone's membership in a social group other than the one that defines itself as "the majority." The great statements of this tradition have become classics, and deservedly so:

> On any of the great open questions . . . if either of the two opinions has a better claim than the other, not merely to be tolerated, but to be encouraged and countenanced, it is the one which happens at the particular time and place to be in the minority. That is the opinion which, for the time being, represents the neglected interests, the side of human well-being which is in danger of obtaining less than its share. (Mill, *On Liberty*)
>
> The entire history of social improvement has been a series of transitions, by which one custom or institution after another, from being a supposed primary necessity of social existence, has passed into the rank of a universally stigmatised injustice and tyranny. So it has been with the distinctions of slaves and freemen, nobles and serfs, patricians and plebeians; and so it will be, and in part already is, with the aristocracies of colour, race, and sex. (Mill, *Utilitarianism*)
>
> If there is any principle of the Constitution that more imperatively calls for attachment than any other it is the principle of free thought—not free thought for those who

agree with us but freedom for the thought that we hate. (Justice Oliver Wendell Holmes Jr., dissenting in *U.S. v. Schwimmer*, 1929)

Our Constitution is color-blind, and neither knows nor tolerates classes among citizens. In respect of civil rights, all citizens are equal before the law. The humblest is the peer of the most powerful. (Justice John Harlan, dissenting in *Plessy v. Ferguson*, 1896)

Why, it seems reasonable to ask, should this tradition of equal citizenship for all be so much on the defensive in a democratic culture? Most obviously, liberalism stands in a very uneasy relationship to democracy, which enshrines majority rule. Even leaving aside the institution of judicial review, the principles of liberal tolerance and equality call for an incredible degree of self-restraint on the part of those who think of themselves as a majority—silent or vocal. Where the majority is white-skinned, liberals demand equality for people whose skins are of a different color. Where the majority believes in traditional religious values and behaviors, liberals demand equality not just for people who have different values and behaviors but even for those who loudly flaunt them. Liberals can give their overt assent to conventionally honored buzzwords such as "family" and "community," and their sympathetic attention to those who live and die by those concepts; but when push comes to shove, liberals cannot give equal respect to patriarchal families that oppress women, or to communities that practice bigotry and exclusion. Liberalism is hopelessly cosmopolitan in a world of parochialisms; tolerant of every deviation imaginable but scornful of intolerance, even when intolerance of one kind or another is the way of life of the ordinary person; respectful of religious diversity but unable to respect dogma or fanaticism.

It's sometimes claimed that liberalism has lost its cachet because it has forsaken its origins, the allegedly single-minded dedication to private accumulation of Locke or Smith. That may be true for the Bushes and Quayles among us, who suffer the indignity of having to run for offices they once would have inherited. But the attacks on liberalism by the wealthy and their spokespersons should not resonate so intensely among other classes merely because liberals appear to them to have accommodated to the wealthy! For although liberalism stands in such an uneasy relationship to democracy, that does not explain why conservatism, its most visible opponent, has been able to reap the benefit of that difficulty. For conservatism, as opposed to liberalism, is actively hostile to democracy. Since the inception of socialist and social democratic movements, conservatives have had to make peace with democratic values, but that has rarely been from conviction, only from opportunism. For their actual views one has only to look at the obscene posture of the Bush Administration toward the Motor Voter Registration Bill; or the evisceration of the right to strike or even to organize labor unions after twelve years of conservative dominance.

Similar to those attempts to thwart popular mobilization are the Reagan/Bush efforts to shut down all avenues toward open government, and to hide information from the public; to extend presidential prerogative to the point of excluding any representative voice at all in the conduct of foreign affairs, and to develop a secret, illegal, unelected government for that purpose. As Theodore Draper has pointed out, the entire purpose of the Iran/contra scheme was to shelter policymaking not from the nation's "enemies," who knew perfectly well what was going on, but from the American people themselves, the only ones who were in the dark.

Whatever liberals seem to stand for, then, contemporary conservatives stand for bureaucratic autocracy and corporate plutocracy as much as they do for "free markets." And yet conservatism, in the version that British sociologist Stuart Hall calls "authoritarian populism," can also pretend to stand for "the people" in a manner debarred to liberalism. For the authoritarian populist version of conservatism purports to represent a self-conceived monolithic majority that, even when angry, is resigned to its exclusion from power and wealth no matter who rules, but correctly believes that conservatives will better defend the only prerogatives it has remaining to it, e.g., to determine who is going to move in next door, or to police the sexual behavior of its children.

In addition, liberalism has an even deeper difficulty. Where democracy invokes the people and the majority, and imagines that through simple acts of honest representation their virtuous will can be made into virtuous law, liberalism substitutes an intellectual policy elite of administrators and judges. The problem is not who runs liberal institutions—whether it is the allegedly "undemocratic" Supreme Court, or even "pointy-headed bureaucrats"—but what they do and how they do it. The unpleasant truth, first elucidated by Max Weber, is that in the modern democratic age "democracy" is the facade behind which administrative experts, in one guise or another, get the real job done. To take a historically crucial example: For simple, apparently populist solutions to economic crises, like the use of greenbacks in place of specie, or free silver, liberalism substituted what has become the impenetrable system of the Federal Reserve. Or again, for democratic class conflict, liberalism substitutes a legal right to strike, a right that is less a guarantor of action than a system of formal legal constraints on it. Thus it often appears that liberal government is not on the side of the working class but is instead neutral when labor clashes with what John L. Lewis called its "deadly adversary" (and even worse than neutral when conservatives take over administration and make institutions like the National Labor Relations Board into handmaidens of business power). In other words, everywhere the putative democratic majority looks, it sees what it thought was its power dissolve into the evanescent web of administrative relationships, and what it thought was its moral virtue scathingly criticized by the moral experts of liberal tolerance. Liberal reform often represents the replacement of mass uprising and mass resistance by professionally defined regulation and control; and a critique of traditional mass values by philosophical ethics.

Moreover, liberal reform has a fatal predilection for weakening its primary tool—government. Since Bentham and Mill, liberals have insisted that government is the only agency capable of reforming the conditions that make democratic equality unachievable. Under the sway of liberal reformers, however, government promises much but delivers very little, and so government in general comes to bear the onus of failure to achieve a real measure of that equality. Liberalism thus pays a price for its unfulfilled pretenses, and its lack of credibility worsens as conservatives, when they control government, deliberately corrupt and cripple it.

This weakness of liberal government, moreover, is based in large part on the conviction that the private sector is itself not "political," a conviction that stems from liberalism's own founding myth of private property and free enterprise. Liberals, committed to that belief along with a belief in the individual and minority rights rather than class struggle, thus find it difficult to make an unequivocal alliance with the only class that has an interest in challenging that myth.

For better or worse, then, Dan Quayle is not totally off the mark when he attacks the "liberal cultural elite" that allegedly dominates our public discourse. Liberalism's commitment to social reform, as opposed to conservatism's dedication to ideological revanchism, requires and has always brought to the forefront a class of intellectual (and, more recently, therapeutic) experts: policy-makers and policy exponents who speak a language of progress through science, education and an ideal of tolerance that is modern liberalism's equivalent of moral virtue. Like Senator Roman Hruska defending the nomination of G. Harrold Carswell to the Supreme Court on the ground that even mediocre people deserve representation, the buffoonish Vice President speaks for those who lack access to that language of progress. (That his speeches are written for him and his positions articulated by paid-up members of the cultural elite such as William Kristol is another matter—though of course, not really.)

Furthermore, Quayle is also correct in another important respect. "Liberal" is exactly the word to describe, for example, Diane English, creator of *Murphy Brown*, or Hillary Clinton or Bill Clinton's good friend Linda Bloodworth-Thomason of *Designing Women*—and, like Dukakis before them, Clinton and Albert Gore. By the standards of Mill, John Dewey, John Rawls, Teddy Kennedy or Hillary Clinton, Clinton and Gore may not be very good liberals, but liberals are indubitably what they are; as Joe Louis said of one of his opponents, he can run but he can't hide. The whole bag of sleazy diversions, from slavering over executions to denouncing Sister Souljah, will not fool any of the new redbaiters, who can look at Gore's high rating on Americans for Democratic Action's roll-call vote scale, or Clinton's remarks about "denial" and "neglect" after the Los Angeles riots and his proposal for public works investment in urban areas, or his calls for a tougher income tax on the wealthy. But as the electorate eventually becomes skeptical of their self-evidently evasive tactic of chastising the name-callers for calling names, what should compromised liberal politicians do—always keeping in mind that there is no such thing as an uncompromised politician of any kind?

Most simply, they ought to understand that Louis Hartz was right about America being a liberal milieu. He may have underestimated the corrosive effects of race, gender and sexuality on the polity. Yet it is, in the end, an undeniably liberal polity, and aspects of that heritage are worth standing on no matter how divisive they may seem at present; worth standing on not merely for those who want to be morally correct but for those who want to win as well. Yes, there are many illiberal votes for censorship of avant-garde art, but anyone who runs on a ticket of that and "right to life" is going to lose in most parts of the nation. The right to be let alone by the government is fundamental to Americans; there are no votes to be lost, and many to be gained, by emphasizing its application to abortion policy. The same is true of the right to vote, the cornerstone of equal citizenship; a liberal who is not in a constant rage about the Republican opposition to simplified voter registration is not committed to either democracy or liberalism, and will deserve the apathy with which a large portion of the potential electorate will greet his candidacy.

As for liberal reform, it is obvious that we cannot expect ringing endorsements of affirmative action in the present political climate, despite its being a fundamental and typical instance of liberal rectification. We can expect, though, that a liberal President will (learning a lesson from his conservative counterparts) appoint judges who will preserve rather than eviscerate it. And if we can't expect even liberal democrats today to join enthusiastically in an antiracism crusade, we can expect them at least to be committed to other fundamental aspects of liberal equality. The basis of equal citizenship is that all people should have the chance to perform up to their fullest capabilities, and this is an ideal that in principle few Americans will deny. Thus liberals should be unashamed to stand on the utilitarian notion that every time a potentially productive worker is lost to drugs, crime, illiteracy, unemployment or underemployment, we are all losers. "Workfare" may be a political necessity these days, but it is an illusion; education, though, is the real thing, and proposals for universal access to education from Head Start through graduate school (and for educational rather than military solutions to the drug problem) are both liberal and "American," and genuinely productive as well. So too is compensatory aid to cities, to rectify years not just of neglect but of policies deliberately designed to reward white suburbs and strangle nonwhite inner cities. So too is effective day care, for women who want to or who must participate in the nondomestic work force; and proper health care, for all who deserve it because they are ill, not because they have one level of income instead of another. And although liberal and not-so-liberal Democratic politicians may be in thrall to the banks and insurance companies and communications empires and fractions of industrial capital that finance their campaigns, none of this need prevent them from the obvious step of guaranteeing organized labor's bottom line for attacking the imbalance between capital and the working class: a law forbidding the hiring of replacement workers during strikes, and the promise of appointments to the N.L.R.B. that will at least treat the right to strike as a right, and the right to strikebreak as an abomination.

These are only examples; my point is not to come up with one more potpourri of liberal programs but to suggest that there is still an American liberalism, combining both rights and reform, that political leaders can successfully embrace rather than shun. And if none of this will even begin to solve the profound structural problems of the American economy, the armchair radicals who never tire of pointing this out do not have the faintest realistic idea themselves what might be done.

As for the traditional attitude of the radical left toward liberals, the first thing that ought to be evident to anyone capable of coherent thought is that there is not going to be a revolutionary Marxist system or an androgynous utopia or even a social democratic commonwealth in the United States in the near future, or perhaps any future. Yes, given liberalism's origins, liberals have to be reminded that capitalism by its nature reproduces exploitation and injustice; and that the opportunity to fulfill individual capacities is considerably more available to well-born white men than to the children of the poor or people of color or women. Still, the horror with which radicals perennially discover that liberals are really liberals—that they are committed to impartial government, class neutrality, tolerance of manifest evil, and lesser-evil reform rather than revolution—has become a tiresome imitation of Claude Rains in *Casablanca*: "I'm shocked, shocked to find that gambling is going on in here!" We ought to give it a rest. We ought also to be aware of making implicit unholy alliances with the right by attacking liberal tolerance because it falls short of embracing racial, ethnic or sexual "difference"; the welfare state because it perpetuates private property and wage labor; government because it entails bureaucracy; free speech because hurtful things get said.

Liberal tolerance and the liberal version of civic equality, though perhaps they can be improved on, are in the end not dispensable. An American society without liberalism would be a sinkhole of racism, sexism and every form of unabashed bigotry. It would be a society in which black men got tried by juries of white men and routinely executed for crimes they may not have committed; in which people of color couldn't go to public schools or colleges and universities of their own choice; books like *Our Bodies, Ourselves* couldn't get distributed; union organizers couldn't speak to potential members anywhere without fear of being beaten up or arrested; gays wouldn't dare speak their name; blasphemy against Christian dogma would be a crime; and so on. There isn't much civility in American society today, but most of what there is has been nurtured by liberal policies and attitudes.

What the left should finally recognize is that conservatives are right. Liberalism, properly considered, makes immense demands on the social order; it indeed deserves, or at least can deserve, the epithet of "creeping socialism." From the moment of formation of the First International, if not before, liberals, as Mill's *Principles* testifies, have been under constant pressure to extend their understanding of the extensiveness of the changes necessary to make good the promises of liberal equality; and they have constantly done so. Thus the "Reagan Democrats" who consistently tell interviewers that the Democratic Party has "gone too far" in representing black people have a sadly inaccurate idea of what civil-rights legislation and affirmative action have actually accomplished; but they are a lot closer to the truth than those on the left who castigate liberals for "not really" opposing racism. The task for radicals, then, is never to let up their pressure, always to point out how much remains to be done after the latest bout of liberal reform, but not to treat liberalism as their primary enemy. It is not classical liberalism but rather a compromised and half-hearted version of it that makes supine compromises with political power brokers or corporate moneybags. What's wrong with liberals, usually, is not that they're liberal but that they're not liberal enough.

As for liberals, their real task is to have the guts to go on being liberal, however they may feel they have to treat the word itself; and however they may have to modify contemporary liberal rhetoric. Liberalism may not be the American way, but it is indeed an American way, and despite all its limitations still the best one realistically available to us.

★ ME AND MY ★ ZEITGEIST

Andrew Cohen

From *The Nation*, July 19, 1993

Today's Zeitgeist-watchers strike a special note of apocalypse when they describe the spirit we twentysomethings are said to share. In his novel *Generation X*, Douglas Coupland calls it a "mood of darkness and inevitability"; *Business Week* speaks of our "collective sense of fore-boding"; and Neil Howe and Bill Strauss, in their book *13th Gen*, detect a "tone of physical frenzy and spiritual numbness" in what they call our "carnival culture."

In the popular image being constructed, we are a Peter Pan genera-tion afraid of adulthood, the "lost boys," and girls, of a generation gone slumming. Our "fatalism," writes William Raspberry of the *Washington Post*, is turning us into a "generation of animals," with no opinions, no expectations and no clear future: a bunch of bicycle messengers with master's degrees; a caravansary of down-and-out slackers, *Wayne's World* computer hackers, *New Jack City* gangster rappers and MTV fiends; the doom-stricken Baby Bust behind the Baby Boom.

A few years ago, in the early days of the recession, the press was most interested in those of us who had moved back home and become Baby Boomerangs. The self-proclaimed spokesmen of our generation—and they were mostly men—explained that we were struggling at twenty-five to live as well as we had at fifteen; that we were the first American generation not destined to live better than the previous one.

Today, a psychosocial profile has been attached to the plain facts of downward mobility. Bret Easton Ellis claims "We are clueless yet wizened, too unopinionated to voice concern." Also too ignorant. The *Washington Post* recently ran the headline "Students Don't Protest Over Vietnam Now—They Don't Even Know Where It Is." And in a roundup review of Bridget Fonda movies ("Mommy! might be the unspoken rallying cry behind the slew of films about people in their twenties"), the *New York Times* lectured about our "career avoidance," "low expectations" and childishness.

The name for this syndrome, usefully provided by Douglas Coupland, sniglet-master of the new Zeitgeist, is "successophobia"—"the fear that if one is successful . . . one will no longer have one's childish needs catered to." Those not afflicted with successophobia are often instead gripped by a generalized rejectionism—like the kids in Richard Linklater's movie *Slacker*, who live off dead-end jobs (or graduate school stipends) while they hatch conspiracy theories, jam in garage bands, shop for plaid shirts in thrift stores or declare that "withdrawal in disgust is not the same as apathy."

Coupland's novel *Generation X*, stocked with young slackers stuck in various "McJobs" in Palm Springs, California, has become the unofficial guide to this twentysomething Schadenfreude. One character torches a car with an "I'm spending my children's inheritance" bumper sticker and wants to avenge himself on yuppies "rusting" in place above him. What Coupland's young people, like virtually all of these projected emblems of an age, share is a peculiarly conservative and middle-class disappointment— sense of entitlement gone sour.

Some monitors of the Zeitgeist look upon this and detect fertile ground for generational warfare. In *13th Gen*, Howe and Strauss try to turn all this youthful disgust and disappointment to political purposes. To the twentysomethings who "feel like all the air has been sucked up by the generations before them," the authors—white middle-class guys in their forties—say it's not too late to fight back. Their most ardent disciples can be found in the Lead or Leave Campaign, a new student organization that identifies the enemy as old folks with their Social Security benefits and spendthrift middleagers who are mortgaging the future.

Howe and Strauss have at least exploded the idea that all twentysomethings are apathetic; in its place, they substitute the notion that we are all natural neoliberals. People of my generation, they say, "don't care much for the senior and labor lobbies," "prefer recession to an out of kilter balance sheet," believe "race should only be a private issue" and think that the most pressing concern of our time is the federal deficit. What begins as a call to generational arms turns out to be some intergenerational advice, as, behind the rhetoric, the sturdy symmetries of class reassert themselves from one era to the next.

LOSING GROUND IN A GENERATION
How many hours, weeks or years of continuous labor does it take for an American to pay for some of the staples of middle-class life today as compared with twenty years ago?

PURCHASE TIME WORKED	1972	TODAY
Median-price home	3.7 years	5.4 years
Year of private college	20.6 weeks	39.6 weeks
Total annual expenses for an average household	67.4 weeks	82.2 weeks
Chevrolet sedan	25.4 weeks	42.0 weeks
Doctor's office visit	2.5 hours	7.5 hours
Emergency room visit	7.0 hours	23.1 hours

SOURCE: New York City Department of Consumer Affairs

A COUPLE OF WHITE GUYS SITTING AROUND TALKING

Jon Cowan has two days' stubble and a bloodshot look, and he believes the deficit is "our generation's Vietnam." He wrestles with it like an old soldier, barking commands at a young woman hunched over a calculator ("Well, then cut out all foreign aid!") in his spacious office at the

Lead or Leave Campaign in Washington. Lead or Leave, which Cowan started last year with his friend Rob Nelson, exists to pressure politicians to sign a pledge: They will cut the deficit in half in the next four years, or leave office. The idea was originally Ross Perot's. It's not the first agenda item that springs to mind for a youth movement.

"The deficit will destroy our future," Nelson says simply. "Lost jobs, hunger and homelessness, untreated AIDS babies. Generational war is inevitable if we don't do something about it."

Cowan, twenty-seven, and Nelson, twenty-nine, have, more success-fully than any other twentysomethings, identified themselves as symbols of the age—in magazine articles, on *Nightline* and *Good Morning America*, and on Op-Ed pages across the country. They were even invited to the White House. Buoyed by $42,000 worth of Perot's largesse and an approximately equal amount from Republican financier Pete Peterson, they left jobs on Capitol Hill (Cowan was Representative Mel Levine's press secretary, Nelson a consultant at Malchow & Co., fundraising for Greenpeace and Gay Men's Health Crisis) to turn Lead or Leave into a national campus organization. They claim ten thousand members.

The two appeared on the cover of *U.S. News & World Report* in February under the heading "The Twentysomething Rebellion," posing with a motorcycle and sporting the look of outdoor adventurers. Given that image, their office came as a surprise: the floor-to-ceiling windows, the posh Connecticut Avenue address (across from Cartier and the Mayflower Hotel, conveniently next door to the Gap). The place smelled like generations of Big Macs. This is not rebellion as one would expect it. By today's standards, however, any twentysomething show of purpose evokes a stunned tribute.

But Lead or Leave is less a rebellion than it is an exercise in the politics of innocence. Cowan and Nelson call themselves liberals but, willy-nilly, espouse Reaganesque economic theories. These can be briskly put to rest. They insist, for example, that deficits raise interest rates and "crowd out" private investment, but the Federal Reserve sets interest rates, and there's a fair body of evidence to show that government spending encourages, or "crowds in," private investment. As a percentage of G.N.P. the U.S. deficit is far lower than it was in 1945 (and apart from G.N.P., the deficit is meaningless, since, with governments as with people, the ability to repay a loan is determined by income). When the U.S. debt-to-income ratio peaked, just after World War II, interest rates were around 2 percent.

France and Italy have deficits that are far larger than the U.S. government's. Also, the size of the U.S. deficit is debatable because the government makes no distinction between everyday expenses and investments, posting both as losses [see Robert Heilbroner, "Thedeficit," January 27, 1992]. But beyond all that, the national debt is a class issue, not a generational one. Paying it off quickly would enrich wealthy bondholders in each generation at everyone else's expense. Because proportionately more people between the ages of 16 and 30 are at the bottom of the income ladder, deficit busting—otherwise known as austerity—would actually hurt them the most.

At least implicitly, Lead or Leavers seem to understand that at base the deficit involves a conflict over the priorities of government. So it is revealing that their main target thus far has not been military spending or government waste but Social Security. A demonstration of some one hundred people on the steps of the headquarters of the American Association for Retired Persons was the opening salvo in what Lead or Leavers like to call a "fight for generational equity."

Their argument runs something like this: The government pays retirees out of the payroll taxes it collects each year from younger workers. Today there are roughly 3.4 people in the work force per Social Security beneficiary; in 2030, by which time some seventy-five million Baby Boomers will have retired, there will be only 1.9 workers per geezer, leaving nothing in the till when people in their twenties are ready to collect. The Social Security Administration and the A.A.R.P., they say, have conspired to paper over this oncoming debacle with rosy economic projections, and therefore the government should consider "privatizing" the entire program.

They are right to add that the Social Security payroll tax is regressive and the cap on it a silly idea, since millionaires pay no more than the moderately well-off. But there's no reason to go private. The Social Security trust fund will actually accumulate a surplus of $4.3 trillion by 2015. Thanks to Ronald Reagan's hike in the payroll tax, the government is taking in more than three times the amount that it is paying out in Social Security benefits; it invests this surplus in special-issue Treasury notes, which is another way of saying that the money goes to finance the national debt. If the government exhausts the surplus, it can always issue fresh debt to pay for the notes that have come due; U.S. government bonds are gilt-edged that way, and if they ever become irredeemable, more than the Social Security system will be in trouble.

All that aside, why would anyone try to organize a youth movement around the fear that when young people reach their sixties, they may not get Social Security? In the first place, the very idea of a movement is as concocted as the guide to grunge culture slang ("lamestain," "harsh realm") that a mischievous music critic recently slipped past the editors of the *New York Times* Styles section. The Zeitgeist industry is in fact a closely held corporation of a few authors and "activists" who swap ideas liberally but share a conservative ethos. Unaware of this cross-pollination, the media generated dozens of stories supported by only one or two sources, all fixed on the notion of deficit-busting and all passing it off, incredibly, as a preoccupation of people in their twenties.

In the second place, youth is only tangential to the project at hand. Before he thought of *13th Gen*, Neil Howe wrote a book with Wall Street bond broker and Lead or Leave benefactor Pete Peterson, titled *On Borrowed Time: How the Growth in Entitlement Spending Threatens America's Future*. Howe has also collaborated with Phillip Longman, founder of the Americans for Generational Equality (AGE), a now-defunct D.C.-based granny-bashing outfit that lobbied for the last Social Security payroll tax hike. Howe later wrote a Lead or Leave pamphlet with *13th Gen* co-author Bill Strauss, called "Deficits in Your Face." There Howe and Strauss told twentysomethings that "older Americans are waging a generational war against YOU. . . . like Vietnam, it's going to take the youth of America to stop it." They also predicted that we will all face a 37 percent tax rate. When Cowan and

Nelson borrowed Howe and Strauss's agent and began to shop around a book proposal of their own, they upped that figure: "If current policies are not dramatically altered, today's youth can expect to pay up to 70% of their income in taxes by the middle of our careers."

Howe and Strauss refer reporters to Lead or Leave for an example of "today's activists," who don't care much about labor or race, who worry about Social Security (Coupland, by the way, cites the retirees-per-worker figures in the appendix to *Generation X*) and who, according to *13th Gen*, "question many of the old liberal orthodoxies on drugs and crime." Cowan and Nelson, who refer reporters to Howe and Strauss for statistical data, gladly assume the mantle of today's activists. The book proposal they circulated before landing a deal with Penguin includes a list of "controversial" political choices they planned to consider: "Eliminate the deficit in five years," "End race-based affirmative action," "Put peacekeeping troops in the inner cities to control crime," "Allow abortion in the first trimester but turn over all other decisions to states," "Legalize addictive drugs such as 'crack.'" Cowan and Nelson insist they never advocated any of those ideas—except of course eliminating the deficit—and say they decided with Penguin that none of those other issues would be discussed. Stay tuned.

THE FORGOTTEN ONES

One mile from the Lead or Leave office, at a public school in Washington's Anacostia district, Jonathan Kozol asked the principal what he found most frustrating about working with young people today. "On Fridays in the cafeteria," the older man said, "I see small children putting chicken nuggets in their pockets. They're afraid of being hungry on the weekends."

The parents of these children are the twentysomethings who disappear in the Zeitgeist manufacturers' generational profile. According to a recent *Business Week* survey, eighteen- to twenty-nine-year-olds spent $15 billion last year on children's clothing, among the top five expenditures for this age group. (Eating out, at $30 billion, was the highest.) These young parents don't fit any of the twentysomething stereotypes. Baby Boomerangs never seem to have children; they're busy paying off their college loans. Granny-bashers aren't exactly the family type. Neither are the slackers, who, having grown up to expect "life options," now opt for temporary poverty.

The consensus is that the dark and airless mood of the twentysomething times has been set by money troubles, but the scope of those troubles has gone unexamined. As the table on page 98 shows, it is much harder to afford a house, a car or a college education today than it was twenty years ago. *Rolling Stone* had a piece on the growing number of college-educated twentysomethings taking jobs that require only high school degrees, but it didn't mention that more than half the people in this generation don't go to college at all. The unglamorous working-class truth is that in 1990, one-third of the families headed by someone under 30 lived below the federal poverty line; 58 percent of the families headed by someone who is black and under 30 are living in poverty. Real wages are lower than they were in 1963, and as a consequence, Americans are working more hours in the paid labor force than at any time since 1948.

Even Howe and Strauss acknowledge that falling wages have determined the too-obtrusive fate of twentysomething families. In the margin of their book they cite Children's Defense Fund figures, saying, "In 1979, 74 percent of working Americans under age twenty-five were earning an hourly wage which—if received full-time and year-round—exceeded the cash poverty level for a family of three. By 1991, that share had fallen to 47 percent." So Howe and Strauss are not ignorant of this generational reality; they're just not interested.

The monopolists of the Zeitgeist industry have already agreed that racism, low wages and poverty are not among our problems, because they've agreed who "we" are. "We" are not poor black and Latino families, or the children of immigrants; we wear penny loafers, ride mountain bikes (this according to *Time*) and have large discretionary incomes because we moved back home after college. "Our" problems are different; we want to live as well as our parents accustomed us to living, so that one day "we" can be on top.

Maybe the Zeitgeist is not so much the essence of an age as the battleground for those who would define it. Any "choice of a new generation," in terms of Pepsi or politics, is bound to come up against its contradiction in a society that is growing more polarized. Given class differences and the persistence of outright segregation in schools and in cities, *Schoolhouse Rock* and *Sesame Street* can hardly be the basis for a collective consciousness. Nor can the narrow and misguided fight against the federal deficit be a generational call to arms. A movement is a moral thing. Capital budget accounting will not be our Freedom Ride; Ross Perot is not the Reverend King. The alternative to deficit-busting cuts in social services is a drive to create better jobs, better schools and better chances. Today in Washington such pinched efforts as there are in those directions go under the heading of "investment in human capital." But if cost-effectiveness is the principal criterion of governance, and investment its best metaphor, then perhaps it will take a true youth movement to reinvigorate the politics of the possible. We can make all the penny-niggly arguments we want to suit the climate in Washington, or we can learn at long last that the alternative to austerity is simply justice.

★ A SOCIALISM OF ★ THE SKIN

Tony Kushner

From *The Nation*, July 4, 1994

Is there a relationship between homosexual liberation and socialism? That's an unfashionably utopian question, but I pose it because it's entirely conceivable that we will one day live miserably in a thoroughly ravaged world in which lesbians and gay men can marry and serve openly in the Army and that's it. Capitalism, after all, can absorb a lot. Poverty, war, alienation, environmental destruction, colonialism, unequal development, boom/bust cycles, private property, individualism, commodity fetishism, the fetishization of the body, the fetishization of violence, guns, drugs, child abuse, underfunded and bad education (itself a form of child abuse)—these things are key to the successful functioning of the free market. Homophobia is not; the system could certainly accommodate demands for equal rights for homosexuals without danger to itself.

But are officially sanctioned homosexual marriages and identifiably homosexual soldiers the ultimate aims of homosexual liberation? Clearly not, if by homosexual liberation we mean the liberation of homosexuals, who, like most everyone else, are and will continue to be oppressed by the depredations of capital until some better way of living together can be arrived at. So then are homosexual marriages and soldiery the ultimate, which is to say the only achievable, aims of the gay rights movement, a politics not of vision but of pragmatics?

Andrew Sullivan, in a provocative, carefully reasoned, moving, troubling article in the *New Republic* a year ago, arrived at that conclusion. I used to have a crush on Andrew, neocon or neoliberal (or whatever the hell they're called these days) though he be. I would never have married him, but he's cute! Then he called me a "West Village Neil Simon," in print, and I retired the crush. This by way of background for what follows, to prove that I am, despite my wounded affections, capable of the "reason and restraint" he calls for at the opening of his article, "The Politics of Homosexuality."

Andrew divides said politics into four, you should pardon the expression, camps—conservative, radical, moderate, and liberal—each of which lacks a workable "solution to the problem of gay-straight relations." Conservatives (by which he means reactionaries, I think, but he is very polite) and radicals both profess an absolutist politics of "impossibilism," which alienates them from "the mainstream Moderates" (by which he means conservatives) who practice an ostrich-politics of denial, increasingly superseded by the growing visibility of gay men and lesbians. And liberals (moderates) err mainly in trying to legislate, through antidiscrimination bills, against reactive, private-sector bigotry.

Andrew's prescription is that liberals (with whom he presumably identifies most closely) go after "pro-active" government bans on homosexual participation in the military and the institution of marriage. Period. "All public (as opposed to private) discrimination against homosexuals [should] be ended and every right and responsibility that heterosexuals enjoy by virtue of the state [should] be extended to those who grow up different. And that is all." Andrew's new "liberal" gay politics "does not legislate private tolerance, it declares public equality. . . . Our battle is not for political victory but for personal integrity."

The article is actually a kind of manifesto for gay conservatism, and as such it deserves scrutiny. Every manifesto also deserves acolytes, and "The Politics of Homosexuality" has earned at least one: Bruce Bawer, who appeared this year in the *New Republic* with "The Stonewall Myth:

Can the Gay Rights Movement Get Beyond the Politics of Nostalgia?"
Bruce, however, is no Andrew. He's cute enough; he looks rueful and
contemplative on the cover of his book, *A Place at the Table*, though if
you've read it you'll know Bruce doesn't like it when gay men get dishy
and bitchy and talk sissy about boys. He thinks it makes us look bad for
the straights. Bruce is serious, more serious even than Andrew, as the big
open book in the cover photo proclaims: He's read more than half of it!
(Lest anyone think I habitually read the *New Republic*, the playwright
David Greenspan gave me Andrew's article, and Andrew Kopkind
among others drew my attention to Bruce's.)

Bruce is not only more serious than Andrew, he's more polite, no easy
trick; he's so polite I almost hate to write that he's also much easier to
dismiss, but he is. His article is short and sloppy, and he has this habit
of creating paper tigers. Take the eponymous "Stonewall Myth," to
which "many gay men and lesbians routinely" subscribe: According to
Bruce, these "many" believe that gay history started with Stonewall and
regard the riot as "a sacred event that lies beyond the reach of objective
discourse." Huh? I don't know anyone who believes that, and I've never
encountered such a ridiculous statement in any work of gay criticism or
reportage or even fiction. But Bruce goes on for pages tilting at this
windmill and the "politics of nostalgia" that accompanies it. He's also,
and I mean this politely, a little slow. It took him five years to figure out
that maybe a gay man shouldn't be writing movie reviews for the
viciously homophobic *American Spectator*. In his book he is anguished:
"Had I been wrong to write for so reactionary a publication? If so, then
how did one figure out where to draw the line? Should I refuse to write
for the *Nation* because its editors frequently appeared to be apologists
for Communism," etc.

In the article Bruce decides that our real problem is a fear of acceptance, fear of failure, a "deep unarticulated fear of that metaphorical place
at the table," and so we march in front of TV cameras in our underwear,
confirming for all the world that we really are sick. (Clothes, worn and
discarded, are always bothering Bruce; spandex and leather, business
suits and bras, his writing is littered with the stuff.) I'll focus mostly on

Andrew's meatier, seminal (oops!) text. (For a polite but mostly thorough reaming of *A Place at the Table*, read David Bergman in the Spring '94 issue of *The Harvard Gay and Lesbian Review*.)

In "The Politics of Homosexuality," Andrew concedes quite lot of good will to those farthest to the right. He draws an odd distinction between the "visceral recoil" of bigots and the more cautious discomfort of homophobes—those who "sincerely believe" in "discouragement of homosexuality," who couch their sincere beliefs in "Thomist argument," in "the natural law tradition, which, for all its failings is a resilient pillar of Western thought." Bigotry, too, is a resilient pillar of Western thought, or it was the last time I checked. Andrew realizes bigotry "expresses itself in thuggery and name-calling. But there are some [conservatives] who don't support antigay violence." Like who? George Will, Bill Buckley and Cardinal O'Connor have all made token clucking noises about fag-bashing, but the incommensurability of these faint protests with the frightening extent of the violence, which has certainly been encouraged by the very vocal homophobia of "conservatives," might force one to question the sincerity of their admonitions, and further, to question the value of distinguishing "Thomist" homophobes from the "thugs" who in 1993 attacked or killed more than 1,900 lesbians and gay men (at least those are the hate crimes we know about).

Andrew takes a placid view of people on the reactionary right because he is convinced their days are numbered. But does he really believe that Pat Buchanan is now "reduced to joke-telling"? Such a conclusion is possible only if one ignores the impressive, even terrifying, political energies of the religious right. Since Andrew decides political discourse can countenance only "reason and restraint," he of course must exclude the Bible-thumpers, who are crazy and loud. But the spectrum is more crowded, and on the right less well-behaved, than a gentleman like Andrew cares to admit. His is an endearing reticence, but it is not wise.

Andrew is at his best describing the sorts of traumas homophobia inflicts on its victims (though to nobody's surprise he doesn't care for the word "victim"), yet despite his sensitivity, he's alarmingly quick to give up on the antidiscrimination legislation of those he calls liberals. "However effective or comprehensive antidiscrimination laws are, they cannot reach far enough." They can't give us confidence, and they only "scratch the privileged surface." "As with other civil-rights legislation, those least in need of it may take fullest advantage: the most litigious and articulate homosexuals, who would likely brave the harsh winds of homophobia in any case."

It's unclear whether Andrew opposes such legislation, which, it seems to me, is worthwhile even if only moderately effective. I assume that in limiting the gay rights movement's ambitions to fighting "pro-active" discrimination, he is arguing against trying to pass laws that impede "reactive" discrimination, though I can't find anything in his very specific article that states this definitively. (In any case, his distinction between "reactive" and "pro-active" discrimination falls apart as soon as one considers adoption laws or education or sexual harassment.) Perhaps he's vague because he knows he hasn't much of a case. What worries him especially is that the right will make effective propaganda out of the argument that "civil rights laws essentially dictate the behavior of heterosexuals, in curtailing their ability to discriminate." And he believes further that this argument contains "a germ of truth."

The argument is unquestionably good propaganda for homophobes, but it's identical to the N.R.A.'s argument for giving every nutbag in the country access to a semiautomatic. We have to argue such propaganda down, not run away from the legislation that inspired it. As for the "germ of truth," Andrew writes:

> Before most homosexuals have even come out of the closet they are demanding concessions from the majority, including a clear curtailment of economic and social liberties, in order to ensure protections few of them will even avail themselves of. It is no wonder there is opposition.

This is a peculiar view of the processes by which enfranchisement is extended: Civil rights, apparently, are not rights at all, not something inalienable, to which one is entitled by virtue of being human or a citizen, but concessions the majority makes to a minority if and only if the minority can promise it will use those rights. Antidiscrimination laws are seen as irrelevant to creating a safer environment in which closeted or otherwise oppressed people might feel more free to exercise their equality; laws apparently cannot encourage freedom, only punish transgressions against it.

The argument that antidiscrimination laws violate "majority" freedoms has already been used to eliminate the basis of most of the legislation from the civil-rights movement. Affirmative action, housing and employment laws, and voter redistricting can all be said to curtail the freedom of bigots to discriminate, which is, of course, what such measures are supposed to do. The connection that such legislation implies between gay rights and other minority rights displeases Andrew, who resists the idea that, as forms of oppression, homophobia, and racism have much in common.

With homosexuality, according to Andrew, "the option of self-concealment has always existed," something that cannot be said about race. (I could introduce him to some flaming creatures who might make him question that assessment, but never mind.) "Gay people are not uniformly discriminated against; openly gay people are." Certainly there are important differences of kind and degree and consequence between racism and homophobia, but the idea that invisibility exempts anyone from discrimination is perverse. To need to be invisible, or to feel that you need to be, is to be discriminated against. The fact that homophobia differs significantly from racism—and, loath as I am to enter the discrimination olympics, I'd argue that the consequences of racism in America today are worse than those of homophobia—does not mean that people engaged in one struggle can't learn from another, or that the tools one oppressed people have developed can't be used to try to liberate others.

Andrew is joined by Bruce in his anxiety to preserve the differences among various kinds of oppression, but they both seem less interested in according each group its own "integrity," as Andrew rightly calls it, than in keeping gay rights from being shanghaied by the radical left. "The standard post-Stonewall practice . . . indiscriminately link[s] the move-ment for gay equal rights with any left-wing cause to which any gay leader might happen to have a personal allegiance . . . " (this is Bruce). "Such linkages have been a disaster for the gay rights movement: not only do they falsely imply that most gay people sympathize with those so-called progressive movements, but they also serve to reinforce the idea of homosexuality itself as a 'progressive' phenomenon, as something essentially political in nature." Andrew, meanwhile, warns against the "universalist temptation," which exercises "an enervating and dissipating effect on gay radicalism's political punch."

Gay radicalism's political punch is not something either Andrew or Bruce wishes to see strengthened. Conservative gay politics is in a sense the politics of containment: Connections made with a broadly defined left are what must be contained. The pair predicts the emergence of increasing numbers of conservative homosexuals (presumably white—in both Andrew's and Bruce's prophecies they come from the suburbs), who are unsympathetic to the idea of linking their fortunes with any other political cause. The future depends not on collectivity and soli-darity but on homosexual individualism—on lesbians and gay men instructing the straight world quietly, "person by person, life by life, heart by heart" (Andrew), to "do the hard, painstaking work of getting straight Americans used to it" (Bruce).

Like all assimilationists, Andrew and Bruce are unwilling to admit that structural or even particularly formidable barriers exist between them-selves and their straight oppressors. And for all their elaborate fears that misbehaving queers alienate instead of communicate, nowhere do they express a concern that people of color or the working class or the poor are not being communed with. The audience we are ostensibly losing is iden-tified exclusively as phobic straights, "families" which one suspects are two-parent, middle-class) and gay teenagers.

Bruce and Andrew are very concerned about young gay people. Watching a "lean and handsome" fifteen-year-old leaf through the *Native* at the start of his book, Bruce worries that queer radicalism, sexual explicitness and kink frighten gay kids and the families from whence they come. Probably it is the case that teenagers are freaked by photo ads for *The Dungeon*. But the *Native* is not produced for teenagers. Images of adult lesbian and gay desire can't be tailored to appeal to fifteen-year-olds and their straight parents. Our culture is the manifest content of our lives, not a carefully constructed recruiting brochure. True, there aren't readily available, widely circulated images of homosexual domesticity or accomplishment or happiness, but I'm more inclined to blame the homophobic media than gay radicalism for that. Nor does the need for such images mandate the abandonment of public declarations of the variety of sexual desire, the public denial and repression of which is after all The Problem. Lesbian and gay kids will have less trouble accepting their homosexuality not when the Gay Pride Parade is an orderly procession of suits arranged in monogamous pairs but when people learn to be less horrified by sex and its complexities.

Out of the great stew of class, race, gender and sexual politics that inspirits the contentious, multiplying, endlessly unfixed lesbian and gay community in America, gay conservatism manages to make a neat division between a majority that is virtually indistinguishable in behavior and aspirations and Weltanschauung from the straight world, and a minority of deviants and malcontents who are fucking things up for everyone, thwarting the only realizable goal, which is normalcy.

Andrew says up front that politics is supposed to relieve anxiety. I'd say that it's supposed to relieve misery and injustice. When all that can be expected from politics, in the way of immediate or even proximate social transformation, are gay weddings and gay platoons, the vast rest of it all, every other agony inflicted by homophobia, will have to be taken care of by some osmotic process of quiet individualized persuasion, which will take many, many, many years. It's the no-government, antipolitics approach to social change. You can hear it argued now against school desegregation, or any attempt to guarantee equal education; you can hear it argued against welfare or jobs programs. It's the legacy of trickle-down, according to which society should change slowly, organically, spontaneously, without interference, an approach that requires not so much the "discipline, commitment, responsibility" that

Bruce exhorts us to—we already practice those—but a great, appalling luxury of time (which maybe the editor of the *New Republic* and the erstwhile movie critic of the *American Spectator* can afford), after the passage of which many, many, many more miserable lives will have been spent or dispensed with. I am always suspicious of the glacier-paced patience of the right.

Such a politics of homosexuality is dispiriting. Like conservative thought in general, it offers very little in the way of hope, and very little in the way of vision. I expect both hope and vision from my politics. Andrew and Bruce offer nothing more than that gay culture will dissolve invisibly into straight culture, all important differences elided.

I think both Andrew and Bruce would call this assessment unfair, though I don't mean it to be. Andrew's politics may be roomier than Bruce's; Andrew is more worldly and generous (except, apparently, when it comes to the theater). Both men have a vision. They see before them an attainable peaceable kingdom, in which gay men and lesbians live free of fear (of homophobia, at least), in which gay kids aren't made to feel worthless, or worse, because they're gay.

But what of all the other things gay men and lesbians have to fear? What of the things gay children have to fear, in common with all children? What of the planetary despoilment that kills us? Or the financial necessity that drives some of us into unsafe, insecure, stupid, demeaning and ill-paying jobs? Or the unemployment that impoverishes some of us? Or the racism some of us face? Or the rape some of us fear? What about AIDS? Is it enough to say, Not our problem? Of course gay and lesbian politics is a progressive politics: It depends on progress for the accomplishment of any of its goals. Is there any progressive politics that recognizes no connectedness, no border-crossings, no solidarity or possibility for mutual aid?

"A map of the world that does not include Utopia is not worth even glancing at, for it leaves out the one country at which Humanity is always landing." This is neither Bruce nor Andrew, but that most glorious and silly gay writer, Oscar Wilde. Because this is the twenty-fifth anniversary of Stonewall, that mythic moment that lies beyond all objective discourse (just kidding, Bruce!), we are all thinking big. That's what anniversaries are for, to invite consideration of the past and contemplation of the future. And so, to lift my sights and spirits after the dour, pinched antipolitics of gay conservatism, I revisited Oscar, a lavish thinker, as he appears in political drag in his magnificent essay, "The Soul of Man Under Socialism."

Oscar, like our two boys, was an individualist, though rather more individual in the way he lived, and much less eager to conform. It would be stretching things to say Oscar was a radical, exactly, though if Bruce and Andrew had been his contemporaries, Lord knows how they would have tut-tutted at his scandalous carryings-on.

Oscar's socialism is an exaltation of the individual, of the individual's immense capacities for beauty and for pleasure. Behind Oscar's socialist politics, wrote John Cowper Powys, is "a grave Mirandola-like desire to reconcile the woods of Arcady with the Mount of Transfiguration." What could be swoonier? Or, with all due deference to Andrew and Bruce's sober, rational politics of homosexuality, what could be more gay?

Powys wrote that Oscar's complaint against capitalism and industrialism is "the irritation of an extremely sensitive skin . . . combined with a pleasure-lover's annoyance at seeing other people so miserably wretched." If there is a relationship between socialism and homosexual liberation, perhaps this is it: an irritation of the skin.

"One's regret," Oscar tells us, "is that society should be constructed on such a basis that man has been forced into a groove in which he cannot freely develop what is wonderful, and fascinating, and delightful in him—in which, in fact, he misses the true pleasure and joy of living." Socialism, as an alternative to individualism politically and capitalism economically, must surely have as its ultimate objective the restitution of the joy of living we may have lost when we first picked up a tool. Toward what other objective is it worthy to strive?

Perhaps the far horizon of lesbian and gay politics is a socialism of the skin. Our task is to confront the political problematics of desire and repression. As much as Bruce and Andrew want to distance themselves from the fact, Stonewall was a sixties thing, part of the utopian project of that time (and the sixties, Joan Nestle writes, is "the favorite target of people who take delight in the failure of dreams"). Honoring the true desire of the skin, and the connection between the skin and heart and mind and soul, is what homosexual liberation is about.

Gay rights may be obtainable, on however broad or limited a basis, but liberation depends on a politics that goes beyond, not an antipolitics. Our unhappiness as scared queer children doesn't only isolate us, it also politicizes us. It inculcates in us a desire for connection that is all the stronger because we have experienced its absence. Our suffering teaches us solidarity; or it should.

★ LOOKING BACKWARD ★

Adolph Reed Jr.

FROM *THE NATION*, NOVEMBER 28, 1994

A review of *The Bell Curve: Intelligence and Class Structure in American Life*. By Richard J. Herrnstein and Charles Murray.

Charles Murray first slithered into American public life a decade ago, when he published *Losing Ground: American Social Policy, 1950–1980*, in which he argued that the cause of poverty among black Americans is the very effort to alleviate poverty through social provision. He purported to show, by means of a mass of charts and straw formulations he called "thought experiments," that the social welfare system institutionalizes perverse incentives encouraging indolence, wanton reproduction, and general profligacy. He proposed, appropriately for a book bearing a 1984 publication date, that the poor would be best helped by the elimination of all social support; a regime of tough love would wean them from debilitating dependency, on pain of extermination. (Now we have to wonder how the lazy dreck had enough sense to identify and respond to the incentives, but that was, after all, a different book for a different day.)

Losing Ground made a huge splash, catapulting Murray into prominence as the Reagan Administration's favorite social scientist and winning him luminary status in the social policy research industry. One can only wonder what heights of popularity Thomas Malthus would attain if he could come back into a world stocked with computers that perform multiple regression analysis!

Murray has returned to the center of the public stage now with publication of *The Bell Curve*, the product of a diabolical collaboration with Richard Herrnstein, the late Harvard psychologist known outside the academy—like his Berkeley counterpart, Arthur Jensen—for a more than twenty-year crusade to justify inequality by attributing it to innate, and therefore supposedly ineradicable, differences in intelligence.

As their title implies, Herrnstein and Murray contend that the key to explaining all inequality and all social problems in the United States is stratification by a unitary entity called intelligence, or "cognitive ability"— as measured, of course, in I.Q. This claim has surfaced repeatedly over the past seventy-five years only to be refuted each time as unfounded class, race and gender prejudice. (See, for instance, Stephen Jay Gould's *The Mismeasure of Man*.) *The Bell Curve* advances it with the same kind of deluge of statistical and logical sophistry that has driven its predecessors, as well as Murray's opus of tough love for poor people.

Herrnstein and Murray see rigid I.Q. stratification operating through every sphere of social life. And they put two distinct wrinkles on this long-running fantasy. First is Herrnstein's old claim that I.Q. stratification is becoming ever more intense in a postindustrial world that requires cognitive ability over all else. As democratic institutions have succeeded in leveling the playing field, differences of individual merit become all the more pronounced. Second, the demonic duo back coyly away from the implications of their eugenic convictions (no doubt because cultural memory decays slowly enough that people still remember the Nazi death camps). Instead of directly endorsing extermination, mass sterilization and selective breeding—which nonetheless implicitly shadow the book—they propose a world in which people will be slotted into places that fit their cognitive ability, in which each of us will be respected for what we actually are and can be (which will amount to more or less the same thing).

The effect of this reform will be, as they see it, to end ressentiment from and against those who seek more than their just deserts or aspire beyond their natural capacities. Of course, we'll need to have controls to make sure that dullards do what is best for them and don't get out of line. But that is a necessary price to stem the present tide of social breakdown. We shall, that is, have to destroy democracy to save it.

The Bell Curve's message about the inevitability of existing patterns of inequality rests on a series of claims concerning intelligence. These are: (1) that human intelligence is reducible to a unitary, core trait that is measurable and reliably expressed as a single numerical entity, I.Q.; (2) that I.Q. increasingly determines (or strongly influences—Herrnstein and Murray frequently try to hide behind the weaker claim while substantially assuming the stronger one) socioeconomic status and behavior; (3) that I.Q. is distributed unevenly through the population in general and by race in particular; and (4) that cognitive ability is given and "substantially" (another bogus hedge) fixed by genetic inheritance. These claims are highly dubious. Some of them are preposterous and loony. All are marinated in self-congratulatory class prejudice and racism.

The book begins with a lengthy attempt to rehabilitate the old reductionist notion that there is a biologically based hereditary "general factor of cognitive ability," a variant of the semi-mystical entity that Charles Spearman, a pioneer psychometrician (i.e., intelligence tester), labeled "g" in the early 1900s. The defense rests largely on protests that proponents of hereditarian I.Q. theories—for example, explicit racists like William Shockley and Arthur Jensen and the racist and fraud Cyril Burt—have been maligned and persecuted by ideologically motivated environmentalists and egalitarians. (Hereditarians, of course, are only tough-minded scientists who pursue trust courageously in the face of personal danger and ostracism.) The authors even try to sanitize psychometry's sordid history of eugenicist affiliations bordering on genocide. "[D]uring the first decades of the century," they coo, "a few testing enthusiasts proposed using the results of mental tests to support outrageous racial policies," such as forced sterilization, racist immigration restrictions and the like. By contrast, Daniel Kevles (*In the Name of*

Eugenics) and others have amply documented prominent psychometricians' active and extensive involvement in shaping eugenicist public policies in the United States that affected thousands of lives in the first third of the century and beyond. Stefan Kuhl (*The Nazi Connection: Eugenics, American Racism and German National Socialism*), moreover, details the close connections and mutual admiration between American and German Nazi eugenicists throughout the 1930s and for years after. *The Bell Curve*'s tepid acknowledgment smacks of white Southerners' claims that the original Ku Klux Klan consisted of pranksters whose high jinks sometimes got out of hand—sort of the DKEs of the Reconstruction era.

Having, at least in their view, rescued psychometry's reputation from its own heinous past, the authors then offer a two-pronged, ostensibly pragmatic defense of their version of "g." They point to the tendency of tests of mental aptitude to converge, such that performance on some tests correlates with performance on others. For Hernnstein and Murray, as for Spearman and his epigones, that convergence indicates that the tests variously measure a single, fundamental property-general cognitive ability. They also adduce the authority of "the top experts on testing and cognitive ability" in support of the contention that this "g" exists.

As Gould and others (for example, R.C. Lewontin, Steven Rose and Leon J. Kamin, *Not in Our Genes: Biology, Ideology, and Human Nature*) have pointed out, though, the numerical representation of a vector of test scores does not necessarily denote a real, empirical entity. To presume that it does is to succumb to a fetishism of numbers that inverts the relation between statistical analysis and the world it is intended to illuminate. The hard certainty of the formal mathematical abstraction imbues it with an apparent reality of its own: If a firm statistical relation exists, then it must correspond to something in the empirical world. (Gould characterizes this idealist fallacy, which lately has been resurgent among social scientists, as "physics envy.") In the absence of neurological or other physiological evidence, there is no reason to believe that the numerical "Intelligence Quotient" captures anything but a mathematical relation among a battery of test scores. This relation, in addition, is doubly arbitrary. It is not the only mathematical relation thinkable among the tests, nor are the tests themselves self-evidently measures of innate abilities that can be arrayed hierarchically. And since we can know "g" only through test scores and their correlation, determination of a test's accuracy in identifying core cognitive ability becomes to some degree a function of the extent to which the scores converge in variance. There is at least a potential for idealist circularity in this argument: We know a test is a reliable measure of intelligence because we stipulate that intelligence is indicated when the test's parts correlate well with one another.

In fact, both prongs of *The Bell Curve*'s defense of the reductionist notion of intelligence rest on circular argument. Appealing to the consensual authority of psychometricians to validate I.Q. testing is like appealing to the consensual authority of creationists to validate creationism. Psychometry by and large is intelligence testing, so it would be more than stunning to find a consensus of psychometricians that didn't endorse I.Q. testing. Similarly, the contention that the vector of test scores measures a core cognitive ability depends on a prior assumption that what tests measure is indeed core intelligence. As Lewontin et al. note, to determine whether a test is accurate requires some pre-existing notion of what it should measure and what results it should yield. We know that early psychometricians took girls' outperformance of boys on certain items to indicate flawed test design. And other scientific racists of that era, when confronted with blacks' greater possession than whites of some trait or other thought to be desirable, simply reversed their interpretations of that trait's significance.

Herrnstein and Murray consistently bend over backward to give the benefit of the doubt to research whose conclusions they find congenial, and they dismiss, misrepresent or ignore that which contradicts their vision. For instance, they decline to engage the work of Harvard psychologist Howard Gardner (*Frames of Mind: The Theory of Multiple Intelligences and Multiple Intelligences: The Theory in Practice*) or Yale's Robert Sternberg (*Beyond IQ*), among others, who argue for multiple fields of intelligence that are not hierarchically organized. They don't even mention the work of Gardner's colleague David Perkins, whose *Learnable Intelligence: Breaking the IQ Barrier* appears in the same Free Press catalogue as *The Bell Curve*. They also repeatedly and disingenuously accuse anti-hereditarians of contending that genes play no part in social life. Hernnstein and Murray justify their insistence on the I.Q. standard, to the exclusion of other ways of construing intelligence, primarily by pointing to the apparently strong positive relationship between I.Q. and school performance, income and other measures of success. This presumably shows that I.Q. is the critical form of intelligence because it is such an important predictor of life chances. At the same time, they insist that I.Q. is not just or even mainly an artifact of class position. They frequently even take education or socioeconomic status as proxies for I.Q. when they lack actual test scores. This circularity reaches its zenith—and reveals the ideological motor that drives the authors' vision—in the following formulation:

> The broad envelope of possibilities suggests that senior business executives soak up a large portion of the top IQ decile who are not engaged in the dozen or so high-IQ professions. . . . A high proportion of people in those positions graduated from college, one screen. They have risen in the corporate hierarchy over the course of their careers, which is probably another screen for IQ. What is their mean IQ? There is no precise answer. Studies suggest that the mean for . . . all white collar professionals is around 107, but that category is far broader than the one we have in mind. Moreover, the mean IQ of four-year college graduates in general was estimated at about 115 in 1972, and senior executives probably have a mean above that average.

Let's pause a moment to marvel at the elegant precision of science.

Herrnstein and Murray seek to avoid the appearance of circularity through two strains of statistically based argument. On the one hand, they claim that the relation between I.Q. and social performance persists even when all environmental differences are taken into account. On the other, they revert to the stock-in-trade that has always underscored the hereditarian camp's sideshow quality; I mean, of course, the studies of separated twins.

I admit to not having tracked down and examined closely the research they cite to support these two lines of defense. Four points nevertheless suggest cause for skepticism. First, social environments are complex, and it is very difficult—especially in a large aggregate sample like the National Longitudinal Survey of Youth, on which *The Bell Curve* principally relies in this regard—to wash out confidently the multifarious consequences of social stratification. Simply controlling for parental income, as these studies typically do, is hardly sufficient. The effects of stratification can work in subtle and indirect ways that persist through momentary parity of income. For instance, the child of a first-generation middle-class black or Puerto Rican family is likely to have fewer social resources—given the effects of ghettoization and discrimination in access to sources of personal capital (mortgages and other bank loans, accumulation of capitalizable home equity, investment opportunities, inherited wealth)—than her white counterpart, and to shoulder an additional burden of everyday racial discrimination. Hernnstein and Murray are crudely, and strategically, insensitive to this level of complexity, as they show when dismissing the possibility that racial discrimination might account for persisting black/white differences in I.Q. scores:

> An appeal to the effects of racism . . . requires explaining why environments poisoned by discrimination and racism for some other groups—against the Chinese or the Jews in some regions of America, for example—have left them with higher scores than the national average.

Second, as Lewontin and Richard Levins (*The Dialectical Biologist*) reflect a consensus among professional geneticists [see Susan Sperling's essay in the November 28, 1994, issue of the *Nation*] in painstakingly arguing, the attempt to apportion definitively the separate effects of heredity and environment is hopelessly wrongheaded and naive. I quote them at some length because of the importance of the point:

> All individuals owe their phenotype to the biochemical activity of their genes in a unique sequence of environments and to developmental events that may occur subsequent to, although dependent upon, the initial action of the genes. . . . If an event results from the joint operation of a number of causative chains, and if these causes "interact" in any generally accepted meaning of the word, it becomes conceptually impossible to assign quantitative values to the causes of that individual event. . . . It is obviously . . . absurd to say what proportion of a plant's height is owed to the fertilizer it received and what proportion to the water, or to ascribe so many inches of a man's height to his genes and so many to his environment.

Herrnstein and Murray presume that in measuring patterns of variation in I.Q. scores in a way that neutralizes the effects of selected aspects of environment, they can distill the part played by heredity in determining cognitive ability. Thus they repeatedly invoke the claim that intelligence is at least 40–80 percent determined by inheritance. This presumption and the claim derived from it are plain stupid.

Third, even if we grant their crackerbarrel view of causation and variation, their case is defeated by the weight of its own numbers. By their own precious calculations, I.Q. accounts for no more than between 10 and 20 percent of the variation they discover between individuals and "races" on most measures, and usually closer to the lower end. (Howard Gardner makes this point also in his important forthcoming review of *The Bell Curve* in *The American Prospect*, where he also discusses at length other approaches to theorizing human intelligence that Herrnstein and Murray ignore.) If, as they take as a consensual figure, I.Q. derives 60 percent from genetic inheritance (and what could that statement possibly mean as a practical matter, anyway?), then heredity accounts for no more than 6–12 percent of the total variation they find. Why should the tail wag the dog for all those leaden, deceitful pages?

Fourth, we come to the twin studies. Hernnstein and Murray report that Thomas Bouchard at the University of Minnesota (about whom more later) has found the same strikingly high correlations in I.Q. among his sample of supposedly real twins raised apart that Sir Cyril Burt found among the imaginary twins in his fraudulent "research." (Burt, by the way, was easily the most respected psychometrician of his time, knighted for his accomplishments as a theorist of scientific racial hygiene.) Perhaps, though the possibility that life would so faithfully and dramatically imitate art ought to give pause, particularly considering that few other twin impresarios had ever reported the consistent strength of relationship that Burt claimed. And then there is the troubling issue of what exactly one means by separated twins.

Lewontin, Rose and Kamin in *Not in Our Genes* examine the samples on which the best-known twin studies prior to Bouchard's were based. They note, first, that pure cases of twins separated at birth and raised completely apart would be exceedingly difficult to locate because they would most likely not know each other's whereabouts or even that either sib was in fact half of a twin set. As it turns out, most of the putatively separated twins lived with close family members and most of those who didn't lived with nearby family friends. Nearly all lived within a few miles of and had regular if not constant contact with each other. According to research notes, one English set lived within a few hundred yards of each other, played together regularly and wanted to sit at the same desk at the school they both attended. Another English set had been separated until age five, then finished growing up under the same roof and were in continuous contact thereafter until they were interviewed for the study at age fifty-two. A set in a famous Danish study were "cared for by relatives until the age of seven then lived together with their mother until they were fourteen." The research notes indicate that

> they were usually dressed alike and very often confused by strangers, at school, and sometimes also by their stepfather.

> . . . [They] always kept together when children, they played
> only with each other and were treated as a unit by their
> environment.

Such is the twin research that is the hereditarians' trump card.
(Maybe they can make dog-faced boys the next scholarly frontier.)

Several of *The Bell Curve*'s reviewers have detected a damning empirical flaw in the logic of its case. On the one hand, Hernnstein and Murray contend that I.Q. is largely fixed by nature and cannot be improved. On the other, they note that studies inside their own paradigm have recorded a steady upward trend in test scores across time. They squirm mightily to make those points fit, but they can't. Nor can they face up to the entailments of that contradiction, because the point of the book, like the point of every line that Murray has ever written, as well as every syllable of Hernnstein's I.Q. research, is only to advance a reactionary, racist, and otherwise anti-egalitarian ideological agenda by dressing it with a scientistic patina.

Beneath the mind-numbing barrage of numbers, this book is really just a compendium of reactionary prejudices. I.Q. shapes farsightedness, moral sense, the decisions not to get pregnant, to be employed, not to be a female household head, to marry and to remain married to one's first spouse (presumably the divorced and remarried Murray has an exemption from this criterion), to nurture and attend to one's offspring, and so on.

Simply being stopped—but not charged—by the police becomes evidence of an I.Q.-graded tendency to criminality. White men who have never been stopped have an average I.Q. of 106; those stopped but not booked have to schlepp along at 103; those booked but not convicted check in at 101; the convicted but not incarcerated peer dimly from a 100 wattage; and those who go to jail vegetate at 93. Even putting aside the bigotry embedded in their cops' view of the world, this is batty. Not only is the slope of this curve—as with so much of their data—too perfectly straight but the suggestion that minute increments of difference could portend such grave consequences is numerical fetishism gone off the deep end. Two points on an I.Q. test can separate conviction from acquittal!?

Instructively, the authors restrict their analysis of white criminality to a male sample and parenting to a female sample. Parents = mothers. And while they examine abuse and neglect of children (found to be almost the exclusive province of the lower cognitive orders) among this female sample, spousal abuse is mentioned nowhere in the book, much less considered a form of male criminality.

In his review Howard Gardner accuses Herrnstein and Murray of practicing "scholarly brinkmanship." The description is apt. They repeatedly leave themselves enough wiggle room to avoid responsibility either for the frightening implications of the line they advance so insistently or for defending the crackpot pseudoscience on which they ultimately base their interpretation. Just a few examples of the way the authors try to have it both ways: Early in the book—and Murray has repeated this canard ad nauseam in his soft-spoken, carefully measured tones on news chat shows since publication—they announce piously that they want all to understand that "intelligence is a noun, not an accolade." Small matter that the book is entirely an attempt to justify the opposite view. Similarly, they end with an equally pious call to treat every person as an individual and declaim against making judgments about groups, when group difference has been the central organizing principle of their entire argument.

This kind of mendacity is one of their narrative's main tropes. When forced by the logic of their own account to a point at which they would have to declare explicitly as militant hereditarians, they say, Well, it really doesn't matter ultimately whether or not I.Q. is inherited because the environmental changes required to increase I.Q. are impossibly huge. Yet that argument depends completely on the hereditarian justification of inequality that they spend the whole book trying to establish.

Nowhere is the authors' dishonesty clearer than with respect to race. Their analysis of white variation in I.Q. is ultimately a front to fend off charges of racism. What really drives this book, and reflects the diabolism of the Murray/Herrnstein combination, is its claim to demonstrate black intellectual inferiority. They use I.Q. to support a "twofer": opposition to affirmative action, which overplaces incompetent blacks, and the contention that black poverty derives from the existence of an innately inferior black underclass.

Murray has protested incessantly that he and Herrnstein wanted in no way to be associated with racism, that the book isn't even about race, which is after all the topic of only one of *The Bell Curve's* twenty-two chapters. But in addition to the infamous Chapter Thirteen, "Ethnic Differences in Cognitive Ability," three others center on arguments about black (and, to varying degrees, Latino) inferiority. The very next chapter, "Ethnic Inequalities in Relation to IQ," is a direct attempt to explain existing racial stratification along socioeconomic lines as the reflection of differences in group intelligence. The other two chapters in Part III seek to pull together claims about racial differences in intelligence and behavior. Those four chapters set the stage for the book's only two explicitly policy-driven chapters, "Affirmative Action in Higher Education" and "Affirmative Action in the Workplace," both of which are about initiatives directed toward blacks, and both slide into stoking white populist racism with "thought experiments" positing poor or working-class whites shunted aside in favor of underqualified, well-off blacks.

Murray's protests do suggest something about his views of race, however; it's apparently a property only some of us have. *The Bell Curve* makes a big deal of restricting the eight chapters of Part II to discussion of whites alone. If we assume that they are no less a "race" than everyone else is, then well over half the book is organized around race as a unit of analysis. Moreover, the theme of racially skewed intelligence and its significance for public policy runs through the entire volume. (In the third chapter the authors speculate about how many billions of dollars the Supreme Court's 1971 *Griggs v. Duke Power Company* decision, striking down the use of all but performance-based tests for employment and promotion, has cost the "American economy," and they argue gratuitously for choosing police by I.Q.) And how could it be otherwise in a book whose punch line is that society is and must be stratified by intelligence, which is distributed unequally among individuals and racial groups and cannot be changed in either?

Despite their concern to insulate themselves from the appearance of racism, Hernnstein and Murray display a perspective worthy of an Alabama filling station. After acknowledging that genetic variations among individuals within a given "race" are greater than those between "races," they persist in maintaining that racially defined populations must differ genetically in significant ways because otherwise they wouldn't have different hair texture or skin color. And besides, they say, there must be differences between races because races "are by definition groups of people who differ in characteristic ways."

Despite Murray's complaints that it has been misinterpreted, *The Bell Curve* is committed to racial inequality. Admitting that they can't isolate biologically pure racial categories, Hernnstein and Murray opt to "classify people according to the way they classify themselves." But this destroys the possibility that their statistical hocus-pocus does any of the hereditarian work they claim for it. What they describe at most is race as a category of common social experience. Therefore, whatever patterns they find among racialized populations can only reflect that experience.

Most tellingly, however, they attempt quite directly to legitimize J. Philippe Rushton, whose most recent excrescence is reviewed by Susan Sperling in the November 28, 1994, issue of the *Nation*. They announce self-righteously that "Rushton's work is not that of a crackpot or a bigot, as many of his critics are given to charging." This about a man who presents racial rankings on "Criteria for Civilization" (only "Caucasoids," naturally, consistently meet all twenty-one items on his checklist) and "Personality and Temperament Traits," in addition to erect penis size (by length and circumference, no less), as well as the rest of the stock-in-trade of Victorian scientistic racism, and who computes an "Interbreeding Depression Score" to help clarify his statistical findings!

Rushton is in fact only the tip of the iceberg. *The Bell Curve* is embedded in the intellectual apparatus of the cryptofascist right. The central authorities on whom Herrnstein and Murray rely for their claims about I.Q., race and heredity are nearly all associated with the Pioneer Fund, an ultrarightist foundation that was formed in the 1930s to advance eugenicist agendas. The fund boasts of having been almost entirely responsible for funding I.Q. and race and heredity research in the United States in the past twenty years, and much of it worldwide. Rushton, along with nearly all those who contribute jacket blurbs for his book, is a major recipient of Pioneer grants. This includes Thomas Bouchard of the Minnesota twins, as well as Richard Lynn, on whom Herrnstein and Murray draw extensively, describing him as "a leading scholar of racial and ethnic differences." Among Lynn's leading scholarship to which they refer are the following articles: "The Intelligence of the Mongoloids," *Personality and Individual Differences* (1987); "Further Evidence for the Existence of Race and Sex Differences in Cranial Capacity," *Social Behavior and Personality* (1993); and "Positive Correlations Between Head Size and IQ," *British Journal of Educational Psychology* (1989). In addition, Lynn is editor of *Mankind Quarterly*, the Pioneer Fund's flagship journal. (Readers interested in the history and current involvements of the Pioneer Fund should consult my column in the December issue of *The Progressive*; Ruth Conniff's "The War on Aliens" in the October 1993 *Progressive*; Stefan Kuhl's *The Nazi Connection*; and John Sedgwick's "The Mentality Bunker" in the November 1994 *GQ*.)

Herrnstein and Murray take pains to sugarcoat and hedge their more outrageous claims, but their nasty political agenda, always visible in the wings, occasionally comes to center stage. They warn of the "dysgenic" effects for the nation of low-I.Q. women's relatively greater fertility and that the "shifting ethnic makeup" resulting from immigration of low-I.Q., high-breeding populations will "lower the average American IQ by 0.8 points per generation."

What makes this international vipers' nest of reactionaries so dangerous is that many of its members maintain legitimate academic reputations. Rushton, for instance, as recently as 1988 won a Guggenheim Fellowship. Others routinely do contract research for the U.S. military. Most hold respectable university appointments.

This brings me to the final and perhaps most important point to be made about this hideous book. It is worthwhile to pause for a moment to compare the appearance of *The Bell Curve* to the last significant eruption of pseudoscientific, hereditarian political reaction into American public life. Only two decades ago, the same Herrnstein, Jensen and Shockley flooded the channels of the public information industry with essentially the same arguments I've been discussing here.

At that time I refused to attend to the controversy, partly out of a conviction that it is both beneath my dignity and politically unacceptable to engage in a debate that treats as an open question that I might be a monkey. Progressive forces were still at least a residual presence in American politics, however, and liberal intellectuals could be counted on to fight the foes of minimal human equality. I am still convinced that having to do what I've done in this review besmirches my dignity. It's a statement about the right's momentum that *The Bell Curve* makes such a splash that the *Nation* has to devote so much space to arming our troops against it.

Mainstream racial discourse is dishonest and polluted enough to take the book seriously. Jason DeParle, in his *New York Times Magazine* puff piece, can't decide whether the Charles Murray who burned a cross in his youth, who alleges that the Irish have a way with words, Scotch-Irish are cantankerous and blacks are musical and athletic, and who proposes a separate but equal world in which "each clan will add up its accomplishments using its own weighting system . . . and, most importantly, will not be concerned about comparing its accomplishments line-by-line with those of any other clan," is a racist.

New Republic editor Andrew Sullivan opines that "the notion that there might be resilient ethnic differences in intelligence is not . . . an inherently racist belief." Now liberals of all stripes—and even illiberals like Pat Buchanan, John McLaughlin and Rush Limbaugh, which should make us wonder what exactly is going on—are eloquently dissenting from Herrnstein and Murray's unsavory racial messages. It's necessary to remind them that more than any other force in American politics, they are responsible for this book's visibility.

Murray has always been the same intellectual brownshirt. He has neither changed over the past decade nor done anything else that might
redeem his reputation as a scholar. And it doesn't matter whether he is a
committed ideologue or an amoral opportunist. Nazis came in both
varieties—think of Alfred Rosenberg and Paul de Man—and in real life
the lines separating the two are seldom clear. We can trace Murray's
legitimacy directly to the spinelessness, opportunism and racial bad faith
of the liberals in the social-policy establishment. Although Murray's dra-
conian conclusions seemed unpalatable at first, they have since come to
inform common sense about social policy, even in the Clinton White
House. Liberals have never frankly denounced Murray as the right-wing
hack that he is. They appear on panels with him and treat him as a
serious, albeit conservative, fellow worker in the vineyard of truth. They
have allowed him to set the terms of debate over social welfare and bend
over backward not to attack him sharply.

Many of those objecting to Herrnstein and Murray's racism embrace
positions that are almost indistinguishable, except for the resort to
biology. Mickey Kaus in his scurrilous tract *The End of Equality* presents
a substantive agenda for American politics quite like theirs, minus the
I.Q. and explicit hereditarianism. Herrnstein and Murray note the sim-
ilarities and draw on him for their absurd concluding chapter. Although
William Julius Wilson in *The Truly Disadvantaged* criticizes Murray's
thesis in *Losing Ground*, he does so only by suggesting alternatives to
Murray's interpretation of data. Wilson reserves harsh moral judgment
for left-liberals, whom he scolds for not being tough-minded enough
about pathologies among the poor. He urges a pre-emptive focus on
"ghetto-specific cultural characteristics," thus ceding important ground
to Murray's perspective. Many of those so exercised in the *New
Republic*'s special feature on *The Bell Curve* have joined Murray in mean-
spirited bashing of "political correctness" and affirmative action. And
many more join him in writing about inner-city poor people as an alien
and defective Other, a dangerous problem to be administered and
controlled—not as fellow citizens. I have argued recently (in the February 1994 *Progressive*) that the difference between racially inflected

"underclass" ideology and old-fashioned biological racism is more apparent than real. Racist ideologies in the United States have always come in culturalist and biologistic, and often overlapping, strains. The point is the claim of essential inequality, not the location of its source.

While reading Hernnstein and Murray and the literature on which they draw, I often felt like a mirror image of Julian West, Edward Bellamy's protagonist in *Looking Backward*, who fell unconscious at the end of the nineteenth century and awoke at the end of the twentieth. And indeed, the authors' strategic hedging of their hereditarian claims could presage the return of an updated version of the Lamarckian race theory popular a century ago. As "culture" has increasingly become a euphemism for "race"—an expression of inherent traits—it is only a short step to characterizations of group difference more overtly inflected toward biology, yet avoiding what remains, for the moment anyway, the stigma of biological determinism.

There's not much reason for optimism. This past July, Daniel Patrick Moynihan announced at his Senate Finance Committee hearing on welfare reform that we could be witnessing the processes of "speciation" at work among the innercity poor. Nodding their agreement were the Secretary of Health and Human Services, Donna Shalala, and her two world-class poverty researcher under secretaries, Mary Jo Bane and David Ellwood (the originator of the "two years and off" welfare policy, who incidentally shows up in *The Bell Curve*'s acknowledgments). Just how different is that from Rushton or the Aryan Nations or the old White Citizens Council?

As I was writing this essay I learned of the untimely death of Erwin Knoll, editor of the *Progressive*. He adds to the list of our recent losses and will be sorely missed. The more the realization settles in, the deeper the sadness becomes.

★ MARTYRS AND FALSE ★
POPULISTS

Adolph Reed Jr.

FROM *THE PROGRESSIVE,* OCTOBER 1995

In desperate times we strain to find something to celebrate. There is an understandable tendency to romanticize the oppressed, and to grasp at anything that looks like alternative politics.

Hence the recent, disturbingly knee-jerk reactions within the left to such disparate phenomena as the militia movement and the Mumia Abu-Jamal case.

I was surprised by the letters in the *Nation* and the *Progressive* from readers who were affronted by negative coverage of the militias in each magazine. I've heard the same kind of position taken in conversations with people I know personally who identify with the left. The substance of this ostensibly progressive defense of the militia movement goes something like this: the militia supporters are by and large working class; they often are recruited from especially depressed local economies; their membership expresses their alienation from politics-as-usual; therefore, we shouldn't dismiss their populist frustrations.

It is true that militia members want to curtail the repressive power of the state and complain about the predatory power of large corporations. They oppose NAFTA and want to assert popular, community control of government. But defending them on these grounds is naive and short-sighted, and reflects a broader, perhaps more insidious tendency—including a kind of accentuate-the-positive bias toward whatever looks like autonomous, populist action. This is the same tendency that willfully inflates any sort of apparently group-conscious activity—for instance, youth fads—into the status of political movements.

On the militia issue, the first problem is that class origin, or for that matter class identity, isn't an adequate criterion for making judgments about political positions. The principle that if it comes from the oppressed, there must be something OK about it is not only simplistic; it can have truly reactionary implications. This kind of thinking has too often led down the road to complete accommodation to the worst strains arising from working classes. In fact, it's almost routine now that calls for sympathetic understanding of working-class bigotry—"We need to recognize the genuine fear of loss of control of the family, traditional values, close-knit neighborhood, jobs, way of life, etc., etc."—are the first steps down the road to full-scale retreat from commitment to equality and social justice. Think about the Democratic Leadership Council.

There is a long history of rationalizing working-class nativism and racism. It helped sanitize the regime of terror that was the Southern Redemption, restoring unadulterated white-supremacist rule after Reconstruction. The architects of that restoration's ideology characterized the racist putsch in the South as a revolt of the common people against a corrupt elite that cynically used blacks to further unpopular aims.

The same mindset counseled sympathetic understanding for labor's rabid anti-Asian racism in the West in the late nineteenth century, and tolerated the New York draft riot of 1863, anti-feminist and anti-abortion activism, and whites' anti-busing riots. One version even sympathized with official resistance in Yonkers, New York, to court-ordered remediation of a lengthy, nefarious history of racial discrimination. Yonkers, the line went, was being penalized as a working-class/lower-middle-class suburb that can't afford to use exclusionary zoning to keep blacks and Hispanics out.

Of course, most leftists who have a warm spot for the militia movement would not support these positions. But the differences are more of degree than of kind. Today, we hear arguments that we should focus on common class interests like living-wage jobs for all rather than affirmative action, and "universalistic" rather than "race-based" social policy. In his new book, *Turning Back: The Retreat from Racial Justice in American Thought and Policy*, Stephen Steinberg discusses how this ostensibly farther-reaching alternative often masks a retreat from the struggle for equality within the working class. Sometimes, he notes, it yields a racial trickle-down argument that the best way to fight racism or sexism is to direct benefits or strategy to whites and men.

Racist and fascist movements always have some popular, working-class base. Mussolini came out of the Italian Socialist party, and National Socialism sought actively to compete for the hearts and minds of politically unsophisticated German workers disposed to authoritarian, conspiratorial, and scapegoating theories. In both cases, the movement drew energy from the same kind of superficially anti-capitalist rhetoric that the militias project—complete with their versions of "black helicopter" fantasies. The Nazis also pioneered, in their conspiratorial mythology about German defeat in World War I, the "stab in the back" theory that underlies the POW/MIA lunacy running through the ideological pools in which the militia movement swims.

And, besides, their anti-statism really isn't the same as ours, or it shouldn't be anyway.

But confusion on this score points up another problem in the left. We often aren't clear enough about distinguishing opposition to the actions of particular governments and regimes from hostility to the actions of government in principle. As a result, we sometimes over-value anything that looks like an insurgency against concentrated power.

It's easy, for instance, to paint ordinary Not In My Back Yard politics at the local level as something grander and more progressive. Mobilization by residents of a threatened neighborhood to stop a corporate development project can be a very good thing. But the visions that support such mobilizing aren't necessarily progressive; they can rest on the same kind of parochial territorialism that prompts demonstrations against housing desegregation. In fact, opponents of open housing routinely see themselves as the victims of oppressive government and evil realtors. Even the slow-growth movement in local politics isn't unambiguously democratic or anti-corporate. Often enough it simply represents the efforts of those who arrived last week to keep anyone else from arriving next week. We have to recognize such struggles' ambiguity if we are to realize their best tendencies.

We have to recognize that not every popular mobilization is progressive just because it arises from the grassroots. Having experienced the underside of populist rhetoric in segregationism and opposition to civil rights, I'm perhaps especially sensitive to the fact that a lot of nastiness can lie under labels like "the people." Lynch mobs were, after all, a form of popular, direct action.

No matter what Alexander Cockburn says, I haven't seen anything to suggest that I shouldn't judge the militiamen by the company they keep politically. Nor have I seen any signs among them of a substantive vision for political and economic reorganization that would allay my fears.

I confess, as well, to being toward the statist end of the left, at least among those of us whose politics were formed in the 1960s and after. I'm always uneasy when we get fuzzy about the distinction between our objections to actions taken by those who control the American state and a more general objection to the State as an abstraction. Yes, government is ultimately a means of coercion. Therefore, it needs to be accountable to the citizenry. At the same time, government needs to be insulated from the whims of fleeting, potentially tyrannical majorities.

The experience of being black in the United States highlights the dangers of a simplistically majoritarian notion of democracy. Decentralization of public authority in the name of popular democracy—from "states' rights" to the "new (and newer) federalism"—has been a rallying cry of opponents of black civil rights for more than a century and a half.

The state is the only vehicle that can protect ordinary citizens against the machinations of concentrated private power. Even though it does function as an executive committee of the ruling class, the national state is the guarantor of whatever victories working people, minorities, gays, women, the elderly, and other constituencies we embrace have been able to win—often enough against the state itself. And this applies both to formalizing those victories as rights and using public policy to redistribute resources that make them practical reality.

The public sector is the area of the economy most responsive to equal-opportunity employment. And the national state—ours as well as others—is the only entity powerful enough to control the activities of piratical multinational corporations. That's what the fights against NAFTA and GATT are all about—preserving the state's capacity to enforce social, economic, and environmental standards within its own territory.

And that's just the defensive side of the struggle. We need to press for a more active use of the state in international economic and foreign policy to combat the multinationals' depredations across the globe.

It always seemed to me that our struggle, to rehearse a long-outdated slogan, wasn't really to smash the state, but to seize it and direct it to democratic and egalitarian purposes.

I don't get a sense of anything compatible with this perspective from the militia movement. Empty cliches like, "The government is the child of the people and has to be spanked when it gets out of line," don't inspire confidence. Who do the militiamen have in mind when they evoke the image of "the people"? What do they consider appropriate uses of public authority?

As Chip Berlet and others point out in the June issue of the *Progressive*, there's not much reason to think that the militia movement's politics are anything other than paranoid proto-fascist. To say that they're not all racist, sexist, or xenophobic is both bizarre and beside the point. Organizationally and ideologically they're plugged into the most vicious, lunatic, and dangerous elements of the right. No matter that some individuals may think, or want to think, or want gullible journalists to think that they're just out playing a more strenuous version of *Dungeons and Dragons*.

So what if this puts me on the same side as the Justice Department? We're also on the same side when we demand enforcement of voting rights or redress from Ku Klux Klan violence or prosecution of corporate criminals. And, even if I weren't a former object of COINTELPRO-era surveillance and harassment, I would have no illusions about the really existing law-enforcement authorities—at whatever level of the federal system—being dependable allies. I grew up in inner cities where municipal police were clearly an occupying force. I lived through the civil-rights movement when the state police and FBI worked hand-in-hand with the Klan. Nevertheless, it's important for us to recognize that in principle at least the state belongs to us as much as to any other interests in the society, and part of our fight must be to make it responsive to us.

The issue of our relation to the criminal-justice system highlights another problematic tendency in the left, one that appears most topically in the Mumia Abu-Jamal support movement. We often have trouble keeping straight that being a victim of injustice has no necessary relation to the quality of one's politics or character. A friend in Atlanta, in the aftermath of Wayne Williams's conviction in the city's missing-and-murdered-children case that drew national attention in the early 1980s, observed that the state probably had just railroaded a guilty man. We have to recognize that that is always a possibility in the messy world of social experience.

This is true of organizations as well as individuals. Members of the MOVE cult in Philadelphia certainly should not have been bombed by the city, but it was reasonable to evict them after years of their neighbors' complaints of harassment and public-health violations.

I don't presume to pronounce on Abu-Jamal's guilt or innocence. At this moment only three issues should concern us: that there are very persuasive reasons to believe that he didn't receive a fair trial, quite likely for political reasons; that his freedom of speech has been violated; and that he is an atypically visible victim of the barbarity of capital punishment. We must avoid the temptation to exalt him as a symbol of progressive politics. All that most of us know about his politics, apart from his speaking out against police brutality, is that he has some connection to MOVE—a group with pretty wacky ideas. Certainly he is an activist, but there are a lot of activists, some of whom have bad politics. Being victimized by the state should not in itself confer political stature.

First of all, the evidence to which we have access leaves open a possibility that Abu-Jamal could actually be guilty of the crime with which he is charged. Second, whether he's guilty or innocent, his ordeal doesn't indicate anything about the substance of his politics. It's certainly right and important to rally and organize to support his case. But we must take care neither to rush to make him a hero nor to let his appeal as an individual divert us from broader, more complex concerns.

Norma McCorvey (Jane Roe of *Roe v. Wade*), in her recent conversion to Operation Rescue's brand of holy rolling, should give us pause about loading too much significance onto individuals whose personal circumstances momentarily embody larger political concerns.

Some of us can recall as well the case of Joanne Little in the 1970s. Little's was an especially tragic story of an impoverished young woman from a small North Carolina town. While incarcerated on a breaking-and-entering charge, she escaped from jail after killing a white jailer who allegedly attempted to rape her in her cell. The state declared her an outlaw, which amounted to a shoot-on-sight order. Little became a *cause célèbre* for the women's movement in particular. But she was in far over her head as a celebrity. Her subsequent forays into petty criminality left the movement with egg on its face.

Even under the best of conditions a movement built around a single individual can go only so far. This approach trades on the imagery of martyrdom; yet its goal is to ensure that the putative martyrs are rescued. Rescued martyrs, however, are always a potential problem because they live on as fallible human beings.

The difference between James Meredith, who integrated the University of Mississippi and was later shot on a solitary march through the state, and Martin Luther King and Malcolm X is instructive. Unlike the others, Meredith survived and went on to follow the twists and turns of post-segregation politics in increasingly pathetic and perverse ways, bottoming out as an aide to Jesse Helms. Martyrs work best when they're dead.

The *cause-célèbre* phenomenon, like fuzzy-mindedness about the militia movement, reflects a romantic, almost opportunistic tendency in the left. It is part of a soothing, "warm-bath" politics, a politics that is counterproductive because it imagines a specious, quick-fix alternative to the tedious, frustrating work that we most need: building support by organizing to create a base for a concrete, coherent political program.

Especially now, in this most dangerous of times, we need to be much clearer than that.

★ DARK AGE ★

Thomas Frank

From *The Baffler*, #6 and 8, 1995–96

The Cultural Miracle

Have you heard? The "affluent society" is over! Virtually every respectable organ of public opinion has now officially acknowledged its demise: The warm old world of general prosperity is gone forever; poverty and economic insecurity have made a triumphant comeback; the wealth of the nation has concentrated itself rapidly into fewer and fewer hands. Meanwhile every innovation in public policy further impoverishes those who work for a living: "Welfare reform" turns out to mean creating a docile workforce, desperate for any kind of employment; so does any change in labor law; so does "free trade"; so does the explosion of the prison population; so does the growth of the temp industry. But for our cybermasters, displaying their lifestyles in the *New York Times Magazine*'s 1995 special issue on "The Rich," things just keep getting better and better. Tiring of our lo-res problems, they have decided that it's best simply to secede from Second-Wave notions of public responsibility altogether, to seal the perimeter of the gated community, climb into their skyboxes, and jet off into the fully-secured sunset.

For all its great cable channels, the excellent new global cyber capitalism is turning out to be a lot like the simple, grinding, exploitative capitalism of a hundred years ago. The astonishment that so many commentators express at this fact, however, is in one sense profoundly dishonest. Only the most naive can be surprised when a decade of policies designed to crush organized labor, enrich the rich, and render our entire national life subservient to the whims of the market achieve exactly those ends. But in a broader sense the alarm so commonplace on today's editorial pages is genuine. As we learned in the "Deprivation Theory" unit back in Sociology 101, inequality of this kind always begets social upheaval. It's virtually a mathematical certainty: Immiseration brings radicalization. We're walking blithely down the road to disaster; we're asking for a replay of the 1930s, for strikes and interfering brain-trusters; we're pushing what's known euphemistically in this country as "the middle class" to the known limits of its complacency, and this time it won't just be a bunch of suburban kids flipping us off and smoking pot when we told them not to.

And yet the seismographs of public opinion show barely the faintest signs that Americans are preparing to redress what's been done to them. Instead, we on the receiving end of the new inequality are turning out majorities that reaffirm the very politics that have so afflicted us, we are tuning in enthusiastically to hear millionaires and their hired spokesmen pose as rebels, revolutionaries, defenders of the forgotten man. We're rising as one, a song on our lips, to strengthen the hands of those who smite us; we're up on the rooftops of our flooded homes praying fervently for rain; we're offering smiling shoeshines to the people who have come to take possession of our foreclosed farm.

Were the man in the skybox inclined to view events in long-term perspective, perhaps he would be more impressed by the world-historical cultural wonder of which he is the beneficiary. Perhaps he would get on his cell-phone *right now* and pledge ten or twenty thousand to the local televangelist. For this is the doing of the Almighty Invisible Hand as surely as were the "economic miracles" of postwar Germany and Japan, a deliverance from the fate of the strife-and-strike-fatigued Mexicans, French, and British that is so ineffable it can only be attributed to divine intervention. By some act of economic providence the American population seems to have become incapable of acting on its own behalf; "rational choice," at least for us sub-CEOs, has disappeared without a trace from the sociological radar screen. Every day the market commits some new outrage, offers some new demonstration of its worthlessness as a way of ordering human civilization; and every day the organs of official opinion respond with louder and louder declarations of faith in the providence of the market, tributes to the glory of the global economy, zealous denunciations of any organization that would check the market's omnipotence.

Call it, then, the Cultural Miracle, an unprecedented unlinking of economic cause and social effect: a parting of impoverishment and action, of social reality from political consequences. It's the cultural equivalent of the economists' "black box": In one side go the objective circumstances—the most vicious attack on the public well-being by private wealth in decades; and out the other comes the mysterious response—the most abject reverence for private wealth to characterize our public culture in decades. The nation's owners are free to do their worst now, since there's no longer any substantial force out there that can counterbalance, challenge, or even question their choices. The only political "incentives" we have created encourage them to make things worse for us still. Layoffs and lowered wages not only increase profits, they appear to translate directly into hosts of new converts to the Limbaugh Legion, fresh ranks of grumblers vowing revenge against the "politically correct."

We've all heard about the problem of conformity in flush times. The Cultural Miracle, though, is complacency in years of economic privation; it is the spectacle of both parties in free-fall to the right; it is Cold War military policies that, though now lacking any external justification, continue to propel themselves along for no reason but inertia; it is armies of temps and junior executives and blue-collar workers who imagine that the correct response to their own newfound economic precariousness is to smash what's left of the welfare state.

The Cultural Miracle is the Great Disconnection of the American intellect, the virtual extinction of popular thinking in terms of social class at the exact moment when social class has made a most dramatic return. It is a prodigious uncoupling of the language and imagery of everyday life from that whole plodding Second Wave world in which "interests" were organically connected to action and in which economics provided identifiable "motives" for social behavior.

Even economics, it seems, is no longer concerned with the production of things but with the manufacture of imagery, with the health of a Culture Trust whose every arcane fluctuation or celebrity-swap receives the instant scrutiny of both business and lifestyle editors nationwide. Culture causes and simulacrum is in the saddle to a degree that perhaps only Jean Baudrillard can imagine, that the laughably archaic studies linking TV to real-world violence can only begin to suggest. Notions of objective social reality have themselves become objects of easy retro derision, as distant and clichéd as the strange impulses that once prompted our ancestors to attempt to control the world around them.

What desultory feelings of discontent that manage to penetrate the veil quickly assume a savagely retrograde aspect. As in previous hard times, the language of rebellion, of class resentment, and of egalitarianism have taken center stage; once again the elemental battle of the People against the Elite is joined. But don't look for a Clifford Odets comeback or a Eugene Debs postage stamp anytime soon. The characteristic political expression of these miraculous times is a stunningly misguided variant of the old populist formula, this time turned neatly inside out. When we talk about the People we're talking about businessmen; when we heap scorn on snobbish elites, it's those meddling unions and their pals in the government who are our target.

Vox Mercatus, Vox Dei

Right-wing populism has a long history, marked prominently by the racism with which earlier leaders sought to turn the working class against its own interests. But whether its current avatar is Steve Forbes, Newt Gingrich, or Rush Limbaugh, the Cultural Miracle is driven by a different and far more powerful ideological fuel, an anti-intellectualism that is almost metaphysically resolute in its hostility to ideas. However its various nostrums and slogans—the flat tax, the Contract with America, the gold standard, the protective tariff—flicker across the national media consciousness, the guiding impulse of the new cultural dominant remains the same: to think about exerting human control over the marketplace (unless you're a CEO) is somehow elitist. Sometimes, of course, the language that its Republican devotees use is familiar Jacksonian stuff: rantings against effete Harvard, ravings against treasonable experts and their values-eroding expertise, and boasts of their own offensiveness to established policy institutes and schools of government administration. And, as usual, they make their announcements of cultural mistrust not in small-town PTAs and letters to sundry editors, but from positions of real power: magazines and newspapers subsidized by some of the largest fortunes in the country, radio and TV programs that reach vast audiences, the floor of the House of Representatives.

But the latest bearers of the proud tradition of Joe McCarthy, Billy Sunday, and Davy Crockett unleash their powerful new version of the assorted old prejudices not simply against thinkers or the college-educated—many of the inquisitors hold assorted Ph.D.s and MBAs themselves—but against particular kinds of thought. Nor is it merely tradition or that Old Time Religion that they want to defend from the ravages of modernity: On the contrary, for the new Right these are Second Wave ideas as obsolete as ink and paper. The adepts of the Cultural Miracle are fundamentalists of a different sort, prophets not of the angry God of Jonathan Edwards but of the omnipotent market. Read a handful of the sharp-edged editorials of the *Wall Street Journal*, through which the faithful are called to action; scan the pages of the latest business advice books: The market is eternal, the market is unchanging, the market is all-solving, the market is all-seeing, the market is everywhere. The market is both the natural condition of mankind and the unique blessing of the American Eden. The market is also synonymous with democracy: Since it gives the People what the People want, the market is, by definition, the incarnation of the People's will. Those who speak for the market speak with the *vox populi*. Most importantly, though, the market is a fantastically jealous god, deeply offended by the puny efforts of mere mortals to improve on its creations with government, tariffs, unions, or culture.

Having replaced God with the market, the new anti-intellectuals take on targets more colossal than their forebears could have ever imagined. For Gingrich and Co., the elitist enemy is not mental ability per se but Enlightenment itself, portrayed now as the exclusive affectation of bureaucrats and professors, as an intolerable affront to Nature and the omnipotent market. The heresy that must be rooted out is the basic notion that people can control their world, can, through exertion of human intelligence, improve their situation; the bedrock value with which it must be replaced is a Zen-like doctrine of no mind, of bodily and spiritual attunement to the deep rhythms of the market. Buying and selling arc holy acts, the source and end of human meaning; all else is empty sophistry and deceptive tricks by which scheming professors propose to get themselves ahead.

This, then, is the new consensus worked by the Cultural Miracle: The market is natural, normal, and irresistible. Efforts to control its vagaries, however, are artificial, dictatorial, arrogant—and undemocratic. One can watch the new faith that buttresses the cultural Miracle emerging in documents like Terry Teachout's reworking of H. L. Mencken, in which the great scoffer is no longer the hated tormentor of the booboisie, but the ally of the marketwise peasants in their eternal battle against the verbal prestidigitations of the know-it-all bureaucrat. Or in Rush Limbaugh's recent statement of theoretical principle, borrowed almost verbatim from the stripped-down Social Darwinism of William Graham Sumner: Nobody has any obligation to anyone else, under any circumstances (unless they've signed a contract). With a contemptuous snort he dismisses a hundred years of social theory as so much airy fantasy, needless complexities taking us away from the straight and true faith of Gilded Age capitalism. Or consider the bizarre speech given a few years ago by P. J. O'Rourke to the Cato Institute, the thinking Hun's think-tank, in which he declared himself for "no political cause whatsoever" and hailed the group's dedication to "nothing," all of which he derives from a hostility to intellect and a relativism that should make those hated deconstructionists envious:

> I don't know what's good for you. You don't know what's good for me. We don't know what's good for mankind. And it sometimes seems as though we're the only people who don't.

But while the public is coached with a steady chant of *stop thinking*, the market proceeds on its benevolent way, unhindered by the corrosive disbeliefs of the New Right: It *does* know what's good for us. The errant ways of bureaucrats and the hubris of policy makers are to be excoriated in resentful small-town editorials without number, but the market moves serenely along, now and forever, beyond our earthly powers of reckoning. Its booms and busts are as natural as earth and sky, and our duty is not to engage in insolent schemes by which we might control the market, but to reconcile ourselves to its majestic ways; to make our own culture as "flexible" as Third Wave capitalism demands; to offer up unquestioningly the prosperity of generations when "competitiveness" calls. To appease the market we will surrender every vestige of self-government, abandon the ways and beliefs and tastes and faiths of centuries, turn our cities into warehouses of the "amenities" by which the mobile, transnational yuppie can be served. And history is the baggage needed least of all, the dethroned god whose every trace the zealots of the market seek to efface, rationalize, or enclose conveniently in a glass display case.

It's a strange species of populism that declares the people's will to be the destruction of the people's way of life. But the crowning mind-fuck of this panorama of intellectual obscenity has to be the perversity of the label fancied by the architects of this chaos—they like to call themselves "conservatives."

The People, Maybe!

If the characteristic political maneuver of the Cultural Miracle is a Buchananesque transformation of inchoate public resentment of business depredations into support for pro-business policies, its characteristic intellectual maneuver is even more counterintuitive: endless lessons about "reality" and adjusting ourselves to it. The cover story of the January 8, 1996, issue of *Newsweek*, a choice bit of pseudo-history penned by journalist Robert Samuelson, offers a useful glimpse of the mental processes of the Cultural Miracle in action. Things *have* gotten worse for ordinary people in the last few years, the pundit admits. But the problem is not business ("what we today call 'the market,'" Samuelson notes in a pious aside)—it's us. All these years we've been thinking about things wrong, expecting too much, waltzing irresponsibly through an "Age of Entitlement" during which we believed that prosperity was somehow our right. Most importantly, we never understood "the market" correctly: For years we thought of it as a big "machinery" that we could adjust and control.

Now we know better, Samuelson smugs. The market is not something we can alter, but an elementary force of nature that stands outside history altogether, "a vast river" that floods and recedes regardless of our petty desires. But it's a well-meaning deity, if its ways seem whimsical: When it fires people, puts others on twelve-hour shifts, and smashes wage scales, we must remember that it is acting in the best possible interests of all, that "the process can be harsh and crude, and although some suffer, more benefit." Our response to these petty misfortunes should not be to challenge the market's omnipotence, but to reconcile ourselves to its overarching wisdom. And there is a long litany of lessons that we must relearn as we humble ourselves, do our penance, and prepare to resume the path "toward reality" that was forsaken after World War II: everything from shopworn notions about "human nature" (you know, that basic acquisitive urge that never, ever, ever changes) to the entrepreneur-worship of Tom Peters to the fundamental tenets of the new apostle's creed. Government cannot help and must stop trying; if we're poor, it's our own fault.

More importantly, there are a few historical facts that we must forget. We must not think about where we came up with this mistaken social system in the first place. Apparently it just happened one day when that abstract and irresponsible entity, Big Government, started promising people things. Above all we must not remember that social change happened because people organized themselves in unions, co-operatives, and political parties and *made* them happen; that the non-rich once had power because they *took* power. Such behavior is doctrinally impossible, and any evidence that it ever occurred must be ignored: Only the market has the ability to act with historical effect. And we must strive to erase any recollection of events that was not filmed in color, to convince ourselves that Big Government is a product not of the 1930s but of the misguided generosity of the postwar boom; now that prosperity has departed, so must that Government.

Clifford Odets's 1935 drama of economic information and its forgetting, *Till the Day I Die,* is a populist fantasy of exactly the phenomenon Samuelson denies. The play opens on a group of German communists surreptitiously cranking out leaflets with which to plaster Nazi Berlin. One hero boasts to a comrade that "This particular leaflet's going to make some of our Nazi friends perspire once it gets into the workers' hands. Workers might like to know . . . wages are down one-third and vital foods are up 75 per cent." The Nazis, meanwhile, maintain their grip on power by keeping such inherently explosive facts from the people and by torturing to the point of mental collapse those who dissent openly. Information is connected unproblematically to unrest in Odets's world; if the people know what is happening to them, the people act.

The Cultural Miracle is Odets's 1930s turned upside down, information severed from action and populism itself tamed and in the service of its old archenemy. The people can have all the data they want, but it turns out they'd much rather have the sappy Hollywood screenplays Odets was eventually hired to write. The culture of the nineties looks a lot like that of the thirties, with all the old genres intact but—just as the daily terrors, political battles, and strange passions of that time now seem as mysterious to us as events on another planet—with the poles of meaning neatly inverted, the symbols and the metaphors magically reversed.

It's not that we don't feel the old anomie: Just as the audience at the first performance of Odet's *Waiting for Lefty* joined the actors chanting

"Strike!", we can be easily worked up against the mysterious forces that make life so unfulfilling. But for us rebellion has come disconnected from the tangible change it once promised. Now it only appears publicly as an existential thing, a sort of limp craving for self-expression so closely associated with consumer products and brand loyalty that we are virtually incapable of imagining it without a corporate sponsor of some kind.

Just as in the 1930s, we push the envelope of "realism" ever further, but reality seems to work differently now. Bigger Thomas reappears as Clarence Thomas, surviving a persecution mounted by crazed leftists this time. Studs Lonigan is back as a character on *Cops*, a selfish union worker being gratifyingly taken down by the market he tried to defy. Forget the millionaires who run the place; what we want is TV vengeance against the poor Lonigan next door, we want his union broken, we want his unemployment benefits stopped, we want his health care taken away, we want stiff laws demanding that he behave just so, we want him locked up; and we want to watch the resulting tragedy on television, see him hauled off half-naked and bleary from drinking too much Colt 45, pleading pathetically with some stern law enforcement officials.

Broadcast demagoguery, never in eclipse for long, has made a triumphant comeback. Limbaugh battles Buchanan for Father Coughlin's old market niche and the antidemocratic nightmare from Frank Capra's *Meet John Doe* is acted out in real life, with thousands of common folk crowding into convention centers and mouthing empty slogans at the behest of some power-mad millionaire. But the Cultural Miracle does Capra one better—not only are the millionaires no longer required to conceal their involvement or hire "John Does" to do their populist fronting, but we find it hard to imagine mass movements (or magazines, for that matter) that have arisen *without* a responsible millionaire at their helm. Being men of the market, millionaires *are* the people, and we cheer them ecstatically as they ascend their skybox to watch the performance of the Gary Cooper character, played by Bruce Springsteen, of course.

The saga of Everyman continues during the commercials, filmed always in Olympian slow-motion as he relaxes on the jet plane, gazes out the window of his office, carries the way of the market to all those benighted lands that have yet to experience American culture. It's hard times, so the thing to do is to get those CEOs up on those pedestals as fast as possible, take that federal government apart as quickly as we can, surrender any notion of controlling the market, and learn our place in the great global scheme. You'll get that raise when you stop thinking about that union.

The Will to Forget

Only the most unabashed partisans of business supremacy are willing to boast openly about the larger change that has made the Miracle possible, to speak the name of the great foe whose vanquishing now permits the market to stride the globe unchecked. Francis Fukuyama, the right's favorite pre-Limbaugh intellectual, put it most plainly in a famous 1989 essay: Business has *ended history.* Not just in the Hegelian sense, the simple victory dance over the corpse of the Soviet Union that was the essay's primary purpose, but in a philosophical way as well. While America's arms expenditures triumphed over the Red Menace, its comfortable consumer banalities triumphed everywhere over local and inherited culture, language, and ideas, and literally ended people's ability to think historically. The visibility of Western consumer goods throughout the world signals the success of what Fukuyama hails as the combined Western effort "to create a truly universal consumer culture that has become both a symbol and an underpinning of the universal homogenous state." And while Fukuyama readily admits that "The End of History" does not mean that all economic and social conflict has been resolved, that universal capitalism means universal happiness, he gloats that without the faculty of cultural memory our unhappiness, however grinding, just doesn't matter. People can no longer think about their social position in a manner that might lead to conflict, that might threaten Western business interests.

Fukuyama's pronouncements may have marked a new hostility to history, but pastlessness is as American as Microsoft. Visiting the new country in the mid-nineteenth century, de Tocqueville was deeply moved by its willful rejection of the class rankings and tastes of the

European past, by the settlers' tendency to forget the Old World and to abandon the ways of the countless generations before them. Casting off the dead weight of the ages has always been a favorite conceit of American writers less frightened by democracy than was the aristocratic de Tocqueville: Deracination has in many ways been the centerpiece of the nation's self-understanding. The golden fable of opportunity—of an empty land where anyone could, like Jay Gatsby, remake himself unhindered by the artificial constraints of civilization—is, after all, the basic theme in the great American stories of immigration and western expansion. Even our atrocities obeyed this primal cultural impulse, this imperative to forget: Slavery demanded a cultural uprooting of those who did not come to the New World willingly. But by and large our literature praises the power of the melting pot, celebrates the democracy of the frontier, sings the glories of getting out of the Old and into the Cold.

For ideologues of American business, the suspicion of history is a longstanding article of faith. In the frequent denunciations of the past voiced by the great Captains of industry one finds not mere assimilationist longings, but profound disdain for any entangling traditions that could interfere with efficiency and restrict the absolute freedom of every individual to pillage every other individual. Henry Ford's famous outburst, "History is bunk," was a statement of fundamental business ideology, not merely a response to an immediate annoyance. According to the great capitalists' "practical" worldview, as Richard Hofstadter has noted, "The past was seen as despicably impractical and uninventive, simply and solely as something to be surmounted." In its quest for efficiency, the pre-Information business "community" set itself against the peculiar and backward-looking ways of tradition and human particularity in almost every way it could. Its famous time-motion studies aimed to suppress factory workers' humanity, transforming them into robots like the hapless line worker in Charlie Chaplin's *Modern Times*. Its glass-and-steel office towers were efficiency-maximizing machines for the paper-shuffling labor of its Organization Men, stripped of any concessions to human tastes and comfort; its suburbs and tenements, sterile boxes for the propagation of obedient underlings.

Alongside the hyper-rational, hyper-efficient Organization envisioned by America's premier managers there also developed an emotional and religious conception of business practice, a cult of positive thinking that was even more hostile to cultural memory than was the dominant cult of efficiency. In the writing of the postive thinkers, anti-historicism reached a new plateau of sophistication: The annoyances of history and cultural particularity were not just to be over-paved, but *leveled*, reduced to a convenient flatness where every epoch was exactly like the present as far back as the eye could see. The economic struggle of daily life was and had *always been* a matter of individual men and God, a question of just how positively each up-and-coming entrepreneur could think, just how blindly he could pursue success. The cold statistics of the bureaucrats were ultimately insignificant, nor did social class or local economic conditions really matter: All you needed to succeed was a salesman's disposition and an open-faced readiness to work. All human history—and especially the doings of its big figures, favorites like Jesus, Lincoln, Charlemagne, and Joan of Arc—could be understood as parables for the struggling executive of the twentieth century. Theories of efficiency may have intentionally ignored history, but positive thinking went them one better: For its believers the past was fundamentally identical to the now. Capitalism is the immutable way of God and nature, the unchanging condition of mankind. To wonder how things ever got to the sorry state they were was to engage in idle and even counterproductive conjecture: Society *never* developed or changed (although, as Samuelson would point out, it would occasionally embark on some sort of folly like the New Deal), it simply produced a series of interesting executives and leaders from whose exploits we might learn a thing or two.

With the coming of the Age of information this anti-historicism has blossomed into a full-blown secular antinomianism. Cause and effect itself is a meaningless illusion, the new business thinkers argue, for the Information Age is an *Age of Unreason*, of instant, world-wide change and constant flux. The world is mad, they insist, it's spinning chaotically out of control, and to remain profitable, businessmen must become mad themselves, become creatures immersed totally in the present (or, better still, the future) and intentionally ignorant of whatever developments have put us where we are. "How people and companies did things yesterday doesn't matter to the business re-engineer," write the authors of 1994's ubiquitous management text, *Reengineering the Corporation*. The hero of the Information Age, according to its authors, is the businessman who is able to violate most violently, to separate himself most completely from both his own and his company's past—to *forget*. The virtue of forgetting is the book's essential message. Its dust jacket carries this enticing legend: "Forget what you know about how business should work—most of it is wrong!" With total seriousness its authors recommend that businessmen adopt an epistemology of constant forgetting, of positive militancy against cultural memory. "At the heart of business re-engineering," they write, "lies the notion of *discontinuous thinking*—identifying and abandoning the outdated rules and fundamental assumptions that underlie current business operations." In the wave after wave of manuals that have appeared since then the language of permanent-overthrow is simply ratcheted up a few notches. Now we fill our commuting time penetrating the mysteries of concepts like "Thinking outside the box," "radical change," and "transformation." So thick have the ranks of the corporate Jacobins grown that "The will for change has itself become banal," advertising executive Jean-Marie Dru writes—just before proposing his own scheme for more effective and total corporate deracination: "disruption." ("If a brand rests on its heritage, fails to question itself, and builds only on its past, before long it will come to appear complacent or static.")

Unlike his Organization predecessors, who merely wanted to destroy annoying obstacles to efficiency like city blocks and the sleeping habits of laborers, the information businessman dreams of what Russell Jacoby once called "social amnesia," a collective inability to recall who did what *yesterday*, never mind last year or last century. Freed from the gravitational pull of worldly history, he floats deliriously on a rushing stream of detached signifiers, the flotsam and jetsam of centuries of civilization having become just so many shiny trinkets floating meaninglessly by (it's not a coincidence that Dru quotes appreciatively from Baudrillard and

Tom Peters from Ludwig Wittgenstein). The constant flux that supports us all, consumerism's endless piling of new upon new, can be bound by no tradition, reason, language, or order other than the simple mandates of ceaseless, directionless change.

Among media decision-makers themselves the curtailment of our historical attention span is assumed quite matter-of-factly, with what one imagines is a fair amount of pride, to be an accomplished fact. Thus the convention on "objective" news programs of discussing events of last week or a few months ago as though they were dim memories of the distant, unenlightened past: References to Iraq must be prefaced by the reminder that the U.S. was at war with that nation a few years ago; news from Somalia must begin by informing us that, quite recently, this country was occupied by American soldiers. Otherwise, it is understood, we just wouldn't remember: Naturally we're too caught up in whatever the current patriotic frenzy is to recall those of the recent past. If we're lucky the logistical problems associated with this need to constantly remind viewers of what was once common knowledge may one day expand to the point where TV news becomes impossible altogether, with almost all of the 45-minute program devoted to telling us what country we live in, that other cities and nations exist, who our elected officials are, and so on. The only thing that will never require explaining, of course, is the glowing box itself, the central position it occupies in our dwellings, and the reasons why we come back to stare at it, day after day.

THE APOCALYPSE THAT REFRESHES

Freedom from the past, however, does not necessarily bode well for other freedoms. In fact, no effective challenge to the rule of business can be mounted without solid grounding in precisely the sort of cultural memory that Information Capitalism, with its supersonic yuppie pannationalism and its worship of the instantaneous, has set itself out to destroy. Without memory we can scarcely understand our present— what strange forces in the dim past caused this agglomeration of seven million unhappy persons to be deposited here in the middle of a vast continent, clinging to the shores of this mysteriously polluted lake?—

much less begin to confront the systematic depredations of the system that has made our lives so miserable. In contrast to American business's insistent denial of pastness, Richard Hofstadter continues,

> In Europe there has always existed a strong counter-tradition, both romantic and moralistic, against the ugliness of industrialism—a tradition carried on by figures as diverse as Goethe and Blake, Morris and Carlyle, Hugo and Chateaubriand, Ruskin and Scott. Such men counterposed to the machine a passion for language and locality, for antiquities and monuments, for natural beauty; they sustained a tradition of resistance to capitalist industrialism, of skepticism about the human consequences of industrial progress, of moral, aesthetic, and humane revolt.

Without an understanding of particularity, of the economic constructedness of our lives, this kind of critical consciousness becomes impossible. All we can know is our own individual discomfort, our vague hankering for something else—an else that can be easily defined away as a different product choice, a new lifestyle, a can of Sprite anti-soda, or a little rule-breaking at Burger King.

This century's technological advances are often described as victories over the primal facts of nature: hunger, cold, disease, distance, and time. But the wiring of every individual into the warm embrace of the multinational entertainment oligopoly is a conquest of a different sort, the crowning triumph of the marketplace over humanity's unruly consciousness. The fact that the struggle has been a particularly long one does not alter the fact that business authorities seem to be on the verge of a spectacular and final victory. It is fitting that, as this century of horrors draws to a close, our masters rush to perfect the cultural equivalent of the atom bomb, to destroy once and for all our ability to appreciate horror. With no leader but the "invisible hand," with no elite but the mild and platitudinous Babbittry of the American hinterland, Western capitalism will soon accomplish what the century's more murderous tyrants, with all their poisonous calculation, could only dream of doing: effacing the cultural memory of entire nations. For there is no tradition, religion, or language to which business owes any allegiance greater than momentary convenience; nor does any tradition, religion, or language remain that can muster a serious challenge to its cultural authority. It is capitalism, not angry workers, unhappy youth, or impoverished colonial peoples that is "the bull in the china shop of human history," David Rieff wrote in 1993. "The market economy, now global in scale, is by its nature corrosive of all established hierarchies and certainties. . . ."

When the twentieth century opened, business was only one power among many, economically and culturally speaking, a dangerously expansive but more or less contained participant in a larger social framework. While it might mistreat workers, break unions, bribe editors, and buy congressmen, its larger claims and authority were limited by an array of countervailing powers. It does not require a rosy sentimental view of any past period to recognize that today there are no such countervailing forces. Not only is labor toothless and feeble, seemingly capable only of slowing its own demise, but there is no cultural power on earth—save maybe the quixotic imagination of each isolated "reader" of the corporate text*—that can stand independent from or intrude upon the smooth operation of capital. With its advanced poststructuralist powertrain, its six-barrel rock 'n' roll assimilator, and its turbocharged fiber-optic speed, multinational capital is able to run cultural circles around our ponderous old notions of democracy, leaving us no imaginable means through which the culture of business might be resisted, no vantage point from which "the public" might be addressed, not even any way to approach the subject without lapsing into cliché. It's night in America, and we can feel ourselves slipping into a sleep from which we can't imagine ever waking.

---

*Fukuyama's dismissal of Cultural Studies' argument about reception of Western culture-products is significant: "For our puposes, it matters very little what strange thoughts occur to people in Albania or Burkina Faso. . . ." Not being "embodied in important social or political forces and movements," they just aren't "part of world history."

Thomas Frank

Meanwhile the last twenty years have brought a palpable undoing of the American fabric, a physical and social decay so unspeakably vast, so enormously obscene that we can no longer gauge the destruction with words. We all know this: there it is every night on TV, there it is as you drive through the South Side of Chicago on your way to work (thank God for the virtual office!). And yet it matters nothing, because we don't live in that America anymore: Our home is *literally* the TV, the interactive wonder, the simulation that is so much more exciting, fulfilling, and convenient than any possible permutation of physical reality. We can do nothing but watch the world crumble because—our collective imagination being as much a construct of business necessity as the government's various trade agreements—we cannot imagine it being any other way.

Out here in the great flyover, ground zero of the Information Revolution, you can *feel* the world dissolving, everything from the hard verities of the industrial past to the urban geography beginning to melt away in the pale blue CRT fog. Our archetypes and ideas and visions and memories, the accumulation of centuries, are yielding as easily to corporate reengineering as has our landscape, built and torn down and renamed and reshuffled, everything forgotten instantly and relegated overnight to the quaint land of sepiatint. This year we'll live in beautiful Passiondale, just down the road from Cambry Estates. Next year the noise and mud aren't so charming; wreck it down and move to a new box in a better fortified enclave: meaningless upon meaningless, stretching out across the infinitely malleable Illinois prairie.

Even while we are happily dazed by the mall's panoply of choice, exhorted to indulge our taste for breaking rules, and deluged with all manner of useful "information," our collective mental universe is being radically circumscribed, enclosed within the tightest parameters of all time. In the third millennium there is to be no myth but the business myth, no individuality but the thirty or so professionally accepted psychographic market niches, no diversity but the happy heteroglossia of the sitcom, no rebellion but the preprogrammed search for new kicks. Denunciation is becoming impossible: We will be able to achieve no distance from business culture since we will no longer have a life, a history, a consciousness apart from it. It is making itself unspeakable, too big, too obvious, too vast, too horrifying, too much of a cliché to even begin addressing. A matter-of-fact disaster, as natural as the supermarket, as resistable as air. It is putting itself beyond our power of imagining because it has *become* our imagination, it has *become* our power to envision, and describe, and theorize, and resist.

★ A LAMENT FOR ★ BOSNIA

Susan Sontag

FROM *THE NATION,* DECEMBER 25, 1995

I went to Sarajevo for the first time in April 1993, one year after the start of the Serb-Croat campaign to carve up the newly independent multiethnic Bosnian state. Leaving Sarajevo after that first stay, I flew out as I had come in, on one of the Russian UNPROFOR cargo planes making a regular run between Sarajevo and Zagreb. The heart-stopping drive into the besieged city by the switchback trail over Mount Igman lay far in the future, on my seventh and eighth stays; and by that time, the winter and summer of 1995, my standards of peril and my tolerance of the shock of Sarajevo would have eased. Nothing ever equaled the first shock. The shock of Sarajevo itself, the misery of daily life in the shattered city under constant mortar and sniper fire. And the aftershock of reentry into the outside world.

To leave Sarajevo and be, an hour later, in a "normal" city (Zagreb). To get into a taxi (a taxi!) at the airport . . . to ride in traffic regulated by traffic signals, along streets lined with buildings that have intact roofs, unshelled walls, glass in the windows . . . to turn on the light switch in your hotel room . . . to use a toilet and flush it afterward . . . to run the bath (you haven't had a bath in several weeks) and have water, even hot water, come out of the tap . . . to take a stroll and see shops, and people walking, like you, at a normal pace . . . to buy something in a small grocery store with fully stocked shelves . . . to enter a restaurant and be given a menu. . . . All this seems so bizarre and upsetting that, for at least forty-eight hours, you feel quite disoriented. And very angry. To speak to people who don't want to know what you know, don't want you to talk about the sufferings, bewilderment, terror, and humiliation of the inhabitants of the city you've just left. And even worse, when you return to your own "normal" city (New York) and your friends say, "Oh, you're back; I was worried about you"—to realize that they don't want to know either. To understand that you can never really explain to them—neither how terrible it is "there" nor how bad you feel being back, "here." That the world will be forever divided into "there" and "here."

People don't want to hear the bad news. Perhaps they never do. But in the case of Bosnia the indifference, the lack of effort to try to imagine, was more acute than I ever anticipated. You find that the only people you feel comfortable with are those who have been to Bosnia too. Or to some other slaughter—El Salvador, Cambodia, Rwanda, Chechnya. Or who at least know, firsthand, what a war is.

A few weeks ago—I'm writing in late November—I returned from my ninth stay in Sarajevo. Although once again I came in by the only land route, this was no longer my sole option (U.N. planes were again landing on a corner of the destroyed Sarajevo airport), and the rutted dirt trail over Mount Igman was no longer the most dangerous route in the world. It had been widened and graded by U.N. engineers into . . . a road. In the city there was electricity for the first time. The shells were not exploding, snipers' bullets were not whizzing past everyone's heads. There would be gas for the winter. There was the promise of running water. Since my return, an agreement has been signed in Ohio that promises an end to the war. Whether peace, an unjust peace, has actually come to Bosnia I am reluctant to say. If Slobodan Milosevic, who started the war, wants the war to end and can impose this decision on his proxies in Pale, then the successful campaign to destroy Bosnia by killing or relocating or driving into exile most of its population is, in most senses, finished. Finished, too, is what the Bosnians had held out for: their internationally recognized unitary state.

So Bosnia (an utterly transformed Bosnia) is to be partitioned. So might instead of right has triumphed. Nothing new in that—see Thucydides, Book V, "the Melian dialogue." It's as if the eastern advance of the Wehrmacht had been halted in late 1939 or early 1940 and the League of Nations called a conference among "the warring parties," at which Germany was awarded half of Poland (the western part), the invading Russians got 20 percent of the east, and while the 30 percent of their country in the middle that the Poles were allowed to keep did include their capital, most of the territory surrounding it went to the Germans. Of course, no one would have claimed that this was very fair by "moral" criteria—quickly adding, Since when have moral standards prevailed in international politics? Because the Poles had no chance of successfully defending their country against the superior forces of Hitler's Germany and Stalin's Russia, they would have to be content with what they got. A least, the diplomats would have said, they still have some of their country; they were on the verge of losing it all. And of course the Poles would have figured as the most difficult at the negotiations, since they didn't see themselves as simply one of three "warring parties." They thought they had been invaded. They thought they were the victims. The diplomats brokering the settlement would have found them quite unreasonable. Divided among themselves. Bitter. Untrustworthy. Ungrateful to the mediators trying to stop the slaughter.

If before, people didn't want to know—you often heard that the war in Bosnia is so complicated, it is hard to know which is the "right" side—now more people do understand what happened. They also understand that the war—that is, the Serb and Croat aggression—could have been stopped at any moment in the past three years in exactly the same way and by the same minimum application of force by NATO (entirely sparing soldiers on the ground as well as civilians) as finally took place this past August and September. But the Europeans didn't want to stop the conflict (both the British Foreign Office and the Quai d'Orsay are traditionally pro-Serb), and the Americans, the only major power to acknowledge that justice was on the Bosnian side, were reluctant to get involved. Now that the war has, or seems to have been, stopped, it suddenly looks less complicated. The mood is retrospective now.

One question I'm often asked after returning from a stay in Sarajevo is why other well-known writers besides myself haven't spent time there. Behind this lies the more general question of how to explain the widespread indifference, or lack of solidarity, in Europe (most notably in Italy and Germany) with the victims of an appalling historical crime, nothing less than genocide—the fourth genocide of a European minority to take place in this century. But unlike the genocide of the Armenians during World War I and of the Jews and the Gypsies in the late 1930s and early 1940s, the genocide of the Bosniak people has taken place in the glare of worldwide press and TV coverage. No one can plead ignorance of the atrocities that have taken place in Bosnia since the war started in April 1992. Sanski Most, Stupni Do, Omarska and other concentration camps with their killing houses (for hands-on, artisanal butchery, in contrast to the industrialized mass murder of the Nazi camps), the martyrdom of East Mostar and Sarajevo and Gorazde, the rape by military order of tens of thousands of women throughout Serb-captured Bosnia, the slaughter of at least 8,000 men and boys after the surrender of Srebrenica—this is only a portion of the catalogue of infamy. And no one can be unaware that the Bosnian cause is that of Europe: democracy, and a society composed of citizens, not of the members of a tribe. Why haven't these atrocities, these values, aroused a more potent response? Why have hardly any intellectuals of stature and visibility rallied to denounce the Bosnian genocide and defend the Bosnian cause?

The Bosnian war is hardly the only horror show that has been unfolding in the past four or five years. But there are events—model events-that do seem to sum up the principal opposing forces of one's time. One such event was the Spanish Civil War. Like the war in Bosnia, that struggle was an emblematic one. But intellectuals—the writers, theater people, artists, professors, scientists who have a record of speaking up on important public events and issues of conscience—have been as conspicuous by their absence from the Bosnian conflict as they were by their presence in Spain in the 1930s. Of course, it's speaking rather too well of intellectuals to think that they constitute something like a perennial class, part of whose vocation is to take up the best causes—as it's unlikely that only every thirty years or so is there a war somewhere else in the world that should inspire even would-be pacifists to take sides. Most intellectuals are as conformist, as willing to support the prosecution of unjust wars, as most other people exercising educated professions. The number of people who have given intellectuals a good or (depending on your point of view) a bad name—as troublemakers, voices of conscience—has always been very small. Still, the standard of dissent and activism associated with intellectuals is a reality. Think of Havel, Pasolini, Chomsky, Sakharov, Grass, Michnik. . . . Why so little response to what happened in Bosnia?

There are probably many reasons. Heartless historical clichés certainly figure in the paltriness of the response. There is the traditional bad reputation of the Balkans as a place of eternal conflict, of implacable ancient rivalries. Haven't those folks always been slaughtering one another? (This is comparable to having said when confronted with the reality of Auschwitz: Well, what can one expect? You know, anti-Semitism is an ancient story in Europe.) Not to be underestimated, too, is the pervasiveness of anti-Muslim prejudice, a reflex reaction to a people the majority of whom are as secular, and as imbued with contemporary consumer-society culture, as their other Southern European neighbors. To bolster the fiction that this is, at its deepest source, a religious war, the label "Muslim" is invariably used to describe the victims, their army and their government—though no one would think of describing the invaders as the Orthodox and the Catholics. Do many secular "Western" intellectuals who might be expected to have raised their voices to defend Bosnia share these prejudices? Of course they do.

And this is not the 1930s. Nor the 1960s. Actually, we are already living in the twenty-first century, in which such twentieth-century certainties as the identification of fascism, or imperialism, or Bolshevik-style dictators as the principal "enemy" no longer offer a framework (often a facile one) for thought and action. What made it obvious that one should side with the government of the Spanish Republic, whatever its flaws, was the struggle against fascism. Opposing the American aggression in Vietnam (which took over the unsuccessful French effort to hold onto Indochina) made sense as part of the worldwide struggle against Euro-American colonialism.

If the intellectuals of the 1930s and the 1960s often showed themselves too gullible, too prone to appeals to idealism to take in what was really happening in certain beleaguered, newly radicalized societies that they may or may not have visited (briefly), the morosely depoliticized intellectuals of today, with their cynicism always at the ready, their addiction to entertainment, their reluctance to inconvenience themselves for any cause, their devotion to personal safety, seem at least equally deplorable. (I can't count how many times I've been asked, each time I return to New York from Sarajevo, how I can go to a place that's so dangerous.) By and large, that handful of intellectuals who consider themselves people of conscience can be mobilized now solely for limited actions against, say, racism or censorship—within their own countries. Only domestic political commitments seem plausible now. Among once internationally minded intellectuals, nationalist complacencies have renewed prestige. (I should note that this seems true more of writers than doctors, scientists, and actors.) There has been a vertiginous decay of the very notion of international solidarity.

Not only has the global bilateralism (a "them" versus "us") characteristic of political thinking throughout our short twentieth century, from 1914 to 1989—fascism versus democracy; the American empire versus the Soviet empire—collapsed. What has followed in the wake of 1989 and the suicide of the Soviet empire is the final victory of capitalism, and of the ideology of consumerism, which entails the discrediting of "the political" as such. All that makes sense is private life. Individualism, and the cultivation of the self and private well-being featuring, above all, the ideal of "health"—are the values to which intellectuals are most likely to subscribe. ("How can you spend so much time in a place where people smoke all the time?" someone here in New York asked my son, the writer David Rieff, of his frequent trips to Bosnia.) It's too much to expect that the triumph of consumer capitalism would have left the intellectual class unmarked. In the era of shopping, it has to be harder for intellectuals, who are anything but marginal and impoverished, to identify with less fortunate others. George Orwell and Simone Weil did not exactly leave comfortable upper-bourgeois apartments and weekend country houses when they volunteered to go to Spain and fight for the Republic, and both of them almost got themselves killed. Perhaps the stretch for intellectuals between "there" and "here" is too great now.

For several decades it has been a journalistic and academic commonplace to say that intellectuals, as a class, are obsolete—an example of an analysis willing itself to be an imperative. Now there are voices proclaiming that Europe is dead, too. It may be more true to say that Europe has yet to be born: a Europe that takes responsibility for its defenseless minorities and for upholding the values it has no choice but to incarnate (Europe will be multicultural, or it won't be at all). And Bosnia is its self-induced abortion. In the words of Emile Durkheim, "Society is above all the idea it forms of itself." The idea that the prosperous, peaceful society of Europe and North America has formed of itself—through the actions and statements of all those who could be called intellectuals—is one of confusion, irresponsibility, selfishness, cowardice . . . and the pursuit of happiness.

Ours, not theirs. Here, not there.

★ LIFE IN PRISON: ★ CORRECTIONS COWBOYS GET A CHARGE OUT OF THEIR NEW SCI-FI WEAPONRY

Anne-Marie Cusac

FROM *THE PROGRESSIVE,* JULY 1996

Introducing the penal industry's latest toy: It's called a stun belt. An electronic shocking device secured to a person's waist, it is the hot new item in corrections gear. Guards love it because they don't have to get near prisoners who wear the belt. They can set off the eight-second, 50,000-volt stun from as far away as 300 feet.

The manufacturer of the device is Stun Tech, a company based in Cleveland, Ohio. It claims that the R.E.A.C.T. (Remote Electronically Activated Control Technology) belt is "100 percent nonlethal." Sales have been booming since 1994, when the federal Bureau of Prisons decided to use the belt in medium- and high-security lockups. Since then, the U.S. Marshals Service and more than 100 county agencies have employed the belt for prisoner transport, courtroom appearances, and medical appointments. Sixteen state correctional agencies currently use the belt. Seven more are considering it.

But human-rights groups are aghast. "The stun belt looks to be a weapon which will almost certainly result in cruel, inhuman, or degrading treatment," a violation of international law, says Brian Wood of Amnesty International, which will launch an international campaign against electronic stun devices this summer. The use of the stun belt in

U.S. prisons "will inevitably encourage prison authorities—including those in torturing states—to do likewise," says Wood, who believes the chances are very high that the belt will eventually be used for torture.

Stun Tech's promotional materials recommend the belt as a psychological tool, an effective deterrent for potentially unruly inmates, and a humane alternative to guns or nightsticks.

The Stun Tech R.E.A.C.T. belt is available in two styles: a one-size-fits-all minimal-security belt (a slim version designed for low visibility in courts), and the high-security transport belt, complete with wrist restraints. Both come attached to a nine-volt battery. When activated, the stun belt shocks its wearer for eight seconds, with three to four milliamps, and 50,000 volts of "continuous stun power." The painful blast, which Stun Tech representatives advertise as "devastating," knocks most of its victims to the floor, where they may shake uncontrollably and remain incapacitated for as long as fifteen minutes. Two metal prongs, positioned just above the left kidney, leave welts that can take up to six months to heal.

According to two physicians, and a 1990 study by the British Forensic Service, electronic devices similar to the belt may cause heart attack, ventricular fibrillation, or arhythmia, and may set off an adverse reaction in people with epilepsy or on psychotropic medications.

Stun Tech denies that its belt could cause fatalities. But the recent death of a Texas corrections officer, who suffered a heart attack shortly after receiving a shock from an electric shield similar in design to the stun belt, raises serious questions about the belt's safety.

Like many other Texas corrections workers, Harry Landis was in training to use the electric riot shield. Like the stun belt, the taser, and the stun gun, the shield is an electronic shocking device. Guards frequently use the shield when removing prisoners from their cells. But on December 1, 1995, something went terribly wrong. As part of the training, Landis was required to endure two 45,000-volt shocks. Shortly after the second shock, Landis collapsed and died.

The Texas Department of Criminal Justice, which had used the shields to subdue prisoners since September 1995, immediately suspended their use. Meanwhile, John McDermit, president of Nova Products, Inc., the maker of the shield, denied that it had killed Landis. "We're very sorry this happened," McDermit said. "But there certainly was no connection between his training and his death."

But Jimmy Wood, the Coryell County justice of the peace who conducted an inquiry into Landis's death, has a different story to tell. "Landis was in fairly decent shape as far as physical appearance is concerned," he says. "He did have a history of heart problems. But was he going to die this day if he didn't experience an electric shock? No, he wasn't."

According to Jimmy Wood, Landis's autopsy showed that he died as a result of cardiac dirhythmia due to coronary blockage following electric shock by an electronic stun shield. "The electric shock threw his heart into a different rhythmic beat, causing him to pass away," he says.

"The shield worked as it was intended to," says Mark Goodson, an engineer who conducted tests on the shield following Landis's death. "Now comes the problem. The manufacturer puts in its literature that the shield will not hurt anyone, including people with a heart condition. But they have not done studies on people with heart conditions. They haven't done studies on people at all. They conducted their tests on animals—anesthetized animals. Do you see the danger here? In one word: adrenaline."

Goodson explains that this is a problem with all pulsed electrical stun technology. "No one can even define a safe voltage," he says. "We don't even have an idea if it is safe or not for the general population."

McDermit continues to believe that Landis's death was mere coincidence. "We think that just happened to be a timing problem," he says.

The stun belt and its relatives are supposed to be non-lethal or, at the very least, less-lethal. At the Law Enforcement and Corrections Technology Conference in Los Angeles, I talk to less-lethal weapons manufacturers, representatives of the National Institute of Justice, officials of the Rome and Phillips laboratories, and executives of correctional facilities. They are all quite proud of the newest "less-lethal" technologies. They tell me about products already on the market: mace, pepper spray, beanbag bullets, rubber bullets, plastic bullets, and the stun belt. They also let me in on some new ideas: a cannon-like instrument that shoots a sticky net, disorienting lights, sounds that cause nausea, sticky foam, aqueous foam "doped with pepper spray," and a gun that heats its victim's body up to 107 degrees Fahrenheit.

Many of these devices inflict significant pain. Some are potentially deadly (sticky foam, for instance, can seal a person's lungs; the sticky net, shot at close range, has knocked the head off of many a dummy).

Michael Keith, president of MK Ballistic Systems, maker of the beanbag bullet (coarse material stuffed with lead shot), explains how such products develop: "All technology starts low-tech," he says. His own beanbag bullet had to go through some adjustments when corrections officials discovered that, at close range, it punctured bodies. Now corrections personnel shoot from farther away. The stun belt, Keith adds, is "just a modified dog collar."

Though his work is in beanbag bullets, not stun technology, Keith has many ideas for improving the belt. He would install a tracking device and a timer, and make the belt impossible for the wearer to remove. An inmate who got away would get a jolt every thirty seconds or so until he was "in need of serious medical attention," Keith says. "The guy would be frog-jumping in the backseat. I wouldn't say it should kill him. That wouldn't go over in our society."

The sponsor of the Los Angeles conference is the American Defense Preparedness Association. It publishes *National Defense* magazine, and organizes many other conferences with such titles as "Enhancing the Individual Warrior," "Undersea Warfare," and "Bomb and Warhead."

Conference participants thrill to the idea of combating "internal enemies." "I don't think our defense against an internal enemy is any different from a defense against an external enemy that might be threatening our borders," says Sherman Block, sheriff of Los Angeles County.

During conference break-out sessions, we watch film clips from *Star Trek*, *RoboCop*, *Star Wars*, *Gunsmoke*, and Clint Eastwood Westerns. "The police firearm is more reminiscent of Wyatt Earp than it is of *Star Trek*'s Captain Kirk. We do indeed have a technology gap," says Alan Bersin, the conference chairman.

To cover the gap, the industry stresses the importance of manipulating the American public's fear of crime. "Think about the public's concern about crime and translate that concern into a national agenda—into new solutions, new technologies," says Jeremy Travis, director of the National Institute of Justice. "How can we build a public demand, and marry that demand to production?"

Stun Tech's advertising material asserts that "merely wearing the belt is not a violation of civil rights. As long as it is not used for officer gratification or punishment, liability is non-existent."

Leaving aside the issue of "officer gratification," the belt seems popular precisely for its punishment potential. And it is being used even before defendants are proven guilty.

In December 1994, Bruce Sons was on trial for the murder of a California highway patrol officer. Sons was forced to wear a stun belt. The belt went off accidentally, shocking Sons. His attorney, Troy Childers, requested that the belt be removed. The judge denied Childers's request, demanding that Sons wear the belt until he testified.

In April 1995, James Oswald stood trial for robbery and the murder of a Wisconsin police officer. The Waukesha, Wisconsin, court system required Oswald to wear the stun belt. Oswald's attorney, Alan Eisenberg, objected.

"I was worried that they would accidentally stun him into the middle of next week—which proved to be a true prediction," says Eisenberg. "I argued that it was a Nazi torture device." Oswald, who appeared in court in a wheelchair throughout his trial, was, according to Eisenberg, unable to walk and unable to run. The court, not convinced that Oswald's disabilities were real, required both shackles and the stun belt.

Authorities acknowledge that the belt was accidentally set off once, shocking Oswald. Oswald claims he was stunned twice, and was being tortured. Eisenberg believes that the court's insistence that Oswald wear the belt "was part of a multiphase effort to torture this guy. Many of the people who had responsibility for him were friends of the deceased. It was like a chicken in a fox coop."

When I ask Stun Tech president Dennis Kaufman to send me a copy of Stun Tech's promotional video for the R.E.A.C.T. belt, he warns me that many viewers find the footage graphic. "There are about thirty people jumping around like Mexican jumping beans," he says.

Kaufman is right: The video is graphic. But it only shows law-enforcement and corrections officers wearing the belt. All have been warned and given time to prepare themselves psychologically before the shock. During the eight-second blast, all are clearly in pain.

The officers in the Stun Tech video fall onto gym mats, or outside onto grass. One guard, panicked by the shock, dives headlong into a portable movie screen and a metal cart. "Watch his head," yells an off-camera voice.

I call Kaufman several days later to check some facts. He asks me if I have received the video. "It makes great party viewing," he says.

Advertising brochures for the R.E.A.C.T. belt come accompanied by an affidavit signed by a single medical doctor, Robert Stratbucker of the University of Nebraska Medical Center. Stratbucker conducted a series of safety tests using the Stun Tech Ultron II—a stun gun—a version of which forms the shock component to the R.E.A.C.T. belt. Stratbucker conducted his tests on anesthetized swine.

An anesthetized pig is very different from a human being in dread of electrocution. In their own way, the Stun Tech representatives acknowledge this. Jim Kronke, a Stun Tech distributor and trainer, calls the belt's effect on prisoners "very psychological," adding that, "at trials, people notice that the defendant will be watching whoever has the monitor." He points out that the belt has never caused anyone to defecate or killed anyone. "If it ever kills anyone," says Kronke, "I think it's going to be from fright."

Kaufman also blames fear for any potential physical danger. "We don't recommend that it be placed on anyone who has a heart condition. The reason is that, if they have to wear it for eight hours, there's a tremendous amount of anxiety. The fear will elevate blood pressure as much as the shock will." But, he adds, "the technology we are using is not capable of causing a heart attack."

A 1990 study by the British Forensic Science Service came to some rather different conclusions. The British scientists found that high-voltage, high-peak, short-duration pulses, such as those which the stun belt inflicts, are dangerous. The study describes stun devices as "capable of causing temporary incapacitation of the whole body: a body-wide-spread immobilizing effect." A one- to two-second shock, said the scientists, would probably cause the victim to collapse. A three- to four-second shock would have an incapacitating effect on the entire body for up to fifteen minutes. Since the shock is distributed via electric currents throughout the entire body, including the brain, the chest region, and the central nervous system, the researchers concluded that "anyone in contact with the victim's body at the time of shocking was also likely to receive a shock," and that they "could not discount the possibility of ventricular fibrillation." This is to say that a stun device could potentially kill someone.

Although Stun Tech advises guards not to use the belt on inmates with a known heart condition, this precaution hardly eliminates all potential dangers. For one thing, some at-risk hearts appear healthy. "You shock someone with 50,000 volts of electricity and that person has some unrecognized congenital problem or conduction mechanism in their heart, and you put them at great risk for arhythmia," says Armand Start, a medical doctor who runs the National Center for Correctional Healthcare Studies. "You can't predict this. You can't determine the conduction mechanism in a heart. Arhythmia mostly happens in healthy hearts."

Corey Weinstein, a physician and co-director of the Pelican Bay Information Project (which monitors human-rights abuses at Pelican Bay prison in California), says that stun belts "have the same problems as tasers. With tasers, people on psych meds have altered neurological responses. People with seizures have real problems."

Start questions Stun Tech's claims that the belt is medically safe. When he served as medical director of the Texas state prison system, stun guns, closely related to the belts, were being employed. The state eventually stopped using them. "Having dealt with the stun gun, I know that that was implemented without a good medical evaluation. If corrections is true to form, they have implemented this the same way. Show me a refereed study on this thing."

Kaufman says an independent, refereed medical study has never been conducted on the R.E.A.C.T. belt.

The stun belt's popularity is linked to the return of the chain gang. States like Wisconsin that are putting prisoners back on the chain gang plan to use the belt to keep them in line.

A new law in Wisconsin assigns twelve-person teams of prisoners to outside work, clearing brush and trash. The teams will wear the R.E.A.C.T. stun belt in addition to leg shackles. The Wisconsin Department of Corrections suggested the belt as a "humane" alternative to chaining prisoners together.

Wisconsin may be the first in line, but it is not likely to be the only state with stun-belted work crews. Kaufman says that the company has already talked with Florida, Alabama, and Louisiana about adapting the stun belt to their chain gangs. "Everyone going back to chain gangs is looking at this," says Kaufman.

Until Wisconsin came up with the idea of stun-belting the chain gangs, most wearers of the belt were people charged with violent offenses, people whom police and correctional officers, or court officials, considered security risks. But under the new Wisconsin provision, this is likely to change. Inmates who are considered escape risks or who are deemed dangerous to the public are usually kept off the chain gangs. Chain-gang members who wear the stun belt will actually be the least dangerous of prisoners.

Justification for the work crews follows the same line of thinking in Wisconsin as it does in other states. "We have a tremendous idleness problem in our medium- and maximum-security prisons," says Bob Margolies, legislative liaison for the Wisconsin Department of Corrections. "Many of our prisoners want work."

Ken Morgan, warden at the Racine Correctional Institution, where the first stun-belt-wearing work crews could start as early as January 1997, agrees that there is an idleness problem. "But it is primarily due to overcrowding," he says.

On the morning when I visit the Racine prison, Morgan informs me that the day's population is 1,297—377 over capacity. "The overcrowding has extended all feeding periods," he says, and doubling inmates in cramped, one-person rooms is common practice. "We have numbers, as you can see, sleeping on the floor. It's almost physically impossible to put bunks in some of these rooms." Morgan holds the door as I peer into a narrow, darkened room where an inmate lies motionless on a small cot, a sheet pulled over his head. As a result of this overcrowding, he says, it's impossible to keep everyone busy, though most of the inmates work at food or janitorial service or grounds-keeping within the fence. About 400 inmates are currently unoccupied.

Morgan's attitude toward the stun-belted work crews is more resigned than enthusiastic: "It's like anything else. We will make it work if it comes into effect. As we increase population-wise, we're going to have to rely more and more on technology."

But is this the technology U.S. prisons should be relying on?

Some correctional officers wonder about the belt's real purpose, particularly when it is combined with chain gangs.

Chase Rieveland, former assistant secretary of the Wisconsin Department of Corrections, who is now serving as secretary of the Washington Department of Corrections, sees the belted work crews as a "symbolic statement," designed to give the public an illusion of increased safety. "The thing that concerns me most is the public image that is left out there that says this is going to fix something, stop crime and violence. I guess I don't believe that. The question becomes, how far do we go in brutalization?"

Robert Ganger, the executive director of the Correctional Association of New York, sees the new work crews as "part and parcel of the excessive practices that we've been engaged with all around the country. The brunt of it falls on unpopular groups like prisoners, so people don't react. They just shrug."

For Ganger, stun belts, like the chain gangs themselves, are a gimmick. "If you engage in sane correctional practice, you can set up totally secure work crews without any of the theatrical accouterments that are unneeded. They're like fluff. It's a form of political show business. Politicians are more interested in their standing in the polls than in good correctional practice."

Under the conditions for the new Wisconsin work crews, two guards will supervise twelve inmates. Each guard will monitor six inmates, all connected via the belt to the same radio frequency. According to Wisconsin State Representative Tammy Baldwin, this means that "there is a lot of potential for stunning the wrong person, or stunning all. If there's an attempted escape or an attack on the guard, that's going to be a split-second decision."

The belt may affect prisoners assigned to work crews differently than it does someone who has not recently undergone strenuous physical activity. "People who are out in the sun, sweating, with dehydration and electrolyte imbalances—those people are also at risk," says Start.

Moreover, once the R.E.A.C.T. belt goes off, there is no stopping it. Although a blast of between one and three seconds is enough to paralyze almost anyone temporarily, the manufacturer set the timer at eight seconds in order to account for differences in bodily resistance to the belt, explains Kronke, the Stun Tech trainer. Even if, as often happens, the belt knocks its wearer to the floor after a half-second, the wearer must endure the entire eight-second stun. And the R.E.A.C.T. belt is not equipped with a switch that would allow a guard to end an unintentional activation.

If this is disturbing, Stun Tech's record for accidental activations is even more so. In the few years that the R.E.A.C.T. belt has been on the market, unintentional activations have matched intentional activations—nine times each, according to Stun Tech president Kaufman. Nevertheless, Stun Tech advertises that every activation has been "100 percent successful."

Kaufman maintains that the chances of a false activation (the result of an interfering radio signal) are "one in twenty-nine million," and suggests that documented accidents are the result of operator error. "Let me put it to you this way," he says. "Every time a plane crashes they blame the plane, not the pilot. And it's usually the pilot's fault." Several months ago, the company began installing a switch guard on all its belts. Kaufman says that this should put an end to unintentional activations.

Still, even Kronke has his doubts about the accidental activations. After James Oswald received an unintended jolt, the Waukesha, Wisconsin, court called Kronke in as an adviser. The belt must have been set off by an interfering radio signal, he says. "I don't know what else it could have been."

As the stun belt catches on nationally, it may become an attractive export. And that has Amnesty International worried. Acts of torture and severe ill-treatment using new electronic devices have been reported in at least fourteen countries, says Brian Wood of Amnesty.

Although the stun belt has not yet been sold abroad, Amnesty has expressed concern about the use of such electroshock weapons for torture. Amnesty has had records of torture with low-voltage cattle prods since the 1970s, but these new varieties of electronic devices—the taser, the stun gun, the electroshock baton, the electric riot shield, and the stun belt—function at a significantly higher voltage than the older variety. According to the British Forensic Science Service study, they are more severe by nearly two orders of magnitude.

Amnesty, the Omega Foundation, and the Journal of the American Medical Association all suggest that the number of "push-button" torture cases is on the rise. Torturers favor the new devices because they are easy to use, and tend not to leave obvious or lasting marks. Countries with records of electrical torture sometimes attempt to obtain samples of these devices in order to manufacture their own, according to an Omega Foundation report.

Amnesty now has cases of torturers shocking children, as well as men and women, with hand-held, high-voltage devices in the most sensitive areas of the human body: "behind their ears, on their necks, in their mouths, in their reproductive organs and rectums." Torturers have been known to give multiple blasts and to run devices continuously over their victims' bodies. People who have undergone this kind of torture have reported intense pain, muscle contractions, lost bowel control, vomiting, and urination.

Although the physical evidence of electrical torture may eventually disappear, the real trauma is psychological—the experience of being shocked into incapacitation and severe pain again and again. "Post-traumatic-stress syndrome describes the reaction to electrical injury as well as to other forms of torture," says Douglas Shenson, director of the Human Rights Clinic at Montefiore Hospital and North Central Bronx Hospital. Shenson claims that 11 percent of the patients he sees at the Human Rights Clinic report electrical torture. The way electrical torture is used, says Shenson, "is often to inflict maximal pain. The electrodes are often applied to the most sensitive parts of the body. That includes the genitals." Patients who have endured this form of torture report lingering psychological symptoms, "anything from depression to loss of appetite."

The stun belt would make an ideal torture weapon, Amnesty fears. The operator does not have to have physical contact with the victim in order to cause pain (manufacturers of a newer version, the R.A.C.C. belt, advertise its ability to shock from as far as 600 feet away). Although Stun Tech limits the R.E.A.C.T. belt's blast to eight seconds, "that doesn't help a prisoner whose torturer may be setting [the belt] off again and again," says Wood. The belt can be set off repeatedly, with only a one-second delay between shocks. The medical affidavit, which accompanies advertising materials on the R.E.A.C.T. belt, and supposedly proves its safety, discusses only a single application of the stun.

Stun Tech's Kaufman is eager to begin marketing the belt to other countries. "Many nations have shown interest," says Kaufman. Stun Tech already sells its device, Ultron II, abroad.

Would Stun Tech willingly market the stun belt to prison facilities in China, Mexico, or Saudi Arabia—three countries known for their human-rights abuses? Yes, says Kaufman, "We can deal with certain countries under the Free Trade Agreement without a problem." I ask if Stun Tech conducts research on the prison systems of the countries it ships to. Kaufman tells me it does not.

Many countries tend to look to the United States to set standards. When the U.S. Bureau of Prisons officially adopts an instrument like the stun belt, "the danger is that this belt—like other U.S. stun technology—will find its way onto the international market and into the hands of dedicated torturers," says Amnesty's Wood.

At nine in the evening, I arrive at the Outagamie County jail in Appleton, Wisconsin, and press the rear-door buzzer. A voice comes over the loudspeaker, requesting my name. The door unlatches. I enter the bright hallway. No one appears to greet me, and I am slightly disoriented, but have little choice in direction—there are no turnoffs or stray passages here. I round a corner and come face to face with a large elevator door, which immediately opens.

Upstairs, I meet Jim Kronke, the Stun Tech trainer. He leads me into a large, glassed-in office, where several stun devices lie carefully arranged on a table. I ask if one of the devices is a stun gun.

"I don't call this a stun gun," says Kronke. "I call it an electric restraining device. If someone calls it a stun gun, I hand it over to the officer and say, 'Please stun yourself with this.' "

He holds the stun device up in the air and presses a button. The device crackles, and a miniature bolt of lightning leaps between the two metal prongs at its tip. The muscles in my stomach clench.

One of the requirements for the eight-hour course necessary for officers who carry stun devices, explains Kronke, is that "you have to stun yourself." Officers in his training courses generally stun themselves in the large thigh muscle—not the place, it occurs to me, where an officer is likely to shock a disobedient inmate. Because of the body's reflex reaction to electrical shock, the stun generally lasts less than half a second—that is, less than the average shock needed to "take someone down," and much less than the stun belt's eight-second discharge.

An eight-second stun is not required for officers undergoing the six-hour training for the stun belt. However, many officers, Kronke assures me, elect to try it.

I ask if the shock from the stun belt hurts. Yes, he says. "It does a number on you. It feels like two needles. And it will leave some pretty severe marks."

He describes the time when he allowed himself to be shocked with the belt. He had built up a tolerance to electricity by taking "hits" with the electronic restraining device. He prepared himself psychologically to withstand the belt. "I had it all planned out. I was going to count 'one thousand one, one thousand two.' I never heard the beep. I was down on my back, spinning around. It was devastating. It hurt tremendously." He tells me the welts on his back took two months to heal.

Despite the pain involved, some officers seem to take pleasure in attempting to defy the belt. As I sit talking with Kronke, a second officer walks in. He, like Kronke, is a big man, larger than many prisoners. "I'd like to try it sometime to see if I could outlast it," he says.

Kronke describes officers at the Appleton facility who bet each other Mountain Dews, claiming that they will be able to remain standing the entire eight seconds of the shock—a very rare feat. For those who do undergo the belt, Kronke offers pocket calculators and T-shirts. He tells me the other officers have nicknamed him "Fifty," for 50,000 volts.

When I ask Kronke if he will allow me to try the stun belt, he turns grave. "You would not want to wear this belt," he says. "I would not recommend it."

So I ask if I can shock myself with the stun gun. Kronke has me sit in a chair, press the prongs against my leg, look up at him, and pull the trigger. I feel a powerful smack and am immediately fatigued. My arm and leg jump apart in reflex. Kronke informs me that I have shocked myself for "much less than half a second."

★ CHILD LABOR IN THE ★ 1990s

Thomas Geoghegan

FROM *THE NEW YORK TIMES*, DECEMBER 1, 1996

This time of year makes me think of a teen-ager I once met who knew the world of child labor like Huck Finn knew the river. He thought holidays were awful. Halloween is bad, he told me, and Thanksgiving weekend is worse.

But Christmas made him shiver, because "then the stores really stay open late." Kids like him, who worked full-time hours, often didn't get home till 2 a.m. It was in 1991, at an all-night supermarket, when I first saw child labor at the midnight hour. As I was grinding coffee beans, I noticed that this store was being manned (if that is the word) by children.

Wasn't this a school night?

"Pardon me," I asked the girl at the cash register, "but how old are you?" She gasped. "No, no," I said. "I mean what's the average age of people working here?"

"Oh, maybe like sixteen to twenty," she said. As if twenty meant "management."

A few nights later, over dinner, a teacher I knew told me that a lot of students worked forty hours a week. "But past midnight?" I asked. "On a school night?"

"What's the alternative?"

"Forbid it."

"That's the only income some of these families have."

I decided to look up some law.

Thanks to the New Deal, we have the Fair Labor Standards Act, which deals with "children" who are sixteen and seventeen. It says the Labor Secretary can prohibit them from occupations that are "physically hazardous" or "detrimental to their health or well-being," like tending bar. I couldn't help but think that working until 1 or 2 a.m. on a school night would be detrimental to their health and well-being.

But only four states have set limits on how late teen-agers can work: New York, Wisconsin, Washington and Oregon. According to the Department of Labor, about 2.6 million sixteen- and seventeen-year-olds worked in 1995, putting in an average of 19.2 hours a week. An additional four hundred thousand were actively seeking jobs. But the Labor Department does not know how late these teen-agers worked and under what conditions. It does not know how many were in school, or how many even younger children were working.

President Clinton and other politicians have called for curfews for teen-agers. Yet curfews typically make exceptions for those who are working. Yes, some of these young people bring in their household's only income. But perhaps there is another reason for widespread teen-age labor: We dare not interfere with the employer's right to manage.

In 1993, with support from the National Safe Workplace Institute, I filed suit in Federal District Court in Chicago to compel the Labor Secretary to set limits on the working hours of sixteen- and seventeen-year-olds. I was representing teachers who were acting, for purposes of the suit, as guardians of students working abusive hours.

One of these kids had grown up in a world of gangs and crime. But what had wrecked his grades, unraveled his life, was the time he spent as a bag boy for Big Business.

"Kids do it for the clothes," he said.

This annoyed me. I asked him what he meant.

"Look, you're a lawyer, right?"

"If you were my dad . . ."

This made me uneasy.

". . . I'd say, 'Look, maybe you're not rich, but you can buy me some threads.' " He frowned. "Kids with good parents, they don't have to work."

"What do you mean by 'good'?"

He thought. "Oh, maybe $15,000 a year." Well, I thought, I make more than that. It suddenly hit me that this kid was talking about basic clothing, not Ralph Lauren.

He took me into the world of child labor: cleaning urinals at 1:30 a.m., sorting endless items by color, wielding butcher knives in delis.

Then there were the big suburban discount stores. "You know what they do? They take the kids out there, and then bring them back in buses, and you don't get back in the city till 2 a.m.," he said.

"Wait. Don't the kids know this?"

"No, man! They don't know! They're just kids! Look, you apply for a job and you say like, 'It's got to be from four to ten.' 'Oh,' they say, 'sure, yeah, like we close at ten.' They close at ten, suuuurrre, but that's when you start working! And then you get on the bus, and then you got to go to the other stores"—to pick up other young workers who are also shuttled in—"and you wait and wait and wait."

I was troubled that people might think the kids were slaving away for designer clothes. I mentioned my concern to a teacher. "Look around," she said. We were in the school cafeteria. "See any kids here in designer clothes?" The kids, brown and white, were drably dressed. It wasn't sub-urban grunge. It was bleaker.

"You can tell when they're working late," the teacher said. "The ones with those jobs have real long jackets that scrape the floor. They flip them over their heads so they can get some sleep." Like carrying around their own bedrolls. Sometimes, she said, she sent them to the infirmary. "The nurse there, she's used to it. She knows they aren't sick. She just tells them to go to bed."

There were other kids in the case. One seventeen-year-old worked more than forty hours a week at an upscale hardware store. Her sister called the store to ask if she could have the night off before the college boards. The answer was no. The school counselor called. No. The girl worked most of the night.

There was a sixteen-year-old, a tall, shy kid. She, too, worked more than forty hours a week, late into the night. Eventually, she got pregnant and dropped out of school.

And there was the sixteen-year-old who worked at the McDonald's called "McCrack," because of its location. By the time she got out— 1:00 a.m.—the buses had stopped running.

Halfway through the case, the kids started to disappear. Quit school. Moved away. The teachers said we should get other plaintiffs. So I met with another group of kids.

"Remember when that guy came in the other night?" said one.

"Naked? He's come in before."

The kids giggled.

"What time does she let you out?" one young woman asked the others, referring to their boss at a fast-food restaurant.

"Oh, one-thirty, and she doesn't pay us after one!"

In the end, I decided not to add any more kids to the case. Why bother? They would wind up dropping out, too.

In the end, we lost our case. But before the end came, we did have a meeting in Washington with a Clinton Administration official.

"Let's assume we have the authority to regulate," the official said. "Why is this so bad? I mean, from the perspective of their parents, maybe this is a way of keeping the kid under control."

"'Under control'?" I said. "These kids are out of control! 'Parents'? What parents? You think these kids have parents?"

Most of the kids I had been representing were living with an older sibling. Down at their income levels—$12,000, $13,000 a year—we don't have families anymore.

Even if these new Democrats do little, at least they give you a meeting. As a lawyer, I can tell you it makes a good impression on the client.

★ SEDUCED BY ★ CIVILITY: POLITICAL MANNERS AND THE CRISIS OF DEMOCRATIC VALUES

Benjamin DeMott

FROM *THE NATION*, DECEMBER 9, 1996

What is the real American malaise? Why is this country in trouble?

Lately the leader classes have been floating a fresh answer to these queries, talking up a new "root cause" of national woes. Not race, not class, not dirty lyrics or cheap scag or toe-sucking consultants, not under- or over-taxation. Our not-so-secret malaise is, in a pet leader-class phrase, the decline of civility. The Republic is suffering from rampant intemperateness on the one hand (loss of the inner check on which social intercourse depends) and distaste for associated living on the other. Citizens are shouting too much, as on Geraldo and talk-radio. They've forgotten how to listen and respect and defer. Furthermore, the once-vaunted native genius for collaborative, volunteer problem-solving is disappearing down the drain, and people feel the disappearance. Putting the country back on track requires a rediscovery, by ordinary folk, of mutuality as a value.

Judged for seductiveness, the emerging orthodoxy on civility ranks high. It has a radiant vocabulary—common good, civic trust, communal participation, social capital. . . . It shrewdly selects, as representative villains, characters with jumbo negatives—not just the uncivil prick in the pickup who gives you the finger as he cuts you off but rabble-rousing Buchanan with his pitchforks, Farrakhan with his demon whites, Robbie Alomar with his wad and (from the past) the demonstrators who chanted "L.B.J., L.B.J., How Many Kids Did You Kill Today?" Two ghastly and unforgettable terrorist acts—the murder of Planned Parenthood clinic workers in Brookline and the Oklahoma City bombing—surface often (seldom relevantly) in discussions of "lost civility" and restraint. The budget wars are also mentioned: Congress and the White House hammering each other daily last winter, with partisan denials of space sending legislators outside the Capitol to discuss Medicare in the rain.

What's more, civility orthodoxy's models of behavior are beyond anybody's faulting. If you've lived awhile in a place where, when sickness and other troubles hit home, the neighbors volunteer to feed and bathe your baby, plow out your car, plant your garden, carry you for months, you're bound to listen hard to bigfoots who deplore Americans' increasing reluctance to lend a hand to neighborhood projects and local improvement organizations.

But seductiveness isn't substance. The incivility railed at by the elite should be seen as a protest by Americans outside the ranks of the publicly articulate against the conduct of their presumed betters. The current orthodoxy on volunteerism and immoderacy shuts its ears to this protest, simultaneously beatifying the undeserving and sapping democratic energy and will. Sold as diagnosis or nostrum, civility is in fact a theater of operations—the classless society's new class war zone.

The decade's sacred civility text is Robert Putnam's "Bowling Alone: America's Declining Social Capital." The article, by a Kennedy School of Government prof, studies communal association, and views membership drops in P.T.A.s, fraternal organizations, church-related groups and the like as signs of an allegedly "mysterious disengagement" by the citizenry from civic life and social trust. Published almost two years ago in the *Journal of Democracy,* "Bowling Alone" went gold overnight among the elites and is still heavily cited by high-profile opinionizers—from editorial board members of the *New York Times* to PBS "essayists." The link between the decline of volunteerism and the demise of civility was forged more explicitly by Putnam's well-placed fans than by the prof himself. David Broder, who ranked "Bowling Alone" as last year's most important magazine article, writes columns recommending the "strengthening of civic life and the return of civility in our public discourse"; the idea is to connect—somehow, anyhow—the upsurge of political nastiness with dwindling enrollment in service groups. And the notion of a commutative relationship between volunteerism and good civic manners is widely endorsed.

The sitting President is among the endorsers. Before the election and after, in speech after speech, Clinton developed civility and common-ground themes, and at the same time plumps for a proposed $10 million program to reward high school student volunteers. The President has huddled frequently enough with Putnam to turn him into a guru. Clinton inspired his alma mater, Yale, to devote an alumni weekend to a symposium on civility. A Yale Law teacher Clinton admires—Stephen Carter—is finishing a book-length treatise on civility. And the various ripples widen. New York's Ethical Culture Society runs an assembly on civility and the media. Columnists, talk-show hosts, editor-spinners, spinner-editors—Ellen Goodman, Paul Samuelson, Hendrik Hertzberg, Ken Bode, Charles Krauthammer, Mary Matalin, Bill Kristol, Rush Limbaugh, many more—hold forth on civility. *The Chronicle of Higher Education* looks saucer-eyed at growing incivility in academe—professors calling each other assholes and cunts at department meetings and elsewhere, administrators struggling to establish rules of "collegiality." *US News & World Report* devotes eight pages to "The American Uncivil Wars." Paeans to civility fill the Congressional Record. Colin Powell and Tipper Gore salute civility at their political conventions. So, too, do Al Gore and Jack Kemp during their debate. Post-debate, post-Alomar rumination garnished with "civil" and "civility" resounds on the networks and crams editorial pages from the *Houston Chronicle* to the *Wall Street Journal*. A week after Election Day, Miss Manners, speaking at the Woman's National Democratic Club in Washington, describes the election itself as a "pro-civility landslide." ("We had a national referendum on whether we want a civil society," says Miss M., aka Judith Martin, and the results establish that "the American romance with rudeness is over.") Days later, Supreme Court Justice Anthony Kennedy reveals he is preparing a speech on civility for the American Bar Association, and Bill Bennett and Sam Nunn announce the formation of their new "Forum on Civility."

In a word, a miniboom in progress.

CAN'T YOU BE MORE CIVIL?

Most leader-class discussion is preoccupied with causation—with the question, Why has civility declined? In answering, the discussants analyze others, never themselves, and invariably the perspective is de haut en bas. Self-scrutiny doesn't exist.

In the dearth of it lies the great disgrace. For some time now, a knowledge explosion has been delivering into your hands and mine, hour by hour, day after day, unprecedented quantities of source-checked data regarding top-dog patterns of conduct, top-dog feelings and attitudes toward personal privilege, top-dog understandings of good/bad, right/wrong. Partly because it meshes with mid-twentieth-century eruptions against the patriarchy and racism and class privilege, the information in question has different clout from that achieved by yesteryear's muckrakers. The material lays down a blunt, useful challenge both to national mythologies (one nation indivisible) and to popular attitudes and feelings that, broadly positive and hopeful, once granted those mythologies an automatic pass.

Non-mainstream figures joke about the challenge, even as they exploit it (Buchanan grinning at the idea of Buchanan heading up a pitchfork brigade against the selfish rich). But mainstream voices, especially editorial voices, tend to adopt graver tones, counseling officialdom against taking the challenge lightly, and advising against cover-ups: You only make it worse; everything is bound to come out.

And come out it does—masses of documentation flowing from sunshine law disclosures, survey research, advances in computing and duplicating, better-financed investigative reporting in scandal sheets and elsewhere. Numbers: how much money is made how quickly and cunningly (as "welfare mothers" are nickeled and dimed and worse) by the can't-lose "investments" of senators or wives of governors or majority leaders—or by corporation executives whose huge, self-immunizing "deferred compensation" schemes screw fellow workers by the thousand—or by whichever celebrities are sinning their way to fortunes this month (a call girl reports that a presidential consultant is a client, whereupon the consultant's publisher renegotiates his book contract upward into the millions). Paper trail documentation of official lies: executive oaths that nicotine isn't addictive, that our firm would never dump poisons into suburban canals, that survival concerns alone dictate downsizing, that the U.S. government absolutely would not allow one of its agencies to wink at drug trading that enslaves African-Americans and others by the tens of thousands, that U.S. top brass absolutely would not hide the facts about soldiers' exposure to chemical weapons, that the White House absolutely would not conceal from the people that it was escalating a foreign war.

More: details filling out elite attitudinal profiles—evidence that the well-placed admire successful stonewalling, rate "reputation for integrity" above integrity, disbelieve that persons of modest means or inferior coiffure can attain distinction or escape shame, believe that it's acceptable for university presidents to keep trustees in their pockets by buying them $200 bottles of Cheval Blanc with dinner at one's club. Videotaped proof of police brutality by ranking officers. Strong evidence that a heroicized Chief Executive welcomed prostitutes into his White House bedroom at a time when he was acceding to the proposition that taxpaying blacks deserved physical abuse for seeking the vote. Proof that the U.S. officer class engaged in mass murder on foreign soil. Proof that the Vietnam draft policy—a policy that, by exempting the well-off from service, contravened the national value of shared sacrifice in wartime—was actually conceived as a means of gulling the educated into ignoring the war. Proof that, under pressure from the corporate health megalith, thousands of doctors have broken their oaths of personal responsibility for the care of their patients. Proof that racism is rife among top oil-company executives. Data disclosing that the reduction of the U.S. producer class to the status of hamburger flippers or unemployables is looked upon with equanimity not only by the managers in place but by significant numbers of their someday replacements: subfreshmen ticketed for training in gatekeeper institutions of higher learning. And so forth. Material of this sort is often accompanied, in the media, by low-key coaching on how to shrug off corruption (yesterday was worse, nobody's perfect, etc.). But the coaching seems not to have taken. The University of Michigan's Center for Political Studies polls voters biannually on their views of the leader class. Decades ago when the center first asked, "Are government officials crooked?" 24 percent answered, "Quite a lot." Two years ago 51 percent gave that response. The center also asks: "Would you say the government is pretty much run by a few big interests looking out for themselves or that it is run for the benefit of all people?" Thirty years ago 64 percent of the respondents answered, "For the benefit of all." In 1994 that figure had dropped to 19 percent.

Mistrust of the authorities runs in the native grain, as everybody knows. But quantitative changes in levels of mistrust are capable of producing qualitative differences—witness the current dismissal by an apparent majority of "character" as a requirement for high public office.

Returning to civility: While the citizen disengagement from public life that civility promoters term "mysterious" is clearly a complex phenomenon, some influences on it aren't arcane. Rude, abusive speech and action reflects, in one of its dimensions, belief in the need for an attitude—some kind of protection against sly, sincerity-marketing politicos and boss-class crooks. "Uncivil" refusal by ordinary citizens to labor unpaid in the cause of points-of-light good works reflects, in one of its dimensions, the daily exposure of ordinary citizens to powerful anti-mutuality instruction from above—oblique but persuasive lessons on how to pull your oar ceaselessly for the benefit of Number One; how not to fret about hungry children in the street; how to feel good when, in the age of homelessness, a corporate bright boy spends $45 million on his own one-family dwelling; how to avoid being suckered into caringness. The "new incivility" needs to be recognized, in short, for what it is: a flat-out, justified rejection of leader-class claims to respect, a demand that leader-class types start looking hard at themselves.

FRIENDS OF CIVILITY

Which, as I said, is exactly where civility discourse encourages them not to look. Unsurprisingly, leader-class talk about civility and incivility deals neither with justified withdrawals of respect nor with impotent fury at corroded leader-class values and standards. And it avoids basic elements of civility such as considerateness, modesty, faith in the rough rightness of democratic values—items readily comprehensible and well suited to plain speech. Talkers sift trends that social science or Tory whimsy finds relevant to the "decline of civility," measuring the degree of their influence. Putnam's "Bowling Alone," the sacred text, is set up as a whodunit. The "crime" is the murder of citizen solidarity, mutual concern, volunteerism. The author casts himself as a detective bent on solving the crime; the "suspects" include longer working hours, women in the labor market, rising racism, mobility (geographical and social), several others. Introduced and assessed with an array of stats and graphs, the suspects are at length dismissed, Poirot-style, one by one. At the conclusion comes the unveiling. "The culprit is TV." Volunteering is declining and civic trust is withering, Putnam explains, because Everyman and Everywoman are bemused by the tube.

Similar etiological dabblings occur at Friends of Civility parleys, public and private. (Bids to civilitarian parleys go out to the right, left and muddled; civilitarianism is vain of its inclusiveness.) And here, as in Putnam's pages, there's zero self-scrutiny. Consider the symposium on civility at the Yale Law School meeting mentioned earlier. The group assembled to ruminate for the edification of law school alumni included accomplished men and women. Arthur Schlesinger Jr. delivered the keynote, and a panel of editors, authors and teachers (Gertrude Himmelfarb, Hilton Kramer, Victor Navasky, Randall Kennedy, Martin Peretz) spoke for the world of ideas; Representative Barney Frank, David Garth and Peggy Noonan spoke for practical politics.

Kramer threw off in familiar vein on scum demonstrators, quoting old anti-L.B.J. chants; he also slammed "vulgarity and ignorance based on the precipitous decline in public discourse." But he found his central example of bottom-dog dimness and unsophistication in the press. Kramer recounted how he learned—during a "long Paris lunch" with Flora Lewis—the secret of mounting stupidity among reporters. (He personified reporters as "some young man" from the provinces who knew no better than to get close to "the trenches.") The secret, according to Lewis, was that

> The *New York Times* had had to send, in effect, relays of mostly young men, although there were one or two women, to cover the [Vietnam] war. . . . Most of these young reporters had little if any experience of the world outside the United States. And what they discovered, or believed they discovered in Vietnam, was that the world was divided into two parties: the evil party, which was the United States, and the rest of the world, which was the good party. . . . Those reporters had to be rewarded with more glamorous assignments. And wherever they were sent out into the world, they were still reporting the Vietnam War, where America was to blame for whatever was wrong with the world, and the locals—the natives, whether they were in Moscow or wherever—were to be given the benefit of the doubt.

Himmelfarb's bottom-dog targets were ill-educated black teachers unwisely allowed to participate in public forums. "Civility, like conversation," she opined, "assumes a commonality—a commonality of purpose, of beliefs, of manners and morals, a common human nature"—but minority multiculturalists have destroyed the commonalities. "I am told," said Himmelfarb, "that in speaking of shared values, I evoke memories of exploited black sharecroppers. Now these are not-off-the-cuff remarks thrown out in the heat of debate or at a private dinner table. They come from very reputable professors in public forums, generally speaking from a prepared text. . . . We are in a culture war. And one of the first casualties of war is civility."

Arthur Schlesinger Jr. had still different targets: bottom-dog boorishness and inability to follow arguments. He wittily reviewed lowbrow griping at White House high style, and went on to claim that the chief difference worth mentioning between yesterday and today is that in the past "the tradition of scurrility" had "a real offset"—namely, a "countertradition of gravitas" (political argument and oratory published fulllength in newspapers and elsewhere). Today, said Schlesinger, "our attention-span-challenged audiences" have abolished the countertradition. Had this been another kind of meeting, each of these Friends of Civility—several others at the parley as well—might have been set straight. Kramer might have been told that a sector of the public has lately awakened to the truth that the American imperium is something different from the selfless light of the world shown in the approved portrait, and that the agents of this awakening over the decades have been the few American reporters who, by giving the benefit of the doubt to natives rather than official briefers, produced the only reliable reporting from a long string of places—Mexico, Chile, the Dominican Republic, El Salvador, a dozen more.

Himmelfarb might have been told that many blacks are aware that their exclusion for centuries from schooling and power continues to have appalling caste consequences for most brothers and sisters, and that privileged whites who harp on "shared values" and commonalities are implicitly and infuriatingly asserting that nothing separates black history from white history. Schlesinger might have been reminded that entertainment conglomerates shape tastes as well as reflect them, and that blaming TV viewers for dumbed-down politics oversimplifies a number of highly knotty matters. All three might have been chastised for coupling intellectually and morally irresponsible oversimplifications with the kind of supercilious insult characteristic of—so Matthew-Arnold thought—barbarian-aristos.

This, though, was a civility fete, hence Kramer, Himmelfarb, Schlesinger et al. heard little or no direct critique. Behaving decorously, respondents turned away from fatuity, greed and obliviousness near at hand to the fairly distant past or else engaged in explicating paradoxes (civility as incivility and vice versa). Randall Kennedy emphasized that nineteenth-century civility promoters had indicted abolitionists for incivility: "The people who marched under the banner of civility, the people who were the compromisers, the people who were being afraid of being labeled as radicals and extremists, were the people who were willing to allow slavery to continue."

Venturing close to the present, Victor Navasky, publisher and editorial director of the *Nation*, addressed himself directly to Kramer and Himmelfarb, averring that the sit-ins gave him his example of a "supremely civil and civilized act." No sooner had Navasky spoken than civilitarian whistles commenced shrieking. Kramer cried that the speaker "violated the standards of civility." Himmelfarb rapped the blackboard, warning that "We seem to be not only discussing incivility, we seem to be on the verge of practicing incivility." Angered, Kennedy told the room that "If you're in an argument with a thug, there are things much more important than civility." For a minute it seemed possible that the inhibiting, intimidating power of civility discourse might not be absolute.

But they who define the issues win the debate. The subject at Yale was the decline of civility, not of fairness, justice or decency among the privileged. And that definition of the subject certified that the problem under consideration had to do with inferiors, not superiors; no tie was made between it and disrespect for the leader classes stemming from thuggish leader-class beliefs and behavior. Kennedy didn't press on with his case. The vision of the "civility problem" as, at its core, one of bottom-dog manners rather than top-dog morals underwent no sustained examination.

OFFENDING OUR BETTERS

The current civility boom is, of course, only one of several indicators of rising establishment impatience with the notion that, on these shores, class interests stand in ever sharper conflict. The most obvious indicator was the 1996 campaign itself, which saw Dole and Clinton vying with each other for the title of politician most angered by allusions to U.S. classlessness as a "myth." (Clinton noodled on "common ground" through every whistle stop; Dole shouted, "We're not a class society; we're a classless society," to audiences from Russell to Hartford.) Other indicators include establishment refusal to accord courtesy to any insider critique of the mega-rich, and establishment eagerness to bash those who dare to murmur moral objections to the moeurs of the stylish professional classes.

Item: Ted Turner recently let fall that the Forbes Four Hundred Richest list is "destroying our country." He argued that the "skinflints" and "Scrooges" on the list "won't loosen up [as philanthropists] because they're afraid they'll reduce their net worth and go down the list." He added: "They're fighting every year to be the richest man in the world. Why don't they sign a joint pact to each give away a billion and then move down the Forbes list equally?"

In her *New York Times* column on Turner, "Ted's Excellent Idea," Maureen Dowd veered between nervous giggles and hints that the man is a kook. She had some of Turner's comments set in caps ("THEY [multibillionaires] SHOULD DO IT [namely, curb their greed and part with serious money for urgent public needs] No-o-w!"), communicating that he's a loudmouth. She referred to Turner variously as a "Rhett Butler romantic," "America's flashiest extrovert," "Captain Outrageous" and "the Mouth of the South." The impression her column left wasn't that a member of the megarich had offered sane counsel to his fellows (in an idiom updated from Andrew Carnegie's essay on "Philanthropy") but rather that Turner is one more self-aggrandizing know-it-all, shooting off his mouth for publicity purposes.

Item: Yesterday the moneyed classes heeded the prudent rule of silence against responding to those who make noise about greed, obliviousness or fatuity—but not now. Evidently convinced that the populace as a whole shares their repugnance for those who refer unashamedly to moral standards, they greet such critics not with silence but with explosions of hatred and countercharges of hypocrisy and sanctimony.

Benjamin DeMott

During a recent interview with the *New York Observer*, Jonathan Kozol spoke slightingly of frequenters of the city's luxo restaurants. He said he was "far more scared in Manhattan [than in the South Bronx, setting of his most recent book], because that's when I feel my soul is in peril, when I have to go to the Four Seasons." The simple message was that a culture that treats hundreds of thousands of children as garbage while consecrating three-star lunches and $45 million hideaways probably ought to look to its soul, and that complicity with such a culture for the length of a meal betrays whatever knowledge one possesses of suffering.

Pow. the *New Republic* fired in fury, jeeringly quoting Kozol's fears for his soul, accusing him of having "made a career of his immunity to transgression," and slaughtering him for moral pride: "He dined for our sins."

It doesn't matter, in sum, whether the critical whisper comes from an ascetic or a billionaire. The leader classes sense that their weapons in hand (civility discourse isn't the least of them) suffice to still any insurgence in an instant.

Idealizers of the civilitarian impulse aren't found exclusively on the right. The religious left, once admirably clearheaded about the difference between substantive and marginal political questions, today evinces a desire to fold a wide range of concerns, moral, political and economic, into the issue of civility. The September/October *Sojourners* has an article by the editor, the Rev. Jim Wallis—a decent man with strong left-activist credentials—titled "A Crisis of Civility." The piece says barely a word about incivility as a response to an unendurable surfeit of corruption. It begins with the usual animadversions on abusive campaigning and concludes that "honesty, respect, principle, openness, fairness, accessibility, and involvement are all issues of civility."

The sentence sounds the theme that tightly binds old myths of classlessness to new scams of civility—that inequity is verbal; flows from tone, not structure; bears no relation to power differentials. Sanitizing and miniaturizing the worst of the past and present, this theme—the language of civility and incivility as a whole—sweeps away human meaning from slavery, the civil rights struggle, one episode after another of murderous cruelty and greed. It has similar effect on differences of opportunity and education: drains them of meaning, persuades the privileged that insulting the weak keeps up standards, encourages those who surmount "disadvantage" to forget that they didn't rise unaided, hence owe others help, not insult. In this cloud of abstraction nothing survives except pieties of the airheaded: faith that no talk on earth is more exalted than talk about talk.

In theory it should be easy to counter such faith—but try it. Criticize a civility promoter, and you hear that you're a fan of rap lyrics about cop-killing, or that you're the sort of nutcake who tries to silence by boos any idea you happen to disagree with, or that you believe differences of opinion on large matters preclude collaborative work toward limited objectives, or that you lack feeling for the glories of civil discourse in the public square to which Hannah Arendt sang her lyric in *On Revolution*. In short, civility boosters can't be defeated, they can only be held out against, with arguments built on patient repetition of truisms about the nature of our kind of polity, viz.:

Democracy continues to oblige citizens to resist—as Richard Hoggart once put it—"the constant pressure to undervalue others, especially those who do not inhabit 'our own' publicly articulate world."

Democracy continues to oblige citizens to render serious, right-valued judgments on others as well as upon themselves.

Democracy can coexist with the belief that all humans are sinners but not with the belief that all sins are equal.

Democracy has within each of its camps, not excluding the civilitarian camp, thugs in number. And when you're in an argument with a thug, there are things much more important than civility.

★ UNCHAINED MELODY ★

Marshall Berman

FROM *THE NATION*, MAY 11, 1998

A review of *The Communist Manifesto: A Modern Edition.* By Karl Marx and Frederick Engels. With an introduction by Eric Hobsbawm.

The best story I've ever heard about *The Communist Manifesto* came from Hans Morgenthau, the great theorist of international relations who died in 1980. It was the early seventies at CUNY, and he was reminiscing about his childhood in Bavaria before World War I. Morgenthau's father, a doctor in a working-class neighborhood of Coburg, often took his son along on house calls. Many of his patients were dying of TB; a doctor could do nothing to save their lives, but might help them die with dignity. When his father asked about last requests, many workers said they wanted to have the *Manifesto* buried with them when they died. They implored the doctor to see that the priest didn't sneak in and plant the Bible on them instead.

This spring, the *Manifesto* is 150 years old. In that century and a half, apart from the Bible, it has become the most widely read book in the world. Eric Hobsbawm, in his splendid introduction to the handsome new Verso edition, gives a brief history of the book's reception. It can be summed up fast: Whenever there's trouble, anywhere in the world, the book becomes an item; when things quiet down, the book drops out of sight; when there's trouble again, the people who forgot remember. When fascist-type regimes seize power, it's always on the short list of books to burn. When people dream of resistance—even if they're not Communists, even if they distrust Communists—it provides music for their dreams. Get the beat of the beginning and the end. First line: "A spectre is haunting Europe—the spectre of Communism." Last lines: "The proletarians have nothing to lose but their chains. They have a world to win. WORKING MEN OF ALL COUNTRIES, UNITE!" In Rick's bar in Casablanca, you may or may not love France, but when the band breaks into "La Marseillaise," you've got to stand up and sing.

Yet literate people today, even people with left politics, are amazingly ignorant of what's actually in the book. For years, I've asked people what they think it consists of. The most popular answers are that it's (1) a utopian handbook on how to run a society with no money or property, or else (2) a Machiavellian handbook on how to create a Communist state and keep it in power. People who were Communists didn't seem to know the book any better than people who were not. (At first this amazed me; later I saw it was no accident. Classical Communist education was Talmudic, based on a study of commentaries, with an underlying suspicion of sacred primary texts. Among Orthodox Jews, the Bible is a sort of adult movie—a yeshiva-bucher is exposed to it only after years of Talmudic training, to insure that he will respond in orthodox ways. Similarly, a trainee at a party school would begin with Stalin, until 1956; then the great indoctrinator Lenin; then, with some hesitation, Engels; Marx came in only at the very end, and then only for those with security clearance.)

Now that security is gone. In just a few years, so many statues and magnifications of Marx have vanished from public squares; so many streets and parks named for him are going under other names today. What does it all mean? For some people, like our Sunday morning princes of the air, the implosion of the U.S.S.R. simply confirmed what they had believed all along, and released them from having to show respect. One of my old bosses at C.C.N.Y. said it concisely: "Nineteen eighty-nine proves that courses in Marxism are obsolete." But there are other ways to read history. What happened to Marx after 1917 was a disaster: A thinker needs beatification like a hole in the head. So we should welcome his descent from the pedestal as a fortunate fall. Maybe we can learn what Marx has to teach if we confront him at ground level, the level on which we ourselves are trying to stand.

So what does he offer? First, startling when you're not prepared for it, praise for capitalism so extravagant, it skirts the edge of awe. Very early in the *Manifesto*, he describes the processes of material construction that it perpetrates, and the emotions that go with them, especially the sense of being caught up in something magical and uncanny:

> The bourgeoisie has created . . . more massive and more colossal productive forces than have all preceding generations together. Subjection of nature's forces to man, machinery, application of chemistry to industry and agriculture, steam navigation, railways . . . clearing of whole continents for cultivation, canalization of rivers, whole populations conjured out of the ground—what earlier century had even a presentiment that such productive powers slumbered in the lap of social labour?

Or a page before, on an innate dynamism that is spiritual as well as material:

> The bourgeoisie cannot exist without constantly revolutionizing the instruments of production, and thereby the relations of production, and with them the whole relations of society. . . . Constant revolutionizing of production, uninterrupted disturbance of all social conditions, everlasting uncertainty and agitation distinguish the bourgeois epoch from all earlier ones. All fixed, fast-frozen relations, with their train of ancient and venerable prejudices and opinions, are swept away, all new-formed ones become antiquated before they can ossify. All

that is solid melts into air, all that is holy is profaned, and man
is at last compelled to face with sober senses, his real conditions of life, and his relations with his kind.

Part 1, "Bourgeois and Proletarians," contains many passages like
these, asserted in major chords with great dramatic flair. Somehow,
many readers seem to miss them. But Marx's contemporaries didn't miss
them, and some fellow radicals—Proudhon, Bakunin—saw his appreciation of capitalism as a betrayal of its victims. This charge is still heard
today, and deserves serious response. Marx hates capitalism, but he also
thinks it has brought immense real benefits, spiritual as well as material,
and he wants the benefits spread around and enjoyed by everybody
rather than monopolized by a small ruling class. This is very different
from the totalitarian rage that typifies radicals who want to blow it all
away. Sometimes, as with Proudhon, it is just modern times they hate;
they dream of a golden-age peasant village where everyone was happily
in his place (or in her place behind him). For other radicals, from the
author of the *Book of Revelation* to the Unabomber, it goes over the edge
into something like rage against reality, against human life itself. Apocalyptic rage offers immediate, sensational cheap thrills. Marx's perspective is far more complex and nuanced, and hard to sustain if you're not
grown up.

Marx is not the first communist to admire capitalism for its creativity;
that attitude can be found in some of the great utopian socialists of the
generation before him, like Saint-Simon and Robert Owen. But Marx is
the first to invent a prose style that can bring that perilous creativity to
life. His style in the *Manifesto* is a kind of Expressionist lyricism. Every
paragraph breaks over us like a wave that leaves us shaking from the
impact and wet with thought. This prose evokes breathless momentum,
plunging ahead without guides or maps, breaking all boundaries, pre-
carious piling and layering of things, ideas and experiences. Catalogs
play a large role in Marx's style—as they do for his contemporaries
Dickens and Whitman—but part of the *Manifesto*'s enchantment comes
from our feeling that the lists are never exhausted, the catalog is open
to the present and the future, we are invited to pile on things, ideas and

experiences of our own, to pile ourselves on if we can. But the items in the pile often seem to clash, and it sounds like the whole vast aggregation could crash. From paragraph to paragraph, Marx makes readers feel that we are riding the fastest and grandest nineteenth-century train through the roughest and most perilous nineteenth-century terrain, and though we have splendid light, we are pressing ahead where there is no track.

One feature of modern capitalism that Marx most admires is its global horizon and its cosmopolitan texture. Many people today talk about the global economy as if it had only recently come into being. The *Manifesto* should help us see the extent to which it has been there all along:

> The need of a constantly expanding market chases the bourgeoisie over the whole surface of the globe. It must nestle everywhere, settle everywhere, establish connections everywhere.
>
> The bourgeoisie has through its exploitation of the world market given a cosmopolitan character to production and consumption in every country. All old established national industries have been destroyed or are being daily destroyed. They are dislodged by new industries, whose introduction becomes a life and death question for all civilized nations, by industries that no longer process indigenous raw material, but raw material drawn from remotest zones; industries whose products are consumed, not only at home, but in every quarter of the globe. . . .
>
> The cheap prices of its commodities are heavy artillery with which [the bourgeoisie] batters down all Chinese walls, with which it forces the barbarians' intensely obstinate hatred of foreigners to capitulate. It compels all nations, on pain of extinction, to adopt the bourgeois mode of production; it compels them to introduce what is called civilization into their midst, i.e. to become bourgeois themselves. In one word, it creates a world after its own image.

This global spread offers a spectacular display of history's ironies.

These bourgeois are banal in their ambitions, yet their unremitting quest for profit forces on them the same insatiable drive—structure and infinite horizon as that of any of the great Romantic heroes—as Don Giovanni, as Childe Harold, as Goethe's Faust. They may think of only one thing, but their narrow focus leads to the broadest integrations; their shallow outlook wreaks the most profound transformations; their peaceful economic activity devastates every human society like a bomb, from the most primitive tribes to the mighty U.S.S.R. Marx was appalled at the human costs of capitalist development, but he always believed that the world horizon it created was a great achievement on which socialism must build. Remember, the grand appeal to Unite with which the *Manifesto* ends is addressed to "WORKING MEN OF ALL COUNTRIES."

A crucial global drama was the unfolding of the first-ever world culture. Marx, writing when mass media were just developing, called it "world literature." I think it is legitimate at the end of this century to update the idea into "world culture." The *Manifesto* shows how this culture will evolve spontaneously from the world market: In place of the old wants, satisfied by the production of the country, we find new wants, requiring for their satisfaction products of distant lands and climes. In place of the old local and national seclusion and self-sufficiency, we have intercourse in every direction, universal interdependence of nations. And as in material, so also in intellectual [or spiritual—*geistige* can be translated either way] production. The intellectual [spiritual] creations of individual nations become common property . . . and from the numerous national and local literatures, there arises a world literature.

This vision of world culture brings together several complex ideas. First, the expansion of human needs: the increasingly cosmopolitan world market at once shapes and expands everybody's desires. Marx doesn't elaborate on this in detail; but he wants us to imagine what it might mean in food, clothes, religion, music, love and in our most intimate fantasies as well as our public presentations. Next, the idea of culture as "common property" in the world market: Anything created by anyone anywhere is open and available to everyone everywhere. Entrepreneurs publish books, produce plays and concerts, display visual art and, in our century, create hardware and software for movies, radio, TV, and computers in order to make money. Nevertheless, in this as in other ways, history slips through the owners' fingers, so that poor people get to possess culture—an idea, a poetic image, a musical sound, Plato, Shakespeare, a Negro spiritual (Marx loved them)—even if they can't own it. Culture stuffs people's heads full of ideas. As a form of "common property," modern culture helps us to imagine how people all around the world could share all the world's resources someday.

It's a vision of culture rarely discussed, but it is one of the most expansive and hopeful things Marx ever wrote. In our century, the development of movies, television and video, and computers has created a global visual language that brings the idea of world culture closer to home than ever, and the world beat comes through in the best of our music and books. That's the good news. The bad news is how sour and bitter most left writing on culture has become. Sometimes it sounds as if culture were just one more Department of Exploitation and Oppression, containing nothing luminous or valuable in itself. At other times, it sounds as if people's minds were empty vessels with nothing inside except what Capital put there. Read, or try to read, a few articles on "hegemonic/counterhegemonic discourse." The way these guys write, it's as if the world has passed them by.

But if capitalism is a triumph in so many ways, exactly what's wrong with it? What's worth spending your life in opposition? In the twentieth century, Marxist movements around the world have concentrated on the argument, made most elaborately in Capital, that workers in bourgeois society had been or were being pauperized. Now, there were times and places where it was absurd to deny that claim; in other times and places (like the United States and Western Europe in the fifties and sixties, when I was young), it was pretty tenuous, and Marxist economists went through strange dialectical twists to make the numbers come out. But the problem with that discussion was that it converted questions of human experience into questions of numbers: It led Marxism to think and talk exactly like capitalism! The *Manifesto* occasionally makes some version of this claim. But it offers what strikes me as a much more trenchant indictment, one that holds up even at the top of the business cycle, when the bourgeoisie and its apologists are drowning in complacency.

That indictment is Marx's vision of what modern bourgeois society forces people to be: They have to freeze their feelings for each other to adapt to a coldblooded world. In the course of "pitilessly tear[ing] asunder the motley feudal ties," bourgeois society "has left remaining no other nexus between man and man than naked self-interest, than callous 'cash payment.' " It has "drowned" every form of sentimental value "in the icy water of egotistical calculation." It has "resolved personal worth into exchange-value." It has collapsed every historical tradition and norm of freedom "into that single, unconscionable freedom-free trade." The worst thing about capitalism is that it forces people to become brutal in order to survive.

For 150 years, we have seen a huge literature that dramatizes the brutalization of the bourgeoisie, a class in which those who are most comfortable with brutality are most likely to succeed. But the same social forces are pressing on the members of that immense group that Marx calls "the modern working class." This class has been afflicted with a case of mistaken identity. Many readers have always thought that "working class" meant only factory workers, or industrial workers, or manual workers, or blue-collar workers, or impoverished workers. These readers then note the changing nature of the work force over the past half-century or so increasingly white collar, educated, working in human services, in or near the middle class—and they infer the Death of the Subject, and conclude that all hopes for the working class are doomed. Marx did not think the working class was shrinking: In all industrial countries it already was, or was in the process of becoming, "the immense majority"; its swelling numbers would enable it to "win the battle of democracy." The basis for his political arithmetic was a concept that was both simple and highly inclusive:

> The modern working class, developed . . . a class of labourers, who live only so long as they find work, and who find work

only so long as their labour increases capital. These labourers, who must sell themselves piecemeal, are a commodity, like every other article of commerce, and are consequently exposed to all the vicissitudes of competition, to all the fluctuations of the market.

The crucial factor is not working in a factory, or working with your hands, or being poor. All these things can change with fluctuating supply and demand and technology and politics. The crucial reality is the need to sell your labor to capital in order to live, the need to carve up your personality for sale—to look at yourself in the mirror and think, "What have I got that I can sell?"—and an unending dread and anxiety that even if you're O.K. today, you won't find anyone who wants to buy what you have or what you are tomorrow, that the changing market will declare you (as it has already declared so many) worthless, that you will find yourself physically as well as metaphysically homeless and out in the cold. Arthur Miller's *Death of a Salesman*, a twentieth-century masterpiece, brings to life the consuming dread that may be the condition of most members of the working class in modern times. The whole existentialist tradition dramatizes this situation with great depth and beauty, yet its visions tend to be weirdly unembodied. Its visionaries could learn from the *Manifesto*, which gives modern anguish an address.

A great many people are in the working class but don't know it. Many are the people who fill up the huge office buildings that choke all our downtowns. They wear elegant suits and return to nice houses, because there is a great demand for their labor right now, and they are doing well. They may identify happily with the owners, and have no idea how contingent and fleeting their benefits are. They may not discover who they really are, and where they belong, until they are laid off or fired—or deskilled, outsourced, downsized. (It is fascinating how many of these crushing words are quite new.) And other workers, lacking diplomas, not dressed so nicely, working in cubicles, not offices, may not get the fact that many of the people who boss them around are really in their class. But this is what organizing and organizers are for.

One group whose working-class identity was crucial for Marx was the group to which he himself belonged: intellectuals.

The bourgeoisie has stripped of its halo every occupation hitherto honoured and looked up to in reverent awe. It has transconverted the physician, the lawyer, the priest, the poet, the man of science, into its paid wage labourers.

Marx is not saying that in bourgeois society these activities lose their human meaning or value. If anything, they are more meaningful and valuable than ever before. But the only way people can get the freedom to make discoveries, or save lives, or poetically light up the world, is by working for capital—for drug companies, movie studios, boards of education, politicians, H.M.O.s, etc., etc.—and using their creative skills to help capital accumulate more capital. This means that intellectuals are subject not only to the stresses that afflict all modern workers but to a dread zone all their own. The more they care about their work and want it to mean something, the more they will find themselves in conflict with the keepers of the spreadsheets; the more they walk the line, the more they are likely to fall. This chronic pressure may give them a special insight into the need for workers to unite. But will united workers treat intellectual and artistic freedom with any more respect than capital treats it? It's an open question; sometime in the twenty-first century the workers will get power somewhere, and then we'll start to see. Marx sees the modern working class as an immense worldwide community waiting to happen. Such large possibilities give the story of organizing a permanent gravity and grandeur. The process of creating unions is not just an item in interest-group politics but a vital part of what Lessing called "the education of the human race." And it is not just educational but existential: the process of people individually and collectively discovering who they are. As they learn who they are, they will come to see that they need one another in order to be themselves. They will see, because workers are smart: Bourgeois society has forced them to be, in order to survive its constant upheavals. Marx knows they will get it by and by. (Alongside his fury as an agitator, the *Manifesto*'s author also projects a brooding, reflective, long patience.) Solidarity is not sacrifice of yourself but the self's fulfillment. Learning to give yourself to other workers, who may look and sound very different from you but are like you in depth, gives a man or woman a place in the world and delivers the self from dread.

This is a vital part of the moral vision that underlies the *Manifesto*. But there is another moral dimension, asserted in a different key but humanly just as urgent. At one of the book's many climactic moments, Marx says that the Revolution will end classes and class struggles, and this will make it possible to enjoy "an association, in which the free development of each is the condition for the free development of all." Here Marx imagines communism as a way to make people happy. The first aspect of this happiness is "development"—that is, an experience that doesn't simply repeat itself but that goes through some sort of change and growth. This model of happiness is modern, and informed by the incessantly developing bourgeois economy.

But bourgeois society, although it enables people to develop, forces them to develop in accord with market demands: What can sell gets developed; what can't sell gets repressed, or never comes to life at all. Against the market model of forced and twisted development, Marx fights for "free development," development that the self can control.

In a time when crass cruelty calls itself liberalism (we're kicking you and your kids off welfare for your own good), it is important to see how much ground Marx shares with the best liberal of all, his contemporary John Stuart Mill. Like Marx, Mill came to see the self's "free development" as a fundamental human value; like Marx, he believed that modernization made it possible for everybody. But as he grew older, he became convinced that the capitalist form of modernization—featuring cutthroat competition, class domination, social conformity and cruelty— blocked its best potentialities. He proclaimed himself a socialist in his old age.

Ironically, the ground that socialism and liberalism share might be a big problem for both of them. What if Mister Kurtz isn't dead after all? In other words, what if authentically "free development" brings out horrific depths in human nature? Dostoyevsky, Nietzsche and Freud all forced us to face the horrors, and warned us of their permanence. In response, both Marx and Mill might say that until we have overcome social domination and degradation, there is simply no way to tell whether the horrors are inherent in human nature or whether we could create benign conditions under which they would wither away. The process of getting to that point—a point where Raskolnikovs won't rot on Avenue D, and where Svidrigailovs won't possess thousands of bodies and souls—should be enough to give us all steady work.

The nineties began with the mass destruction of Marx effigies. It was the "postmodern" age: We weren't supposed to need big ideas. As the nineties end, we find ourselves in a dynamic global society ever more unified by downsizing, de-skilling and dread—just like the old man said. All of a sudden, the iconic looks more convincing than the ironic; that classic bearded presence, the atheist as biblical prophet, is back just in time for the millennium. At the dawn of the twentieth century, there were workers who were ready to die with the *Communist Manifesto*. At the dawn of the twenty-first, there may be even more who are ready to live with it.

★ PLUCKING WORKERS ★

Christopher D. Cook

FROM *THE PROGRESSIVE,* AUGUST 1998
Government and business officials in Missouri have developed an efficient way to slash the welfare rolls: order recipients to gut chickens or pigs for Tyson Foods, ConAgra, or Premium Standard Farms, or else lose their benefits. Under an initiative called Direct Job Placement, the companies have hired hundreds of former welfare recipients. But turnover has been high, and many—balking at the prospect of gutting fifty chickens per minute—have disappeared or been dropped from the welfare rolls by the state.

As one woman on welfare discovered, even having a newborn baby and no means of transportation is no excuse. When the thirty-year-old mother, whose name was withheld for confidentiality, informed her case managers of these extenuating circumstances, they were not sympathetic.

"They told her she had to work at Tyson's even if she had to walk to get there [a six-mile trek]," says Helen Chewning, a former family advocate with the Missouri Valley Human Resource Center in Sedalia. "They sanctioned her while she was pregnant" and then ordered her to work at Tyson when her baby was just eleven days old, Chewning recalls. "She hasn't had any income for six months. How are they supposed to live?"

The single mother is one of more than 110,000 Missourians who have left welfare since January 1993, a stunning 43 percent decline in caseload. Under Direct Job Placement, since May 1995, the state has placed more than 5,400 people in jobs, if temporarily.

But in Missouri and nationwide, these plummeting caseloads are deceptive. According to the *Washington Post*, nearly 40 percent of those who left welfare during a three-month period last year were cut off for breaking the rules—not because they landed jobs.

In the cold calculus of welfare reform, a closed case means success, regardless of what happens to the recipient. As President Clinton celebrates the nation's lowest welfare count since 1969, evidence is piling up across the country that thousands are being coerced into hazardous, short-term jobs or simply kicked off welfare.

Missouri has cut caseloads with such zeal that Clinton used the state as a backdrop last August to announce that 1.4 million people have left welfare since 1996. "We now know that welfare reform works," he proclaimed in a speech to business executives in St. Louis. Clinton touted Missouri's Direct Job Placement approach as a national model. "Thirty-five other states have allowed Missouri to show them that this is a good reform, and they are also doing it," he said.

But state records tell a different story. Missouri is on a sanctioning binge of astounding proportions, pushing thousands off welfare without getting them into jobs. "Since January 1993, the monthly number of welfare recipients who have had their TANF [Temporary Assistance for Needy Families] grant reduced for not looking for work or accepting a job has increased from twenty-seven to 7,345—saving taxpayers over $3 million," according to the state Department of Social Services. The records show soaring numbers of people are being sanctioned by the state: They've been cut off welfare for refusing a job or missing an interview. The caseload has plummeted from 5,228 per month in 1993 to just 265 this May, but much of the caseload decline is simply due to sanctions.

One impetus behind the sanctions, critics assert and state officials acknowledge, is the threat of working in poultry plants or in hog slaughterhouses, where assembly-line jobs involve processing animal parts at a feverish pace in a dirty and dangerous environment.

"It's the same as slavery," says Jerry Helmick, business agent for the United Food and Commercial Workers in Kansas City. "The government sends you there for an interview. If you can stand up and walk, Tyson is going to offer you a job, and you either take it or you're out of the system altogether."

Tyson and other meat-processing companies with high rates of injury and constant employee turnover are corralling the new captive labor force created by welfare reform. In a welfare-to-work program begun by the state in 1995, Missouri welfare agencies send recipients directly to labor-starved, low-wage employers. State documents describe the Direct Job Placement program as "a cooperative effort between local employers and the Division of Family Services," in which "employers experiencing labor-market shortages fill vacancies with recipients."

It's the ultimate public-private partnership, supplying business with a steady reserve of cheap labor while enabling social-service agencies to meet intense caseload-reduction targets set by federal and state officials.

The program includes several Tyson plants, ConAgra chicken processors, Premium Standard's hog-raising and processing plants, and numerous temp agencies and nursing homes. In rural areas with tight labor markets, large companies have near-monopoly control over job placement—and they have transformed county welfare offices into their own private hiring halls.

In the north-central Missouri town of Milan near the Iowa border, a Premium Standard pork-processing plant and a ConAgra chicken-processing factory are the main beneficiaries of the new welfare-to-work regime.

"We have been lucky in Milan because Premium Standard Farms opened up here," says Karen Fay, the Division of Family Services caseload manager for the area. "If we have a person that applies for food stamps who is eligible to work, we send them to Premium Standard Farms. Their job is to cut apart whatever part they get. At Premium

Standard Farms, the pigs are fastened on a belt, and they cut the same part of each pig."

Fay recognizes that people in the welfare-to-work program have few other options. "All we have is PSF [Premium Standard Farms] and ConAgra," she says.

Lisa Garison, human-resources director for Premium Standard's plant in Milan, says the welfare pool has aided the company's expansion. "We continue to try to grow, and any resource that is here in this area, our goal is to tap it." The welfare supply, she says, "has been a key in helping us staff. . . . We hire as many of them as we can. They [case managers at the Division of Family Services] give us as many as they can."

Garison says recipients' work experiences have been mixed: "Some people we've had wonderful success with, and then others find it's a real challenge to enter the work world at the pace that we work at."

Roger Allison, executive director of the Missouri Rural Crisis Center, says Premium Standard's vast hog-raising houses spew noxious methane and hydrogen sulfite gases that reek from fifteen miles away. "These are people who are captive in a workplace that is abusive and environmentally unhealthy," he says. But since the pig farms are classified as agricultural operations, they are not subject to inspections or regulation by the Occupational Safety and Health Administration. (Premium Standard's processing plants do fall under OSHA jurisdiction.)

Garison rejects the charge that it's captive labor. "I don't see those folks as only having one way out of that situation," she says. "There should be plenty of opportunity for people to find the kind of work they want to do; they may have to do something they don't like for awhile."

People who accept a Tyson job are in for a rude awakening. "The first job they get is the puller job—pulling the internal organs out," says Tim Barchak, Missouri political director for the Service Employees International Union. "A lot of these workers will lose their fingernails in two or three weeks from the bacteria and chicken fat." Nearly one-third of Missouri's 103,000 poultry workers suffered an injury or illness in 1995, according to the Bureau of Labor Statistics.

Former Tyson worker Jason Wolfe, twenty-three, toiled for a year and a half on the "thighing line," hanging dead birds on metal shackles for $6.75 an hour. "They want you to hang forty or fifty of these birds in a minute for four to six hours straight, without a break," he says. "If you miss any, they threaten to fire you." The work is so stressful, Wolfe says, that at times, "I'd wake up in the middle of the night and catch my arms rehanging chickens."

Adding insult to injury, Tyson fires people who have too many "occurrences," the company's term for sick days. According to Wolfe, Tyson terminates workers who miss more than five days in a year for any reason. "I was fired because of an occurrence problem because I had to go to the doctor a couple of times," Wolfe says.

"Tyson is very bad about firing people if they are sick or their children are sick," says Chewning. "It's happening all the time. I have people coming in who can't pay their rent because of that. If you have a sick child, you have to take them to the doctor. If you don't, social services will come after you for neglect."

Ed Nicholson, a top spokesman at Tyson headquarters in Springdale, Arkansas, confirms this policy. "If there are six occurrences, a person can be terminated," he says. "If a person is out for three days with an ailment and they have a doctor's note, that would be one occurrence." But each time an employee misses work due to a new ailment, according to Nicholson, it counts as another occurrence.

The grueling and hazardous work means an annual turnover rate of roughly 75 percent according to Greg Denier of the United Food and Commercial Workers in Washington, D.C. Many stay on the job for just a few months before succumbing to injury or sheer exhaustion. The harsh conditions and high turnover create a constant need for new workers. And as unemployment rates dipped well below 5 percent across the Midwest in the mid-1990s, the industry saw its supply of available workers begin to dry up.

Rather than improve conditions to attract employees, the pig and poultry industries have resorted to importing workers from Mexico and housing them in temporary mobile-home facilities. At Premium Standard, "they're actually having to ship Mexicans into and out of housing to fill these jobs, because they can't get enough people to work there," says Brenda Proctor, a consumer economist with the University of Missouri.

According to numerous union officials and former Tyson worker Jason Wolfe, Tyson advertises for Mexican workers to come to its Midwestern plants and even transports them to Missouri. "Sometimes [Tyson's recruiters] get a freezer truck and load them up and take them up here," says Wolfe, who talked with Mexican workers at the plant.

Ed Nicholson denies that the firm recruits or imports Mexican workers. "We have not transported anyone across the border," he says. Instead, Tyson offers bonuses for employees who bring in new workers, he says. "Some of that literature got passed along to people down there [in Mexico], and it gave the impression that we were advertising down there. The word gets out that jobs are available and people show up from Mexico, Texas, or Guatemala."

If low-wage, immigrant workers are good for Tyson and other companies, the idea of a captive labor force provided directly by the state is even more appealing. In 1995, as welfare reform swept the nation, Tyson lobbied to gain easy access to the abundance of cheap workers thrust onto the labor market.

The Direct Job Placement program "was born out of Tyson's need for additional workers," says Linda Messenger, welfare director for Pettis County, where the program began.

When Tyson opened shop six miles west of Sedalia, "It couldn't find enough folks to fill these jobs because the work is messy, and there's lots of carpal tunnel," says Proctor. The company, lured there by Sedalia's powerful state senator, James Mathewson, spent six months advertising in area newspapers and job centers, with little success. "Tyson had trouble with the labor supply and was getting upset."

So Tyson "began doing some informal visiting with Senator Mathewson about their need for more workers," recalls Messenger. According to Proctor, "Mathewson sponsored a bill after this erupted and got

D.F.S. [the Division of Family Services] to try a pilot where, if somebody applied for benefits, they were sent directly to Tyson. If they declined, they were refused benefits for sixty days."

Tyson personnel manager Jennifer Cave says Senator Mathewson was "the driving force" helping the company link up with the welfare department, but she doesn't recall who initiated the discussions.

The program is tailor-made for Tyson. "They have pretty much a constant need for employees because there's a high turnover there. So our offices keep in touch with their employment needs," says Deb Hendricks, information officer for the Missouri Division of Family Services.

Before the Direct Job Placement program, adds welfare director Messenger, "we had clients who were job-ready, who for one reason or another had not responded to Tyson's job advertisements on their own. They have a reputation. It's hard work, sometimes cold and dirty. It's not a glamorous job, and some people were turned off by that."

But once the program was in place, the agency—and Tyson—had leverage. Members of Messenger's staff visited the Tyson plant and "were able to get [clients] to the point of agreeing to an interview," she says. "We would set them up with an appointment, and if they failed to keep the interview we sanctioned them, and that meant they lost their food stamps. Actually, some of them did choose to lose their benefits instead of going to Tyson's."

In fact, the program has driven far more people off welfare than into jobs. Of the 195 recipients sent to one Tyson plant in Pettis County this year for mandatory interviews, just twenty-two accepted entry-level, assembly-line jobs paying $6.70 an hour. Meanwhile, thirty-nine were sanctioned. Local welfare administrators concede they have no idea what happened to the other 134 recipients, who have disappeared from the county rolls.

While the state regards these disappearances as success stories, officials acknowledge that it's a case of out of sight, out of mind. "If they just generally leave welfare, we don't know what they are doing," says Division of Family Services spokeswoman Christine Grobe. Caseload manager Karen Fay acknowledges that she doesn't have data on how many recipients are still working at the jobs where the state placed them. "We have not had to collect those, so we don't have them," she says.

Federal law doesn't require states to ensure that the people who are cut off welfare get jobs, says Mark Greenberg of the Center for Law and Social Policy in Washington, D.C. Instead, the government offers "case-load-reduction credits" to states that trim their rolls sufficiently. It's possible, says Greenberg, for a state to "fully satisfy federal participation rates without getting anybody a single job."

Job retention is virtually nonexistent. Since 1995, the Tyson plant in Pettis County has hired seventy-five people from the welfare offices in Sedalia and neighboring Johnson and Henry counties, according to plant personnel manager Jennifer Cave. But, she says, just "five or less" are still working at the plant, which employs a total of 1,360.

"The processing industry just has high turnover," Cave says breezily. "It's repetitive-motion, unskilled labor."

Union officials say that's precisely the problem. "These are not jobs that give people a career," says Barchak of the Service Employees union. "Jobs in poultry-processing plants are temporary because people burn out quickly. Nobody who burns out in six months is taking with them any skill they can apply to the rest of the American work force."

Crystal Wolfe, Jason's brother, a nineteen-year-old former Tyson lineworker with two children, puts it more bluntly: "If you're just coming off welfare and you haven't worked in awhile, that place will make you never want to work again."

★ THE END OF ★ IMAGINATION

Arundhati Roy

From *The Nation*, September 28, 1998

"The desert shook," the Government of India informed us (its people).
"The whole mountain turned white," the Government of
Pakistan replied.

By afternoon the wind had fallen silent over Pokhran. At 3:45 p.m., the timer detonated the three devices. Around 200 to 300 m deep in the earth, the heat generated was equivalent to a million degrees centigrade— as hot as temperatures on the sun. Instantly, rocks weighing around a thousand tons, a mini mountain underground, vaporised . . . shock-waves from the blasts began to lift a mound of earth the size of a foot-ball field by several metres. One scientist on seeing it said, "I can now believe stories of Lord Krishna lifting a hill."—*India Today*

May 1998. It'll go down in history books, provided, of course, we have history books to go down in. Provided, of course, we have a future.

There's nothing new or original left to be said about nuclear weapons. There can be nothing more humiliating for a writer of fiction to have to do than restate a case that has, over the years, already been made by other people in other parts of the world, and made passionately, eloquently and knowledgeably.

I am prepared to grovel. To humiliate myself abjectly, because, in the circumstances, silence would be indefensible. So those of you who are willing: Let's pick our parts, put on these discarded costumes and speak our secondhand lines in this sad secondhand play. But let's not forget that the stakes we're playing for are huge. Our fatigue and our shame could mean the end of us. The end of our children and our children's children. Of everything we love. We have to reach within ourselves and find the strength to think. To fight.

Once again we are pitifully behind the times—not just scientifically and technologically (ignore the hollow claims), but more pertinently in our ability to grasp the true nature of nuclear weapons. Our Comprehension of the Horror Department is hopelessly obsolete. Here we are, all of us in India and in Pakistan, discussing the finer points of politics, and foreign policy, behaving for all the world as though our governments have just devised a newer, bigger bomb, a sort of immense hand grenade with which they will annihilate the enemy (each other) and protect us from all harm. How desperately we want to believe that. What wonderful, willing, well-behaved, gullible subjects we have turned out to be. The rest of humanity may not forgive us, but then the rest of the rest of humanity, depending on who fashions its views, may not know what a tired, dejected, heartbroken people we are. Perhaps it doesn't realize how urgently we need a miracle. How deeply we yearn for magic.

If only, if only, nuclear war was just another kind of war. If only it were about the usual things—nations and territories, gods and histories. If only those of us who dread it are just worthless moral cowards who are not prepared to die in defense of our beliefs. If only nuclear war was the kind of war in which countries battle countries and men battle men. But it isn't. If there is a nuclear war, our foe will not be China or America or even each other. Our foe will be the earth herself. The very elements— the sky, the air, the land, the wind and water—will all turn against us.

Our cities and forests, our fields and villages, will burn for days. Rivers will turn to poison. The air will become fire. The wind will spread the flames. When everything there is to burn has burned and the fires die, smoke will rise and shut out the sun. The earth will be enveloped in darkness. There will be no day. Only interminable night. What shall we do then, those of us who are still alive? Burned and blind and bald and ill, carrying the cancerous carcasses of our children in our arms, where shall we go? What shall we eat? What shall we drink? What shall we breathe?

The head of the Health, Environment and Safety Group of the Bhabha Atomic Research Centre in Bombay has a plan. He declared that India could survive nuclear war. His advice is that if there is a nuclear war, we take the same safety measures as the ones that scientists have recommended in the event of accidents at nuclear plants.

Take iodine pills, he suggests. And other steps such as remaining indoors, consuming only stored water and food and avoiding milk. Infants should be given powdered milk. "People in the danger zone should immediately go to the ground floor and if possible to the basement."

What do you do with these levels of lunacy? What do you do if you're trapped in an asylum and the doctors are all dangerously deranged?

Ignore it, it's just a novelist's naivete, they'll tell you, Doomsday Prophet hyperbole. It'll never come to that. There will be no war. Nuclear weapons are about peace, not war. "Deterrence" is the buzzword of the people who like to think of themselves as hawks. (Nice birds, those. Cool. Stylish. Predatory. Pity there won't be many of them around after the war. Extinction is a word we must try to get used to.) Deterrence is an old thesis that has been resurrected and is being recycled with added local flavor. The Theory of Deterrence cornered the credit for having prevented the cold war from turning into a Third World War. The only immutable fact about the Third World War is that if there's going to be one, it will be fought after the Second World War. In other words, there's no fixed schedule. In other words, we still have time. No, the Theory of Deterrence has some fundamental flaws.

Flaw Number One is that it presumes a complete, sophisticated understanding of the psychology of your enemy. It assumes that what deters you (the fear of annihilation) will deter them. What about those who are not deterred by that? The suicide bomber psyche—the "We'll take you with us" school—is that an outlandish thought? How did Rajiv Gandhi die?

In any case, who's the "you" and who's the "enemy"? Both are only governments. Governments change. They wear masks within masks. They molt and reinvent themselves all the time. The one we have at the moment, for instance, does not even have enough seats to last a full term in office, but demands that we trust it to do pirouettes and party tricks with nuclear bombs even as it scrabbles around for a foothold to maintain a simple majority in Parliament.

Flaw Number Two is that Deterrence is premised on fear. But fear is premised on knowledge. On an understanding of the true extent and scale of the devastation that nuclear war will wreak. It is not some inherent, mystical attribute of nuclear bombs that they automatically inspire thoughts of peace. On the contrary, it is the endless, tireless, confrontational work of people who have had the courage to openly denounce them, the marches, the demonstrations, the films, the outrage—that is what has averted, or perhaps only postponed, nuclear war. Deterrence will not and cannot work given the levels of ignorance and illiteracy that hang over our two countries like dense, impenetrable veils.

India and Pakistan have nuclear bombs now and feel entirely justified in having them. Soon others will too. Israel, Iran, Iraq, Saudi Arabia, Norway, Nepal (I'm trying to be eclectic here), Denmark, Germany, Bhutan, Mexico, Lebanon, Sri Lanka, Burma, Bosnia, Singapore, North Korea, Sweden, South Korea, Vietnam, Cuba, Afghanistan, Uzbekistan— and why not? Every country in the world has a special case to make. Everybody has borders and beliefs. And when all our larders are bursting with shiny bombs and our bellies are empty (Deterrence is an exorbitant beast), we can trade bombs for food. And when nuclear technology goes on the market, when it gets truly competitive and prices fall, not just governments but anybody who can afford it can have their own private arsenal—businessmen, terrorists, perhaps even the occasional rich writer (like myself). Our planet will bristle with beautiful missiles. There will be a new world order. The dictatorship of the pro-nuke elite. But let us pause to give credit where it's due. Whom must we thank for all this?

The Men who made it happen. The Masters of the Universe. Ladies and gentlemen, the United States of America! Come on up here, folks, stand up and take a bow. Thank you for doing this to the world. Thank you for making a difference. Thank you for showing us the way. Thank you for altering the very meaning of life.

From now on it is not dying we must fear, but living.

It is such supreme folly to believe that nuclear weapons are deadly only if they're used. The fact that they exist at all, their very presence in our lives, will wreak more havoc than we can begin to fathom. Nuclear weapons pervade our thinking. They are the ultimate colonizer. Whiter than any white man that ever lived. The very heart of whiteness.

All I can say to every man, woman and sentient child here in India, and over there, just a little way away in Pakistan, is: Take it personally. Whoever you are—Hindu, Muslim, urban, agrarian—it doesn't matter. The only good thing about nuclear war is that it is the single most egalitarian idea that man has ever had. On the day of reckoning, you will not be asked to present your credentials. The devastation will be indiscriminate. The bomb isn't in your backyard. It's in your body. And mine. Nobody, no nation, no government, no man, no god, has the right to put it there. We're radioactive already, and the war hasn't even begun. So stand up and say something. Never mind if it's been said before. Speak up on your own behalf. Take it very personally.

THE BOMB AND ME

In early May (before the bomb), I left home for three weeks. I thought I would return. I had every intention of returning. Of course, things haven't worked out quite the way I had planned. While I was away, I met a friend of mine whom I have always loved for, among other things, her ability to combine deep affection with a frankness that borders on savagery.

"I've been thinking about you," she said, "about The God of Small Things—what's in it, what's over it, under it, around it, above it."

She fell silent for a while. I was uneasy and not at all sure that I wanted to hear the rest of what she had to say. She, however, was sure that she was going to say it. "In this last year—less than a year actually— you've had too much of everything—fame, money, prizes, adulation, criticism, condemnation, ridicule, love, hate, anger, envy, generosity—everything. In some ways it's a perfect story. Perfectly baroque in its excess. The trouble is that it has, or can have, only one perfect ending." Her eyes were on me, bright with a slanting, probing brilliance. She knew that I knew what she was going to say. She was insane.

She was going to say that nothing that happened to me in the future could ever match the buzz of this. That the whole of the rest of my life was going to be vaguely unsatisfying. And, therefore, the only perfect ending to the story would be death. My death.

The thought had occurred to me too. Of course it had. The fact that all this, this global dazzle—these lights in my eyes, the applause, the flowers, the photographers, the journalists feigning a deep interest in my life (yet struggling to get a single fact straight), the men in suits fawning over me, the shiny hotel bathrooms with endless towels—none of it was likely to happen again. Would I miss it? Had I grown to need it? Was I a fame junkie? Would I have withdrawal symptoms?

The more I thought about it, the clearer it became to me that if fame was going to be my permanent condition it would kill me. Club me to death with its good manners and hygiene. I'll admit that I've enjoyed my own five minutes of it immensely, but primarily because it was just five minutes. Because I knew (or thought I knew) that I could go home when I was bored and giggle about it. Grow old and irresponsible. Eat mangoes in the moonlight. Maybe write a couple of failed books—worstsellers—to see what it felt like. For a whole year I've cartwheeled across the world, anchored always to thoughts of home and the life I would go back to. Contrary to all the inquiries and predictions about my impending emigration, that was the well I dipped into. That was my sustenance. My strength.

I told my friend there was no such thing as a perfect story. I said in any case hers was an external view of things, this assumption that the trajectory of a person's happiness, or let's say fulfillment, had peaked (and now must trough) because she had accidentally stumbled upon "success." It was premised on the unimaginative belief that wealth and fame were the mandatory stuff of everybody's dreams.

You've lived too long in New York, I told her. There are other worlds. Other kinds of dreams. Dreams in which failure is feasible. Honorable. Sometimes even worth striving for. Worlds in which recognition is not the only barometer of brilliance or human worth. There are plenty of warriors that I know and love, people far more valuable than myself, who go to war each day, knowing in advance that they will fail. True, they are less "successful" in the most vulgar sense of the word, but by no means less fulfilled.

The only dream worth having, I told her, is to dream that you will live while you're alive and die only when you're dead. (Prescience? Perhaps.)

"Which means exactly what?" (Arched eyebrows, a little annoyed.)

I tried to explain, but didn't do a very good job of it. Sometimes I need to write to think. So I wrote it down for her on a paper napkin. This is what I wrote: To love. To be loved. To never forget your own insignificance. To never get used to the unspeakable violence and the vulgar disparity of life around you. To seek joy in the saddest places. To pursue beauty to its lair. To never simplify what is complicated or complicate what is simple. To respect strength, never power. Above all, to watch. To try to understand. To never look away. And never, never to forget.

I've known her for many years, this friend of mine. She too is an architect.

She looked dubious, somewhat unconvinced by my paper napkin speech. I could tell that structurally, just in terms of the sleek, narrative symmetry of things, and because she loves me, her thrill at my "success" was so keen, so generous, that it weighed in evenly with her (anticipated) horror at the idea of my death. I understood that it was nothing personal. Just a design thing.

Anyhow, two weeks after that conversation, I returned to India. To what I think/thought of as home. Something had died but it wasn't me. It was infinitely more precious. It was a world that has been ailing for awhile, and has finally breathed its last. It's been cremated now. The air is thick with ugliness and there's the unmistakable stench of fascism on the breeze.

Day after day, in newspaper editorials, on the radio, on TV chat shows, on MTV for heaven's sake, people whose instincts one thought one could trust—writers, painters, journalists—make the crossing. The chill seeps into my bones as it becomes painfully apparent from the lessons of everyday life that what you read in history books is true. That fascism is indeed as much about people as about governments. That it begins at home. In drawing rooms. In bedrooms. In beds.

"Explosion of Self-Esteem," "Road to Resurgence," "A Moment of Pride"—these were headlines in the papers in the days following the nuclear tests. "We have proved that we are not eunuchs anymore," said Mr. Thackeray of the Shiv Sena. (Whoever said we were? True, a good number of us are women, but that, as far as I know, isn't the same thing.) Reading the papers, it was often hard to tell when people were referring to Viagra (which was competing for second place on the front pages) and when they were talking about the bomb—"We have superior strength and potency." (This was our Defense Minister after Pakistan completed its tests.) "These are not just nuclear tests, they are nationalism tests," we were repeatedly told.

This has been hammered home, over and over again. The bomb is India. India is the bomb. Not just India, Hindu India. Therefore, be warned, any criticism of it is not just antinational, but anti-Hindu. (Of course, in Pakistan the bomb is Islamic. Other than that, politically, the same physics applies.) This is one of the unexpected perks of having a nuclear bomb. Not only can the government use it to threaten the Enemy, they can use it to declare war on their own people. Us.

When I told my friends that I was writing this piece, they cautioned me. "Go ahead," they said, "but first make sure you're not vulnerable. Make sure your papers are in order. Make sure your taxes are paid."

My papers are in order. My taxes are paid. But how can one not be vulnerable in a climate like this? Everyone is vulnerable. Accidents happen. There's safety only in acquiescence. As I write, I am filled with foreboding. In this country, I have truly known what it means for a writer to feel loved (and, to some degree, hated too). Last year I was one of the items being paraded in the media's end-of-the-year National Pride Parade. Among the others, much to my mortification, were a bomb-maker and an international beauty queen. Each time a beaming person stopped me on the street and said, "You have made India proud" (referring to the Booker Prize I won, not the book I wrote), I felt a little uneasy. It frightened me then and it terrifies me now, because I know how easily that swell, that tide of emotion, can turn against me. Perhaps the time for that has come. I'm going to step out from under the fairy lights and say what's on my mind.

It's this: If protesting against having a nuclear bomb implanted in my brain is anti-Hindu and antinational, then I secede. I hereby declare myself an independent, mobile republic. I am a citizen of the earth. I own no territory. I have no flag. I'm female, but have nothing against eunuchs. My policies are simple. I'm willing to sign any nuclear nonproliferation treaty or nuclear test ban treaty that's going. Immigrants are welcome. You can help me design our flag.

My world has died. And I write to mourn its passing. Admittedly it was a flawed world. An unviable world. A scarred and wounded world. It was a world that I myself have criticized unsparingly, but only because I loved it. It didn't deserve to die. It didn't deserve to be dismembered. Forgive me, I realize that sentimentality is uncool—but what shall I do with my desolation?

I loved it simply because it offered humanity a choice. It was a rock out at sea. It was a stubborn chink of light that insisted that there was a different way of living. It was a functioning possibility. A real option. All that's gone now. India's nuclear tests, the manner in which they were conducted, the euphoria with which they have been greeted (by us), is indefensible. To me, it signifies dreadful things. The end of imagination. The end of freedom actually, because, after all, that's what freedom is. Choice. On August 15 last year we celebrated the fiftieth anniversary of India's independence. Next May we can mark our first anniversary in nuclear bondage.

Why did they do it?

Political expediency is the obvious, cynical answer, except that it only raises another, more basic question: Why should it have been politically expedient?

The three Official Reasons given are: China, Pakistan, and Exposing Western Hypocrisy.

Taken at face value, and examined individually, they're somewhat baffling. I'm not for a moment suggesting that these are not real issues. Merely that they aren't new. The only new thing on the old horizon is the Indian government. In his appallingly cavalier letter to the U.S. President (why bother to write at all if you're going to write like this?) our Prime Minister says India's decision to go ahead with nuclear tests was due to a "deteriorating security environment." He goes on to mention the 1962 war with China and that "we have suffered three aggressions in the last fifty years [by Pakistan]. And for the last ten years we have been the victim of unremitting terrorism and militancy sponsored by it . . . especially Punjab and Jammu and Kashmir."

The war with China is thirty-six years old. Unless there's some vital state secret that we don't know about, it certainly seemed as though matters had improved slightly between us. The most recent war with Pakistan was fought twenty-seven years ago. Admittedly, Kashmir continues to be a deeply troubled region, and no doubt Pakistan is gleefully fanning the flames. But surely there must be flames to fan in the first place? Kashmir, and for that matter, Assam, Tripura, Nagaland—virtually the whole of the Northeast—Jharkhand, Uttarakhand and all the trouble that's still to come—these are symptoms of a deeper malaise. It cannot and will not be solved by pointing nuclear missiles at Pakistan.

Even Pakistan can't be solved by pointing nuclear missiles at it. Though we are separate countries, we share skies, we share winds, we share water. Where radioactive fallout will land on any given day depends on the direction of the wind and rain. Lahore and Amritsar are thirty miles apart. If we bomb Lahore, Punjab will burn. If we bomb Karachi then Gujarat and Rajasthan, perhaps even Bombay, will burn. Any nuclear war with Pakistan will be a war against ourselves.

As for the third Official Reason: Exposing Western Hypocrisy—how much more exposed can it be? What decent human being on earth harbors any illusions about it? These are people whose histories are spongy with the blood of others. Colonialism, apartheid, slavery, ethnic cleansing, germ warfare, chemical weapons—they virtually invented it all. They have plundered nations, snuffed out civilizations, exterminated entire populations. They stand on the world's stage stark naked but entirely unembarrassed, because they know that they have more money, more food, and bigger bombs than anybody else. They know they can wipe us out in the course of an ordinary working day. Personally, I'd say it is more arrogance than hypocrisy.

We have less money, less food, and smaller bombs. However, we have, or had, all kinds of other wealth. Delightful, unquantifiable. What we've done with it is the opposite of what we think we've done. We've pawned it all. We've traded it in. For what? In order to enter into a contract with the very people we claim to despise. In the larger scheme of things, we've agreed to play their game and play it their way.

All in all, I think it is fair to say that we're the hypocrites. We're the ones who've abandoned what was arguably a moral position, i.e.: We have the technology, we can make bombs if we want to, but we won't. We don't believe in them.

We're the ones who have now set up this craven clamoring to be admitted into the club of Superpowers. For India to demand the status of a Superpower is as ridiculous as demanding to play in the World Cup finals simply because we have a ball. Never mind that we haven't qualified, or that we don't play much soccer and haven't got a team.

We are a nation of nearly a billion people. In development terms we rank No. 138 out of the 175 countries listed in the UNDP's Human Development Index. More than 400 million of our people are illiterate and live in absolute poverty, over 600 million lack even basic sanitation and about 200 million have no safe drinking water.

A nuclear bomb isn't going to improve any of this.

We in India are an ancient people learning to live in a recent nation. The nuclear bomb and the demolition of the Babri Masjid in Ayodhya are both part of the same political process. They are the hideous byproducts of a nation's search for herself. Of India's effort to forge a national identity. To define what being Indian means. The poorer the nation, the larger the numbers of illiterate people and the more morally bankrupt her leaders, the cruder and more dangerous the notion of what that identity is or should be.

The jeering, hooting young men who battered down the Babri Masjid are the same ones whose pictures appeared in the papers in the days that followed the nuclear tests. They were on the streets, celebrating India's nuclear bomb and simultaneously "condemning Western Culture" by emptying crates of Coke and Pepsi into public drains. I'm a little baffled by their logic: Coke is Western Culture, but the nuclear bomb is an old Indian tradition?

Yes, I've heard—the bomb is in the Vedas. It might be, but if you look hard enough, you'll find Coke in the Vedas too. That's the great thing about all religious texts. You can find anything you want in them—as long as you know what you're looking for.

But returning to the subject of the non-Vedic 1990s: We storm the heart of whiteness, we embrace the most diabolical creation of Western science and call it our own. But we protest against their music, their food, their clothes, their cinema and their literature. That's not hypocrisy. That's humor.

It's funny enough to make a skull smile.

We're back on the old ship. The SS Authenticity & Indianness.

If there is going to be a pro-authenticity/antinational drive, perhaps the government ought to get its history straight and its facts right. If they're going to do it, they may as well do it properly.

First of all, the original inhabitants of this land were not Hindu. Ancient though it is, there were human beings on earth before there was Hinduism. India's tribal people have a greater claim to being indigenous to this land than anybody else, and how are they treated by the state and its minions? Oppressed, cheated, robbed of their lands, shunted around like surplus goods. Perhaps a good place to start would be to restore to them the dignity that was once theirs. Perhaps the government could make a public undertaking that more dams like the Sardar Sarovar on the Narmada will not be built, that more people will not be displaced.

But, of course, that would be inconceivable, wouldn't it? Why? Because it's impractical. Because tribal people don't really matter. Their histories, their customs, their deities, are dispensable. They must learn to sacrifice these things for the greater good of the nation (which has snatched from them everything they ever had).

OK, so that's out.

For the rest, I could compile a practical list of things to ban and buildings to break. It'll need some research, but off the top of my head, here are a few suggestions.

They could begin by banning a number of ingredients from our cuisine: chilies (Mexico), tomatoes (Peru), potatoes (Bolivia), coffee (Morocco), tea, white sugar, cinnamon (China)—they could then move into recipes. Tea with milk and sugar, for instance (Britain).

Smoking will be out of the question. Tobacco came from North America.

Cricket, English and democracy should be forbidden. Either kabaddi or kho-kho could replace cricket. I don't want to start a riot, so I hesitate to suggest a replacement for English (Italian? It has found its way to us via a kinder route: marriage, not imperialism). We have already discussed (earlier in this essay) the emerging, apparently acceptable alternative to democracy.

All hospitals in which Western medicine is practiced or prescribed should be shut down. All national newspapers discontinued. The railways dismantled. Airports closed. And what about our newest toy—the mobile phone? Can we live without it, or shall I suggest that they make an exception there? They could put it down in the column marked "Universal." (Only essential commodities will be included here. No music, art, or literature.)

Needless to say, sending your children to university in the United States or rushing there yourself to have your prostate operated upon will be a cognizable offense.

It will be a long, long list. It would take years of work. I couldn't use a computer because that wouldn't be very authentic of me, would it?

I don't mean to be facetious, merely to point out that this is surely the shortcut to hell. There's no such thing as an Authentic India or a Real Indian. There is no Divine Committee that has the right to sanction one single, authorized version of what India is or should be. There is no one religion or language or caste or region or person or story or book that can claim to be its sole representative. There are, and can only be, visions of India, various ways of seeing it—honest, dishonest, wonderful, absurd, modern, traditional, male, female. They can be argued over, criticized, praised, scorned, but not banned or broken. Not hunted down.

Railing against the past will not heal us. History has happened. It's over and done with. All we can do is change its course by encouraging what we love instead of destroying what we don't. There is beauty yet in this brutal, damaged world of ours. Hidden, fierce, immense. Beauty that is uniquely ours and beauty that we have received with grace from others, enhanced, reinvented and made our own. We have to seek it out, nurture it, love it. Making bombs will only destroy us. It doesn't matter whether we use them or not. They will destroy us either way.

India's nuclear bomb is the final act of betrayal by a ruling class that has failed its people.

However many garlands we heap on our scientists, however many medals we pin to their chests, the truth is that it's far easier to make a bomb than to educate 400 million people.

According to opinion polls, we're expected to believe that there's a national consensus on the issue. It's official now. Everybody loves the bomb. (Therefore the bomb is good.)

Is it possible for a man who cannot write his own name to understand even the basic, elementary facts about the nature of nuclear weapons? Has anybody told him that nuclear war has nothing at all to do with his received notions of war? Nothing to do with honor, nothing to do with pride? Has anybody bothered to explain to him about thermal blasts, radioactive fallout and the nuclear winter? Are there even words in his language to describe the concepts of enriched uranium, fissile material and critical mass? Or has his language itself become obsolete? Is he trapped in a time capsule, watching the world pass him by, unable to understand or communicate with it because his language never took into account the horrors that the human race would dream up? Does he not matter at all, this man? Shall we just treat him like some kind of a cretin? If he asks any questions, ply him with iodine pills and parables about how Lord Krishna lifted a hill or how the destruction of Lanka by Hanuman was unavoidable in order to preserve Sita's virtue and Ram's reputation? Use his own beautiful stories as weapons against him? Shall we release him from his capsule only during elections, and once he's voted, shake him by the hand, flatter him with some bullshit about the Wisdom of the Common Man and send him right back in?

I'm not talking about one man, of course. I'm talking about millions and millions of people who live in this country. This is their land too, you know. They have the right to make an informed decision about its fate and, as far as I can tell, nobody has informed them about anything. The tragedy is that nobody could, even if he wanted to. Truly, literally, there's no language to do it in. This is the real horror of India. The orbits of the powerful and the powerless spinning further and further apart from each other, never intersecting, sharing nothing. Not a language. Not even a country.

Who the hell conducted those opinion polls? Who the hell is the Prime Minister to decide whose finger will be on the nuclear button that could turn everything we love—our earth, our skies, our mountains, our plains, our rivers, our cities and villages—to ash in an instant? Who the hell is he to reassure us that there will be no accidents? How does he know? Why should we trust him? What has he ever done to make us trust him? What have any of them ever done to make us trust them?

The nuclear bomb is the most antidemocratic, antinational, anti-human, outright evil thing that man has ever made.

If you are religious, then remember that this bomb is Man's challenge to God. It's worded quite simply: We have the power to destroy everything that You have created.

If you're not religious, then look at it this way. This world of ours is four thousand, six hundred million years old.

It could end in an afternoon.

★ THE DEATH OF ★ LIBERAL OUTRAGE

Patrick H. Caddell and Marc Cooper

FROM *THE WALL STREET JOURNAL*, DECEMBER 23, 1998

Democrats in Congress have a point when they accuse President Clinton's critics of politicizing the law. Republicans cross the limits of credibility when they inflate the seriousness of Mr. Clinton's transgressions into the equivalent of Watergate or Iran-contra. But we expect our Republican adversaries to act that way. What discourages us more has been the behavior of our friends, Mr. Clinton's defenders on the left.

We can only hope that when they stood vigil for Mr. Clinton last week on Capitol Hill, led by the Rev. Jesse Jackson, they said a prayer for Rickey Ray Rector. For Rector's story symbolizes how liberals have sheared off their principles in order to squeeze into that little black box that is Mr. Clinton's moral universe.

In early 1992, as then-Governor Clinton struggled to salvage his presidential candidacy in the face of the Gennifer Flowers scandal, convicted murderer Rector sat on Arkansas's death row. When his time came for execution, Mr. Clinton flew home from New Hampshire just in time to deny Rector a stay of execution. Rector, an African-American, had turned his gun on himself after killing a police officer at his mother's house. He blew his brains out, but he survived—condemned to function with the mind of a five-year-old. As he was put on his feet to walk to the death chamber, and with no trace of irony, Rector asked his guards to say hello to Governor Clinton, whom he had just seen on television, and to save Rector his slice of pecan pie, which he planned to eat when he returned.

It mattered not to Governor Clinton that the law prohibited the execution of someone not competent to understand his crime or his punishment. Rector's life was an insignificant price for candidate Clinton to pay to demonstrate his tough "New Democrat" credentials. In the days following the execution, as Mr. Clinton campaigned in the South, he proudly pointed to his willingness to enforce the death penalty.

Where were the liberals? No Hollywood celebrities—no Rob Reiner, no Barbra Streisand—lobbied to spare Rector's life. There were no NYU emergency speak-outs organized by Sean Wilentz and Arthur Schlesinger Jr. on Rector's behalf. No panels of Ivy League law professors with Alan Dershowitz screaming for due process. Rep. Maxine Waters was too wrapped up co-chairing Mr. Clinton's California campaign to invoke her—and Rector's—"slave ancestors" in a cry for justice as she would six years later on the House floor on behalf of her president. The blatantly pro-Clinton reporters who covered the 1992 campaign—Sidney Blumenthal, Eleanor Clift, Strobe Talbott, Joe Klein—barely found time to hiccup over the outrageous execution of Rickey Ray Rector.

A year later when Marshall Frady in the *New Yorker* wrote a chilling deconstruction of Clinton's political decision to execute Rector, one of us asked a number of Clinton supporters if they believed Mr. Clinton would have executed Rector if he had not been campaigning for president. To a person, their answer was a sheepish no. But they had chosen to remain silent. Such complicity, they argued, was for the greater good—the greater good of finally having a Democrat in the White House. Bill Clinton might not exactly be a new FDR but he was, after all, "electable."

In the past six years, liberals have continued their defense of the Clinton presidency, paying a staggering price: unconditional surrender of their ideals.

Where was the Democratic outrage when in the first months of the Clinton administration eighty-three men, women and children were immolated by federal agents at Waco? The same Democrats now bleating about the violation of Mr. Clinton's rights were eerily silent when, as the 1996 re-election campaign was beginning, the president signed the Effective Death Penalty Act—a dastardly law that quashes nearly all legal appeals from death row.

Democrats denounce the violation of the president's right to privacy. But they have nothing to say when his administration proposes to legalize "roving" wiretaps. They are equally mum on the immigration bill signed by Mr. Clinton that virtually abolished due process and this year alone has resulted in more than 30,000 summary deportations, in many cases of long-term legal residents. And when Mr. Clinton signed the 1996 welfare bill, which requires unwed mothers to name their children's fathers on pain of prosecution, it was left to Jesse Jackson to snuff out the moral fires. When liberals pondered their options of protest at the 1996 Democratic Convention, Mr. Jackson loudly barked the stray dissenters back into the fold.

Likewise, in the current Monicagate fiasco, mainstream feminist organizations have shredded two decades of hard-earned gains in sexual harassment law. True, Paula Jones's case was exploited by Clinton haters. But that's no excuse for the White House to attack her as "trailer trash" or for Mr. Clinton, as a defendant in a sexual harassment case, to lie under oath. Since when is it the task of liberal feminists to intentionally confuse this repugnant act of perjury with what they disingenuously call "just lying about sex"?

But the most disturbing consequence of the surrender to Clinton has been the self-strangulation of the Democratic peace constituency. In August Mr. Clinton ordered missile attacks in Afghanistan and Sudan within days of his disastrous speech about Monicagate. When credible news reports surfaced that the plant demolished by U.S. rockets in the Sudan was a benign pharmaceuticals factory, former President Carter courageously called for an investigation. But Democratic officeholders ignored Mr. Carter's call.

The refusal to speak out on the possible Sudan deception led us directly to last week's tragedy of Operation Desert Fox. As the missiles exploded in Iraq, Democrats cheered. House Minority Leader Dick Gephardt and Minority Whip David Bonior—both of whom voted against the 1991 Gulf War and argued for the right to publicly challenge the wisdom of George Bush's decision—this time pontificated shamelessly about threats to national security. The low point came when Rep. Patrick Kennedy (D., R.I.) on the House floor resurrected—nearly word for word—the scurrilous language the LBJ White House used in 1966 when it questioned the patriotism of his uncle, Robert F. Kennedy, who had begun to speak out against the Vietnam War. Rep. Kennedy even suggested that Congress should ask the CIA for permission to go ahead with the impeachment debate.

As last week came to a close, American liberals staged a bizarre televised pageant of moral suicide. On one channel you could view a third wave of a suspiciously timed American air attack rain down on Baghdad, cruise missiles exploding at a million dollars a pop. On another channel, at the same moment, there were the Reverend Mr. Jackson and the cream of liberalism rallying on the Capitol steps, joining hands and intoning "We Shall Overcome"—praying not for the victims of our ordnance, but for the prevaricating president who signed their death warrant.

The Iraqi people pay their own special price for Monicagate. But we all suffer the collateral damage of this crisis. For their partisan zeal, their failure to distinguish between adultery and crimes of the state, and their bulldozer congressional tactics, the Republicans earned last month's electoral defeat and are now saddled with a couple of high-profile corpses named Gingrich and Livingston. But Democrats and liberals, with their loftier ideals, have fallen further. Many Congressional Democrats privately scorn Mr. Clinton, for his policies and his behavior, with an intensity that rivals the open hatred of GOP Representative Bob Barr. But for narrow partisan political ends, they are willing to hollow out their consciences and close ranks.

We don't think the Senate should remove Mr. Clinton from office for the crimes the Republicans have charged him with. But if he is eventually hoisted on his own petard of the politicization of the rule of law, our sorrow for him will be tempered with the knowledge that—unlike Rickey Ray Rector, whose ghost now hunches anxiously over our shoulders—Bill Clinton will physically survive his political sacrifice. The last supper of his presidency is being paid for with the bankrupting of the liberal moral treasury. Unlike Rector, Mr. Clinton will be able to enjoy his dessert. His historical disgrace, however, will be his just desserts.

★ SEXTUPLE JEOPARDY ★

Jonathan Schell

From *The Nation*, February 22, 1999

In *The Spirit of the Laws*, Montesquieu draws a distinction that is useful in thinking about the impeachment of Bill Clinton. Montesquieu distinguishes between the structure of government, which he calls its "nature"—for example, monarchy, republicanism, tyranny—and the spirit that animates it, which he calls its "principle." For monarchy the principle is honor; for a republic it is virtue; and for tyranny it is fear. The structure, to use a simple analogy, is like the type of a vehicle—for instance, bicycle, car or train—and the principle is the fuel that makes it go (leg-power, gas or electricity).

The "principle" that has fueled the assault on Clinton has been constant throughout and is easily identified. It has been the zeal of the political right in general and of the Republican Party in particular to damage or destroy the presidency of Bill Clinton. The structures of the campaign, however, have been many. They include sexual harassment law, an independent prosecutor and the impeachment provision in the Constitution.

This restless search by an implacable faction for a variety of weapons to use against the President has resulted in a novel situation. The law forbids double jeopardy, but Clinton now faces, if my count is correct, sixfold jeopardy.

The first, of course, is the Senate trial, in which Clinton is likely to be acquitted because the Founders required a two-thirds majority to convict and the attacking party holds only fifty-five of the Senate's hundred seats. This insufficiency has sent the Republicans in search of forms of punishment within its reach.

The second is impeachment itself (as distinct from conviction and removal), which Republicans wish to interpret as condemnation, as if it were now enough to accuse someone of a crime in order to brand him guilty. The problem is that the public, according to every measure of its opinions, condemns Congress for impeaching the President much more harshly than it condemns the President for his misdeeds.

The third is censure, favored by the Democrats, who want to register their disapproval of the President without removing him from office.

The fourth, which has been invented more or less on the spot, is the idea of voting in the Senate on a so-called "finding of fact," by which the Senate would formally define the President's bad behavior even as, in a second vote, it would acquit him. Inasmuch as this "finding of fact"— more accurately named a "finding of conclusions" or a "finding of guilt," inasmuch as the relevant facts were all found long ago—can be passed by a simple majority, it amounts to an end-run around the inconvenient two-thirds rule.

Some Republicans, though, are unsatisfied with this innovation. Sen. Orrin Hatch, for one, worries that if the Senate "finds that perjury and obstruction of justice are not removable" it would send the message that the Senate does not take these offenses seriously. He accordingly invented a variation of the fourth form of jeopardy, in which, after voting the censorious finding, the Senate would simply suspend the trial permanently, depriving Clinton of his acquittal. As part of this now-final judgment, Hatch would buttress the punishment value of impeachment by having the Senate go on record to the effect that "Impeachment Without Removal" (the apotheosis of this sanction through the use of capital letters is Hatch's own) would be designated "the highest form of censure." Here, in a perfect inversion of the rule that a person is innocent until proven guilty, mere accusation (impeachment) is formally transmuted by senatorial declaration not only into conviction but into the sentencing as well.

While all these constitutional novelties were being considered in the Senate, the never-sleeping Ken Starr was concocting a fifth form of punishment—indictment of the President even while he remains in office (as he will for two years after a failure to convict him in the Senate). Taking upon himself the power of judging Presidents that the Constitution gives to Congress, he was in effect saying to the Senate, "If you don't convict him, I will."

The sixth—and, perhaps, most keenly desired—form of punishment is the public humiliation of the President, not only before today's citizens but before all history. With this demand, we leave the realm of law and politics behind and approach the psychosexual substrate—the smoldering, sulfurous, hidden core—of the scandal. Is there any pejorative in the English language that has not been applied to Clinton? Not since Hitler finished himself off in his bunker, it sometimes seems, has a public figure been excoriated as Clinton has. Just last week, Senator Robert Byrd, heaping up damning modifiers and metaphors with a repetitiousness that betrays obsession, announced that he sought a censure that would be "indelibly seared into the ineffaceable record of history for all future generations to see and to ponder"—a condemnation that "can never be erased" and, "like the mark that was set upon Cain, it will follow even beyond the grave." And A.M. Rosenthal, outdoing in promiscuous fury even this verbal flogging, demanded, vampire-like, a judgment on Clinton that would leave a "bite mark" on him "through history." To which one can only add that if the teeth-marks are Rosenthal's, poor Clinton will be at risk of rabies.

However, the main instrument of humiliation was the insistence by the House managers that the Senate either hear live witnesses or release videotapes of their depositions. Defending this demand, manager Asa Hutchinson commented that "only people who have been affected by this real-life drama, speaking from the heart," can sway the senators' "judgment." And Hutchinson's fellow manager Ed Bryant has famously declared, "Wouldn't you want to observe the demeanor of Miss Lewinsky and test her credibility? Look into her eyes?"

Did the managers unconsciously remember, perhaps, that the entire scandal began with Clinton looking into Lewinsky's eyes? Perhaps they had been afflicted by a similar longing. Like psychoanalysts, it seems, they wished to revisit—indeed, to re-enact—the scene that caused the trauma. Isn't it somehow the measure of the folly of this crisis that, in obedience to a pathology we cannot quite put our finger on, the trial perhaps cannot end until almost the entire US government—the House managers, the full Senate, the Chief Justice of the United States—has, following in the misguided, reckless footsteps of Bill Clinton, gazed into the vacant eyes of Monica Lewinsky?

★ THE FALSE DAWN OF ★ CIVIL SOCIETY

David Rieff

FROM *THE NATION*, FEBRUARY 22, 1999

When we put our faith in civil society, we are grasping at straws. Apart from a few principled nationalists, libertarians and Marxists, most well-intentioned people now view the rise of civil society as the most promising political development of the post-cold war era. By itself, that fact only points to how desperate we are, on the cusp of the millennium, to identify any political paradigm offering some realistic prospect of a more humane future. Such hopes give credit to those who entertain them, but they also perfectly illustrate J.D. Bernal's insight that "there are two futures, the future of desire and the future of fate, and man's reason has never learned to separate them."

Civil society is just such a projection of our desires. Worse, it gravely misdescribes the world we actually confront. As a concept, it has almost no specific gravity. It is little better than a Rorschach blot, the interpretations of which have been so massaged and expanded over the past fifteen years that the term has come to signify everything—which is to say nothing. Conventionally, we use civil society to apply to groups, societies and social trends of which we approve: societies based on diversity and tolerance, in which mutual assistance and solidarity are deeply established and the state is responsive rather than repressive.

Civil society is often described as a return to mutuality in political and social arrangements, and as the third force through which the traditional hierarchy of state and subject can be unseated. The term is used somewhat more rigorously by political scientists to encompass all those elements of society, and all those arrangements within it, that exist outside the state's reach or instigation. But in our time, the most general understanding of civil society is as the vehicle for a range of political and social goals. It has become a shorthand way of referring to all those democratically minded groups that have opposed and sometimes brought about the overthrow of repressive regimes in countries as varied as Marcos's Philippines, Abacha's Nigeria and Husak's Czechoslovakia. Where civil society is absent, repressive, tyrannical, even genocidal forces are supposed to have a freer hand; where it is present, it is supposed to constitute a firebreak against war, exploitation, and want.

In short, civil society has come, simultaneously, to be thought of as encompassing everything that is not the state and as exemplifying a set of inherently democratic values. That is why those who tout it as the silver bullet both to "open" repressive societies and to guarantee or deepen democratic liberties and curb state power move with feline grace between using civil society as a descriptive term and as a prescriptive one. To which it might be added that the dogma holding that strengthening civil society is the key to creating or sustaining a healthy polity has come to dominate the thinking of major charitable foundations, as well as human rights and humanitarian organizations.

Those disposed to accept the claims of these groups for the emancipatory potential of civil society should note that the term has been enthusiastically embraced by many government officials in the United States and the countries of the European Union. In the framework of development aid in particular, the shift from channeling assistance to governments, as had been the case well into the eighties, to offering it to local nongovernmental organizations (NGOs) has been justified not simply as the inevitable prudential response to states misusing aid but as a way of building civil society.

That this emphasis on local capacity building, to use the bureaucratic term of art, and on fostering civil society arose at exactly the moment when development aid from most major donor countries was plummeting (in many countries, including the United States, they are now at historic lows) may, of course, be coincidental. But in the development sphere, at least, ideological commitment to making states "responsive" to civil society seems to have been accompanied by a determination to cut funding. When pressed, development specialists who favor this new approach insist that a robust civil society will open the way for the integration of the poor world into the global economy—supposedly the first step toward prosperity.

Viewed from this angle, the idea of civil society begins to look less like a way of fostering democratic rights and responsive governments and more like part of the dominant ideology of the post-cold war period: liberal market capitalism. A perfect example of this synthesis of emancipatory sentiments and faith in free markets can be found in the Executive Summary of the 1997 Carnegie Commission on Preventing Deadly Conflict. Civil society is assigned a pivotal role. "Many elements of civil society," the report states, "can work to reduce hatred and violence and to encourage attitudes of concern, social responsibility, and mutual aid within and between groups. In difficult economic and political transitions, the organizations of civil society are of crucial importance in alleviating the dangers of mass violence." The paragraph then segues, without break or transition, into the following assertion: "Many elements in the private sector around the world are dedicated to helping prevent deadly conflict."

Obviously, the communitarians, human rights activists and liberal foundation executives who first raised the banner of civil society were no more interested in helping refurbish liberal capitalism's ideological superstructure than was the human-rights movement in making its cause the quasi-religious faith of the international new class, but this is nonetheless exactly what they have done. Surely, it is a safe assumption that any term that can be embraced as warmly by the Clinton Administration and the European Commission as "civil society" has been threatens no important vested interests in the rich world.

Again, there is no question of a subterfuge. The idea of civil society simply coincides with the tropism toward privatization that has been the hallmark of these post-cold war times. Far from being oppositional, it is perfectly in tune with the Zeitgeist of an age that has seen the growth of what proponents like Bill Clinton and Tony Blair are pleased to call the "Third Way" and what might more unsentimentally be called "Thatcherism with a human face." As we privatize prisons, have privatized development assistance and are in the process, it seems, of privatizing military interventions into places like New Guinea, Sierra Leone and Angola by armies raised by companies like Sandline and Executive Outcomes, so let us privatize democracy-building. Let's give up on the state's ability to establish the rule of law or democracy through elections and legislation, and instead give civic associations—the political equivalent of the private sector—a chance to do their thing.

The fact that all this comes couched in the language (and the imaginative framework) of emancipation does not, in and of itself, make it emancipatory. Indeed, there are times when it seems as if the advocates of civil society are the useful idiots of globalization. In further undermining the state, they undermine the only remaining power that has at least the potential to stand in opposition to the privatization of the world, commonly known as globalization.

Making the world safe for global capitalism may be one of the effects of the triumph of the ideal of civil society, but it is not, of course, the sole or even the principal reason for its prominence. The ideal of civil society responds to a deeper problem—an intellectual, not to say a moral, void. The most profound legacy of the post-cold war era may prove to be the ideological hollowing-out that all developed countries and many poor ones have experienced. The disappointments, for liberals and leftists, respectively, of nationalism and communism were already largely assimilated well before the collapse of the Soviet empire. What was unexpected was that the end of the superpower rivalry and the victory of market capitalism over state socialism would also reveal just how diminished the nation-state had become over the half-century since the end of the Second World War, and just how ineffectual the international institutions—above all the United Nations and the Bretton Woods organizations—that were established in its wake.

This is the revelation that has come in the package marked "globalization." The cold war had been an era of alliances and battlegrounds. Every nation had its place, whether it wanted one or not. It was above all a militarized environment, and, because only nations could afford modern armies, the nation-state still appeared to be quite strong. But this only shows how the transformation of the world economy could take place without sufficient notice being taken of the implications of those changes.

For all the bluff talk of the United States being "the indispensable nation" or the "only remaining superpower," it is less able to impose its will than it was during the cold war, and internally, no national project with the unifying force of anti-Communism is anywhere to be found. Multiculturalism, global capitalism's consumerist ideological adjunct, has further fragmented any unitary cultural conception of the nation except in its most debased, commodified form.

All the major nations seem to have emerged from the cold war weaker and more incoherent than they were when they entered it. And for good reason. The course of the world economy has been deeply subversive of the established structures of power. But as Robert Hormats, the vice chairman of Goldman, Sachs & Co. International, observed, nobody controls globalization—certainly not national governments, as was demonstrated by the inability of the British government in 1992 to protect the value of the British pound against speculators led by George Soros.

Such perceived and real loss of power has been followed by a loss of legitimacy. It is now politicians who are the supplicants and corporate executives who are viewed as the dispensers of wisdom and authority and the holders of real power. The European Union countries were not able to muster the resolve to end the Bosnian war, but they were able to launch European monetary union at the behest of corporate Europe— an event that in many ways was European capitalism's end run around a half-century-old social contract between capital and labor, now seen to be interfering with the corporate bottom line.

In the United States, a renewed ethnic consciousness has led to what seems like a flowering of a multiplicity of allegiances; in Western Europe, the subsumption of nation-states in the project of the European Union, as well as the arrival of large numbers of nonwhite immigrants for the first time in several centuries, has produced similarly subversive effects on the legitimacy of the nation.

Faced with such confusions, is it any wonder that the ideal of civil society, which does not seek to oppose this fragmentation but rather to capitalize on it, should have become so important? Add to this civil society's seeming moral dimension, and the stew becomes well-nigh irresistible.

Furthermore, this blend of economic and democratic determinism has combined easily with a deep fatalism about the future of the nation-state. Political scientists constantly assure us that we have been going through the most profound change in international relations since the establishment of the Westphalian order in the seventeenth century. Nations have been clearly less and less able to affect investment flows and have thus been judged to be turning into hollow shells. And the future of supranational institutions like the UN system is seen as being, if anything, bleaker still. Better make a virtue of necessity and insist that the new medievalism of civil society, with the NGOs playing the role of the guilds in fourteenth-century Italy, would be an improvement over a world of etiolated nation-states in which even that sine qua non of state power, a monopoly on violence, is in many cases no longer assured.

A world in which the Enlightenment project of universal values seems to have been reduced to human-rights activists' demands for more stringent and binding international legal regimes was bound to be drawn to a faith in localism and single-issue activism. In fairness, the perception of the weakening of the nation and of the impotence of international organizations has not been mistaken. What has been mis-placed is the belief that a network of associations could accomplish what states could not.

David Rieff

Proponents of the effectiveness of civil society point to examples of the successful opposition of popular action to repressive regimes or state policies. People power in the Philippines, the Velvet Revolution in what was then Czechoslovakia, the recent campaign to ban landmines—these are the great success stories of civil society. But it was always an empirical stretch to claim that these historic events were proof that human betterment would henceforth mainly be the product of the struggles of dissidents and grassroots activists.

The idea of civil society has been most coherent when applied to nations where citizens needed protection from a repressive state, as was the case in the Soviet empire. But in other parts of the world this paradigm is either irrelevant or of distinctly secondary importance. There are parts of Africa where a stronger state, one that could bring the various bandits and insurgents to heel, might be of far greater value. It's tempting to add that the United States, after more than two decades of seemingly inexorable privatization, is a country where strengthening the state's role would be preferable to hoping that NGOs will somehow be able to take up the slack.

The suggestion that civil society can cope where nations have failed is, in fact, a counsel of despair in such instances. Without a treasury, a legislature or an army at its disposal, civil society is less equipped to confront the challenges of globalization than nations are, and more likely to be wracked by divisions based on region and the self-interest of the single-issue groups that form the nucleus of the civil society movement.

Why should fragmented groups of like-minded individuals be more effective in, say, resisting the depredations of environmental despoilers than a national government? Remember, the ideal of civil society is being advanced not simply for the developed world, where to a large extent it exists already, but for the world as a whole. And yet, as we know from bitter experience, the leverage of grassroots activists even in the United States, where there are courts to turn to and media to beguile, is not enormous. One can admire the efforts and sacrifices of activists in the poor world without losing sight of the fact that their countries would be better off with honest and effective governments and legal systems, and with militaries that stay in their barracks, than with denser networks of local associations, which may stand for good values or hideous ones.

This last point is essential. Viewed coldly, the concept of civil society is based on the fundamentally apolitical, or even antipolitical, concept of single-issue activism. And yet surely one person's civil society group is another person's pressure group. The assumption of the advocates of civil society is that somehow locally based associations are always going to stand for those virtues the authors of the Carnegie Commission associated them with. When it is said that civil society must be recognized as a new force in international politics, what is meant is a certain kind of civil society—in other words, a certain kind of political movement. But why should this be the case? It is only because what is properly a descriptive term is being misused as an ideological or moral one.

Why, for example, is the International Campaign to Ban Landmines viewed as an exemplar of civil society instead of, say, the National Rifle Association, which, whatever one thinks of its politics, has at least as good a claim to being an authentic grassroots movement? The UN bitterly resisted having to recognize the NRA as a legitimate NGO. And yet if we think of NGO as a description and not a political position, the NRA obviously qualifies.

In any case, to make the claim that civil society is bound to be, or is even likely to be, a force for good is roughly akin to claiming that people, at least when left to their own devices, are good. In contrast, proponents of civil society are often mesmerized by the depredations of states and seem to assume that states, by their nature, are malign or impotent or both. But there are other predators besides government officials, other ills besides those unleashed by untrammeled state power. An example might be the Bosnian Serbs under Radovan Karadzic. During the Bosnian war, it was a liberal conceit that the Serbs acted as they did because of fear or media manipulation. The idea, say, that people are capable, without manipulation, of great evil was dismissed out of hand. And yet as one who spent a good deal of time covering the war in Bosnia, my view is that Karadzic represented the aspirations of ordinary Serbs in that extraordinary time all too faithfully, and could rightfully lay just as great a claim to being an exemplar of civil society as Vaclav Havel.

That Karadzic is an evil man and Havel a good one should go without saying. But where the question of civil society is concerned, it is beside the point, unless, of course, you accept the claim that civil society exists only when the ideals or interests being expressed are good, peace-loving and tolerant. At that point civil society becomes, as it has for its more unreflective advocates, a theological notion, not a political or a sociological one. The example of Rwanda, which, as Peter Uvin has shown in his extraordinary book *Aiding Violence*, was viewed by development experts before the genocide as having one of the most developed civil societies in Africa, should be a warning to anyone who assumes it is a sure measure of a nation's political health or a buffer against catastrophe.

Finally, there is the problem of democracy. Leaders of associations, pressure groups and NGOs—unlike politicians in democracies—are accountable to no one except their members and those who provide them with funds. That may seem a minor question to adherents of a particular cause. Does it matter that Jody Williams was never elected to lead the campaign against landmines? Perhaps it doesn't. But proponents of civil society are claiming that it offers a better alternative, or at least an important additional voice, to that of governments and parliaments, not just on a single issue but on all the pressing questions of our time. And leaders of such groups, unlike politicians, do not have to campaign, hold office, allow the public to see their tax returns or stand for reelection. It is, indeed, the new medievalism, with the leaders of the NGOs as feudal lords.

This, of course, is hardly what most advocates of civil society have in mind. And yet as things stand, it is this unaccountable, undemocratic congeries of single-interest groups that is being proposed as the only viable alternative to the nation-state. It seems to me that were they to achieve the kind of prominence and centrality that is being predicted for them, we would all be far worse off than we are today. And things are gloomy enough already. The premise on which the advocates of civil society have been operating is simply wrong. The nation-state has been weakened, but it is not a spent force. And those who aspire to the better world the magic bullet of civil society is supposed to engineer would do better to fight the political battles they believe need fighting in the full knowledge that we do not all agree on what should be done or how societies should be organized, and we never will.

★ A REVIEW OF ★
IT DIDN'T HAPPEN HERE:
WHY SOCIALISM FAILED
IN THE UNITED STATES

James Weinstein

FROM THE *LOS ANGELES TIMES*, DECEMBER 17, 2000
In 1906, Werner Sombart wrote a book titled *Why Is There No Socialism in America?* He wasn't the first to expound on this aspect of America's divergence from Europe, and he wasn't the last. The honor of having written the latest, if not the last, book on the weakness of socialism in America goes to Seymour Martin Lipset and Gary Marks, whose *It Didn't Happen Here: Why Socialism Failed in the United States* is an intelligent and in many ways a thoughtful book. But do we need it? Do Lipset and Marks look at the question of socialism's failure in a way that opens our minds to rethinking the problem—if it is a problem—of the absence of an organized American left rooted in traditional socialist ideas?

Don't get me wrong. As a lifelong socialist, I am deeply concerned about what has happened to the political movement for socialism in America, but I am even more interested in knowing what has happened to the meaning of socialism and its democratic, libertarian and egalitarian traditions in this era of highly developed corporate capitalism. Lipset and Marks, however, restrict themselves pretty much to a discussion of the fate of the party, or parties, that have called themselves socialist. They write about this movement but fail to explore the transformation of the public's understanding of the term. Nor do they consider the ways in which socialists themselves may have changed in the light of the Soviet experience.

Consider this: Socialism, as it was understood by Karl Marx and by many socialists in the West before 1917, hasn't happened anywhere in the world—not in the United States, not in Europe, not in the Soviet Union, China or Cuba. So in what ways is the United States unique? Perhaps Lipset and Marks should have asked why there is no socialism worldwide. They do raise this question, but only implicitly and obscurely, and then they skim past it. They ignore the problems posed by communist countries that have called themselves socialist but that did not—and probably could not—embody the socialist principles underlying the Western movement before 1917. Instead, they focus narrowly on American exceptionalism—on how the United States is different from Western Europe—and how these differences have affected the history of the left in the United States. And they rely on familiar arguments and assumptions about socialism, at least some of which were fixed in the popular mind by the Russian Revolution and its aftermath.

The arguments Lipset and Marks use have been made by commentators on the American scene from Alexis de Tocqueville in the 1830s to Daniel Bell in the 1950s, by socialists from Friedrich Engels to Lenin and by American historians from John R. Commons and Selig Perlman to Louis Hartz. The authors know this literature well and cite these arguments to good effect, but they don't carry us beyond them onto new ground.

The first reason for the weakness of class-conscious political movements in America, Lipset and Marks tell us, is genealogical: The United States was the first major capitalist country that came into being without significant feudal ancestors. Never having to defeat a domestic feudal ruling class and never having experienced the fixed class divisions—and class resentments—that feudalism entailed, the United States was born free. Thoroughly bourgeois and with a vigorous civil society (except, of course, in the slave states), revolutionary America still had an elite, made up of slave owners in the South and merchants in the North, but the vast majority of the population were independent producers who, as property owners, had the right to vote, a right soon extended to all free males. As Lipset and Marks write, socialism has had limited appeal because its social content "is similar to what Americans think they already have, namely a democratic, classless, anti-elitist society."

Ethnic diversity is another reason that Lipset and Marks explore for socialism's weakness in America. Unlike Europe, where workers in each country shared a common language and culture, in the United States workers were divided by their cultural differences. In its early days the socialist movement in the United States was little more than an import from Germany, isolated by language and culture from most American workers. And, indeed, though premised on working-class solidarity, the movement continued to be plagued by the old-world hostilities of an ethnically divided working class well into the 20th century. Native-born and immigrant Britons and Germans formed an elite stratum of skilled workers as well as the bulk of craft union membership. Southern and Eastern European immigrants—and, in the [American] West, Chinese—were generally relegated to unskilled work. And African-Americans, still only recently freed from slavery and isolated by racism, were employed in the most menial jobs—except when they were being used as strikebreakers, which, of course, further fragmented the working class.

These problems alone would have made the job of building a united working-class movement difficult, but things were made worse because most immigrants were politically and culturally conservative, and their conservatism was encouraged by an actively anti-socialist Catholic Church. As Lipset and Marks make clear, the predominance of immigrants in the American work force worked against the growth of political socialism, despite the movement's largely immigrant origins.

After 1900, when Eugene V. Debs first ran for president and the Socialist Party of America was founded, the Socialists faced yet another, perhaps more daunting, problem: the peculiar structure of the American political system. Ours is a system that militates against the success of third parties. The parliamentary systems of Europe and Canada make it relatively easy for a minority party to be heard and even to become part of a ruling government coalition, because the heads of government are chosen by parliamentary majorities, not separately as in the United States. As the European systems have evolved, minority parties, like the Greens in Germany, have become members of ruling coalitions. Even in France, where the president is elected separately, the parliament is elected by a partial system of proportional representation and minority members are easily elected and sometimes become part of governing coalitions.

In the United States, however, single-member congressional districts and the separate election of the president by nationwide popular vote (constrained by the Electoral College) greatly disadvantage any minority party. No third party, except the Republicans, has ever successfully rivaled a major party in the United States. And the Republicans succeeded only because the Whig party had disintegrated over the question of the extension of slavery, an issue that split the nation. Although since then there have been many third-party efforts, no significant third party except the Socialists has lasted more than two presidential elections. The Socialists survived, at least until 1932, Lipset and Marks suggest, because they were a highly ideological and principled party. But that also prevented them from making the kinds of compromises that might have made them more relevant and influential, though perhaps less distinct.

All of this is well-traveled ground, but two ideas, one presented in the first chapter, the other in the last chapter, hint at a new way of looking at this question. Early on, Lipset and Marks quote Marx's introduction to *Das Kapital* in which he suggests that rather than being an exception, America would be a model for capitalist countries. Only in the last chapter do the authors return to this idea and point out that over the last half century, the left throughout the world has followed America by moving to the right. This has been true throughout Europe and in Japan, especially, Lipset and Marks observe, in England, Australia, and New Zealand, where all three labor parties have become unionist, rather than socialist.

In those countries, the authors write, this has simply been a return to form; "Only during and after World War I did labor parties in these countries adopt socialist programs." This reference to the destabilizing effect of war receives only glancing attention, but perhaps it is the key to the politics of the left in the last century. Consider this: The chaos and devastation of World War I created the conditions in which the Bolsheviks seized power in Russia, the German Social Democrats were elected to office and the British Labor Party turned socialist and was elected. As a result of conditions created by World War II, Mao Tse-tung and his party took control of China, the Communist parties of Italy and France greatly increased their strength, and the British Labor Party swept back into office as Clement Atlee ousted wartime hero Winston Churchill. In short, the world wars weakened state apparatuses and delegitimized the capitalist class of these countries and opened up space for the left, which emerged from the world wars as the champions of a populist nationalism.

Of course, in the United States, the world wars had exactly the opposite effect on the left. Isolated from wartime destruction and enjoying a boom in producing military and other goods for its allies, American capitalism emerged from both world wars greatly strengthened. At home, the wars provided full employment after serious depressions. Wages rose sharply, unions cooperated with management and grew substantially. In both cases, the postwar years saw savage attacks on the left which, because of its own internal weakness, was particularly vulnerable each time. (This is a complex story to which Lipset and Marks do not do justice in their chapter on political repression.) Rebuilding Europe after both wars and Japan after the second war further solidified American capitalism's control over the American state and the world economy. (Interestingly, the only significant growth of the left in the last 50 years was also in reaction to a war: the war against Vietnamese independence. That war did not wreak physical damage on the country, but for millions of Americans it played havoc with the idea of America as a democratic ideology.)

This brings us back to Marx's idea that "the country that is more developed industrially shows to the less developed the image of their future." Lipset and Marks quote this remark as if it were a comment on politics, but Marx meant it as a statement about the developmental logic of capitalist society. And though Marx believed that capitalist development was a prerequisite for socialism, he had little to say about how the political movement for socialism would or should develop. He did believe that Britain, or more likely the United States, would be the first to achieve the level of technological development and the experience of democracy required to make possible a peaceful transition to socialism. So far, history has not proved him wrong in this regard. Indeed, one might argue that the United States has achieved this level of development and awaits the growth of a left to appreciate that potential. If that is so, then perhaps the title of Lipset and Marks' book might better have been *Why Socialism Hasn't Happened Here Yet* rather than *It Didn't Happen Here.*

Asking why it didn't leads to the rehash of already answered questions that this book barely transcends. But asking why socialism hasn't happened encourages thinking about many questions: To what extent, for example, have socialism's principles been incorporated into corporate capitalism and mainstream American culture? And what else in the socialist tradition might revitalize our culture and point the way to a more democratic, humane and egalitarian society?

RIGHT CROSSES

★ INTRODUCTION ★

Christopher Hitchens

I s there a necessary connection between journalism and radicalism? The question seems absurd when first asked: Tory and reactionary pamphleteers have been a gorgeous part of the scribblers' mosaic since letters were first penned. Well, then, is there any assumption about a connection between journalism and radicalism? This inches us nearer to the truth, since many a conservative, and even conservative radical, writer has had to answer the question, from parents or professors, about when he or she is going to get a proper or serious job. Very well, is there any assumption about a connection between journalism and radicalism in America? And here, the answer often seems to be yes. The conservative establishment makes the "liberal bias" of journalism into one of its favorite grumbles. The Left—never happier than when talking about "media bias"—nonetheless deploys its attacking energies more upon concentrations of ownership than upon modes of journalistic expression. In the universities, it is often noticeable that the Party of the Right prefers law or business or the military as its career path, while the Party of the Left is more interested in communications.

Some mainstream journalistic traditions appear to validate this rather fuzzy distinction. Few aspirants now set out to emulate the anti-striking achievements of Henry Ford's *Dearborn Independent,* while prizes are

207

there to be won by those who dream of Watergate, or the "muck-raking" tradition begun by Ira Tarbell and continued through Jessica Mitford. Not unlike the Hollywood "Academy," the juries of official press awards (and what a lot of prizes the profession awards itself) tend to give higher marks to scalding exposes or compassionate narratives. The overall bias of the American press is towards consensus, and the overwhelming bias of its proprietors is towards profit and entertainment, but the stuff still has to be written by somebody, and thus a man like Seymour Hersh can be a hero to a young *New York Times* reporter in a way that William F. Buckley, for example, was never likely to become.

If I had had my way, the anthology you hold in your hands would have been entitled *Between The Bushes*. Not only would this have been a synecdoche for the squalor and triviality of the Clinton years, but it would have described a quasi-real period in political and cultural life. During the Reagan epoch, when I was one of those Washington critics who essentially did not believe a word about, or from, the "Great Communicator," I noticed that the think-tanks and foundations of the conservative movement were changing the pattern I sketched above, and busily incubating their own generation of propagandists. A bright young person from (say) the *Dartmouth Review* could be airlifted from the campus, with not many more battle scars than it took to denounce "political correctness," and dropped into a plausible magazine slot at any one of half-a-dozen foundation-supported right-wing glossies, or at the *Wall Street Journal* or the Moonie-financed *Washington Times*. In those days, I very much scorned this tendency, which seemed to shower patronage on kids who were already spoiled enough. (Punishment for this was to fall upon the Right later on, in the shape of the scuzziness, shallowness and greed of David Brock: a young man who could not get himself believed even when he claimed to be a liar. No other individual touched bottom, or searched it out, with anything like Brock's assiduity. Still, I can remember thinking that one or two of the others had not quite deserved the Head Start that they received.) But there was evidently more talent in that pipeline than I was willing to acknowledge.

The sudden implosion of the first Bush regime, and the consequent appearance of Mr. and Mrs. Clinton upon the Presidential podium, was somewhat contradictory from the conservative point of view. It meant, first, that a rather mediocre and centrist Republican regime no longer needed any apology. And it took place in a context—the much more massive and resounding implosion of party-state socialism—that could be (with a little faith and a little propaganda) retrospectively attributed to the Reagan Revolution. Other touchstone events, like the electoral defeat of the Sandinistas in Nicaragua, seemed to put the dispirited American Left even more on the defensive. And Bush Senior's most signal success in the Persian Gulf, while it by no means put an end to the "Vietnam syndrome" (because nothing will ever do that, at least while any of us alive at the time can still draw breath) at least relaxed some of the inhibitions about the use of American power.

If Mr. Clinton had really been a "New Democrat," he might have been able to triangulate some of this into a new centrism that would have given conservatives relatively few targets. But his flabbergasting combination of corporate fund-raising with ethnic and sexual politics— I am understating matters deliberately—allowed a renaissance of conservative writing and polemic. Much of this, as you will see from the selections made by my learned colleague Mr. Caldwell, was satirical. That in itself was, from the radical left point of view, a bad sign. Nothing so much empowers a magazine or a movement as an ability to be witty and sarcastic; nothing condemns a regime so much as a fear of laughter. I confess that I found myself becoming a regular reader of the *Weekly Standard* because I was, at least at first, in search of a humorous rag. And, just as the lack of a sense of humor is a direct negation of a person's seriousness (here I plagiarise without shame from Martin Amis) so the corollary may hold. . . .

Many liberals believe that there is something essentially mean and · resentful about the American Right, and there is good historical support for this proposition, as well as plenty of contemporary illustration. But I was struck, reading Mr. Caldwell's selections, by how generous in spirit many of these essays are. (I might instance Bill Kaufmann on Dorothy Day, even though I have no time for softness about religion: also Peter

Collier on the Kennedy cult, as well as the operatic and literary parodies executed by David Tell and Francis X. Bacon.) Andrew Ferguson, who was funny long before he hoisted any particular colors, and who is one of the great discoveries of the Right in this epoch, can—as I know to my own cost—be deadly without needing to be nasty. This was a period when much of official liberalism fell back on "speech codes" and identity politics, and adopted a distinctly solemn visage and demeanor. Having proclaimed for years that the personal was political, it did not care for the application of this principle to the first Democrat re-elected since Franklin Roosevelt. It also opened itself to ridicule, and was taken up on the unintended invitation. But as Kenneth Anderson's contribution illustrates, triumphalism on this point can come before a fall.

Of the many permanent contradictions with which the conservative, and especially the American conservative, must live, the most abiding is the problem of "big government." Mr. Caldwell and I, for obvious and sufficient reasons, forbade any extension of this anthology beyond the date of 11 September 2001. But many of his selections show an awareness of the difficulty presented by state power, as it is exerted by a global internationalist colossus at home and abroad. (As a matter of fact, so do many of mine.) Beyond any doubt, the argument about the proper role of government, in controlling the life of the citizen, will be the critical one in the coming decade. The stubborn assertion of a kind of skeptical libertarianism is a thread that is to be found in more than one ideology. Perhaps for this reason, the pre-2001 triumphs of the Right in foreign affairs are given—how shall I phrase it?—only the most muted recognition here.

An attitude towards Washington has also become a factor. In *The Company of Critics*, Michael Walzer wrote that, like most people he knew, he had never really been to the nation's capital except to protest. Most writers from the Left continue to orient themselves towards New York, with side-bets on Cambridge, San Francisco, Chicago and Madison, Wisconsin. The willingness of conservative writerly types to put up with a Washingtonian existence, and to expose themselves to policy matters, is not overrepresented in this selection. But its effect can be felt in a certain assurance on the part of several contributors: a sort of divided realisation that for the Right, the Federal City is both the belly of the beast and a place of opportunity. (By something more than chance, that duality could fairly describe the long-standing attitude of many leftists to America itself.)

The test of a well-conducted argument is not its ability to convert or to persuade. It lies in its capacity to refine or to redefine the positions of the other side. The intellectual fluidity of the decade just past is not something that will suddenly congeal in our new era of what Robert Lowell in another context called "the reign of piety and iron." I hope and trust that my own choices reflect some of the necessary deference to irony and to openness. But I certainly think that these elements are present among those I am proud to call my antagonists.

CHRISTOPHER HITCHENS
Washington, D.C.
11 March, 2002

★ FROM THE TRAGEDY ★ OF MACDETH

Francis X. Bacon

FROM *THE AMERICAN SPECTATOR*, AUGUST 1994

Act I
Scene I—A heath in Arkansas.
[*Enter* MACHDETH *and* LYONS, *jogging*]

MACDETH: How now, my gentle Lyons, what's o'clock?

LYONS: My liege, the moon our sister Artemis,
Like a T-cell new ruptured
By plaguy ill-bred pathogen hath done
Dismissed herself from the field of play. [*Pushes button on wristwatch*]
Six-thirty.

MACDETH: Then let us canny falconers uncage
our Reeboks to th'unruly winds and speed
on wings of Taiwan-sculpted rubber hence,
lest time should turn our stomachs cuckold
and torpor the McBreakfast Special cheat.

[*Enter three* WITCHES]

Yet stand I traitor to mine eyes or they
to me, who credit not their troth?
For these appear not women, nay, nor men,
but antecedents of the pronoun s/he—
three Deans of Gender Studies, it would seem,
the very substance of delirium.

1st Witch: Hail, Macdeth, all hail to the chief!

2nd Witch: Hail, good-lookin! Ro-mance on your mind?

3rd Witch: Hail, Macdeth, both witness and defendant!
Art happy to see me, or is that a Title IX
Enforcement order in thy pocket?

Macdeth: Stay, weird sisters! Download this riddle
Into the syntax of propinquity.
For even as the wench of Little Rock
Doth hide her charms in cotton-poly blend,
Then bends with the remover to remove,
So too methinks your feign'd modesty
Encrypts itself the better to reveal.

1st Witch: Lesser than Robert Reich, and stouter!

2nd Witch: Wetter than Maxine's waters, and whiter!

3rd Witch: Like Teddy for a spouse, but better wive'd!

Witches: All hail! [*Exeunt*]

Macdeth: Hie thee hence to Lady Hillary,
Knock twice—lest haste a Foster husband find—
And quaint her of this morrow's tidings.

Francis X. Bacon

LYONS: Good my Lord. [*Exit*]

MACDETH: What joy, what horror must this be, that makes
My very scalp unseat itself, as when
The tempest scatters sickle'd wheat afield
Or Cristophe runs his fingers through my hair?
What FDA-untested potion sacks
My intellect, and exiles high-enthron'd
Consciousness of Lack of Consciousness
Of Class? Ambition, like a draught
Of cannabis long held (but not inhaled),
Doth prick resentment to a fury, who
Gallops onward riderless, and comes
Uncaptained frothing to her post. But let
Our morning's revels look to botany;
If she's at Rose, then I'll with Flowers be. [*Exit*]

Scene II—The Governor's Mansion.
[*Enter Lady* HILLARY *with* MESSENGERS]

HILLARY: To Salomon go, and short my 20-years,
But do thou fetch me Deutschmarks in their stead,
That I might 'scape inflation's bloody tooth,
And like an alchemist turn dross to joy.

1st MESS.: I hear, your ladyship, and fly. [*Exit*]

HILLARY: And thou,
Ill-gendered knave, get thee to Madison
And teach our gentle cousin we would have
His ear.

2nd MESS.: I go. [*Exit* MESS. *Enter* LYONS]

LYONS: My lady, by your leave . . .

HILLARY: Fair Lyons, I wonder at thy charge, and see
Thy face doth fax a message bearing not
The subtext of serenity.

LYONS: So foul
And fair a ball I have not seen. 'Tis foul,
In curving wide of deep left field; 'tis fair,
But in its agents of accomplishment.
For whilst I and thy noble husband did
This morning mark our wonted course afoot,
Three pollsteresses squat and whiskered stood
Bestride the path and croaked, All hail! All hail,
Mister President! I deem they be
So lipped the flaccid tennis balls of fate
Through triumph's garden hose to inspirate. [*Exit*]

HILLARY: *Mister* President! First Lady, I?
Say rather Empress, partnered with a drone.
By what defect of wit, what folly, what
Dire presentiment, did I then yoke me
Unto obscurity and shame? O come,
Ye Wellesley-spawned Eumenides of spite,
Unsex me here! Replace my blood with quarts
Of chilliest testosterone, and butch
My hair, that no suspicious visitings
Of NOW—nor journalists—might weaken my
Resolve, or set me gagging Socks-like on
Compunction's hairball.

   [*Enter* FOOL]

Fool! Varlet!

Cross-gartered, mincing, single-witted knave,
Remove thee from mine eyes, for but to gaze
On thy ill-favored visage acheth sore.

FOOL: Madam, 'tis I.

HILLARY: Methought thou wast another,
Nearer in bond canonical, though more
Remote in kind.

FOOL: Nay, nay, your ladyship,
For ne'er was cuckold made but in his horns
Discernible, that shame be published by
His brow, or on his saxophone.

HILLARY: Thou art
An arrant whelp! Take caution lest I pull
The stripes from thine Adidas—but to lay
Them on thy back.

FOOL: 'Twould make thee whinny.

HILLARY: How?

FOOL: Marry, not as mare but as Mandela,
Whose Winnie spurneth not the lash, nor yet
Was vex'd by a friend whom time did not
Incinerate.
[sings]An ANC leader I knew
Asked her pals to a strange barbecue
And explaining with sighs,
'Well, smoke gets in your eyes,'
Ignited a dozen or two.
But let me set a riddle, for my head:

How dost thou in thy managements compare
To auguries of Carthage or of Rome?

HILLARY: Thy wit defeats me, naughty Sphinx. Make plain
Thy lesson.

FOOL: 'Struth, that riches haply came
Thy way unearn'd, in chicken futures.

HILLARY: Fie!

FOOL: [*sings*] *A damsel of Lernerite fashion*
Insisted on social compassion:
'The market's degrading.
It's insider trading
That pulls the post-modernist cash in.'

HILLARY: You're fired.

　[*Enter* MACDETH]

MACDETH: How *'bout* them *Hawgs!*

HILLARY: You're hired again.
And what blind beggary of fortune leads
Thee here? No lickerous enticement to
Thy fancy struts within these walls. No drab
Awaits, no bawd, no trollop, slattern, slut
Or concubine, no bacon double-cheese
With extra fries. Or haply hast thou lost
Thy MasterCard, and cruel need restored thee
To our halls?

FOOL: [*sings*] *When she finds on her bed an intruder*

Francis X. Bacon

Like to Mandy Rice-Davies, but nuder,
Slick Willie explains
And forthrightly maintains
First I gave her a job, then I
Hey nonny hey nonny
Hey nonny nonny
Hey now Elizabeth Tudor!

MACDETH: Nay, tire me not in the habiliments
Of wrath, nor taunt me with remorse's sting.
For now is the winter of our discontent
Made Acapulco through the *New York Times*,
And any misdemeanors of the past
Full deeply in the Metro section buried.
Indeed this very day intelligence
Is mine, if I can but New Hampshire or
Nebraska buy, that Little Rock shall lose
Both pimp and pimpernel, and Washington
A fan of Fleetwood find.

HILLARY: Let no device
Remain untried, no artifice untested,
That ruth should beggar opportunity,
Or honor's scruples pauperize success.
The siding from thy mother's mobile home
I'll sell, her dentures pawn, her Elvis lamp,
Her Betty Crocker coupons liquidate!
Come Phaedra, come mistress mine Medea,
Teach your willing daughter true resolve!
My husband I'll dismember for his pelf,
Nor e'en his long-retir'd Jockey shorts
Can rest unmortgaged, but shall serve
Our purposes: as britches of contract,
Brief harbingers of longings sated.

FOOL [*aside*]: That creditor be credulous indeed
who takes in trust such fell collateral.

MACDETH: If we should fail?

HILLARY: You fail! But do thou act
upon thy courage as it is thy wont
to operate upon thy hostesses,
and thou'lt not fail. Did not the bearded crones
give certain prescience of triumph?
Then play the man—or better, play the field,
and I shall summon manliness for both. [*Exeunt*]

FOOL: 'Tis passing strange, that Caesar, in his home
should tempt the "why" of fate,
and stint the Y of chromosome. [*Exit*]

    ACT II
    Scene I—A cavern. In the middle, a boiling cauldron.

1st WITCH: Where hast thou been, sister?

2nd WITCH: Killing swine.

3rd WITCH: Porkers, boars, or gender-chauvinists?

2nd WITCH: Marry, all three, and at a single stroke.

1st WITCH: How now?

2nd WITCH: Vin Foster lieth silenced on the crimson'd turf,
And husband, lawyer, Razorback alike
Are dumb, reposing in the selfsame corse.

Francis X. Bacon

1st WITCH: 'Tis well and bravely done!
Then turn we to our order's liturgy,
Lest Dee Dee's woe be changed to Limbaugh's glee.

WITCHES: Double, treble toil and trouble,
Fan the flamers, prick the bubble,
In the cauldron boil and bake
Packwood's acne, Bobbitt's ache.
Lorena's shiv and Tonya's shank,
Constituents of Barney Frank,
Eye of World Trade Center bomber,
Midnight snack of Jeffrey Dahmer . . .

[*Enter* AUDITOR]

AUDITOR: Oyez! Oyez! [*Reads*]
"Here be it noted in conformity
With H.R. 741 6(e)3:
Provideth funding for this curse, in parts,
The National Endowment for the Arts." [*Exit*]

WITCHES: . . . distill our brew with earwig venom,
Compound with Amy Fisher's denim,
Teddy's poppers, Willie's toke,
Jonestown punch, Anita's Coke,
Janet Reno's rescue tactics,
Magic Johnson's prophylactics,
G-man's sting and he-man's stench,
Powder'd harlot, Liquid Wench,
Jaws of Jersey City mobster,
Claws of Chappaquiddick lobster
(clutching in its briny clickers
Mary Jo Kopechne's knickers),

THE TRAGEDY OF MACDETH

Possum's blister, maggot's wen,
Susan Estrich estrogen—
Macdeth shall thus the networks charm
To spin the news and spare him harm! [*Exeunt*]

★ RACE AND IQ ... ★ ARE WHITES CLEVERER THAN BLACKS?

Andrew Sullivan

From *The Sunday Times* (London.), October 23, 1994

It all began innocently enough. About a year-and-a-half ago I had lunch with Charles Murray, a friend and regular contributor to the American magazine I edit, the *New Republic*. As might be expected, we talked about what he was working on. I goaded him, as is my wont, to write something for me about it. "There's only one problem," he averred. "It's about IQ and race." I told him not to worry; if he was as careful and as smart as he usually is, it would be worth whatever criticism came his way. And, I casually promised, I'd stick up for him.

Eight months later, Murray gave me an early draft of the book, which he had co-authored with a psychology professor, Richard Herrnstein. I read and re-read it. It wasn't, it turned out, about IQ and race; it was about the role of genetically heritable IQ in exacerbating social inequality in America. But since Murray is almost pathologically honest, he included a section very soberly presented on race and IQ.

The data shocked me; there is an enormous amount of very credible evidence that the mean IQ of Asian Americans is a little higher than that of European Americans, which is considerably higher than that of African Americans. This in itself was news to me. Even more shocking was that I could not find any reputable psychometrician who seriously challenged it. The reasons for these racial differences turn out to be complex, and ultimately mysterious. And in this, there were plenty of reputable psychometricians who differed with Murray.

Murray's theory as laid out in the book, *The Bell Curve,* is that genes probably play some part in it; on Murray's best guess, about 60%. The reasons for this guess are contestable and complicated, which is why the article I finally published ran to about 11,000 words, more than eight times the length of the text you are reading. It is also why I felt it important to accompany the article with criticisms and responses, to show the variety of opinions on this delicate matter.

Eminently reasonable, right? Well, I was in for a shock. What I did not count on was the reaction of my colleagues. Almost unanimously they opposed publication of anything at all; either the Murray and Herrnstein essay, or any responses. I had encountered (not for the first time in my life) the existence of a genuine taboo. Murray's argument cannot be true, my colleagues seemed to say, so it cannot be published. My response was merely: it might be true, so why not publish? As long as there was space for dissent and criticism, the issue of the magazine would serve to further debate, rather than to stifle it.

This, though, was not enough. Tempers flared, insults were hurled; for a while some people would hardly speak to me. One editor sent me a letter accusing me of committing an act of "moral and intellectual evil." Another yelled in my office: "But these guys are Nazis!"

The owner of the magazine and even his family were lobbied to stop publication or alter the essay's format. I myself was pressured not to write an editorial defending publication of the piece, and this was after I had promised to let any staffer at the magazine write a dissenting article in the issue carrying the Murray and Herrnstein essay.

It soon became apparent to me that I was not dealing with an issue in which rational debate was going to hold sway. Still, I gamely asked, what were my colleagues' arguments for suppression? First, a suspicion of the motives of the authors. One of my colleagues described them in print as "repellent," "dishonest" and "creepy." But Herrnstein was, until his recent death, a distinguished professor at Harvard; Murray had written many cogent books and articles, not least for the *Sunday Times* on the issue of the British underclass. Neither is a racist. While one always suspects people with a fascination with race to be prone to dark weirdness, neither author was weirder or darker than many other writers we regularly published. They could be tarred perhaps legitimately by association; the field of psychometrics, especially psychometrics and race, is crammed with crackpots and bigots. Ultimately, though, it seemed to me, Murray and Herrnstein had to be judged on their data and their arguments. How could that happen if their data and arguments were not brought to light?

Others argued that even if Murray and Herrnstein were right, it was wrong to publish them. What, I asked myself, could this possibly mean? One rationale was that the sheer indelicacy of the subject required it to be shielded from allegedly vulnerable African Americans. If, however, this view is not racist, what is? (It is interesting that the black writers I asked to respond to Murray and Herrnstein's essay—a third of the respondents were black—were far less worried about publication than many of the whites.)

A more plausible point was that there could be awful consequences for publishing. This indeed was something that had caused me to anguish: what if the *New Republic* could be used by teachers to ignore black students, or impair students' motivation to learn. But the detailed 24-page debate that I finally put together provided no grist to racists; it showed rather how any crude claims on this subject are phoney. And at some point, a writer or an editor cannot be held responsible for the evil ways in which his material can be used.

Another rationale for suppression was that even to conceive of genetically influenced racial differentials in IQ was racist. But it is clearly a difficult subject, with many contentious nuances. To say that a debate simply cannot take place is to enforce a taboo utterly at odds with free inquiry and this, it turned out, was what was really at issue. the *New Republic*, for good or ill, holds a particular place in American journalism. Other, bigger magazines, *Newsweek* and *Time* for example, and the television media are often nervous of being first in controversy, fearing for their advertising or being hobbled by political correctness. These outlets often wait for the *New Republic* (with its broadly liberal reputation) to give them an excuse to wade into treacherous waters.

My colleagues feared that my decision could actually alter the discussion of this volatile issue in American public life. They were right: *Newsweek* followed four days later with a cover story. *Nightline* ran a special show. An acrimonious public debate is now in full sway.

In retrospect, it has been an interesting journalistic experience. Every society, I now realise, has its taboos, even those that seem as permissive as America's. Journalists are actually the guardians of many taboos. They determine what is said and how; they frame the parameters of public debate. They help sustain the fact that debate in a democracy tends to be less about the truth than about the appearance of truth; not about arguing, but about posturing.

Conservatives do this in several ways: in their preposterous cowardice and silence about class, for example, or about homosexuality. In these areas, they would rather curtail discussion than open it up. But liberals have their taboos, too: on the subjects of race and gender, all sorts of things are simply not contestable; they cannot be said. My liberal colleagues, who rarely lose an opportunity to hail their devotion to free speech, were suddenly making every possible effort to shut somebody up.

This instinct, it turns out, is not a matter of ideology; it is not even a matter of journalism. It is a matter of manners. And in the polite, posturing dinner party that is America's discussion of race, I unwittingly belched.

★ WHAT MY FATHER ★ KNEW

Ruth Wisse

FROM *COMMENTARY,* APRIL 1995

On the morning of June 22, 1940 my mother, my elder brother, and I fled the Romanian city of Czernowitz to join my father in Bucharest. The signal for our departure was a phone call from one of my father's former employees, a certain Boncescu, and it had not been entirely unexpected. Boncescu asked for Father and, when told that he was in the capital on business, instructed my mother to prepare a bag for the children and to take the next train there. She had two hours to pack. We left the house where I was born at 4 Urban Jarnik without good-byes. Years later the neighbors' son described to me how he had come to visit my brother as they had arranged, but found the door bolted, his knock unanswered.

My father was by profession a chemical engineer. In 1934 he had been sent to Czernowitz by his Polish employer to build the first rubber factory in northern Romania, and within a year he had Caurum up and running (as it does to this day), employing between 600 and 900 workers in two or three shifts, producing rubber boots, hospital sheeting, tubing, bouncing balls for children. For his achievement he received a medal from King Carol. It was this medal, along with his skills of persuasion and probably significant bribes, that after two months in Bucharest, and on the condition of no return, finally secured for us the exit visas we needed to leave the country. Since my parents' Polish papers would have doomed us, we traveled across Europe as stateless persons, with Lisbon as the port of departure and Montreal our final destination.

Father plotted our future and our itinerary as carefully as he could. South American papers were the easiest to buy, and given his passion for rubber, he should have taken us to Venezuela. But after six years as a Romanian manufacturer, he said he did not want to live again where there were only two classes—the rich and the poor. He decided to join his brothers who had recently immigrated to Canada.

We took the first leg of our journey by train. A photograph of the four of us at the Acropolis shows what improbable tourists we made, standing impassive in brilliant sunshine with our backs to the glory of Greece, white shoes scuffed in the sand. Athens was the high point of the trip. Through the Mediterranean we cruised by boat, anticipating the dangers at each port of call. At age four, with blond hair, my precocity sharpened by the tension, and speaking German as my mother tongue, I was the one the officials questioned at points of inspection, or if not, I was encouraged to volunteer the answers. In Italian waters, where my father had expected trouble from the fascist militiamen, there was only a perfunctory passenger check on board; at British Gibraltar, smiling soldiers in short khakis did their work so scrupulously that some hapless souls were left ashore.

In the way of such things, the real danger came to us as a complete surprise.

We had reached Lisbon in the middle of September, two weeks before our ship was to sail. Our Canadian visa authorization had arrived—how, is another story—but because our ship would be docking in New York (from where we would take the train to Montreal), we were also required to have transit visas for the United States. Before giving us these documents, the American consul wanted proof of our wealth and our health. Instructing my very short-sighted father to undergo an eye examination, he gave him the name of the local opthamologist. The doctor turned out to be away on holiday, scheduled to return several days after our ship would leave port.

No refugee family is without at least one story of this kind, of the moment their lives hung by a hair. We went back to the consulate and Father explained the situation: could the consul please give him the name of another specialist? The consul could not. Father stressed the importance of this journey for us as prospective Canadian immigrants (not as Jews—the dread word was never spoken), and the value of four trans-Atlantic berths. The consul regretted that he could not change the rules. Then Father lost his head, or else chose to gamble. Grabbing the consul's hand, he pointed it at my brother and me and shouted, "You are a crazy man! Will you throw away the lives of these children? Give me the name of another doctor or I will kill you!"

His English was not strong, nor was he, so I cannot imagine that his words struck fear into the consul's heart. Mother, recalling the scene, said she knew we were finished. But perhaps something in Father's desperation forced the American to recognize him as a man. Without saying a word, he extricated himself from Father's grasp and issued us the visas. Consequently, we were able to leave Lisbon aboard the New Hellas on the second day of Rosh Hashanah, 1940—the same day, 36 years later, that my father died.

Having perused many such accounts of Jewish flight across Europe, my reader is now probably imagining us spared the Nazi death camps. But like the history of our time, our family's history was more complicated than that. It was the Soviets, not the Nazis, we were fleeing—and had we not eluded them, my father and probably we, too, would have expired somewhere in the gulag along with many more victims than were killed in the Germans' crematoria.

As general manager and part owner of Romania's largest rubber factory, my father was the very model of the class enemy. He was also a well-read and intelligent political observer. Monitoring the threats from both ends of Europe, but especially from the East, he had asked the trusted Boncescu to wire immediately if the Russians should cross the border and, anticipating their invasion that summer, had already gone to Bucharest to try to get us exit papers. No one could have known yet of what the Nazis were capable, because despite the virulence of their anti-Semitism, the scale of governmentally-organized killing in Germany was still relatively small.

By contrast, Russia had already registered its trademark on state murder. The kulaks lay forcibly starved by the millions. The purges had set a record in the elimination of elites. Many of my parents' friends who had crossed from Poland into Russia to participate in the great socialist experiment were already known to be dead or missing "in Siberia."

But, of course, the main reason my father knew just what he had to fear from the Communists was that he had once been attracted to Communism himself.

"Your mother would shoot me if she knew I were telling you this, but your father Leibl was a Communist in the 1920's." The woman who favored me with this information in Jerusalem in 1980 had grown up with my mother in that legendary life called "Vilna,"* and had stayed on in Communist Poland after the war. She and her second husband had come to Israel only in 1968, when Europe's most durable ideology claimed Poland anew, making reluctant Zionists of yet another group of Jewish internationalists.

Now that she had settled among the Jews, this woman's Communism rested uncomfortably on her conscience, like a mink coat that becomes embarrassing once public opinion clamors for animal rights. That is to say, she felt obliged to apologize for her political views only out of deference to the scruples of others. Assuming the same held true for my father, she thought it unlikely that he would have risked the scowl of his Americanized children by recounting his political past. But she was wrong: my father's experience with Communism was precisely the sort

---

* See Ruth Wisse's "The Most Beautiful Woman in Vilna," *Commentary,* June 1981.—ED.

of thing he was willing to talk about. What better form of moral instruction than to try to understand the nature of error?

Leibl had been initiated into Communism at its source. The story had begun with an earlier expulsion, this one from Bialystok, Poland, in 1914, when the Germans captured the city. The entire family had fled to Russia, where my grandfather and his two elder sons tried to continue the family business by starting up a small textile mill near Moscow while his wife and their three younger children—Leibl being the littlest— sought safety in Saratov on the Volga. In the absence of a Jewish *heder*, Leibl was sent to the local school.

Only in 1917, after the February revolution, was the family reunited in Moscow, and there they reaped the fruits of liberty. The factory my grandfather had started in the nearby town of Pavlovski Passad, employing Russian workers, produced cloth that he could now sell legally in the city, and within a short time he had amassed enough capital to consider expanding the business. Under the czar, Jews had been prevented by discriminatory laws from living in Moscow, but now Grandfather could legally rent a room for his family, legally send his children to school, and legally instruct his youngest son for his bar mitzvah.

But by the time Leibl came to read his portion of the Torah in the small synagogue and to taste his reward of brandy and cake, there had occurred a second revolution. Lenin had replaced the young parliament with a dictatorship of the proletariat and set up the CHEKA, the Extraordinary Commission for the Struggle Against Counterrevolution and Sabotage, or political police, with orders to shoot "speculators" on sight. The press, the schools, the law were nationalized, along with the banks and industries.

The Soviets confiscated Grandfather's business and his savings without any right of appeal; he was told he could stay on as the state's temporary manager. Trying to recoup some of his losses by selling a fraction of the production on the black market, he eluded the CHEKA for three years, once daring to drive a wagon of his goods through the Moscow streets.

While Grandfather tried to exercise his freedom, his youngest son fell in thrall. The year of his bar mitzvah, 1918, Leibl stood among thousands listening to Leon Trotsky (né Bronstein) in Red Square. As between the two Jewish lawgivers, he much admired the perfect orator of Moscow over the all-too-human stammerer of Sinai. By the time the family returned to Poland, he had decided to claim his independence. Refusing to study in a yeshiva, he attended the Polish high school in a neighboring town, then passed the entrance exams for Stephen Bathory University in Vilna. He supported himself through tutoring, and performed prodigious feats of memory. Once, during a set of final examinations in mathematics, he pointed out an error in the test, and after being threatened with expulsion, was vindicated when a supervisor came in to report the mistake.

How shall I characterize Leibl's idealism during his student days in Vilna? Idealism was then as plentiful as food was scarce. With the release of moral energies that Judaism had historically tried to discipline, idealism gushed from Jewish youth as from a thawing mountain, spilling down into many rivers and streams. Historians try to sort out the Communists from the nationalists, the Hebraists from the Yiddishists, the Bundists from the Labor Zionists, the anti-Zionist Orthodox Agudah from the pro-Zionist Orthodox Mizrahi; but, swept up by the yearning for a better world, the young people who had come of age during the war were not always on Sunday what they had been before the latest rally on Saturday.

Leibl, for instance, originally wanted to study agriculture because he had decided to become a farmer in Palestine. When he learned that the university would not accept Jews into agriculture, he settled for chemistry (like Chaim Weizmann). His colleagues in the chemistry lab found him a room in the house of Anna Vladimirova Rosenthal, Vilna's inspiring Bundist leader, for whom Yiddish was a sacred trust but whose Jewish nationalism was thoroughly anti-Zionist.

But it was the Communists who held the moral edge over all the other political groups. Outlawed under Poland's Pilsudski regime, they were the only ones who had to function clandestinely, thus arousing sympathy as well as respect. By contrast, the Zionists who promised to take Jews out of Poland to Palestine seemed at times to be working hand in hand with the Polish nationalist government, and their popularity among some of the wealthier and religious Jews of the city almost lent them a bourgeois respectability.

Leibl put study ahead of politics, but he developed a reputation for foolhardy courage. He brought food to political prisoners, pretending to be their relative. One night, walking with his cousin, he refused the orders of some drunken Endecs, Polish nationalists, to get off the sidewalk, and when one of them brandished a pistol, Leibl tore open his shirt and cried, "Go ahead, shoot!" The Endec was with difficulty restrained by his friends.

The high point of Leibl's political activism came at the request of Chaim S., a childhood friend from Bialystok and an affiliated Communist who planned to slip from Poland into Russia on a party mission carrying 200 rubles in cash. Leibl helped him raise the required sum, and organized the illegal crossing. The two boys hired an experienced border-guide, giving him a down payment and promising the rest upon his return to Vilna with a prearranged password that Chaim would give him once he was safe on the other side. The friends mischievously agreed on the word *k'mat,* Hebrew and Yiddish for "almost"—but, when misspelled, an acronym for the Yiddish *kush mir in tukhes,* or kiss my ass.

Their plan succeeded, up to a point. The guide delivered passenger and password and was paid in full, but Chaim was never heard from again. According to rumor, he had been seized as a Polish spy and deported into the Russian interior. For years afterward, Chaim's mother in Bialystok would hound my grandparents, threatening to denounce Leibl to the authorities, holding their son responsible for her son's death. Grandfather, who was by then completely blind, took to sleeping with a wad of rubles under his pillow for the moment he would have to buy off an arresting policeman. He dubbed Leibl "Fishke the Red," after the beggar-hero of the Yiddish romance *Fishke the Lame* whose tender sympathies exceed his practical abilities. Since Leibl had in fact developed a limp, thought to be caused by rheumatoid arthritis, the epithet exposed the political idealist as an incipient cripple in more than one respect.

To the extent that Leibl had ever "been a Communist," he soon ceased to be one. Trotsky's aura may not have faded all at once, but neither did that non-Jewish Jew become my father's hero. Trotsky's prosecution of revolutionary terror against the rebellious sailors of Kronstadt and other real and imagined enemies weighed on my father's conscience, since he felt he had delivered his friend Chaim into the hands of the bloody regime. Until he left Vilna in 1929 to take his first job as a junior engineer, Leibl warned his Communist friends against slipping into Russia, as many were doing to escape local conditions and in expectation of a finer life. He began to understand the Revolution through its consequences, Marxism through Trotsky's enforcement of it.

But unlike his earlier boyish exchange of Moses for Marx, the collapse of his faith in Communism left his moral yearnings unchanneled. The search for truth that brought him such satisfaction in the laboratory had no parallel in politics. His questions could never be answered: must idealism, in its haste to perfect the species, become a murderous torrent that sweeps human beings away? If a man's good intentions bring evil consequences, is he still entitled to claim innocence? Might the Jews have been right after all to limit the human tendency to wickedness through a strict religious regimen, before aspiring to usher in a messianic age?

The ascetic habits Leibl had developed as a self-supporting student made him stricter than his father when it came to self-imposed discipline, but he lacked the advantage of his father's Sabbath days, which is to say the pleasure his father took in obeying God's law. In the years that I best remember him, my father's Sabbath mornings in Montreal were spent writing checks to charities, cultural projects, and individuals he helped to support. This might seem a decent substitute for the Jewish commandment of *tsedakah,* except that the checkbook does not sing out like a congregation of living Jews when a man is called up to the Torah to pledge his charity aloud.

Father's life in Canada defied the dichotomies of success and failure, rich and poor. What do you call a man who forfeits the profession he loves? From the moment he arrived as a new immigrant, Leibl, now also Leo, tried to find work as an engineer in the Canadian rubber industry; but as it was not yet hiring Jews, he went to work instead in the textile factory his family had bought in Huntingdon, Quebec, about 60 miles south of Montreal.

He did not like textile production as he had adored experimenting with rubber, and having once managed a factory he himself had built, he could not have relished his new job as a small shareholder in the family business. Mother, who took it upon herself to voice his unspoken thoughts, always referred to his work as "slaving for his brothers." He spent most of the week at the mill, staying overnight in a room he shared with one of his brothers at the Huntingdon Chateau. This grand hotel had been built during Prohibition as a whiskey hole for thirsty Americans. Its empty grandeur gave a man the sense that they had both seen better times.

Leo was a good manager and a good negotiator. The mill turned a profit, and as long as my father represented management, there was never a strike. Back in the city, he brought the same negotiating skills to the board of the Jewish day school that his children attended. My father is credited with having led the fight for expanding this school to the upper grades, in appreciation of which the library of Bialik High sports on its wall his name and a picture of him smiling.

As the factory prospered, we moved in 1950 into a splendid old house where each of us (by then) four children had his own bedroom, with a sun porch and basement apartment to spare. Mother used the magnificent living room for literary receptions in support of Yiddish culture. Invitations to her soirees required the purchase of a recent Yiddish book by a local writer, selections from which the author would read as the evening's entertainment. It goes without saying that Father's subsidy had helped to pay the publisher.

And politics? By the end of the war, Communism should have lain buried along with fascism in their respective ruins. Certainly, where we lived in Montreal, the atrocities of the Soviet system were no secret. Many of the refugees who joined us in Montreal had spent the war in Russia; they spoke of Soviet commissars and victims, and of some of the former who had become some of the latter. A number of our acquaintances, sympathizers of the Jewish Bund, continued to mourn the execution by the Soviets of their beloved leaders, Henryk Erlich and Victor Alter, despite many appeals from socialists around the world.

In 1945, Igor Gouzenko, a clerk in the Soviet embassy in Ottawa, gave the Canadian government abundant evidence of Soviet spy rings operating right under its nose. Whether or not his disclosures triggered the cold war, as some historians think, they did lead to the conviction for treason of Fred Rose, a Communist member of the Canadian parliament from the largely Jewish district of Montreal-Cartier. Eventually deported to Poland, Rose did not become a martyr like the executed Rosenbergs in the United States; in particular, having betrayed his Montreal constituents as well as his country, he aroused little sympathy on the Jewish street.

I think I know what people mean when they describe the 1950s as a decade of complacency, lacking in idealism. They mean that the Left in general, and Communism in particular, were losing influence. At the beginning of the decade, in Korea, Communism suffered its first major defeat, challenging the belief that its expansion was historically determined and inevitable. Khrushchev's revelations at the 20th Soviet Communist party conference that under Stalin the dictatorship of the proletariat had been the dictatorship of a tyrant were followed almost immediately by the march of Soviet troops into Hungary, crushing hopes for the promised thaw in Russian politics. Memoirs seeped into the West, any one of which (try Gustav Herling's 1951 *A World Apart*) could have condemned an empire.

Yet even my father felt uncomfortable invoking "fascists and Communists" in a single phrase. He wanted to distinguish between an ideology of power that had realized itself in totalitarianism and (what he saw as) a positive ideology that had deteriorated into totalitarianism. I think he clung to this distinction less for the sake of his own battered beliefs than for the martyred Rosa Luxemburg, Chaim S., and many other friends who had seemed to him pure of heart. He would have liked to condemn the historical consequences of Communism without damning splendid men and women who sacrificed their lives to it. He was not yet ready to give "idealism" a bad name.

Tenderness for the failed ideology was far more complicated within regular party circles. There was no counterpart north of the American border for the investigative mania of Senator Joseph McCarthy, and so Canadian Communists and fellow travelers could not relish a sense of victimization as a substitute for confronting their political sins. Shortly after the death of Stalin, Montreal's United Jewish People's Order (UJPO), the Jewish Communist organization, faced a crisis when one of its leaders traveled to Moscow to see for himself why so many acquaintances had not been heard from; on his return he confirmed that most of the Soviet Jewish intelligentsia had been murdered. Ironically, it had been the wartime visit to Canada of the Soviet theater director Solomon Mikhoels and the Yiddish Communist poet Itsik Feffer that had allowed UJPO to claim the moral high ground in the "united struggle against fascism." Stalin's execution of these men could not be written off as yet another necessary sacrifice on the road to socialism.

Yet neither could the UJPO's members easily disband an organization that had claimed all their loyalties and, in providing for their social needs, defined the circle of their friends. To keep the face of Communism smiling, the organization now adopted the kind of cultural programming that had characterized the Popular Front of the 1930s. It threw its energies into folk music. Long before rock impresarios took to marketing their clients as ambassadors of international good will, some of my Communist friends organized songfests, hootenannies, and festivals of youth, where by joining your voice to tens or hundreds of others you were invited to step into the great Brotherhood of Man.

When I was at college, it was a little galling to realize that I would never hear anyone like Trotsky, never meet anyone like Anna Vladimirova Rosenthal, never have to sleep on straw sacking as my father had done.

Before I learned the word, I considered myself an epigone, descendant of a generation whose deprivation had been so much greater than mine that I could never test myself against the same standard of adversity. I would have been embarrassed to mention to my father the toothless Communism I discovered through folk music, and I was a little embarrassed myself to join the Folk Music Club that replaced the earlier Labor Progressive Party Club at McGill University. Still, I, like so many of my generation, was eager to experience at least some of the afterglow of that great revolutionary idealism that was said to have illumined our century.

In 1949, while on his way to Israel to work on a kibbutz, my brother had picked up a copy of *Youth Sings*, published that summer by the International Union of Students to coincide with the World Festival of Youth and Students in Budapest. When I took up the guitar, this was the hymnal I used to practice my chords. The book's preface, in vintage CP style, was irresistibly phony:

> There is no more pleasant or inspiring way in which to express friendship, international solidarity, and understanding, the deepest and most joyous feelings of young people, than through song. Folk songs, songs of work, student songs, songs of struggle, expressing the finest and best from the national culture of dozens of countries will . . . help to ensure that the spirit of the festival is carried to all the corners of the earth.

Only Pete Seeger ever recited such lines with conviction. Still, the knowledge that one is being manipulated by propaganda never prevented anyone from falling prey to it. Passionate youngsters had composed these songs on their way to creating a perfect world, or, as in Spain, on their way to defeating the black beast of fascism. Singing their music joined us to their faith in an unmediated bond of exaltation. Indeed, their faith was brighter than anything we ourselves had been offered, no one having taught us to pray or to sing on behalf of any other ultimate cause. The songs on those pages, some printed in the Cyrillic alphabet, united us to the "Youth of the World," a more potent abstraction than "God of Our Fathers."

Britain:
    The people's flag is deepest red
    It shrouded oft our martyr'd dead,
    And ere their limbs grew stiff and cold
    Their hearts blood dyed its every fold.
    Then raise the scarlet standard high
    Within its shade we'll live and die!
    Though cowards flinch and traitors sneer,
    We'll keep the red flag flying here!

Germany:
    Spanish heavens spread their brilliant starlight
    High above our trenches in the plain;
    From the distance morning comes to greet us,
    Calling us to battle once again.
    Far off is our land,
    Yet ready we stand.
    We're fighting and winning for you,
    Freiheit!

Ireland:
    Come Workers sing a rebel song,
    A song of love and hate;
    Of love unto the lowly
    And of hatred to the great.
    The great who trod our fathers down,
    Who steal our children's bread.
    Whose hands of greed are stretched to rob
    The living and the dead.

Spain:
    Viva la Quince Brigada
    Rumbala, rumbala, rumbala

WHAT MY FATHER KNEW

Viva la Quince Brigada,
Rumbala, rumbala, rumbala.
Que seha cubierto de gloria
Ay Carmela, Ay Carmela . . .

USSR:
Through the winter's cold and famine,
From the fields and from the towns;
At the call of Comrade Lenin
There arose the Partisans.
Battle-scarred and faded banners
Fluttered bravely on before;
But far deeper was the crimson
Of the recent wounds they bore.

United States of America:
Gwine to lay down my sword and shield
Down by the riverside,
Down by the riverside
Down by the riverside.
Gwine to study war no more.

Among the questions that did not occur to us to ask at the time: Why should Russians be drenched in fighters' blood even as Americans were swearing off war? Why did Russians sing patriotically of "Moscow" and "Motherland" while Americans rejoiced in "Hallelujah, I'm a Bum" and rehearsed the sins of Jim Crow? How strange that the most powerful message of all—"Freedom!"—should be coming to us in German, while Canadians warbled "L'Alouette" and amused themselves with "Nous nous amusons tous, tous, tous, / Nous nous amusons tous."

We did not think ourselves naive. We made fun of some of the cloying phrases as we sang them, mimicking foreign accents, composing our own parodies. All the same, when I plucked my guitar at the folk-music club, or sang along to my Folkways records, I could have sworn that the banks of my country were made of marble with a guard at every door, and the vaults stuffed with silver that the workers sweated for. In defying my manufacturer-father, I began to feel like my revolutionary father's daughter.

In his own way, it was my father who rescued me from this sentimental Communism, just as he had saved my life once before.

One day in my final year of college we were sitting together in the living room, with time to spare before the arrival of guests. I think the family was gathering that evening in celebration of Hanukkah. The snow had been falling for hours, and apart from vague concern for the safety of our visitors in their cars, it brought me an uncommon feeling of security. My mother would soon seat herself at the piano, and sing her favorite medley of winter songs: "Un do in heym iz freylakh reyn / on kelt fargessen mir." Just as the lyrics said, our home was joyously clean, the cold banished from our minds. I was happy to be alone with my father.

The doorbell rang, too early to be guests. Father and I both went to answer it. At the door stood a man with a shovel. He was not one of those professionals with a truck and a plow, but a man on foot, in a worn windbreaker and wool cap, with weary eyes. He asked my father if he could clear our path for $1.50.

The path needed clearing. The professional with the plow had come and gone several hours earlier. In fact, I had been thinking that I ought to go out and do the job myself, but had kept putting it off because it was so sweet inside. Now I was sorry. I prayed that my father would simply hand this man his $1.50, saying, "That's all right, my friend. We'll manage the job ourselves." But Father accepted the man's offer, told him to ring the bell when he was through, and closed the door behind him.

When we returned to the living room, everything had changed. I could hear the sound of the shovel, like a fist on my conscience, striking blow after blow. Out there was a poor man working, and here, over-privileged, sat I inside. I wanted to protest; I would happily change places and do the work in the man's stead. I was angry at the unspoken accusation being leveled against me, and said to my father that he ought to have given the man the money, and let me shovel the walk.

Father looked genuinely surprised. "What does it have to do with you? If a man asks for work, and I have the work to give him, he is lucky and so am I. If he sets a reasonable price on his work, I pay him what he earns." That put an end to our conversation, but not to the questions it raised for me. Why should I have put my guilt ahead of another man's pride? Why did I prefer my father's charity to the thought of him as an employer? Was it compassion for the shoveler that made me want to fob him off with a donation, or tender feelings or myself? Wasn't it Father's greatest achievement to have given employment to so many workers over a lifetime?

It is hard to negotiate the inequalities that—next to the common fate that awaits us all—are the most characteristic feature of the human condition. Our passion for equality may be so great that we cannot bear to employ a man, lest it remind us of the inequality that remains whether we employ him or not. My father, who had known inequality from both sides, was not afraid of the responsibility of being someone's boss. As for me, I would soon enough look for shelter in the academy, where someone else hires, someone else fires, and in the still air of delightful study, the artifice of idealism can be kept alive.

★ THE UNFLAPPABLES ★

Tucker Carlson

FROM *WEEKLY STANDARD*, DECEMBER 25, 1995

Most people get annoyed when salesmen call during dinner. Not at my house. We love it. A call from somebody hawking burial plots or new long-distance service may interrupt the meal, but it also gives us a chance to play Scare the Solicitor, my family's favorite parlor game. The object is to say something so disturbing, so bizarre, to a telemarketer that he'll never call again, maybe even give up phone sales for good. It's harder than it sounds.

"Hi, Mr. Carlson, this is Brandon Mink, from Merrill Lynch."

"Hi." (Voice sounds kind of familiar. Do I know this guy?)

"Mr. Carlson, if you have a second, I'd like to talk to you about some important investment opportunities."

"Well, to tell you the truth, Brandon, I can't. I'm kind of busy. I'm having my other leg amputated in the morning. Got to pack for the hospital."

(Pause. Nervous chuckle.) "You're kidding, right?"

"Unfortunately not." (Did he just ask me if I was *kidding?*) "Had the other one taken off last year. Terrible experience. Just when I was getting used to one prosthesis, they're getting me another. I'm not looking forward to it."

"Wow. Sorry. Well, listen, would you have time to talk when you get out?"

"Actually, Brandon, I'm going out of town after I leave the hospital. Headed up to Minnesota for a couple of months. Going to get some experimental therapy, see if I'll ever walk again. I won't be back till March."

"Hmm. Okay. Well, maybe I could call you then. Will you be at this number?"

Sound callous? Not by the standards of the people who call my house. (Though, to be fair, Brandon from Merrill Lynch did write a follow-up note a few days later. "If your spirits stay high," he wrote in ballpoint at the bottom of the investment pitch, "you'll never be low.")

Just the other night, Sherri from Rollins Protective Services dialed up to see if I wanted to buy some fantastically expensive alarm system. So I told her I was blind.

"Legally blind?" she asked.

"Oh, totally blind," I said. "I was young, a chemistry set blew up in my face."

From across the room my wife grimaced, as if to say I was going too far. Which I was, but then so was Sherri.

"Well, we have a model for the visually impaired," Sherri offered hopefully. "It doesn't have Braille, but the buttons are raised. Alarms are especially important for the handicapped." She didn't miss a beat. "If your house caught fire, the alarm would wake you up and the fire department would come and lead you outside."

She almost had me. "I'm not sure," I said. "I have this terrible drinking problem. I don't think I'd wake up even if the alarm went off."

"Well," she countered, "the firemen would just carry you out."

Clearly nothing was going to deter this woman. Finally, in a desperate move, I slammed the handset against the wall, made a yelping sound and muttered something about hitting my head on a kitchen cabinet. Got to go, I said.

But she ignored me. "Could I at least come over and show it to you?" she pleaded.

"Show it to me?" I harrumphed with what was rapidly becoming real indignation. "I'm blind!"

Over the years, I've tried just about every disease and physical deformity I could think of on phone solicitors, the whole gamut from kidney dialysis and advanced melanoma to more esoteric maladies like lupus and Hansen's Disease. When Greenpeace canvassers would show up at our door begging for money, I'd stare at them in bovine incomprehension without saying a word. Taking their clipboard, I'd write, "I am a deaf-mute" in big, scrawly letters and keep staring. Usually, they'd get uncomfortable and leave quickly (though one patient volunteer spent 10 minutes trying to explain acid rain to me in hand gestures).

But all of these were just short-term solutions. What I really needed was something to scare them off for good, some way to get blacklisted by phone salesmen. By the time Citibank called last summer hoping to hook me on a new credit bargain, I thought I had it all figured out.

"Would you like to take advantage of our new Credit Value Plus Voucher Savings Plan today?" the woman asked.

"Of course, I'd love to," I said. "But I don't know if I should. My future's kind of up in the air at this point. I'd better wait to find out what happens with my appeal."

"Your appeal?"

"Yeah, I'm out on bond right now. Maybe you read about it—I killed three people in a drug-related murder spree a couple of years ago. I'm out now trying to beat the charges. And it's expensive. You wouldn't believe what lawyers cost. So I really don't think I should take advantage of the offer till I win my case."

"I know you're innocent," she said perkily.

"I'm not. I definitely did it. But I'll probably get off anyway. This is America."

"Good luck!" she said.

★ THE END ★
OF THE AFFAIR

Erich Eichman

FROM *THE NEW CRITERION*, DECEMBER 1996

Earlier this year, famously, the physicist and political leftist Alan Sokal submitted a fully footnoted, jargon-filled essay of pure nonsense to the editors of the academic journal *Social Text*, arguing that physical reality was merely a social construct. He didn't believe a word of it, but he was trying to make a point. The editors published the essay, Mr. Sokal announced his hoax, and all hell broke loose.

For many, the hoax did in fact reveal—as Mr. Sokal intended—the vacuousness of academic theory and the absurd incoherence of the language in which it is perpetrated. For others, however, the hoax was an unforgivable act of disloyalty that undermined a political project of great importance, especially in the university: the effort to "interrogate" knowledge and "unmask" the hidden power relations that determine the bourgeois definition of the "truth." This is what academic theory—especially the kind practiced by *Social Text*—claims to be doing much of the time.

Members of both camps showed up at New York University's Meyer Hall on Wednesday evening, October 30, to witness a panel discussion—hosted by NYU's journalism department—entitled "After the Media Event: Politics, Culture & the Social Text Affair." Among the participants were Alan Sokal himself and Andrew Ross, one of the editors of *Social*

Text and by far the most glamorous "cultural studies" professor in the entire universe. Not surprisingly, the auditorium was filled to overflowing. In academic terms, this was a Big Deal.

The evening's moderator was Jay Rosen, a teacher of journalism at NYU, who made it clear from the outset that "After the Media Event" was to be a purely intramural discussion, a "family affair" concerned with the "civic health of the Left." (Given the university venue, this exclusion of rightward views was easily enforced.) Unafraid of cliché, Mr. Rosen argued that it was time to get past the media hullabaloo and "put a different frame around the event," to progress "toward a deeper understanding," to go "into depth about larger issues," to "break new ground"—even to "move the discussion forward." (It somehow does not come as a surprise that Mr. Rosen is an editor at the treacly monthly magazine *Tikkun*.) Toward this end, he announced that, despite the contentiousness of the subject, the panel discussion was "an inquiry, not an inquisition." No one, in short, was to be "on trial."

Implicitly, though, both Mr. Ross and Mr. Sokal were on trial, accused by different leftist family factions of betraying either the Enlightenment or the Revolution or both. Mr. Ross was allowed to defend himself first. This he did in a brief talk delivered in a faintly arch style that seemed to amuse his fans in the audience, to judge by the chortling that greeted even his woollier pronouncements.

It should be said that Mr. Ross's sentences had a certain decentered quality that often made it difficult for the uninitiated to grasp exactly what he was trying to say. The gist was that *Social Text* had nothing to apologize for. *Lingua Franca,* the magazine that had revealed Mr. Sokal's hoax, had perpetrated a "yellow media exposé." The hoax was part of a backlash—on the Left—against "feminism, multiculturalism, and the queer renascence." Mr. Sokal's "needlessly polarizing" stunt in no way delegitimized *Social Text* or its content. Because the Enlightenment had been used to support racism and sexism, it was right to subject it to a critique, which is what *Social Text* had been doing in its notorious Sokal issue. Above all, Mr. Ross made it clear, scientific knowledge was still to be considered "like all other forms of knowledge": that is to say, it was not safe from a postmodern interrogation that would question its "assumptions about universality." He did concede that "language"—that is, the obscurantist language of academic theory—"is a serious problem." "I am no dissenter," he said, "from this complaint." But, he added, "I am not going to sign up for an evangelical clean-up squad." In a final flourish of leftist family values, he argued that "guilt-tripping" and "false polarities" would not help in the fight against economic injustice. All this was greeted with sustained applause, a prelude to Alan Sokal's remarks. Now, it needs to be said that there is a certain aspect of theater to even academic events: Mr. Ross, with his bracelets, earring, loose white shirt and perfectly trimmed, longish black hair, looked as if he had stepped out of a casually hip advertisement in Details magazine. Mr. Sokal, on the other hand, lacked only a pocket protector and a slide rule to fit central casting's image of a clean-cut science geek. In this respect, he was at a disadvantage—given the atmosphere of edgy postmodern subversion emanating from various sectors of the crowded auditorium—but only in this respect.

Mr. Sokal's main argument-true to its theme-was logically structured and conceptually coherent. Truth, he said, was a matter of reason, objectivity, and evidence. The purpose of his *Social Text* hoax was to reveal the sloppy thinking that had infected certain elements of the Left under the influence of postmodern theory. Only by reasoned argument, he felt, could the Left defeat the demagoguery and superstition of its enemies. The "hypersubjectivity" of postmodern theory—which emphasizes group identities-merely "plays into the hands of anti-rationalists" by trumpeting "local knowledges" at the expense of universal truths. Mr. Sokal proudly declared himself a "leftist and a feminist" and thus especially troubled by trends that might "divert us from a leftist social critique."

At this point, Mr. Sokal did something very clever: he referred to a real-world controversy that might demonstrate his point. This startling digression had a momentarily tonic effect, although it caused no end of trouble later on. He cited a recent *New York Times* story about the war of words between archeologists and Native American creationists over the right to study various prehistoric skeletons found on Native American grounds out west. Archeologists almost universally believe that the peoples of North America came here from Asia, across the Bering Strait, as skeletal remains confirm. Tribal creationists, however, believe that their people literally sprang from the ground, and they wish to bury the skeletons before the scientists can use them to advance a "falsehood."

For Mr. Sokal, this controversy showed the foolishness of "local knowledge." Clearly reason, objectivity, and evidence were on the side of the archeologists, and yet one man cited in the article—a nonlocal, empathetic British archeologist, in fact—had maintained that the Zuni world view (the Zunis reside in Arizona, where some of the disputed skeletons can be found) was "just as valid" as that of the archeologists. But how could it be? As Mr. Sokal was at pains to point out, these warring explanations of human origins were mutually exclusive: they could both be wrong, but they could not both be right. Broadly speaking, he said, the principles of the scientific method (emphasizing evidence logically studied) were the best way of adjudicating the matter. The postmodern Left—obsessed with group identities—forgets this at its peril, Mr. Sokal warned. He was especially horrified when a hostile article in Tikkun on the hoax (its author was not Mr. Rosen) included the statement that "truth can be another source of oppression." Mr. Sokal clearly thought this was the wrong road for the Left to travel. His remarks were greeted with respectful applause.

Two other panelists had their say before the free-form questioning began. Ellen Willis, a professor of journalism at NYU and a longtime *Village Voice* contributor, delivered an even-handed, anguished disquisition on the "tensions and weaknesses of the Left" that had been revealed by the Sokal hoax. She was not really willing to condemn the nonsense in Social Text and journals like it—and in fact congratulated postmodern theory for opposing Marxist conceptions of class that overlooked culture—but she was not at all happy with the insularity and hermeticism that now were so much in evidence, and she lamented the "overvaluation of particular identities." The Left, she said with a certain weariness, "is in dismal shape right now" and "paralyzed in the face of all-out class war by global capital."

Ms. Willis was followed by Stanley Aronowitz, a professor at City

University of New York and one of the founding editors of *Social Text,* although apparently he did not participate in the decision to publish the Sokal piece. Mr. Aronowitz is not a thin or a shy man, and much of what he said, although incomprehensible, was refreshingly entertaining simply because it was delivered with such clownish brio. He reminded those who did not know that *Social Text* had been founded seventeen years before to contribute to the "renovation" of the "Marxist project." And "that is still what it is about." He alluded to the Frankfurt School and condemned the media's characterizations of *Social Text* (including, later, "the affair Kimball," that is, the article in this magazine by its managing editor for June 1996). He went on to declare the real issue to be "scientificity" and rambled a bit through postmodern theory before announcing: "We are not relativists."

The truth of this last statement was not entirely evident in the discussion that followed. As Mr. Aronowitz's talk dissolved into commentary by other panelists—Mr. Ross reasserted at one point that "science is not a neutral discourse" and Mr. Aronowitz seconded the idea—the moderator, Mr. Rosen, tried to bring things back down to earth. This was a mistake.

For Mr. Rosen, the *Social Text* hoax was principally about one thing: "Are there any intellectual standards in this corner of the Left?" The bluntness of the question and the allusion to standards set off a bout of hissing from the audience. After a certain amount of to-and-fro, in which Mr. Ross joked about how standards are supposedly always "falling," never "rising" (this was considered hilarious by his claque), Mr. Rosen asked his question about standards again. Mr. Ross responded, with mild heat, that "standards are about ethics," which require that you don't "practice deception." Mr. Sokal recognized this as a jab at his hoax and parried it by pointing out that the editors of *Social Text* had been free to judge the content of his article quite apart from whether he believed it himself, which was irrelevant. So neatly did he make this point that he was rewarded with a brief round of applause. The adulation was short-lived.

In the course of the audience questioning—some of it sensible, most of it not—someone asked Mr. Sokal "how you know truth when you see it." He responded by returning to the archeologists' troubles with the Zuni creationists. He repeated the simple law of contradiction (mutually exclusive ideas can't both be right) and appealed again to evidence and logic. Then a student in the back, with real heat, thundered: "On whose authority should we be forced to answer the question?"

It is difficult to convey how swiftly this query derailed the evening. The questioner angrily went on to complain that the choice required by Mr. Sokal's logic "presented a double bind," for only "particularisms offer resistance to the epistemic violence you're proposing!" At this point there was much appreciative murmuring from the crowd and a few huzzahs of assent.

For Mr. Sokal and Mr. Rosen, though, all this was completely baffling. Mr. Sokal recited the law of contradiction again and restated the need to rule from evidence, which seemed so obvious to him, but he was rewarded for his pains by guffaws from the knowing theory fans in the audience, who clearly considered him blinkered in exactly the way a logocentric hegemonist might be. He finally gave up. "I don't understand your question." Mr. Rosen didn't either. First he couldn't remember the name of the Native American tribe being discussed ("Who are these people again?") and then he naïvely asserted: "Isn't the question, Where do these people come from?" The exasperation of the audience was palpable: It certainly was not!

It was left to Stanley Aronowitz to explain, rather condescendingly, that the inquisitor had raised a "metatheoretical question." (Sighs of relief all round.) In short, the man was asking whether "the framing itself is subject to interrogation." This was considered helpful, and the questioning went on, but the raw collision of theory and reason had finally struck a jarring note. Family etiquette had been breached, and things could not be the same. Todd Gitlin, another NYU professor of journalism, stood up to say a few words on behalf of intellectual standards, which would allow the Left to prove, for instance, that "Charles Murray is a fraud." But the Zunis reappeared when Andrew Ross, inspired by another question and response, turned to Mr. Sokal to say "you cannot dismiss Zuni thinking as prejudice." (It's odd how categorical a category-busting theorist can be.) Another person innocently asked Mr. Ross how one could defend the Zuni world view and not at the same time disarm oneself for combating Jerry Falwell and other Christian fundamentalists who have their own creationist ideas.

This was an obvious and sensible question. A lesser man, when faced with the task of answering it, might have stumbled over his own inconsistencies and beat a retreat. But Andrew Ross is not a famous cultural theorist for nothing. He simply "reframed" the question. He pointed out that it sadly ignored "the inequality of power relations between the two groups" (Zuni, fundamentalist Christian). He then asked Mr. Sokal why he was putting Native Americans "on trial" with his archeology example, since they were the most "screwed over" and "marginalized" group in American history. "That is a very political choice," he said. Fortunately, this sally inspired a certain amount of groaning and hissing from the audience, although probably some percentage of it was aimed at the purblind Mr. Sokal for having misguidedly questioned the Zuni way of knowledge in the first place.

The long evening ended with an editor of *October* magazine standing to declare to the editors of *Social Text,* empathetically, "that she knew what it was to be attacked by Roger Kimball." She then proceeded to speak in a roundabout way of a "crisis in language," which was "symptomatic of a larger crisis." Stanley Aronowitz seemed to agree: "We lack the capacity to understand one another." To Mr. Sokal he magnanimously said: "You've gone far to begin the discussion." And then, in the only direct admission of error in the entire evening, he declared: "Look, *Social Text* fucked up. . . . But the project of *Social Text* is not a fucked-up project!"

I suspect that Mr. Sokal would say that this is another case where the laws of logic might lead one to a different conclusion. If the first statement is true (and it is), then the second statement cannot also be true (and it isn't).

★ WHY A WOMAN CAN'T ★ BE MORE LIKE A MAN

Harvey Mansfield

FROM *THE WALL STREET JOURNAL*, NOVEMBER 3, 1997
Everyone noticed that last month's Promise Keepers rally in Washington, like the Million Man March before it, was for men only. But the event prompted surprisingly little reflection on the state of manliness in our culture. Even Patricia Ireland of the National Organization for Women saved most of her indignation for the supposed religious intrusion into politics. (The feminist slogan "The personal is political" doesn't apply to Christians.)

The Promise Keepers themselves turned the other cheek to Ms. Ireland. They made no attack on feminism and no appeal to manliness. Any vague talk of women submitting to men came from the Bible, they explained, not from us men. The Promise Keepers also did some unmanly things: public confession, weeping, holding hands, seeking support and overemphasizing chastity. Their pronouncements smelled of pop psychology, the embodiment of everything unmanly in our society.

On the other hand, they did take responsibility for their family duties and promised to keep their promises. You might think that one promise is enough, and that there's something suspicious about a second promise to keep the first one. But manly men need to boast a little, and one shouldn't underestimate the difficulty of keeping marital promises these days, when men hear so much about the right to choose. On the whole, then, the Promise Keepers are doing manly things even if they do not say so.

Feminists, for their part, are not really opposed to manliness. What they dislike about men is their exclusivity. Betty Friedan's seminal book, *The Feminine Mystique* (1963), was an attack on femininity, not on manliness. It blamed men for foisting the feminine mystique on women, for getting them to believe that it is better to seem frail, dumb, and submissive. The implication is that it's better for women to be strong, smart, and aggressive—like men.

Yet feminists have feminized America without intending to do so. While claiming the right of equal access to jobs, they have changed the atmosphere of the workplace. How can women have equal access, they demanded, if they are not made to feel as comfortable as men are while working? Thus "sexual harassment" was born, and certain manly excesses come under severe bureaucratic scrutiny.

Nowhere is feminization more obvious than in the military, where feminism faces its ultimate challenge: Are women up to the demands of the most manly occupation there is? The experiment underway in the U.S. military belongs in a comedy by Aristophanes. Instead we have a grim struggle of ideology against nature in which no one is allowed to laugh at the ridiculous, much less state the obvious—that women are not cut out for war. Even if we could "socially construct" women to grow bigger and tougher, would we really want both sexes going off to war? Who would stay at home for the joys of peace?

With women in the military, two bad things are happening at the same time. The military is made more sensitive and less manly, and manliness is set free from the counterweight of feminine sentiment and feminine reason. The military protects the country, as a husband or father protects his family. When a man takes responsibility for others, it is a manifestation of his protective nature.

The protective element of manliness is endangered by women having equal access to jobs outside the home. Women who do not consider themselves feminists nonetheless often seem unaware of what they are doing to manliness when they work to support themselves. They think only that people should be hired and promoted on merit, regardless of sex. I am far from wishing to clap women back in the home—my wife would never go along—but women do need to think about the costs of what they are doing.

Some of that thought should be directed to the question of authority. A responsible man who wants to protect his family needs the authority to do so. Ms. Ireland says that husband and wife should be equal partners, and Maureen Dowd of the *New York Times* writes that men should "stop worrying about who wears the pants. We both do." Man is a pairing animal, said Aristotle. In pairing off, partners can be equal without being alike; they can both make contributions to a common whole. But can they both wear the pants?

Ms. Dowd does not account for the difference between male and female authority, the former challenging and peremptory, the latter gentle and persuasive. While there are hard women and soft men, in general it doesn't work when one sex tries to adopt the style of the other. Men become indecisive; women turn shrill. The two styles of authority do work when they complement rather than compete with each other. To cooperate, however, the gentler sort must defer to the manly sort. This means not that men have to decide, only that they have to appear to decide. Women can get most of what they want without dispelling that appearance.

Someone might ask how a professor like me can act as if nothing has happened in the past 30 years, trying to get by on stereotypes and warmed-over common sense. To which I retort that there is more truth in stereotypes than in ideologically driven "studies," and that our age needs to reduce the reputation of social science and restore that of common sense. It seems to me unlikely that when women compete with men to wear the pants, they will very often succeed, or be pleased when they do. I note that prudent young men already avoid relationships with feminist women. Why ask for trouble?

But let women figure that out for themselves. There is a more important concern about manliness—for both sexes. The reason for deferring to manliness is not to let manly men run wild, but on the contrary to criticize and control their ways. Our society suffers as much from unbridled manliness (consider the crime statistics) as from feminization. One reason is that when women compete with men, they risk ignoring their very reasonable doubts about the worth of competition.

And the feminization of society makes it harder for men to express their manliness in responsible ways. Why go out to compete in the world if there is no one at home to whom you may bring your money or honors? Or from whom to get consolation when you lose—as inevitably you will. Competition may be manly, but home is better than work. That's something women used to know, before they were wised up by feminism.

★ A TALE OF TWO ★ REACTIONS

Mark Lilla

FROM *THE NEW YORK REVIEW OF BOOKS*, MAY 14, 1998

1.

What do we mean by the term "reaction"? Dictionaries tell us that the word first entered the vocabulary of modern political thought in eighteenth-century France, where it was taken over from the scientific treatises of Isaac Newton. In his *Principia* of 1687 Newton had conjectured that every action in nature provokes an equal and opposite reaction. He did not think to apply this principle to politics, but his French disciples, notably Montesquieu, did. *The Spirit of the Laws* sets forth the "generating principles" of a body politic, which are nothing less than the laws of motion determining its political actions and reactions. This treatise established a mechanistic conception of politics in which movement and change are constant but not arbitrary, and where reaction is a predictable force.

A very different concept of reaction developed out of the French Revolution, which changed our understanding of what revolution is and what it means to oppose one. Classical and early modern thinkers, including Montesquieu, took revolution to be a simple upsetting and reordering of society on new principles. But the French Revolution was taken by its partisans and critics alike to have revealed a principle of historical unfolding, and not necessarily a progressive one. While it is true that some of the Revolution's early supporters held to a progressive conception of history, it is probably more accurate to say that most held an eschatological view of the Revolution's place in history, as did its critics. The Revolution represented a rip in the fabric of time, the fulfillment of a historical promise for some, an apocalypse for others. On this score there was perfect eschatological agreement between the revolutionaries, who set the calendars back to the Year 1, and their reactionary opponent Joseph de Maistre, who thought a restoration of the *ancien régime* too tame, and called instead for a new dispensation, "the contrary of the Revolution."

By the early nineteenth century "reactionary" had become a term of abuse leveled by prorevolutionary forces against their opponents, whom they accused of standing on the wrong side of history. But however polemical its intent, the concept also described something quite real, since the reactionaries, no less than the revolutionary party, had placed themselves in the judgment seat of history and had abandoned the field of common political deliberation. This is why reactionary rhetoric so often seems an inversion of revolutionary rhetoric; it is also why both kinds of rhetoric have been employed on right *and* left over the past two centuries, depending on the winds of fortune. When thinkers on the right see themselves trapped on the wrong side of a historical abyss they speak of the death of God, secularization, the last man, the waves of modernity, or the forgetting of Being. When those on the left feel abandoned by Minerva's owl there is talk of the disenchantment of the world, the dialectic of Enlightenment, the occult workings of power and language, or, more prosaically, the machinations of global capitalism, the military-industrial complex, and media conglomerates.

As we know from modern history, the rhetoric of revolution and reaction can have a disastrous effect on a nation's political discourse. To take only the most prominent example, political life in nineteenth-century France was so divided by eschatological struggles over the legitimacy of the Revolution that neither side could brook compromise with its satanic opponent. Dreams of a genuine (not bourgeois) restoration, or of a final solution to the issue of clerical privileges, lasted until the Third Republic, at great cost to the nation. This rhetoric also stifled the development of liberal-democratic thought and habits of mind, as can be felt in French intellectual life even today.

There was, of course, a small stream of liberal thought that we associate with the names Constant, Staël, Guizot, and, most profoundly, Tocqueville. Although these figures had little influence on nineteenth-century French political life, they still have much to teach us about how to think and live in a post-revolutionary age. Their position was based on a dispassionate analysis of the causes and nature of the Revolution, to which they responded subtly. With the revolutionaries, they agreed that the Revolution was a *fait accompli* that had established once and for all the principle of "modern liberty" against "ancient liberty," as Constant put it. But with the reactionaries, the liberals agreed that the Revolution would bring its own cruelties and disasters if revolutionary enthusiasm was not moderated and channeled into reasonable public deliberation. What marked this beleaguered liberal tradition was its lucidity in the face of the modern and antimodern political passions arising out of revolution, and its commitment to meliorist politics in a less than ideal age. It is this lucidity and commitment that have disappeared from American political discourse, rendering ours an age of reaction. American society never experienced a revolution of the French sort, and consequently never bred a similar tradition of thoroughgoing reaction. But if we think of reaction more generally as a mode of political discourse defining itself not by the aims it wishes to pursue but in relation to a real or imagined revolution in social affairs, then there is no doubt that we live in a reactionary age. Over the past four decades, America—and not just America—has experienced two smaller revolutions which have bred their own distinct forms of reaction, and which together have brought serious political reflection down to absolute zero. The two events to which I refer are the cultural revolution that we call "the sixties" and the shift in political and economic attitudes that, for lack of a better word, can be termed "the Reagan revolution." These revolutions are quite real, but to the extent that they have become symbols that excite or dull the political imagination they are also imaginary. The cultural revolution has become the predominant imaginative symbol on the American right, fueling a form of cultural reaction; the Reagan revolution has become the corresponding symbol on the left, generating a political-economic form of reaction.

Because the causes of reaction are both real and imaginary it is a difficult phenomenon to grapple with. One must not only examine its genuine sources of dissatisfaction; one must also try to understand how reactionaries subjectively view the revolutions they reject. Here it is very important to let the reactionaries speak for themselves, rather than imputing motives to them or relying on one's own interpretation of affairs. Two series of articles recently published in the conservative review the *New Criterion* and in the progressive weekly the *Nation* offer an excellent opportunity to do just that. The *New Criterion* series, called "Notes on a Cultural Revolution," which began in September 1997, has been written entirely by the magazine's managing editor, Roger Kimball. The *Nation* series, called "First Principles," which has been running since April 1997, is a forward-looking collection by various authors who set out to define a program for a "progressive majority." Taken together these articles permit us to consider the reactionary rhetoric of our time from two opposed vantage points and to see what they have in common.

Roger Kimball's well-written essays return again and again to "the sixties." I put this term in quotation marks, not to mock it, but in recognition of the fact that although we know *something* happened then, we still don't know what it was or even when it began. Was the Berkeley free speech movement the beginning of the end? Columbia '68? Woodstock? Or was it, as Larkin mused, the sexual revolution of 1963, between the end of the *Chatterley* ban and the Beatles' first LP? The conservative use of the term "the sixties" is imprecise, but there is probably no precise way to mark a cultural revolution—no tennis court oath, no storming of the Bastille, no beheading, no Thermidor. Still, we all recognize a "before" and an "after", and we are all still groping for the meaning of what happened in between.

Mark Lilla

Conservatives today do not speak much about the strictly political consequences of the sixties, perhaps because these have proven ephemeral and few. Congress and the courts have become stronger, the presidency weaker, and every public person must now resign himself to living under the omnipresent klieg lights of the media. Otherwise the American political system today does not look markedly different from the system thirty years ago. But if the conservatives are to be believed, this institutional stability masks more fundamental and threatening transformations in American life. When speaking of the Sixties, as Roger Kimball does in his series, they focus on three transformations: in public authority, the family, and individual morality.

As the conservatives see things, the past thirty years have brought a delegitimization of public authority in virtually every aspect of social life, from policing to the civil service, the schools, the universities, some would even say the armed forces. In some respects these institutions have become more democratic and have been constrained by law; mainly they have been rendered less capable of exercising their important functions in a democracy. When drug pushers and vagrants are permitted to set the tone in public parks, it is not the police who lose. It is poor urban families who lose their backyards. When children are coddled and undisciplined in the schools, they are the first to suffer, their families next. When universities cater to the whimsical tastes of their students and the aggressive demands of political interests, they cease to be retreats for serious cultivation of the self. When pornography is readily available on cable TV or the World Wide Web, the sleaze merchants profit and we are all demeaned. This litany could be extended, but the point is clear: by delegitimizing the exercise of public authority in the name of freedom, the Sixties sanctioned the pollution of public life and the weakening of democratic institutions.

Conservatives see the general decline in social authority and responsibility most clearly in the American family, which they consider a fragile institution. Birthrates are down, illegitimacy is up, and divorce is quickly becoming the rule rather than the exception. The sexual revolution made promiscuity a fashionable ideal (however rarely practiced), thus encouraging young people to postpone marriage and sanctioning its dissolution in the name of self-fulfillment. Parents today are less willing and able to discipline their children, partly because feminism cast a shadow of suspicion on any hierarchy within the family. Children are encouraged in public to have self-esteem but receive no guidance from their parents in private on what behavior is estimable. Given their freedom by the sixties, they now seem sadder and lonelier without the cocoon of love and authority that stable traditional families used to provide.

And finally there is private morality, about which conservatives feel alone in addressing without shame or euphemism. It is not that anyone thinks that incivility, promiscuity, drug use, and irresponsibility are good things. But we have become embarrassed to criticize them unless we can couch our objections in the legalistic terms of rights, the therapeutic language of self-realization, or the economic jargon of efficiency. The moral condition of the urban poor, romanticized in pop music and advertising, shames us but we dare not say a word. Our new explicitness about sex in television and film, and growing indifference to what we euphemistically call "sexual preference," scares the wits out of responsible parents, who see sexual confusion and fear in their children's eyes. But ever since the sixties they risk ridicule for raising objections that earlier would have seemed perfectly obvious to everyone.

These are commonplaces in conservative cultural literature today, and many are repeated in Roger Kimball's *New Criterion* series. But even if one takes them (as I take them) to be largely correct, they raise an obvious question which Kimball and other conservatives evade: Why did such a profound revolution take place in America when it did? Let us call this the Tocqueville question. In the aftermath of the social earthquake that was the French Revolution, Tocqueville was careful not to associate himself with the reactionaries and exiles who passed the time rending their garments and tearing their hair. The Revolution piqued his curiosity and led him to seek its causes deep in the French past, and to imagine its future by looking to the American present. Tocqueville was a thinker and a practical man of politics, not a public moralist, and so he sought social-historical principles that would explain the events and help to master their consequences. These he thought he found in "equality" and "individualism," principles which in their radical form helped to fuel the Terror, but which, he believed, might be reinterpreted institutionally to secure a modern liberal-democratic order.

How do American conservatives understand the causes of our cultural revolution? To judge by the essays of Roger Kimball and other conservatives, the cause of the Sixties was quite simply . . . the Sixties. They just happened, as a kind of miracle, or anti-miracle. Europeans tend to see their own Sixties experiences—which were more political, certainly more violent, but culturally less destructive than ours—in the light of the traumas and affluence of the postwar decades. But the American postwar years were not traumatic, and since conservatives romanticize the affluent fifties they are reticent to seek the causes of the cultural revolution there. And for all their invocations of Tocqueville, they do not look where he sought the causes of all modern revolutions, in the very principles of democratic society. When it comes to the cultural revolution, the conservatives will point to moral weakness, self-indulgence, cowardice, "liberal capitulation," as Kimball calls it; they will even blame the subterranean influence of Continental nihilism. What they refuse to consider is the darker side of our own American creed. Their unspoken motto is: "Blame America last."

Twenty years ago conservative writers had a partial explanation of the cultural revolution. Then they maintained that an alien "new class" of intellectuals, teachers, reporters, and civil servants had sprung up on American soil and captured our leading institutions, and they awaited the day when this putsch would be reversed, thanks to the sound moral instincts of "ordinary Americans." But now that the moral views of "ordinary Americans" are approaching those of this so-called new class, conservatives are stumped. They no longer try to *explain* the cultural revolution; they are content with endlessly recounting its horrors, inspiring the faithful, and putting themselves at the service of whatever questionable political forces might hold back the tide.

There is even an element of monasticism in conservative intellectual rhetoric today, as if the only option for those wishing to protect themselves from the rot was to establish a bunker within the Washington beltway (of all places) among like-minded friends and institutions, waiting for the apocalypse or—who knows?—the lost messiah. In late 1996 a controversy was set off among conservatives when the religious magazine edited by Richard John Neuhaus, *First Things*, published a symposium on "the end of democracy" in which contributors (among them Robert Bork) openly questioned the legitimacy of the American system today, now that, as the editors put it, "law, as it is presently made by the judiciary, has declared its independence from morality." Some neo-conservatives distanced themselves from this view and from the magazine, but in fact these so-called paleoconservatives had a point. If the cultural revolution was as bad as conservatives have been claiming, and if it represents an alien distortion of the American tradition, rather than its plausible metamorphosis, then withdrawal and Old Testament curses are very much in order.

2.

Reaction on the left takes a different form today. If conservative reaction has come to focus almost exclusively on the cultural revolution of the Sixties, progressive reaction—an appropriate oxymoron—is the child of the Reagan revolution of the eighties. One need not think that Ronald Reagan's two terms in office matched the Sixties in social significance to recognize that his presidency capped a tectonic shift in American politics that began (significantly enough) in 1968 and, Nixon's self-destruction apart, has been uninterrupted since. The Reagan years did not herald a cultural counterrevolution, whatever conservatives may think. It did, however, represent a revolution in the way most Americans—and not just Americans—think about political and economic matters. Thanks to Reagan, most Americans now believe (rightly or wrongly) that economic growth will do more for them than economic redistribution, and that to grow rich is good. It is taken as axiomatic that the experiments of the Great Society failed and that new experiments directed by Washington would be foolhardy. Regulation is considered *dépassé*, and unions are seen as self-serving, corrupt organizations that only retard economic growth. These "neoliberal" ideas, as they are called abroad, have also caught on in other industrialized nations whose social-democratic ideas were shaken by the oil shock and the failures of their own welfare states. And when the walls fell in 1989 these ideas seemed to receive historical confirmation, and now have become the creed of those international organizations controlled by the industrialized West.

To judge by the *Nation* series on "First Principles," the left no longer disputes this view of Reaganism, though it thinks there is more to the story. Nearly two decades of Republican government have had a sobering effect, and the characteristic tone on the left is pragmatic today, not eschatological. Still, the explanation of Reaganism that one gets even from a sobered *Nation* is reactionary—that is, it is not an explanation at all.

When searching for causes of this seismic shift in American political attitudes, *Nation* writers appeal most frequently to a corrupt campaign finance system that gives those with money a louder voice in the electoral process. This, they say, creates the illusion of satisfaction with liberal capitalism in America, when in fact figures show that nearly everyone is becoming worse off. They then proceed to prove by statistics that the Reaganite cause is unjust: jobs are less secure, unions are toothless, families have no health insurance, wages are frozen or dropping because of foreign labor competition, and the environment continues to suffer. The real value of redistributive social spending—whether on welfare, schools, or public health—has declined while military spending has remained near the cold war peak. Meanwhile a new shameless breed of corporate executives and venture capitalists has become unimaginably rich and influential in the mindless rush toward a global economy in which only the strong will survive. Yet when this self-evident economic case is made to middle America, it is distracted by a cynical right-wing strategy appealing to people's greed ("no new taxes"), their fears (the "race card"), their pride ("Mr. Gorbachev, tear down this wall"), or nostalgia (family values). Aided by conservative policy intellectuals, in turn supported by right-wing foundations and conspiracy-obsessed million-aires, the Republican Party has a lock on America's political imagination and has moved the Democratic Party step by step in its direction.

When asked to explain the cultural revolution of the Sixties, conservative reactionaries appeal to miracles, or antimiracles. When asked to explain the Reagan revolution of the eighties, progressive reactionaries appeal to smoke, mirrors, and occult powers. The conservatives assume that everyone is aware of the damage caused by the cultural revolution, but that by now they have been too morally corrupt to resist it. The left believes that Americans actually don't understand that the Reagan revolution was a disaster, since if they did, they would overturn it. Although political commentators on the left rarely adopt an apocalyptic tone when discussing politics today, they are still unable to offer a pragmatic analysis of the political revolution with which they are grappling. To put the matter in slightly Hegelian terms, they are incapable of explaining the rational core of the revolution—the deepest reasons why the Reagan revolution happened in America when it did, why it was so popular, and why it persists. To say that mistakes were made and that better packaging is required for the progressive agenda is simply not a serious response.

3.

The reactionary character of contemporary political discourse in America can be measured by a stroll through any decent bookshop. There one will find a long shelf of conservative books documenting the horrific consequences of the cultural revolution, but none that also probes the quite real sense of insecurity many Americans are feeling in the whirlwind of our new economy's creative destruction. There is another shelf, not quite as long as it used to be, purporting to show how the corporate-media-military complex keeps the Reagan revolution going, but again no sober account from the left of the very real, very troubling side effects of the Sixties cultural revolution. And no book I know of confronts squarely what surely is the most surprising phenomenon in postwar American politics: that the cultural and Reagan revolutions took place within a single generation, and have proved to be complementary, not contradictory, events.

Paul Berman's underappreciated essay, "A Tale of Two Utopias," comes closest to explaining the phenomenon. Berman's hypothesis is that the utopian movements of the Sixties, which destroyed themselves through overreaching, violence, and illiberal anti-Americanism, were given a second life in the individualistic liberation movements of the seventies (feminism, gay pride) and the antitotalitarian movements of Eastern Europe in the eighties. He contends that the antibourgeois passions of the sixties and anticommunism in the eighties were generated by the same forces of democratic individualism that, seen in their proper light, are America's legacy to the world. Whatever one makes of Berman's Whitmanesque historical optimism, he is surely on to something. It is only to be regretted that, as a committed writer on the American left, he cannot bring himself to admit the logical implication of his insight: that Reaganism, too, was an extension of the same utopian vision.

To my mind, any analysis of contemporary American politics hoping to escape the rhetoric of reaction would have to confront three uncomfortable facts about our postrevolutionary situation.

1. *The revolution is over.* One reason conservative political discourse is so apocalyptic today is that conservatives have finally come to believe, rightly in my view, that the cultural revolution is complete, successful, and that there will be no restoration of the moral *ancien régime*. Hence their withdrawal to within the beltway and the dark talk of America as Gomorrah (Robert Bork). Hope springs eternal on the left, as we see in the *Nation* symposium, where there is still much talk of new grassroots coalitions, reviving the unions, and restructuring the corporation through aggressive public policies to make it more democratic and "responsible." There is not the slightest chance that of any of this will come to pass. The forces at work in shaping the economy and politics—not just in the U.S., but in the whole developed world—are simply too deep to permit such idle dreaming. And the same is true of

the cultural revolution, which through American popular culture is affecting culture wherever televisions, VCRs, and CD players are to be found on the globe.

2. *The revolution is one and indivisible.* Two decades ago Daniel Bell argued that we were experiencing cultural contradictions caused by the disharmony between the Protestant ethic of capitalism and the hedonistic culture it spawned. Yet Professor Bell himself would probably agree today that any social "contradiction" lasting one generation is not a contradiction, it is a social fact. And the facts are these: the sixties happened, Reagan happened, and for the foreseeable future they will together define our political horizon. As anyone who deals with young people today knows, Americans find no difficulty in reconciling the two in their daily lives. They see no contradiction in holding down day jobs in the unfettered global marketplace—the Reaganite dream, the left nightmare—and spending weekends immersed in a moral and cultural universe shaped by the sixties. They work hard, probably too hard, though no longer to amortize their divine debt or to secure an economic dynasty; they work for ephemeral pleasures and for status and esteem, understood as part of the ethos of democratic individualism. Psychologically at least, the expectations of cultural contradiction have not been borne out, and today we face a question for which neither Tocqueville, nor Marx, nor Weber has prepared us: What principle in the American creed has simultaneously made possible these seemingly contradictory revolutions? How have our notions of equality and individualism been transformed to support a morally lax yet economically successful capitalist society?

3. *The politics of fusion.* If this thesis turns out to be correct—that the cultural and Reagan revolutions are fundamentally harmonious—several corollaries can be drawn from it. One is that some political figure or force in this country will eventually try to exploit that harmony. This already may have begun with Bill Clinton, whose sixties morals and eighties politics do not seem particularly contradictory to the majority of the American public that supports him. His presidency has also taught us why a political agenda making its peace with one revolution

while rejecting the other will be doomed to failure. This does not mean that Clintonism is our destiny, since it would also be plausible for a politician or political movement consistently to reject *both* the cultural and political-economic revolutions of our time. That is what I take Pat Buchanan to be up to in his simultaneous attacks on cultural radicalism and economic free trade. But it seems almost certain that a mixed strategy accepting the culture of the Sixties while rejecting the politics of the eighties (neo-McGovernism), or one that rejects the contemporary culture while applauding the political-economic status quo (neo-Bushism), will collapse under its own incoherence.

The politics of fusion is not particularly appealing, at least to me. A perceptible distinction between right and left is a necessary condition of healthy democratic politics, which depends on clear choices and alternating party government. There is every reason to expect that such a distinction will naturally reappear once political factions develop that bear some relation to social reality, but today they do not. The political discourse of reaction is too pervasive, the habits of mind formed by an earlier cultural and political situation simply too ingrained. Yet facts are facts, and eventually they will out: the revolution *is* over, and the revolution *is* one. The challenge for those genuinely concerned about our liberal-democratic future is the same as in Tocqueville's day: to study dispassionately the forces at work in the revolution of our time, to see if anything decent can be made of it.

★ RICH REPUBLICANS ★

David Brooks

FROM *THE WEEKLY STANDARD*, JUNE 22, 1998

Shallow people are greedy for money, but profound people are greedy for real estate. The shallow person wants fast cars and glitz, but anyone with a broader worldview longs for the kind of home they have in Winnetka, Illinois. The million-dollar houses stretch for mile upon mile through the North Shore suburbs of Chicago. Some are Tudor Revival, others are Prairie School or Queen Anne, but they are all massive and immaculate. There are no weeds in Winnetka. Each house is surrounded by a huge spread of flawless lawn and masterfully landscaped grounds, with hedges so neatly sculpted they look like they're made of green marble. Even the garages are spotless inside, with baby joggers hanging neatly from pegs, the Little Tykes kiddie cars arrayed in perfect rows, and the floors swept and mopped. The renovators appear inside the house every seven years or so like cicadas and install a new refrigerator with even deeper sub-zero capability, a new master-bedroom suite bigger than some zip codes, and maybe new cherry paneling in the rotunda. From the time the Winnetkans wake up in the morning and first set foot on their preheated bathroom floor, to the waning moments of the evening, when they hit the remote to turn off the gas fireplace, they are reminded that life is good, America is just, and nothing should ever change. They claim that fantastic real estate does not guarantee them family happiness, ward off evil, or prevent death, but on the face of the evidence, I'm afraid I find that impossible to believe. Real estate matters; ye shall judge them by their deeds.

I've come to Winnetka to investigate the mystery of the Rich Republicans. The mystery is that, at least on national and ideological issues, they are becoming less and less Republican. The *National Journal* recently reported that the Democratic vote in America's richest 261 towns has risen in every presidential contest over the past two decades. The Democrats won 25 percent of the rich vote in 1980 and 41 percent in 1996. In this last election, Bill Clinton carried thirteen of the seventeen richest congressional districts in the country. And Winnetka embodies the trend. In 1960, Richard Nixon beat John F. Kennedy in New Trier Township—which encompasses Winnetka and several similar North Shore suburbs—by 71 percent to 29 percent. In 1996, on the other hand, Bill Clinton edged out Robert Dole in New Trier; and in the Senate race, New Trier voters decisively preferred the Democratic candidate, Dick Durbin, to the conservative Republican, Al Salvi.

Winnetka still has a Republican congressman, John Porter, but you wouldn't exactly call him a Gingrich or a Lott or even a Dole Republican. His voting record makes him an extremist in the pursuit of moderation: He scores about a 50 percent in the liberal/conservative vote ratings year after year. He opposed more of the items in the Contract With America than any other Republican but one. He tends to support spending cuts but oppose Republican tax cuts. He enthusiastically backs federal funding for the arts, gun control, and environmental initiatives (he's been endorsed by the Sierra Club). He's also pro-choice, rejecting the gag rule that would have banned abortion counseling at federally funded clinics.

When you ask Winnetkans why they are disenchanted with the Republican party, they sometimes go an entire six or seven seconds before they mention the religious Right. To be elected in Winnetka you have to demonstrate you are on the correct side of the cultural divide that splits the GOP between the sane moderates and the Bible-thumping crazies.

The most important symbolic issues in this regard are abortion and gun control. In 1996, Democrat Jeff Schoenberg and Republican Tina Escamilla were running neck and neck in a race for state representative. But just before Election Day, Schoenberg sent out a mailing accusing Escamilla of accepting money from the conservative United Republican Fund and therefore not being as fervently pro-choice and pro-gun control as she claimed she was. Escamilla responded by calling Schoenberg's charges "McCarthyite," but the letter may have had an effect. Escamilla lost.

Basically, Rich Republicans feel that the problem with their party is that it doesn't have a sufficiently tough membership committee. The GOP was trundling along pretty well when suddenly all these people with Democratic parents started pouring out of their oversized churches and think tanks, calling themselves Republicans and screaming for revolution. (Since when does Gary Bauer count as a Republican anyway?) Moderate Republicans may not be as loud as these conservatives—there are no moderate Republican magazines or moderate Republican pundits (at least since Robert Novak and George Gilder went right). But at least they are normal human beings. The country is at peace, the economy is booming, crime rates are dropping, and there is an ever-growing number of excellent family-vacation destinations. But instead of going out and enjoying life, the rabid conservatives treat happiness like it's some sort of calamity. They storm around the country warning about the decline of civilization, gnashing their teeth because Bill Clinton hasn't yet been flayed and quartered, and going into ballistic rages because some polluter somewhere might be over-regulated.

From the perspective of the Rich Republicans, the conservatives are addicted to strife. Right-wingers screech out an endless stream of radical and loopy ideas—destroy the IRS, scrap the tax code, voucherize the schools—though in reality they have no practical knowledge of anything. They rant and rave on *Crossfire*. They go hunting through the backwoods of academia looking for seminars to be outraged by. They seem to feel best about themselves when they are antagonizing others, challenging whatever is said, being negative about everything, hating every movie, feeling superior to every trend. They're so caught up in their sense of themselves as countercultural they even wind up in the lap of the tobacco companies. No wonder they drive away voters.

From the perspective of the conservatives, on the other hand, Rich Republicans get their opinions the way they get their dress shoes: They just go to Saks Fifth Avenue and pick up whatever is fashionable this season. If the *New York Times* tells them that soft money is hurting democracy, they're for whatever might go by the name of campaign-finance reform. If their trophy wives tell them that being pro-choice carries more prestige with the ladies on the exercycles, then they write a check to Planned Parenthood. This hunger for political status, conservatives believe, turns the Rich Republicans into perpetual dupes. If a fashionable play attacks rich suburbanites, they flock to it. If a politician comes up with a noble-sounding scheme to redistribute their wealth, they support it. If a university wants to hire another Queer Theorist, they endow a chair. They couldn't see a hidden agenda if it hit them in the nose. And they've never met a foe they didn't want to appease. Whether it's Communists in Russia and China or extortion-practicing activists here at home, moderates think the solution to every dispute is to give money and make nice. Rich Republicans are, in the view of right-wingers, narrow, gutless, unimaginative, materialistic, selfish, and bland. Conservatives say they admire the stolid bourgeois values, but when they actually see them embodied by Rich Republicans, conservatives find them appalling.

This cultural divide within the GOP is probably unbridgeable, but it is deeply revealing about the mindset of today's rich, and about the character of today's conservatism. For example, when you look at the way the two sides in this dispute actually live, you find that the "moderates" often have more conservative lifestyles than the so-called conservatives. Winnetka is an extraordinarily traditional town. The men go off to Chicago every morning in their white shirts and gray suits on the 7:14 commuter train. The women, by and large, stay home.

In 1960, the local Republican party ran an ad just before Election

Day that included the instruction, "Ladies, please reserve voting time from 6-9 A.M. for the wage earner." You couldn't get away with an ad like that today; the consciousness of Republican women has been transformed. But when it comes to the way people actually live, little has changed. On weekdays, Winnetka is a female-dominated place. The stores, cafes, and restaurants are filled with women and their kids, with a sprinkling of male retirees. There are more realtors than people on the North Shore, but every storefront that isn't a real-estate agency seems to be a children's clothing store; there's even a store that sells hiking gear for toddlers. And if you walk through the residential neighborhoods, every block or so you come across a young mother looking a little bored as her toddler crouches to inspect a pebble. We were always taught that it was this sort of solitude and ennui that leads to feminism. But I saw few nannies here. It seems that in Winnetka, where these mostly college-educated women can afford to—the majority opt to stay home.

The elementary schools in Winnetka send most of their kids home for lunch. There was a move recently on the part of the working parents to have lunch facilities put into the schools. But it went nowhere, so some kids brown-bag it, while the others head for Mom's kitchen. One afternoon, I was walking south from Winnetka into the neighboring town of Kenilworth when I came across a street that had 40 or 50 Range Rover-type vehicles idling along both curbs. I wondered what a bunch of vehicles designed for places that don't have roads were doing in a place that doesn't even have weeds. But then kids started pouring out of the Joseph Sears Elementary School, and mothers popped out of the SUVs in great clusters (you can fit six kibbitzing mothers in one Chevy Suburban). For a few minutes it was all happy pandemonium as the kids, carrying their musical instruments, baseball gloves, and collages, found their moms, bounding about with their extraordinary high cheekbones, thin hips, and running shoes—and after a little dance of greetings and "See what I made?," they all tumbled back into their Range Rovers to go home and snack in their Corian-countered kitchens and frolic on their backyard playsets. If this isn't the sort of scene Phyllis Schlafly dreams about when she sleeps at night, I don't know what is.

Winnetkans spend an extraordinary amount of time thinking and talking about their schools. The homeowners have paid a $100,000 to $150,000 premium to get into this school district, and they are getting their money's worth. The median Winnetka 7th grader scores near the 90th percentile on state and national tests. This year, New Trier High School is sending 8 kids to Stanford, 7 to Johns Hopkins, 10 to Northwestern, 24 to Michigan, and 20 to the Ivy League, out of a graduating class of 765. The high school is growing out of its facilities, and there is a local debate about whether to replace it with one large campus or two. The letters-to-the-editor columns are stuffed with proposals, and the packed town meetings are evidence of the townsfolk's passionate attachment to their public-education system. Some of the parents have heard, however, that there are some barbaric Republican radicals in Washington who are talking about school choice and vouchers that would endanger the institution that serves them so well.

Every year an organization called the Winnetka Caucus sends out questionnaires to poll the residents on local issues. Reading through the responses for the past few decades, you are struck by how hawklike Winnetkans are when it comes to preserving local order. They are not big spenders: In 1994, 71 percent of the respondents said they were against tax increases, and 64 percent said they'd rather see the library close one day a week than raise property taxes. But they are tough proponents of zoning. Year after year, the residents call for tighter zoning regulations and stricter enforcement of the current ones. They want to regulate noise, fast foods, bars, tree-cutting, multi-family dwellings, store sizes, house additions, and "tear-downs" (someone buys a small house and then tears it down to put up a massive home that takes up the entire lot). We're often told that, since the 1960s, individual choice has emerged as the dominant value in American society, but in Winnetka the desire for order often takes precedence, along with that most conservative of values, the urge to make the future more like the past.

"The watchword in Winnetka, like that of the whole North Shore, might be 'preservation,' " reads the first sentence of the 1921 report of the Winnetka Planning Commission. That's at least as true today as it was then, and one might even say that preservation has by now developed into an entire political philosophy. There is a tremendous attachment to the past here. You can buy Winnetka coloring books that introduce children to local history and architectural styles. There is an active historical society, which publishes guides to local homes and their histories. There are strict regulations to ensure that new construction hews to the patterns of the past. And, one suspects, there is even stricter social pressure to make sure that Winnetka traditions are maintained.

All of this means that Winnetka has retained its archaic formality. Most of the homes were built during the first quarter of the century, when a dignified reticence was prized by the upper class, and the houses have kept that spirit even in our more casual age. There are almost none of those cutesy suburban flags that hang above the doorways in many suburbs. There are almost no bumper stickers on the cars, or loose toys or decorations scattered about the lawns. For anybody used to the hodgepodge variety of city life, the atmosphere can be a little intimidating. A few years ago the writer Joseph Epstein took his friend Edward Shils up from Chicago for dinner at the WASPy Winnetka Grill. Shils looked around and said, "I have felt more at home in Africa and India than I do in this restaurant." At the end of their meal, Shils commented, "Thank you for this lovely dinner. And thank you for the intellectual profit of it. Until this evening, Christendom was merely a concept for me."

We talk about property rights a lot these days, but we don't often dwell on how possessing property—great gobs of it—influences a person's worldview. In the 18th and 19th centuries, when the franchise was being extended beyond the propertied classes, the subject was more on people's minds. Edmund Burke called the owners of great property the "ballast in the vessel of the commonwealth." The owners of large properties, the theory went, have a stake in the long-term health of the country, since they hope to pass their lands down through the generations. They are more interested in preserving the wonderfulness of the present than in taking a flier on the future. Therefore, they are moved not so much by abstract notions or social theories as by the need to preserve tangible objects and institutions. (George Bush captured a remnant of this ethos when he expressed his discomfort with the "vision thing.") In short, the large property owners are conservative in the old-fashioned sense of the word, treasuring stability more than change, concrete possessions more than abstract notions.

The American conservative movement has moved a long way from this original conservatism. We now have a weird situation in which it's the Republican moderates who want to preserve the status quo and the people we call conservative who are hungry for change. These days, movement conservatives rail against elites; they don't work up justifications for them. They come to politics with ambitious agendas, not strategies for preserving the status quo. They tend to value creative destruction and entrepreneurial dynamism more than social stability. They go in for intellectual combat and confrontation, not compromise and Bismarckian tactical retreat. It used to be, if you hated rich people, you became a liberal, but now you can find resentment of the sluggish rich on the right at least as much as on the left. That leaves the Winnetkans in the position of affluent orphans: Newt Gingrich doesn't speak for them, and neither does Dick Armey or Trent Lott. Not that anybody's feeling too sorry for them or anything, but where do they go for leadership?

The clearest difference between the preservationism of the Rich Republicans and the activist conservatism of the modern American Right is illuminated in the two sides' approach to the culture war. The Right wants to fight. It wants to confront radical feminism, multiculturalism, identity politics, "Piss Christ," and all the rest. The Rich Republicans, on the other hand don't fight, they co-opt.

Once, 70 or 100 years ago when the homes in Winnetka were built, the American upper classes did have a fighting faith. They saw themselves as the American elite, obligated to serve as the guardians of America's ideology, the instructors to the masses in matters of etiquette and behavior, the leaders and standard-setters in cultural, economic, and political affairs. In those days the upper classes had an ideology inherited from the European elites. They were conscious of their distinct social role (Michael Knox Beran calls that period the "risorgimento of the well-to-do"). But over the past many decades, that aristocratic ethos, that sense of noblesse oblige, has been pounded into dust. Thorstein Veblen ridiculed the rich. A hundred novelists attacked them. A thousand movies made them villains. Just consider the recent films set on Chicago's North Shore—*Risky Business, Ferris Bueller's Day Off, Home Alone, Ordinary People, The Breakfast Club.* If there is one constant in all those movies, it is that the adults in affluent suburbs are smug, stupid, cold, and selfish. There is no ideal personality type that rich people are supposed to aspire to these days, except to pretend that they're not rich or at least don't care about money.

Where that is the prevailing cultural climate, of course, people don't go around launching cultural counteroffensives. Compared with the right-wingers, who are always quick to detect an assault on their values, the Rich Republicans seem to have developed a bland obliviousness to cultural attack. They lack ideological antennae. At the World Financial Center in New York, for example, there is a sculpture that shows greedy capitalists in top hats worshiping money, spanking one another, and trampling people into the dirt. And this work is paid for by the rent collected from Merrill Lynch, American Express, Dow Jones, and Oppenheimer Securities. Don't the corporate bigwigs notice that they are paying for art that depicts them as devils?

Similarly, in Winnetka one is constantly confronted by odd juxtapositions, mingling bourgeois traditionalism with anti-bourgeois radicalism. The newsletter of the Women's Exchange features pictures of handsome suburban matrons and the organization's prim slogan, "Self, Skills, Service." But then if you look at the topics for the discussion groups, you come across "The Creation of a Feminist Consciousness" and "The Creation of the Patriarchy." And to start things off, the officers have included an introductory quotation from a Women's Studies professor at Duke: "We stand at the beginning of a new epoch in the history of humankind's thought, as we recognize that sex is irrelevant to thought, that gender is a social construct . . ." Can it really be possible that those women idling outside the Joseph Sears Elementary School in their Chevy Suburbans are chatting about gender as a social construct? It's as if their lifestyles were fashioned by *Architectural Digest* but their cultural attitudes were crafted by the *Nation.*

The Winnetkans seem to sense that the way to preserve their beloved community is not to fight hostile ideas, but simply to absorb them and render them anodyne. Many of the accouterments of the 1960s, which were invented as an alternative to suburban life, have now been assimilated by the suburbanites and sit cheek by jowl with the traditional *objets* they were meant to repudiate. If you're looking to fill your ample living room in Winnetka, for example, you can go to the old-fashioned stores with names like Knightsbridge to get traditional English-style furniture, paintings of fox hunts, and clunky silver tea services. Or you can rebel against the furniture of the colonialists and ally yourself with the colonial victims. You can go to stores like Cassella Interiors that sell African living-room chairs, masks, and wall totems—Frantz Fanon decor for the haute bourgeoisie. Up the road, a store called Material Possessions sells a Moroccan bird-house for $295 for your multicultural mantelpiece, and Zig and Tig sells oversized Indian furniture for those who favor the funky chateau look. The avant-garde used to produce terrorists to blow up the capitalist overlords. Now on the North Shore, the corporate masters can get their makeover at the Avant Garde Hair Salon. All that is hostile can be reconciled by the balm of consumerism.

Conservatives would say that you can't go on absorbing radical feminism or multiculturalism or New Left egalitarianism for too long without pretty soon seeing your own values co-opted out of existence. You become so diverse, nonjudgmental, and relativistic that you lose your moral bearings. Conservatives argue that the community institutions that Winnetkans enjoy are actually based on certain principles about the different roles of men and women, about the structure of families, and about the application of religious notions to daily life. If you don't defend those principles, but instead blithely dabble in the fashionable ideas of tenured radicals, then your suburban stability will eventually topple. Your kids will grow up without moral instruction and will flounder. Your family and community life will decay.

It's not really possible to say who wins the argument between the conservatives and the moderates, because the debate is rather one-sided. The conservatives make their case, they write their devastating essays, but the Rich Republicans never respond. They just go on living their lives. And truth be told, if you had to bet on which branch of the GOP will have more influence on the nation in the coming few years, you would not put your money on the articulate right-wingers. Because as the country gets richer, more people start thinking and behaving like the Rich Republicans in Winnetka. Affluence produces preservationists. Affluence produces environmentalists. Affluence produces moderates who detest the heat and strife of a culture war and like instead the diverse pleasures of multicultural commercialism. There are now 8.3 million American households with incomes over $100,000. From 1992 to 1997, federal tax revenues rose at an annual rate of 7.6 percent. Consumer confidence is at a record high. This spreading affluence is a recipe for a nation of Winnetkas, or at least the temporary triumph of Winnetkan cultural hegemony. The North Shore suburbs represent only the uppermost strata of the American income distribution, but if the current political mood signifies anything, it is that the large mass of suburban middle-class Americans for the time being share the propertied and satisfied outlook of the burghers of Winnetka, Wilmette, and Lake Forest.

It used to be liberals who railed against the complacency of the American electorate, but now it's conservatives who long to see a little more mass outrage. It used to be liberals who based their politics on abstract notions more than concrete realities, but now it's conservatives who like to emphasize that ideas have consequences. It used to be liberal intellectuals who longed for the drama and turmoil that put them center stage, but now the habits of the New Class, both good and bad, have migrated rightward. And when movement conservatives rail against the Republican middle, they are actually condemning people who lead conservative lives and embody the conservative temperament. The Rich Republicans may not always sparkle with idealism or intellectual rigor, but at least they have their feet planted on the ground—as you would too if your particular ground had been so meticulously aerated, weeded, de-thatched, fertilized, and mown.

★ THE WAY OF LOVE: ★ DOROTHY DAY AND THE AMERICAN RIGHT

Bill Kauffman

FROM *CHRONICLES,* NOVEMBER 1998

The title "Dorothy Day and the American Right" promises a merciful brevity, along the lines of "Commandments We Have Kept" by the Kennedy Brothers. After all, the founder of the Catholic Worker movement and editor of its newspaper lived among the poor, refused to participate in air-raid drills, and preferred Cesar Chavez to Bebe Rebozo.

But there is more to the "right" than a dollar bill stretching from the DuPonts to Ronald Reagan, just as the "left" is something greater than the bureau-building and bomb-dropping of Roosevelts and Kennedys. Maybe, just maybe, Dorothy Day had a home, if partially furnished and seldom occupied, on the American right.

The Catholic reactionary John Lukacs, after attending the lavish 25th anniversary bash for *National Review* in December 1980, held in the Plaza Hotel, hellward of the Catholic Worker House on Mott Street, wrote:

> During the introduction of the celebrities a shower of applause greeted Henry Kissinger. I was sufficiently irritated to ejaculate a fairly loud Boo! . . . A day or so before that evening Dorothy Day had died. She was the founder and

saintly heroine of the Catholic Worker movement. During that glamorous evening I thought who was a truer conservative, Dorothy Day or Henry Kissinger? Surely it was Dorothy Day, whose respect for what was old and valid, whose dedication to the plain decencies and duties of human life rested on the traditions of two millennia of Christianity, and who was a radical only in the truthful sense of attempting to get to the roots of the human predicament. Despite its pro-Catholic tendency, and despite its commendable custom of commemorating the passing of worthy people even when some of these did not belong to the conservatives, *National Review* paid neither respect nor attention to the passing of Dorothy Day, while around the same time it published a respectful R.I.P. column in honor of Oswald Mosley, the onetime leader of the British Fascist Party.

National Review, dreadnought of postwar American conservatism, occasionally aimed its scattershot at Day. Founder William F. Buckley, Jr., referred casually to "the grotesqueries that go into making up the Catholic Worker movement"; of Miss Day, he chided "the slovenly, reckless, intellectually chaotic, anti-Catholic doctrines of this good-hearted woman—who, did she have her way in shaping national policy, would test the promise of Christ Himself, that the gates of Hell shall not prevail against us."

The grotesqueries he does not bother to itemize; nor does Buckley—whose only memorable witticism was *Mater, Si, Magistra, No*—explain just what was "anti-Catholic" about a woman who told a friend, "The hierarchy permits a priest to say Mass in our chapel. They have given us the most precious thing of all—the Blessed Sacrament. If the Chancery ordered me to stop publishing the *Catholic Worker* tomorrow, I would."

If Buckley and Kissinger were the sum of the American right, mine would be a very brief article indeed. But there is another American right—or is it a left, for praise be the ambidextrous—in which Miss Day fits quite nicely. Indeed, I think she is more at home with these people than she ever was with Manhattan socialists. They are the Agrarians, the Distributists, the heirs to the Jeffersonian tradition. The keener of them—particularly the Catholics—understood their kinship with Day. Allen Tate, the Southern man of letters and contributor to the 1930 Southern Agrarian manifesto, *I'll Take My Stand*, wrote his fellow Dixie poet Donald Davidson in 1936:

> I also enclose a copy of a remarkable monthly paper, the *Catholic Worker*. The editor, Dorothy Day, has been here, and is greatly excited by our whole program. Just three months ago she discovered *I'll Take My Stand*, and has been commenting on it editorially. She is ready to hammer away in behalf of the new book. Listen to this: The *Catholic Worker* now has a paid circulation of 100,000! [Tate neglects to say that the price is a penny a copy] . . . She offers her entire mailing list to Houghton-Mifflin; I've just written to Linscott about it. Miss Day may come by Nashville with us if the conference falls next weekend. She has been speaking all over the country in Catholic schools and colleges. A very remarkable woman. Terrific energy, much practical sense, and a fanatical devotion to the cause of the land!

The program that so excited Miss Day was summarized in the statement of principles drawn up at the Nashville meeting of Southern Agrarians and Distributists. Mocked as reactionary for their unwillingness to accept bigness as an inevitable condition, the conferees declared (*inter alia*):

> —The condition of individual freedom and security is the wide distribution of active ownership of land and productive property.
> —Population should be decentralized as well as ownership.
> —Agriculture should be given its rightful recognition as the prime factor in a secure culture.

Though Day was absent from Nashville, she was to speak the language of the Southern Agrarians, without the drawl, many times over the years. "To Christ—To the Land!" Day exclaimed in the January 1936 issue. "The *Catholic Worker* is opposed to the wage system but not for the same reason that the Communist is. We are opposed to it, because the more wage tamers there are the less owners there are . . . how will they become owners if they do not get back to the land."

Widespread ownership was the basic tenet of the Agrarians' Catholic cousins, the Distributists. The *Catholic Worker* published all the major Distributists of the age, among them Chesterton and Belloc, Vincent McNabb, Father Luigi Ligutti, and the Jesuit John C. Rawe (a Nebraska-born "Catholic version of William Jennings Bryan"). On numberless occasions Dorothy Day called herself a Distributist. Thus her gripe with the New Deal: "*Security* for the worker, not ownership," was its false promise; she despaired in 1945 that "Catholics throughout the country are again accepting 'the lesser of two evils'. . . . They fail to see the body of Catholic social teaching of such men as Fr. Vincent McNabb, G.K. Chesterton, Belloc, Eric Gill and other distributists . . . and lose all sight of *The Little Way*."

Dorothy Day kept to the little way, and that is why we honor her. She understood that if small is not always beautiful, at least it is always human.

The *Catholic Worker* position on economics was expressed quite clearly:

> [W]e favor the establishment of a Distributist economy wherein those who have a vocation to the land will work on the farms surrounding the village and those who have other vocations will work in the village itself. In this way we will have a decentralized economy which will dispense with the State as we know it today and will be federationist in character . . . We believe in worker ownership of the means of production and distribution as distinguished from nationalization.

This to be accomplished by decentralized cooperatives and the elimination of a distinct employer class.

The American name for this is Jeffersonianism, and the failure of Distributism to attract much of a stateside following outside of those Mencken derided as "typewriter agrarians" owes in part to its Chesterbellocian tincture. "Gothic Catholicism" never could play in Peoria.

Nor could it stand upon the Republican platform. Carry Wills recalls this exchange during his first visit with William F. Buckley, Jr.: "'Are you a conservative, then?' [Buckley asked.] I answered that I did not know. Are Distributists conservative? 'Philip Bumham tells me they are not.' It was an exchange with the seeds of much later misunderstanding."

Were the Distributists conservative? Was Day conservative? Depends. Herbert Agar, the Kentucky Agrarian and movement theorist, wrote in the *American Review* (April 1934), "For seventy years, a 'conservative' has meant a supporter of Big Business, of the politics of plutocracy," yet "the root of a real conservative policy for the United States must be redistribution of property." Ownership—whether of land, a crossroads store, a machine shop—must be made "the normal thing."

"Property is proper to man," insisted Dorothy Day, though she and the Distributists—and much of the old American right—meant by property something rather more substantial than paper shares in a Rockefellerian octopus. "Ownership *and* control are property," declared Allen Tate, making a distinction between a family farm—or family firm—and a jointstock corporation, the artificial spawn of the state.

Like Tate and the Southern Agrarians, Day was no collectivist, eager to herd the fellaheen onto manury unromantic Blithedales. "The Communists," she said, sought to build "a sense of the sacredness and holiness and the dignity of the machine and of work, in order to content the proletariat with their propertyless state." So why, she asked, "do we talk of fighting communism, which we are supposed to oppose because it does away with private property. We have done that very well ourselves in this country." The solution: "We must emphasize the holiness of *work*, and we must emphasize the sacramental quality of *property* too." ("An anti-religious agrarian is a contradiction in terms," according to Donald Davidson.)

Day described the Catholic Worker program as being "for ownership by the workers of the means of production, the abolition of the assembly line, decentralized factories, the restoration of crafts and the ownership of property," and these were to be achieved by libertarian means, through the repeal of state-granted privileges and a flowering of old-fashioned American voluntarism.

During the heyday of modern American liberalism, the 1930s, when Big Brother supposedly wore his friendliest phiz, Day and the Catholic Workers said No. They bore a certain resemblance to those old progressives (retroprogressives)—Senators Burton K. Wheeler, Gerald Nye, and Hiram Johnson—who turned against FDR for what they saw as the bureaucratic, militaristic, centralizing thrust of his New Deal. The antithetical tendencies of the *Catholic Worker* and the thirties American left were juxtaposed in the November 1936 issue of the *Catholic Worker*. Under the heading "Catholic Worker Opposition to Projected Farm-Labor Party," the box read:

> Farm-Labor Party stands for:
> Progress
> Industrialism
> Machine
> Caesarism (bureaucracy)
> Socialism
> Organizations
>
> Catholic Worker stands for:
> Tradition
> Ruralism
> Handicrafts
> Personalism

Communitarianism
Organisms.

And never the twain shall meet.

An anarchistic distrust of the state, even in its putatively benevolent role as giver of alms, pervaded the Catholic Workers, as it did the 1930s right. But then as the late Karl Hess, onetime Barry Goldwater speech-writer turned Wobbly homesteader, wrote, the American right had been "individualistic, isolationist, decentralist—even anarchistic," until the Cold War reconciled conservatives to the leviathan state.

The 1930's dissenters—the old-fashioned liberals now maligned as conservatives; the unreconstructed libertarians; the cornbelt radicals—proposed cooperatives and revitalized village economies as the alternative to government welfare. The Catholic Workers agreed. The holy fool Peter Maurin, Day's French peasant comrade, asserted that "he who is a pensioner of the state is a slave of the state." Day, in her memoir *The Long Loneliness*, complained,

> The state had entered to solve [unemployment] by dole and work relief, by setting up so many bureaus that we were swamped with initials. . . . Labor was aiding in the creation of the Welfare State, the Servile State, instead of aiming for the ownership of the means of production and acceptance of the responsibility that it entailed.

"Bigness itself in organization precludes real liberty," wrote Henry Clay Evans, Jr., in the *American Review*, a Distributist journal. The home—the family—was the right size for most undertakings. And so the home must be made productive once more. In the April 1945 *Catholic Worker*, Janet Kalven of the Grallville Agricultural School for Women in Loveland, Ohio, called for "an education that will give young women a vision of the family as the vital cell of the social organism, and that will inspire them with the great ambitions of being queens in the home." By which she did not mean a sequacious helpmeet to the Man of the House, picking up his dirty underwear and serving him Budweisers during commercials, but rather a partner in the management of a "small, diversified family farm," who is skilled in everything "from bread-making to bee-keeping." For "the homestead is on a human scale"—the only scale that can really measure a person's weight.

The Agrarians and Distributists dreamed of a (voluntary, of course) dispersion of the population, and Day, despite her residence in what most decentralists regarded then and now as the locus of evil, agreed: "If the city is the occasion of sin, as Fr. Vincent McNabb points out, should not families, men and women, begin to aim at an exodus, a new migration, a going out from Egypt with its flesh pots?" asked Day in September 1946. This revulsion against urbanism seems odd in a woman whose base was Manhattan, symbol of congestion, of concentration, of cosmopolitanism rampant. Yet she wrote of the fumes from cars stinging her eyes as she walked to Mass, of the "prison-gray walls" and parking lots of broken glass. "We only know that it is not human to live in a city of ten million. It is not only not human, it is not possible." The Southern Agrarians would not demur.

World War II destroyed agrarianism as an active force in American intellectual life just as it fortified the urban citadels of power and money. Foes of America's involvement in the war, heirs to the non-interventionist legacy of George Washington, were slandered, most notably Charles Lindbergh, whom the *Catholic Worker* defended against the smears of the White House.

Despite Day's disavowal of the "isolationist" label, the *Catholic Worker* of 1939-41 spoke the diction of the American anti-war movement, which, because it was anti-FDR, was deemed "right-wing." Sentences like "We should like to know in just what measure the British Foreign Office is dictating the foreign policy of the United States!" could have come straight from the pages of Colonel McCormick's *Chicago Tribune*. So could the objection to the "*English and Communist Propaganda*" of the New York papers, and the reverence toward the traditional "neutrality of the United States" and the keeping of "our country aloof from the European war."

"The *Catholic Worker* does not adhere to an isolationist policy," editorialized the paper in February 1939, though in fact its position, and often its phraseology, was within the American isolationist grain. The editorial sought to distinguish the paper from the bogeymen "isolationists" by urging "that the doors of the United States be thrown open to all political and religious refugees"—a position also taken by many isolationists, for instance H.L. Mencken, who wanted our country to be a haven for the persecuted Jews of Europe.

Day and the Workers dug in for a tooth-and-nail fight against conscription—"the most important issue of these times," as they saw it. Day replied to those who noted that Joseph and Mary went to Bethlehem to register with the census that "it was not so that St. Joseph could be drafted into the Roman Army, and so that the Blessed Mother could put the Holy Child into a day nursery and go to work in an ammunition plant."

Or as Peter Maurin put it:
    The child does not belong to the state;
    it belongs to the parents.
    The child was given by God to the parents;
    he was not given by God to the state.

This was by now a quaintly reactionary notion. What were children if not apprentice soldiers? Like their isolationist allies, the Catholic Workers suffered years of "decline, suspicion, and hatred" during the Good War. Circulation of the *Catholic Worker* plummeted from 190,000 in May 1938 to 50,500 in November 1944. By 1944, only nine of 32 Houses of Hospitality were operating.

The Cold War transmogrified the American right: anticommunism became its warping doctrine, yet a remnant of cantankerous, libertarian, largely Midwestern isolationists held on, though the invigorating air of the 1930s, when left and right might talk, ally, even merge, was long gone. The fault lies on both sides.

The unwillingness of the *Catholic Worker*'s editors to explore avenues of cooperation with the Old Right led them, at times, to misrepresent the sole popular anti-militarist force of the late 1940s.

In denouncing the North Atlantic Treaty which created NATO, the *Catholic Worker* claimed that "the only serious opposition in the Senate is from a group of the old isolationist school, and their argument is that it costs too much." This is flatly untrue—the isolationist case was far more sophisticated and powerful, and it rested on the same hatred of war and aggression that underlay the Catholic Workers—but to have been honest and fair would have placed the Catholic Worker on Elm Street and Oak Street, whose denizens might have taught the boys in the Bowery a thing or two.

Postwar Catholic isolationists would be condescended to as parochial morons by the Cold War liberal likes of James O'Gara, managing editor of *Commonweal*, who snickered at those mossbacks who refused to recognize that "American power is a fact" and that "modern science has devoured distance and made neighbors of us all." What good is personalism in a world of atomic bombs? What mattered the small? Fr. John C. Rawe's experimental school of rural knowledge, Omar Farm, near Omaha, was shattered when all but two of its students were drafted to fight World War II. Liberal Catholics continued to support the conscription against which pacifists and right-wingers railed, although, as Patricia McNeal has written of the League of Nations debate, "the majority of American Catholics supported the popular movement towards isolationism and rejected any idea of collective security." But the League aside, we all know which side won. The state side. The liberals who do not know us but, as they so unctuously assure us, have our best interests at heart.

"The greatest enemy of the church today is the state," Dorothy Day told a Catholic audience in 1975, sounding much like the libertarian right that was her natural, if too little visited, kin.

The powerful libertarian strain in the *Catholic Worker* was simply not present in other postwar magazines of the "left," excepting *Politics*, edited by Day admirer Dwight Macdonald. American liberals had made peace with—had made sacrifices to—Moloch on the Potomac. As *Catholic Worker* editor Robert Ludlow argued in 1951,

we are headed in this country towards a totalitarianism every bit as dangerous towards freedom as the other more forthright forms. We have our secret police, our thought control agencies, our overpowering bureaucracy. . . . The American State, like every other State, is governed by those who have a compulsion to power, to centralization, to the preservation of their gains. And it is the liberals—The *New Leader, New Republic, Commonweal* variety—who have delivered the opiate necessary for the acceptance of this tyranny among "progressive" people. It is the fallacy of attempting social reform through the State, which builds up the power of the State to where it controls all avenues of life.

which the *New Republic*-style liberals replied: welcome to the real world.

The inevitable Arthur Schlesinger, Jr., in *The Vital Center* (1949), his manifesto of Cold War liberalism, wrote, "One can dally with the distributist dream of decentralization," but "you cannot flee from science and technology into a quietist dreamworld. The state and the factory are inexorable: bad men will run them if good abdicate the job."

Alas, most on the "right" crawled into the devitalizine center. A dispersion of property, a restoration of ownership, the reclaiming of the land, a foreign policy of peace and noninterference: these were the dreams of losers, of fleers from reality, of shirkers of responsibility, of—most damningly—*amateurs.* Non-experts. In 1966, in the just-as-inevitable *National Review*, Anthony T. Bouscaren mocked Day and other "Catholic Peaceniks" because "sinfully, their analysis of the situation [in Vietnam] goes directly counter to that of the distinguished list of academicians . . . who support U.S. defense of South Vietnam." Grounds for excommunication, surely.

In all this worry about the other side of the world, few partisans bothered to notice the dirt under their feet. Distributism was dead. Or was it? For in 1956, long after the Agrarian dream had been purged from the American right, supplanted by the Cold War nightmare, Dorothy Day insisted that "distributism is not dead." It cannot "be buried, because distributism is a system conformable to the needs of man and his nature."

Conforming to their decentralist principles—and presaging a later strategy of "right-wing" tax resisters—the Workers refused payment of federal taxes, though as Day wrote, we "file with our state capital, pay a small fee, and give an account of monies received and how they were spent. We always comply with this state regulation because it is local-regional," and "because we are decentralists (in addition to being pacifists)." This resistance, she explained, was

> much in line with common sense and with the original American ideal, that governments should never do what small bodies can accomplish: unions, credit unions, cooperatives, St. Vincent de Paul Societies. Peter Maurin's anarchism was on one level based on this principle of subsidiarity, and on a higher level on that scene at the Last Supper where Christ washed the feet of His Apostles. He came to serve, to show the new Way, the way of the powerless. In the face of Empire, the Way of Love.

How beautiful: in the face of Empire, the Way of Love.

It is only in the local, the personal, that one can see Christ. A mob, no matter how praiseworthy its cause, is still a mob, said Day, paraphrasing Eugene Debs, and she explained, in Thoreauvian language, her dedication to the little way:

> Why localism? . . . [F]or some of us anything else is extravagant; it's unreal; it's not a life we want to live. There are plenty of others who want that life, living in corridors of power, influence, money, making big decisions that affect big numbers of people. We don't have to follow those people, though; they have more would-be servants—slaves, I sometimes think—than they know what to do with.
>
> We don't happen to believe that Washington, D.C., is the

moral capital of America. . . . If you want to know the kind of politics we seek, you can go to your history books and read about the early years of this country. We would like to see more small communities organizing themselves, people talking with people, people *caring* for people . . . we believe we are doing what our Founding Fathers came here to do, to worship God in the communities they settled. They were farmers. They were craftspeople. They took care of each other. They prayed to God, and they thanked Him for showing them the way to America! A lot of people ask me about the influence on our [Catholic] Worker movement, and they are right to mention the French and the Russian and English writers, the philosophers and novelists. But some of us are just plain Americans whose ancestors were working people and who belonged to small-town or rural communities or neighborhoods in cities. We saw more and more of that community spirit disappear, and we mourned its passing, and here we are, trying to find it again.

Dorothy Day found it. Not on the left, and not on the right, but in that place where Love resides. In the face of Empire, the Way of Love.

★ WHAT I SAW AT THE ★ IMPEACHMENT

Andrew Ferguson

FROM *THE WEEKLY STANDARD*, DECEMBER 21, 1998

RAYBURN HOUSE OFFICE BUILDING, TUESDAY MORNING, DECEMBER 8

At last! Finally! It's about damn time! The president has found a counsel who looks like someone you might leave alone in a room with your children. Greg Craig, despite carrying the title of special counsel to the president, dares to be inoffensive. Earnest. Sincere. Good hair. He gives every impression of being a well-meaning fellow doing his darnedest to ensure that everybody just calms down, takes a deep breath, gives a fair reading of the evidence, plumbs his conscience, and then lets the boss off scot-free.

What a contrast. Rahm Emanuel was so oily you could have bottled him for salad dressing. Lanny Davis quivers and snuffles like a man on the verge of a nervous breakdown—long overdue, by the way. David Kendall and John Podesta have faces so pinched and crabbed they can only reflect some soul-deep turmoil. But Craig is normal. You can imagine him going home at night to wife and kids in a center-hall brick colonial in Bethesda and coaching Buddy's soccer team and helping Sis with her Campfire Girls candy sale. Picture James Carville with a bunch of Campfire Girls.

So this is Greg Craig: a spokesman so nice they named him twice. Today is the long-awaited day when the president's men have journeyed up to Capitol Hill to make the president's case, and Greg is the man they have chosen to speak first. As he settles into his opening statement—his voice is like a purr—it becomes quickly apparent that his job is to insult Bill Clinton as thoroughly as possible while still maintaining that basically, deep down, the president is a sweetheart who never lied but feels terrible about all the lies he's told. At least I think I'm getting that straight.

For legal reasons, of course, Greg can't use the word "lied." "Sinful"? Sure, Greg volunteers. "Morally wrong"? You bet. And "evasive" and "misleading" and "blameworthy" and "maddening." But not a liar. "Open your heart," he advises members of the committee. (Since when did the White House decide that Republicans have hearts?) Greg is reasonable and calm and he promises the moon. "By the close of tomorrow, all the world will see one simple and undeniable fact," he says. "There is nothing in the record—in either the law or the facts—that would justify his impeachment and removal from office."

Greg's velvety presentation goes over very well with the committee; the deployment of the word "sinful" is a masterstroke. (Top that, Mr. Bauer!) His statement lasts a full fifteen minutes, and normally, according to the traditional work schedules of congressional committees, this would be a good time for the honorable members to call a recess and knock off for some well-earned R&R. But Chairman Hyde has promised to run today's session straight through, without breaks for bathroom time or even feeding. So we are on to yet another panel of experts—panels of experts being this committee's stock-in-trade—beginning with a pudgy Princeton historian named Sean Wilentz, whose area of expertise is condescension.

Professor Wilentz broaches two themes that are becoming *de rigueur* as the president's defenders make their case. The first is that, as a defender of the president, Wilentz is absolutely emphatic that he is not defending the president, who is "reckless" and "devious." (Doesn't anybody like this guy?) Wilentz even cites an article he wrote in the *New*

Republic, proving that he thought the president was scum as far back as 1996. The second theme is a delightful inversion of common sense: that the "rule of law" is under assault not by a chief executive who lied under oath in legal proceedings and employed the vast resources of his office to impede the administration of justice but by the congressmen who are now following the constitutional procedure to remove him for doing that. At least I think I'm getting this straight.

To coax committee members gently toward accepting his view, Professor Wilentz calls them myopic cowards, fanatics and zealots, guilty of "a degradation of conscience," and tells them that, if they disagree with him, "history will track you down and condemn you for your cravenness." I bet he's a tough grader. As the professor sputters away and steam begins to seep slowly from the ears of the assembled congressmen, poor Greg Craig stares at his hands. His shoulders sag. It's not hard to imagine what he's thinking. No sooner has the heroic counsel achieved what heretofore had been deemed impossible—defending Bill Clinton and seeming like a decent guy, all at the same time—than in a wink his hard work comes undone through the self-righteous mewling of this pasty Princeton puke. Greg himself is a Harvard man.

TUESDAY AFTERNOON AND EVENING, DECEMBER 8

For the second panel, the White House has assembled a trio of former Democratic congressmen who served on the House Judiciary Committee in 1974. O Days of Blessed Memory! This afternoon is for wallowing in Watergate, and as a Nixon-hater who lapped up every yummy morsel of the scandal as it happened, I fully understand the impulse. For Democrats of Clinton's generation, Watergate in general, and the committee's impeachment vote in particular, endures in memory as a sacramental occasion, a divine consummation, a moment of unearthly bliss whose perfection rests somehow on the condition that *it never, ever be repeated* until they can figure out a way to do it to another Republican president. And now the vulgarians, these Republicans with their clip-on ties and Wal-Mart Sansabelt slacks, are threatening to violate the memory. And it cannot be tolerated.

I think I'm getting this straight: Because Richard Nixon was almost impeached for asking the CIA to mess with the FBI, for misusing the IRS, and for authorizing the plumbers (the plumbers! the very word brings a thrilling shudder!), a president cannot be impeached unless he has done the same thing. This seems to be the argument made, chorus-like, by the three Watergate veterans brought before the committee. But there's more. Fr. Robert Drinan speaks dreamily of the "dignity of the majesty of the Rodino committee" and seems at times to be lapsing into reverie. Or maybe napping. Liz Holtzman thinks the president is "reprehensible," and the third panelist, an ex-politician from Utah who keeps referring to himself appropriately as an "old has-been," says President Clinton almost certainly perjured himself before the grand jury. I'm beginning to think the president needs some new friends.

They are followed this evening by James Hamilton, a Washington lawyer. He calls the president "disgraceful." He is joined by Richard Ben-Veniste, another Watergate veteran who served under the second Watergate special prosecutor, St. Leon of Jaworski. I notice that when he settles himself at the witness table, Ben-Veniste, a short fellow, perches atop a copy of the thick appendix of supporting materials that Ken Starr submitted to the committee. Talk about contempt for the evidence. Ben-Veniste says the president's behavior was "improper," since all the other insults have already been taken. Like their predecessors, the two lawyers insist that any article of impeachment has to be approved on a "bipartisan basis," which means that there can't be an impeachment unless the people who oppose impeachment vote to impeach. Am I getting this straight?

WEDNESDAY AFTERNOON, DECEMBER 9

Committee Republicans keep complaining that the White House is not addressing the facts of the case, but now, when chief White House counsel Charles Ruff appears before the committee ostensibly for that purpose, the Republicans scarcely ask him any factual questions at all. All the members labor under the traditional "five-minute" rule, allotting everyone 300 seconds to address the witness. The reasoning behind the rule reveals all you need to know about the purpose of congressional hearings. It allows every member a chance to have attention (and TV cameras, if present) focused on himself, while simultaneously making it impossible to elicit substantive information in any sustained manner.

As a result, Ruff's potentially illuminating Q & A proceeds at the customary stuttering pace. Everyone succumbs to drowsiness. I'm sitting behind the president's personal attorney, David Kendall, and I notice he's taken to doodling in a notebook. He draws three boxes and labels them "Draft Articles of Impeachment." In the first box he writes "A"; in the next he writes "An"; and "The" in the third. *Articles,* get it? He elbows his law partner Nicole Seligman, sitting next to him, and points to his doodle. She giggles. Heh-heh. A little impeachment humor. Which confirms my suspicion: This man knows how to party.

Suddenly the atmosphere changes. I notice a couple of Republicans have passed on their allotted five minutes, and when the questioning comes to the next-to-last Republican, Lindsey Graham of South Carolina, I see why. "Mr. Ruff," says Graham, in his Huck Finn drawl, "do you know Sidney Blumenthal?"

Lewinsky scandalphiliacs like me know immediately where he's headed—straight toward one of the more curiously unremarked elements in the case. Presidential aide Blumenthal testified before the grand jury about a conversation he'd had with the president shortly after the scandal broke, in which the president, in some detail, told Blumenthal that Lewinsky was a stalker—one sick little intern. Blumenthal is the White House's Leaker in Chief, and sure enough, stories started to appear in the papers that Lewinsky was . . . a stalker.

Graham starts reading out Blumenthal's testimony, and the air in the hearing room thickens. For the first time in hours Democrats are paying attention.

The minutes tick by, and Hyde announces: "The gentleman's time has expired. The chair recognizes the gentlelady from California, Ms. Bono."

And Bono says, "I yield my time to Mr. Graham," and Graham continues without pause, reading the press clips about Lewinsky the stalker, including one in which Charlie Rangel, the New York Democrat, repeated the accusation.

The Democrats begin to stir. When Graham's time is up again, another member yields his five minutes to Graham. "This is something that is more than consensual sex," he's saying. "This is something, in my opinion, ladies and gentlemen, where a high public official is using the trappings of his office, the White House, to go after a potential witness who possesses information that would hurt his political and legal interests."

It is—finally!—a moment of great drama, electrifying, even.

Now, powerful men who use their positions to slander young women are a great bugbear of Democrats, as we all know, and by the time Graham is reaching a rhetorical climax they are indeed on their feet, appalled. But they're appalled at Graham, not the president.

"Point of order!" shouts Barney Frank. "Mr. Chairman, a point of personal privilege," hollers Maxine Waters. When order is restored she accuses Graham of sexism and especially of "trying to set [Lewinsky] up to be angry at the President of the United States in case she's called as a witness." This is fast thinking on Maxine's part.

After the hearing concludes, and the hallways empty out, I find Frank sitting alone on a table outside the hearing room. I ask him what he thought of Graham's accusations.

"The single most despicable thing I've ever seen in Congress," he says.

Congressman, you've been in Congress almost twenty years. You mean this was the . . .

He stands up and points his finger. "The most despicable thing I've ever seen in Congress. To drag in a man of Charlie Rangel's integrity . . ."

But what do you think of what he said?

"Graham? He's obviously . . ."

No, the president. Why would the president tell Blumenthal all that?

"I don't know what Blumenthal testified to."

Well . . .

"And neither do you. Have you read his testimony?"

Sure.

"I do not know what Blumenthal testified to. Do you understand what I'm saying? Do we have some kind of language barrier here? I don't know that the president said that."

He said she was a stalker.

"Was she? Maybe she was. But to impugn Charlie Rangel, as though Charlie Rangel is some kind of dupe, as though he's some poor dupe who can't think for himself . . . "

Maybe the Republicans are right. Maybe there's no point in asking questions any longer.

★ THE AMERICAN ★ INQUISITION

Kenneth Anderson

FROM THE (LONDON) *TIMES LITERARY SUPPLEMENT,* JANUARY 29, 1999
Like most Americans, I am unmoved by and uninterested in the trial of
Bill Clinton, as I am increasingly uninterested in and unmoved—
repelled, rather—by politicians and all their hangers-on, journalists, lobbyists, lawyers, bureaucrats, pundits, policy analysts, pollsters and
academics, inside Washington and out. I was not glued to the television
news when the House of Representatives read out its articles of impeachment last month, and as the United States Senate opened its ostensibly
historic trial of the President the week before last, I was out shopping at
the mall. And if the trial grinds to an inglorious end in the next few
days, I shall not grieve.

This disenchantment with politics and politicians is not because I
think Bill Clinton does not deserve to be impeached, tried, and removed
from office. On the contrary, I believe Clinton has amply met the standard of "high crimes and misdemeanors" for impeachment and removal.
He is surely guilty of denying, by means of perjury, Paula Jones's right to
a fair trial of her sexual-harassment claim. But, agree or disagree with this
assessment, the trial of Bill Clinton is not about this. Despite the surface
rhetoric of perjury and the rule of law, the trial is about adultery and sin.
Impeachment has become a ritual of confession and redemption, a

religious purge filtered, ironically, through the very morass of laws governing sexuality—sexual-harassment law—that were championed by Clinton and his supporters in the first place. For them, such laws offered a legalistic alternative for the post-religious to the morality of the Ten Commandments. But the outcome has been both a perversion of religion and a failure to focus on the real problem, the urgent need for a reform of what may plausibly be called America's "prosecutorial state."

In my estimation, Clinton perjured himself in order to deprive Paula Jones of the opportunity to claim sexual harassment, the opportunity routinely afforded to educated, upper-middle-class, politically respectable, correctly voting, pro-choice, Democratic women—the Hillary Clintons of this world, and their political clients. True enough, the law today on sexual harassment, as should be broadly apparent, is not a good law. It is the product of a Supreme Court that is plainly aloof from ordinary life, as evidenced by its main contribution to the current constitutional conundrum—a ruling that a tort suit would not greatly inconvenience the chief executive. But if equal protection of the law is the issue, then Clinton has done his illegal best to ensure that one law applies to "white trailer trash" like Jones and another to the self-conceived Uberclass represented by the Friends of Bill and Hillary.

The impeachment proceedings cannot be understood without examining the nature of the elites that surround the Clintons. The singularity of these elites is that their class privileges are defined not merely by education, connections, money, and power, but by the fact that so many of them are lawyers. They take their own access to the law, and their control over others' access to the law, as their privilege. When Paula Jones and her conservative lawyers had the effrontery to assume that they, too, might use the same tactics—those perfected by the Friends of Bill and Hillary for the sake of "deserving" women—it became clear that, in the view of the Clinton elites, this law was reserved exclusively for them—for Jones's betters—and their political clients.

The difficulty with the impeachment trial, and the reason for my lack of interest in it, is that neither the House impeachment vote nor the Senate trial is about this critical issue of the equality of Paula Jones and

Bill Clinton under the law. I say this notwithstanding the numerous speeches by House Republicans which have taken pains to declare exactly this. Rather, the trial is about two issues that differ deeply from equality under the law, and the long shadows of which ensure that, even in the unlikely event of a Senate conviction, it would stand for the wrong things. The first issue is whether Clinton broke, in the eyes of an implacable, unaccountable prosecutor, one of the United States's innumerable, largely unfathomable laws, laws that are distinguished by being simultaneously vague, standardless and yet hyper-technical—this being the special American contribution to jurisprudence. In the hands of the Republicans, the purpose of the trial is not to ensure equal justice for Jones, a full and fair hearing of her claim, but to ascertain whether Clinton, in his capacity as, it is said, America's chief law enforcement officer, broke one of these boundless laws. It is an expression of a new, authoritarian ideal of governance, the prosecutorial state. The other issue is whether the Christian Right—regarding itself as the Lord God's very own political party—will permit an adulterer to occupy the White House. For such theocrats as these, the issue is not justice denied to Paula Jones, but sinful consort with Monica Lewinsky.

No amount of speechifying by Henry Hyde, the chairman of the House Judiciary Committee, can change the reality that the point of impeachment for Republicans is to try, in a political and judicial proceeding, Bill Clinton's alleged sins, not his alleged crimes. If more evidence of this were needed, there is the surprise resignation of Bill Livingston, the House Speaker-to-be, on grounds of adultery. There was no suggestion that Livingston had made misrepresentations under oath or broken any law. The resignation was endorsed by those same House Republicans who claimed that the impeachment of the President was made necessary not by an affair but by the fact that he lied about it under oath. It seems clear that in both cases sin, and not law-breaking, is the real issue for these Republicans and their core conservative Christian constituency, prepared as they are to sacrifice one of their own on the altar of religious virtue. In form, the articles of impeachment may come from Watergate, but in substance they come from Deuteronomy.

To put sin on earthly trial—at long last and praise the Lord—is to the satisfaction not only of the genuine theocrats of the Christian Right. It is also pleasing to Washington's so-called "virtuecrats"—the secular, or at least religiously plural, ideologues of virtue—those believing that virtue could be made the raison d'être of the State, if only they were in charge, this virtuousness to be promoted from the top down to the American peasantry, standing by, presumably, for moral instruction from their television sets. The most prominent among these ideologues is Bill Bennett, former secretary of education under Reagan and U.S. drug policy "tsar." Reinvented as America's very own Liberace of virtue, purveyor of Virtue Lite, he has made a tidy fortune selling a series of books on morality. Alas, in Bennett's *The Book of Virtues, The Book of Virtues for Young People, Adventures from the Book of Virtues*, etc, no virtue goes uncheapened and uncoarsened, save for the two that remain entirely alien to Bennett, modesty and forbearance.

But the politics of personal redemption is not limited to the religious Right or the conservative retailers of national virtue. It is fervently invoked, as well, by those eager to oppose impeachment; they too talk a language of sin, redemption and forgiveness, although in their hands this religious language is indistinguishable from the contemporary secular language of therapy and pop psychology. Hence the noise in the impeachment debate from those who believe that censure, not impeachment or removal, is a sufficient penalty. After all, say these apologists, the Congress of the United States has determined that Bill Clinton has repented most sincerely of his sins with Monica and is judged worthy of forgiveness. Indeed, it is suggested, we must forgive him, in order to heal him and ourselves—one recalls Bill Clinton musing some months ago that the exposure of his affair with Lewinsky might perhaps even be good for America's children. Forgiveness is the Christian as well as the psychologically healthy thing to do, equal justice for Paula Jones being forgotten in the rush to Christian charity and national mental health.

Censure as an alternative panders to the feeling, not unknown among United States senators, that they are godlike, with the power to judge on God's behalf, to forgive on God's behalf, and to bring comfort to the nation and healing to the body politic. Its adherents include, in particular, the ostensibly Mormon Orrin Hatch, who early on offered Clinton a chance to confess his sins and be forgiven—the offer was spurned—and the Orthodox Jew Joseph Lieberman, who was one of the first to shape the national debate by casting matters as personal sin. The White House, eager for the censure alternative, parades the President's personal clergy to provide testimonials of his repentance and Heaven's acceptance of it. (They, no doubt, plan to give testimony to Kenneth Starr, the independent counsel, as to God's state of mind regarding the President; while the independent counsel, in his turn, must dream secretly of indicting God for obstruction of justice and the Holy Trinity for conspiracy.) For those, including me, who profess a certain religious sensibility, it is this arrogation of heavenly prerogatives by earthly political bodies, whether the White House or the Congress, that is the most repellent part of this spectacle. The United States Congress is many wondrous things, but "called of God" is not among them. The Senate is not America's Long Parliament, and Kenneth Starr is not America's Lord Protector. When senators go beyond determining matters of law (which may legitimately include removing the President for violations thereof), and undertake to judge on God's behalf who is a sinner and who has, or has not, been forgiven sufficiently of God to remain in political office, then they usurp powers granted to them neither by God nor by the constitution. Were I a theologian, I might incline to describe them as blasphemers. I would urge them to repentance: less time dwelling on Bill Clinton's sins and more on their own salvation, in fear and trembling and, particularly in the case of Bennett, in silence.

If one fundamental problem of the impeachment proceedings is a religious one, the misuse of the language of redemption and forgiveness, the usurpation of heavenly powers to judge sin and repentance, then the other is thoroughly secular and political. It is the gradual establishment of a powerful and unaccountable prosecutorial state in America, of which the independent counsel is only the most visible current manifestation. The contours of this prosecutorial state can be seen in the difference between the law of perjury and how the American public views the issue. The heart of the case against Bill Clinton is a claim of perjury, predicated on the assumption that perjury is always morally reprehensible and ought always to be subject to legal punishment. Yet I, for one, do not believe this to be so, and neither, I suspect, does a sizable majority of Americans. As James Bowman has argued in these pages (*TLS,* February 20, 1998), lying about sexual matters to protect others even from one's own acts, even reprehensible acts, is often the honorable and morally defensible way of making the best of a bad situation.

Perjury can be defensible for the same reason, that there are some questions to which a person does not owe an answer. It is largely because the American public thinks this that it has shrugged off the charges against Clinton. What the American public understands perhaps less keenly is the extent to which the U.S. legal system, not merely in a sexual-harassment case against the President but to a much broader extent, allows private litigants as well as prosecutors virtually unlimited licence not just to go prowling through the lives of the people involved in a court case, but also to investigate third parties who may once in the past have been someone's lover, or have heard that someone was someone's lover, or just about any other issue of personal relationships that might seem vaguely relevant to establishing character traits. Much of this questioning takes place in "deposition" sessions with only the lawyers present, not in the presence of a judge who might rein in the instrusive questioning. (Not that the presence of a judge would necessarily help: the system of so-called "liberal discovery" of evidence deliberately encourages lawyers to ask anything they please, while judges have long since stopped giving the scope of questioning any seriously critical thought.) This is, after all, how Monica Lewinsky, Kathleen Willey and perhaps others as yet undisclosed became involved in the Paula Jones case and entrapped in the unsavoury web of the independent counsel.

The law, it is commonly said among lawyers, is entitled to every person's evidence. That proposition, however, in a world in which "evidence" is construed as broadly as it is in sexual-harassment law and in Kenneth Starr's investigations, and in which such tactics are frequently used merely to pressure one party or another by threats of personal humiliation through deliberately revealed confidences, seems to me patently false. At some point, it must bump up against some notion of respect for privacy, alien as that notion is to the current Supreme Court, to Kenneth Starr, and to the liberal Clinton constituencies. Lying, under oath or otherwise, is, in fact, the appropriate response to questions which the questioner is not entitled to ask or have answered. It is frequently the case that saying "I won't answer this" or "No comment" can reveal things which are no business of those asking the question. To my mind, it is perfectly moral to lie in order not to give away even that much.

The answer of the lawyers of America is that if Clinton is not held to account for false testimony, then no one else can be held to account for it either, and the judicial system fails. But it seems to me, rather, that the overbearing power granted to lawyers generally, and to prosecutors in particular, to invade lives with questions that they have no business asking already constitutes a massive failure of the judicial integrity of the United States. Noncooperation with its unjust claims seems altogether warranted. Indeed, the only good that might come out of the deeply flawed Clinton investigation, the impeachment, and the trial would be to force a radical rethink of the intrusiveness of judicial process in the United States and arrest thereby the continuing decline of America into a prosecutorial state.

For a remarkable feature of the independent counsel's investigation has been the reactions of former prosecutors around the country to Starr's apparently distasteful tactics—"been there, done that," they repeatedly say, in pursuit of ordinary people and not just presidents. This is not, strikingly, how Clinton's defenders see it. It has become commonplace for them to argue that the Clinton investigation is unique in the unlimited time and resources available to the prosecutor, along with a complete lack of political accountability. Any prosecutor pursuing matters long enough, they argue, could eventually trap people into making false statements under oath. The political implications of this view are twofold. First, it suggests that Clinton is being unequally treated compared with the way, for example, others committing "minor" perjuries would be treated. Second, and more important, it implies that the treatment of Clinton is unique and not at all illustrative of the rest of the American legal system. In this view, it may be necessary to amend the independent-counsel law and its reach over the President, but a more radical reformation of the reach of judicial process as regards the rest of us is not called for. This view is wrong, it seems to me, in both respects. It has been amply documented that ordinary people have been prosecuted, convicted, and served jail sentences for the kinds of perjurious statements alleged against Clinton. The fact that people are doing time for what Clinton has been accused of makes it hard to claim that the President has been singled out unfairly.

More important is what Clinton's case illustrates about the broader conditions of the prosecutorial power in America. The American prosecutorial state is characterized by an empowerment of prosecutors and a corresponding decline in the importance of judges. Contrary to what conservatives believe, outside certain culture-war issues such as abortion, judges play an increasingly peripheral role in the judicial process, ceding their role to private attorneys and prosecutors. In the criminal-law field, the enactment of fixed-sentencing laws and the Supreme Court's repudiation of earlier constitutional protections for the accused have been pivotal in the shift in the balance of power from judges to prosecutors. Judges have found themselves with less discretion, while prosecutors, who have the ability to cut deals with defendants in the form of plea bargains, have ever more.

The answer to this, from America's prosecutorial community, is also illustrated by the Clinton investigation. Time and again, former prosecutors appear on television talk shows, informing the public that the "prosecutor's conscience" and "discretion" ought to have precluded Starr's office from pursuing this action or that. Within the U.S. tradition of the constitutional protection of civil liberties, these are chilling words. They ominously signal that the civil liberties of a potential criminal defendant are no longer secured by the Constitution or by a judge, but merely by the unaccountable conscience of the prosecutor. This is so in a system dominated by the prosecutor's control of plea bargains, vague laws which will always allow indictment for something, and the threat of ruinous costs that will induce any defendant but an O.J. Simpson to cut a deal, no matter what the merit of the charges. Starr, in this light, is not an aberration who has gone outside the system, but the faithful representative of a judicial system gone mad.

Thus the one service that Starr's investigation, by its very lack of conscience, could offer is to bring the fact of this prosecutorial system, and its threat to the civil liberties not merely of the President, but of ordinary people, to public awareness. The matters of judicial process that would require sweeping reform are numerous; they would include not just the independent-counsel statute and sexual-harassment law, but the whole structure of evidence, relevance, perjury, privacy, the disappearing discretion of judges, and the personal accountability of prosecutors for baseless indictments.

No such reform is likely to take place, however, for the simple reason that liberals and conservatives, Democrats and Republicans, all have reasons for liking the prosecutorial state. For conservatives of an authoritarian bent, the reason is easy enough; they like unrestrained police power. But liberals too have got in touch with their authoritarian side; they too have discovered that there are so many, many things that they want to charge people with as crimes. For liberal authoritarians, the prosecutorial state is an alternative path of social engineering in the wake of the failure of the judge-led model. The result is a polity in which conservative and liberal authoritarians egg each other on to criminalize and intrude more and more—a United States that, as Judge Richard Posner pointed out in these pages several years ago, "criminalizes more conduct than most, maybe than any, non-Islamic nations" (*TLS*, September 1, 1995). It is for this reason that Clinton's defenders have been careful to paint the issue not as a matter of the prosecutorial state finally come to roost at the house of liberal authoritarianism, but as a mad independent counsel gunning for the President on purely private sexual matters. Starr's excesses, it is suggested, do not reveal anything about the American justice system as a whole and certainly do not argue for reform of a prosecutorial system that has served elite liberal interests well.

If, however, Congress were prepared to confront the prosecutorial state and undertake to dismantle it, then we could justifiably forget about impeachment and removal. The perjuries that Paula Jones's lawsuit occasioned, including the supposedly "private" lies about Monica Lewinsky, damaged her right to equal treatment under the law. But the laws underlying the lawsuit, the laws allowing such questions to be asked, were never morally defensible in the first place. Even at the cost of procedural injustice to Jones, it would be better to jettison her claims—but only if all the other claims brought by the politically upmarket, educated upper-middle classes and their political clients were jettisoned likewise. And only if all the claims by politicians invoking the powers of God were dismissed also. If the attention of lawmakers could be focused not on heavenly redemption but on reform of an unjust, earthly legal regime, then the impeachment process could be abandoned, and good might yet come of the whole business. But if such a complete reform of the law and the American prosecutorial state is not forthcoming—as it appears not to be—then impeachment and removal ought to proceed. Equality under the law, at least, must prevail: one law for king, peasant and chambermaid.

★ THE REAL STATE OF ★ THE UNION

David Tell

From *The Weekly Standard*, February 1, 1999

While much of America is sleepily rubbing its belly and burping with satisfaction, may we take just a moment to point out that the state of the Union is actually quite *bad*?

Consider, first, the behavior these past two weeks of our print and broadcast press, whose ostensible profession it is to observe, understand, and explain the workings of the government. Gosh, we were told, over and over again, at the start: Henry Hyde and the other impeachment-trial managers have presented a Surprisingly Clear and Compelling Case that the president of the United States has done some genuinely awful things—inconsistent with the health of the Republic.

Surprisingly clear and compelling? True, over three long days January 14 to 16, Hyde and his colleagues mounted an honorable and effective argument that Bill Clinton's grotesque behavior in 1998 warrants his removal from office. But really, now—and it is no criticism of the House managers to say so—they told the Senate nothing, *nothing*, that could possibly have "surprised" anyone who claims to take such questions seriously. The whole of the evidence has been publicly available for months. And the only logical conclusions to be drawn from the evidence have been obvious for even longer. What can it *mean* that all our inkspillers and tele-pundit gabsters were only recently "surprised" to find a strong case against the president? What has American journalism been *doing* all this time?

And how, by this past weekend, could conventional wisdom in Washington have so drastically changed? Now, it was said, Henry Hyde's Surprisingly Clear and Compelling prosecution of the president had been rebutted by a Surprisingly Clear and Compelling defense from the White House. There are objective matters to be resolved here, of course, and the two contending sides in this dispute cannot *both* be clear and compelling. One must be correct and truthful. The other must be incorrect and dishonest. Analytical agnosticism on this question, at this late date, is one of the most irritating aspects of the Lewinsky scandal.

For the White House last week did *not*, in fact, present the Senate with anything close to a convincing demonstration of Bill Clinton's innocence. What the White House proved instead—once more—is that our president surrounds himself with men and women eager to defend even his most elephantine lies. Which fact alone, you would think, might be relevant to a proper judgment on the state of the Union.

It fell to White House counsel Charles F. C. Ruff, last Tuesday, to establish the general themes on which his lieutenants would expand. There was "no basis" for the House of Representatives to impeach the president, he informed the Senate. The charges against Clinton are unfair, "absurd," unconstitutional, even—built on "sand castles of speculation," constructed of "sealing wax and string and spiders' webs," inspired by a conspiracy between Paula Jones's malicious attorneys and an out-of-control Kenneth Starr. Again and again Ruff reminded the senators that "the only two parties who have knowledge" of this or that incriminating conversation have "both denied" they've done anything wrong.

This was rather like a mafia lawyer in a murder trial proposing that, simply because Fat Louie and Sammy the Fish have both testified that Louie never told Sammy to kill anyone, neither Louie nor Sammy can be implicated in the crime. But no senator laughed at Ruff.

White House special counsel Gregory Craig, in turn, launched a lengthy, exquisitely subtle disquisition on how oral sex (still) isn't really sex. Craig then abruptly reversed field, apparently without realizing it, and spent a good bit of time deriding the significance of any fine-tuned distinctions among sex acts. The president, you will recall, acknowledged to the grand jury that Monica Lewinsky had performed fellatio when they were alone together, but denied—defying common sense and Lewinsky's testimony—that he had ever touched her breasts or genitals. The president also insisted to the grand jury, in order to exonerate himself of witness-tampering charges, that he told his aides only "things that were true" when the scandal first became public.

Except that White House aide John Podesta has testified that Clinton explicitly ruled out oral sex with Lewinsky. Any way you cut the evidence, it would seem, Bill Clinton has lied under oath in a federal criminal probe. Gregory Craig called this allegation, felony perjury by the president of the United States, "immaterial," "insubstantial," and "trivial." But no senator laughed at him, either.

Nor did any senator laugh at Clinton attorney David Kendall, who took nearly an hour to explain how it is perfectly natural for the White House senior staff, cabinet and sub-cabinet officials of the executive branch, and the president's best friend all to be continuously on the honker with the CEOs of giant corporations in an effort to secure out-of-town employment for a not particularly impressive 24-year-old administrative assistant. What of the fact that, during the final weeks of this job search, the president had submitted a sworn declaration in the Jones litigation that he'd never had sex with any federal employee—and that Lewinsky was a subpoenaed witness in the case, whose truthful testimony would reveal this declaration to be false? The "big picture" of these impossibly suspicious events, Kendall proclaimed, amounts to "zero."

Needless to say, no senator even dared *think* about laughing at White House deputy counsel Cheryl Mills, whose job it was to emit a further fog about the obstruction of justice counts against Bill Clinton. It is African-Americans, not the president, who are truly now on trial, Mills warned the Senate. Obstruction of justice in the Paula Jones civil rights action against Clinton? The "house of civil rights was never at the core" of that big-haired cracker's lawsuit, according to Mills. The house of civil rights rests instead—entirely—on Bill Clinton's shoulders, since he is right on all the issues, and since his grampaw once owned a store that sold things to black folks. To believe he is guilty, Mills announced, "you must not only disbelieve the president, you must also disbelieve Ms. Currie"—the president's African-American secretary. And that would be "an insult to Betty Currie and to millions of other loyal Americans" just like her. Hint, hint, hint.

Cheryl Mills says that the crime of witness tampering is not a crime at all unless the alleged tampering takes place after a relevant judicial proceeding has already begun. That is not true, and if she is the brilliant, rising-star attorney all the newspapers tell us she is, Mills knows it's not true—but she's saying so anyway. Cheryl Mills says no crime of witness tampering can be committed without some "threat or intimidation." That, too, is a bald-faced misrepresentation of federal law. Cheryl Mills says that when the president had his infamous "We were never alone, right?" interviews with the sainted Betty Currie, witness tampering was the furthest thing from his mind; Clinton was only trying to prepare for a Lewinsky-related media onslaught prompted by Internet gossip Matt Drudge. And that, too, is a lie.

Bill Clinton finished his perjurious Jones-case deposition on the afternoon of Saturday, January 17, 1998. When he got back to the White House, he called Currie at home and asked her to come to work the next day, Sunday, for the first of their questionable conversations. At the time he made this appointment, Matt Drudge's Web site had not yet so much as alluded to Lewinsky's existence.

By Monday, January 19, on the other hand, Washington was abuzz with talk of the intern. And by Tuesday night at nine o'clock, the White House had been fully informed by the *Washington Post*'s Peter Baker about the blockbuster story that paper intended to publish in its Wednesday late editions. Senior White House aides spent the next few hours huddled in Charles Ruff's office, waiting for further news. While they were there, Betty Currie called Ruff to say she'd just been served a subpoena by Ken Starr's grand jury. Sometime later still that Tuesday evening, Clinton called Currie at home to tell her what the next morning's headlines would be.

And it was *after* all this had happened that Clinton and Currie had their second little "We were never alone, right?" chat. By which time the president not only knew he was the subject of a federal grand jury probe, he knew Currie was a subpoenaed witness. The president is guilty. Guilty, guilty, guilty.

But, hey—so what? Rep. Jennifer Dunn, Republican from the state of Washington, voted to impeach Bill Clinton. A healthy state of the Union, you might think she believes, requires Clinton's removal from the White House. But you would think wrong. Responding to the president's State of the Union address last Tuesday night, and *speaking for the Republican party,* Dunn told America that "the state of our Union is strong"—and will remain strong "no matter what the outcome of the president's situation." Got that? He is a criminal, and he must be impeached, but it won't mater a fig if he isn't convicted, because the wheat is high and the crime rate is low. "So what can you expect from Republicans?" Dunn asked, a few minutes further into her remarks. The altogether admirable Henry Hyde and his increasingly lonely allies notwithstanding, that question does sort of hang in the air there, doesn't it?

If so few people any longer even remember what the Union *is,* properly understood—"a government of laws, not men," and a hundred other principles routinely violated by the Clinton presidency—then the only fair conclusion must be that the state of that Union is really *not* so strong at all.

★ GIUSEPPE ★
CONASON'S I DISONESTI

David Tell

Opera in three acts, libretto by the composer, first performed
in Washington during the 1998-99 season

FROM THE *WEEKLY STANDARD*

Act I

SCENE ONE. The Gingricci, an alliance of clerics and enraged albinos
led by Salamandro, have shut down most of the city and surrounded the
Doge's palace. Don Guglielmo, leader of the Disonesti noblemen, con-
fers with his deputy, Podesta, his bodyguard, Carvillo, and his valet, Blumentalio. Don Guglielmo blames the emergency on masculine pride,
and despairs that palace life has withheld from him the worldly counsel
of high-born women ("Che orrore! Mia moglie è frigida e i miei testicoli
sono blu"). Don Guglielmo departs, and, alarmed by his gloom, his
associates ponder their fate. Podesta declares that the Disonesti must
confidently adhere to principle ("Dobbiamo commissionare un
fuocogruppo di Penn e Schoen"). Blumentalio replies that he, a mere
servant, can be confident only of his lowly station ("Sono l'uomo pi-
bello e più intelligente del mondo"). Carvillo calls for moderation and
magnanimity ("Distruggiamo! Massacriamo! Assassiniamo!").

SCENE TWO. Later that evening. Don Guglielmo half-heartedly pastes military dispatches to a ledger on the desk of his adjutant, Giorgio di Stefanopoli. Donna Monica, disguised as a palace intern, arrives with a pizza. Don Guglielmo is made suspicious by his visitor's appearance ("Ha gambe enormi e porta un beretto"), but he accepts the food. While he eats, the lady reveals that she is not a simple intern at all, but a woman of royal birth ("Mi chiamo Monica, principessa ebraica-americana") who has come to help him defeat the Gingricci. Impossible, Don Guglielmo responds; his power is spent. Nonsense, Donna Monica cries, and she urges him to inspect the clever plan she has hidden in her pants ("Molto piccante, no? Venti dollari dal Segreto di Vittoria"). Don Guglielmo is revivified by Donna Monica's support and exults over their meeting ("Buongiorno, un pompino fantastico! Upsidesi—il mio sperma. Scusa"). In his excitement, Don Guglielmo accidentally spills a small drop of Giorgio's paste on Donna Monica's dress.

Act II

Pentagonia, two years later. Out of misguided pity, Donna Monica has befriended an ugly, fat peasant named Linda. She recounts to Linda the story of her profound intellectual partnership with Don Guglielmo, and explains how she has exiled herself to this remote territory purely out of concern that he was eating too much pizza ("Desidero che Nancy Hernreich manga merda"). Linda reassures Donna Monica that no serious person could find scandal in the paste stain on her dress ("Sento l'odore di un gran contratto di libro"). Donna Monica responds that, though Salamandro is now dead, she still fears a resurgence by the Gingricci and worries that Don Guglielmo is not getting the feminine advice he needs ("Ha tette minuscole, Kathleen Willey, ma Eleanor Mondale—vacca!— è provocantissima"). After Donna Monica departs, Linda signals out the window, and the Inquisitore Indipendente enters the room. The Inquisitore reminds Linda that he is acting as a secret agent of the Gingricci, who have promised him a share of their tobacco profits should he succeed in destroying Don Guglielmo ("Ohimè, preferivo veramente una nomina al Tribunale Supremo"). Linda informs the Inquisitore of Donna Monica's soiled garment, and to celebrate the mischief they will make, the two schemers pull the head off a parakeet and drink its blood ("Ha, ha, ha, ha, ha, ha, ha!").

Act III

SCENE ONE. The Doge's palace, a short time later. Egged on by Druggio and Isicoffo, two Gingricci provocateurs, the citizenry is in an uproar over the Inquisitore's false accusation of a liaison between Don Guglielmo and Donna Monica. The Disonesti consider how best to proceed. The Doge's consiglieri, Ruffo and Chendalli, recommend a response of transparent candor and simplicity ("Primo, il privilegio esecutivo, e poi la definizione della parola «solo»"). Because she knows him to be a man of scrupulous rectitude, Don Guglielmo's wife, Rodhama, agrees ("Dirò «è una conspirazione vasta di destra» e spererò di non vomitare"). Don Guglielmo's best friend, Vernono Giordano, offers to arrange for the Duke of Revlona to provide Donna Monica a secure redoubt from the mob ("Parlerò a Don Renaldo di MacAndrews e Forbes, e presto! Una missione completa"). The group's initial optimism is dashed when Podesta reports that Giorgio has defected and denounced Don Guglielmo in the public square ("Ha fatto menzione di «imputazione» in Piazza di Sam e Cokie"). His colleagues depart, and the Doge, crestfallen and distracted, asks his scribe, Bettina, to remind him of their advice, but she has already forgotten what they said.

SCENE TWO. The Grand Council. The oligarchs are debating a Gingricci proposal to expel the council's Moorish members, to whom Don Guglielmo has bravely extended full voting rights. The better to achieve this and other sinister aims ("Niente fluoruro nell'acqua!"), one of the Gingricci, Signor Barro, proposes that Don Guglielmo be replaced as Doge by the ineffectual Don Alberto of Perezzia. Supporting Barro, two of his confederates, Rogano and Lindsigrammo, produce the Inquisitore's fraudulent alchemical analysis of Donna Monica's clothing

("Siamo innamorati dei dettagli pornografichi"). All seems lost until Don Guglielmo dramatically appears and makes clear the truth ("Non ho avuto rapporti sessuali con quella donna"). Moved by his obvious sincerity, the spectators disembowel the Inquisitore and set fire to his liver. A chorus of citizens reaffirm their love for the Doge ("Noi, il popolo, siamo stupidi e immorali"). As the curtain falls, Don Guglielmo rededicates himself to public service ("Mi portate un tamburo di bongo e un sigaro").

★ HEY, KIDS! DON'T ★
READ THIS!

Jonathan Rauch

FROM *THE NATIONAL JOURNAL,* JULY 10, 1999

I don't have children, so I can't say I know much about them. I defer to my many friends in the baby boom generation who are parents. They know everything about children. In fact, they know more about children than was known by all previous generations of parents combined, as becomes clear when you talk to them for more than 60 seconds at a stretch.

I do sometimes wonder, though, if baby boom parents, and baby boom politicians, are always right about absolutely everything. In particular, I wonder if they are right to frame public policy as though adolescents do not exist. My own view—that of a complete amateur, of course, but indulge me—is that this understanding of the world is imperfect. Adolescents exist. It might be better to notice this.

If all you did was read the newspapers and the *Congressional Record,* you might suppose that in America there are two kinds of people, children and adults. The children are all about eight years old, and they are very impressionable and vulnerable, beset on every side by physical and moral perils. The adults are all about forty-five, and their job is to protect the children (though not, as a rule, to discipline them).

Legally, the sharp distinction between majority and minority, although crude, is necessary. Politically, it makes sense to talk about minors as though they were all in kindergarten, since anything done for children is difficult to oppose, and anything done to them is apt to seem constitutional. Still, when baby boom parents and their elected representatives in Washington set out to protect "children" of, say, age sixteen or seventeen, things get peculiar.

After Eric Harris and Dylan Klebold killed thirteen people and themselves at Columbine High School in Littleton, Colorado, the country was treated to a fit of articles and agonies about children who kill. "When Children Kill, Clues Usually There," said a headline in the [Cleveland] *Plain Dealer*. On the floor of the House, Rep. Robert Aderholt, R-Ala., justified his pro-Ten Commandments bill as a step toward "an end of children killing children." Democrats said they wanted more laws to keep guns out of the hands of children. "Children don't need to be held accountable for misusing guns," editorialized the *Atlanta Journal-Constitution*, "they need protection from guns." At the White House, Hillary Rodham Clinton said: "Guns and children are two words that should never be put together in the same sentence."

What seemed odd about the babble about children and guns was that Eric Harris was eighteen years old, and Dylan Klebold was seventeen. "Children"?

On the "protect the children" model of social-policy making, an adolescent is a six-year-old with acne. The way to prevent a "child" of sixteen or seventeen from getting something is to tell him he can't have it, and the way to deflect his interest from the thing is to tell him he's not old enough to handle it. On the "adolescents exist" model, by contrast, such infantilizing tactics may not be ideal. A better way to teach a teenager about responsibility is to give him some.

In 1994, the Justice Department published initial findings of a cluster of studies that tracked delinquency among several thousand children and adolescents in Denver, Pittsburgh, and Rochester. Where youths and guns were concerned, the results seemed to support the "adolescents exist" model. Illegal possession of firearms was a strong predictor of delinquency. For example, 74 percent of boys who illegally possessed guns committed street crimes, compared with 24 percent of boys who had no guns. No surprise there.

Rather more surprising was this: Boys who owned a gun legally (that is, with the advice and consent of their parents) were even less delinquent than boys who had no gun at all. Only 14 percent of boys who legally possessed guns committed street crimes, and 0 percent of them committed any sort of gun crime. "For legal gun owners," the study said, "socialization appears to take place in the family; for illegal gun owners, it appears to take place 'on the street.' " One wonders, then, whether demanding that access to guns be increasingly restricted to adults is a wise policy in a country with about twelve guns for every adolescent.

In the mid-1990s, when he was in charge of the Food and Drug Administration and looking to expand his agency's reach, David A. Kessler made a startling announcement. Nicotine addiction, he said, "is a pediatric disease that often begins at twelve, thirteen, and fourteen, only to manifest itself at sixteen and seventeen when these children [*sic*] find that they cannot quit."

For some years before Kessler sought to redefine the debate, tobacco policy in America had been conducted, roughly, on the "adolescents exist" model. Every effort was made to ensure that Americans of all ages understood that smoking was harmful, and, according to a 1994 report by the Surgeon General, researchers developed a handful of in-school antismoking programs that seemed to have some marginally useful effects. Between 1976 and 1992, the proportion of twelfth-graders who reported smoking one or more cigarettes in the past month declined gradually but steadily, from almost 40 percent to under 30 percent.

In 1992, something happened. After years of progress, the trend reversed. Since 1992, even as adult rates held stable or fell, smoking by twelfth-graders has risen by almost 10 percentage points (and smoking by younger adolescents has also increased, though not as much). No one knows the reason. Antismoking activists sometimes blame Joe Camel, but he came along in 1988. I have what I think is at least an equally plausible theory: As antismoking education graded into something more like antismoking hysteria, adolescents stopped listening. A further speculation is that a campaign to "protect children" from tobacco is likely to miss the mark, for a few reasons.

One is that, pace Kessler, smoking is not like measles, striking innocent tots out of the blue. "Very few twelve-year-olds have even tried a cigarette," writes Mary Grace Kovar, an epidemiologist with the National Opinion Research Center in Washington. "The modal age for trying a cigarette is sixteen." Smoking is not a disease of children; it is a choice made by adolescents, often to distinguish themselves from children.

Moreover, not just anybody smokes. Kovar's analysis notes that smokers age fifteen to seventeen are very much more likely than nonsmokers to be alcohol users and to skip school. Adolescents who smoke tend to be risk takers and rebels. "I think you'll find the same thing through early adulthood, and maybe beyond," Kovar said. "There is a group of risk-taking people. I've always disliked approaches that target an age group instead of targeting people who need certain kinds of help—but that's what we do."

Presumably, adolescents who are attracted to risk and rebellion—the ones who are most likely to smoke—are also the least likely to listen to adults who bluster about making America a land of "tobacco-free kids." Or, worse still, they may listen, and then decide that not being tobacco-free is a good way to show that they aren't kids.

If adolescents don't exist, then a national crusade to put cigarettes out of the reach of "children," on the model of childproof caps, is clearly the way to go. If, on the other hand, they do exist, then calm and respectful education about smoking and risk seems somewhat more sensible.

Am I missing something, or is it odd to suppose that treating the Internet as a threat to "children" will dampen teenagers' curiosity about www.hotsex.com? In June, the House defeated a proposal to ban the sale to "children"—all persons under seventeen—of materials containing "explicit violent material," such as depictions of sadism, torture, and rape. "The Federal government helps parents protect children from dirty air . . . and dirty water," said Rep. Wayne T. Gilchrest, R-Md. "It is only incumbent upon us for the Federal government to help parents protect their children from vulgar, violent videos." If you think such a measure would reduce a teenager's interest in *Natural Born Killers*, you have never met, been, or heard of a teenager.

I imagine that twenty-five years from now people will look back on today's systematic infantilization of adolescents and wonder: How could so many people have forgotten the very most obvious truths about adolescence? Had they never met, been, or heard of a teenager? But then every generation of parents feels obliged to test some outlandishly dumb idea on its children. My parents' generation managed to forget that divorce is bad for children, which was nearly as impressive as forgetting that sixteen-year-olds aren't the same as six-year-olds.

Oh, well. I'm not a baby boom parent. I suppose I don't understand children.

★ CONSERVATIVISM AT ★ CENTURY'S END: A PROSPECTUS

Tod Lindberg

FROM *POLICY REVIEW,* APRIL/MAY 1999

For better or worse, modern ideological conservatism constitutes a completed body of thought. We need not try to settle the issue of how it came to completion, an exercise in intellectual history a bit beyond the scope of these reflections, to note the fact. There was a time, coming to a close perhaps a decade ago, when those of us who took an interest in the development of conservative ideology eagerly reached for our newly arrived periodicals and newly published books in the expectation of finding bold new insights into vexing problems, some of which we did not even realize were problems. This was an exciting time—conservative ideology was a work in progress, and the task had urgency, vitality, and freshness. Part of the task was the development of a thorough critique of liberal and radical ideology and the effects these had throughout our politics and culture. But conservative ideology was not merely negative—merely based in criticism. It had a positive component as well, laying claim to a future it proposed to make better through the defeat of radicalism, the rejection of liberalism, and the implementation of conservative ideas in the policy arena.

This period of intellectual ferment is over. In a way, that is a tribute to its success. One can say of ideological conservatism nowadays that, in general, it knows what the important questions are and it knows the answers to those questions. There remains much detail to work out, but the outlines are clear. Conservatives resolve arguments in favor of the individual rather than the collective, of clear standards of judgment rather than relativistic measures, of personal responsibility rather than the interplay of vast social forces, of the market rather than government economic intervention, of international strength and self-reliance rather than empty promises of security. The Federal government is, in general, too big, taxing too much of the wealth of Americans, doing too many unnecessary and often counterproductive things that get in the way of economic growth, to say nothing of personal liberty. Even as it has indulged in frivolity, the Federal government has been neglectful of the security of Americans in its rush to disarm after the successful conclusion of the Cold War. Meanwhile, a debased high and popular culture shows few signs of recovery.

Among conservatives, one is hard-pressed to find any disagreement on these basic issues. The real questions, instead, are whether, when, and how the American political process will make good on the promises of conservatism. In certain respects, this is a tribute to the triumph of conservative ideology. In the absence of its searching critique of liberalism and its advancement of an alternative vision, it seems unlikely that the old liberal dominance would have faded as it has. The practical import of this triumph is that conservative ideology is no longer merely a theoretical matter. Conservatives would like to implement it, to substitute their ideas for the dead hand of liberalism that guided our politics for decades. The principal activity of ideological conservatism at century's end takes place not in the realm of ideas, but in the world of politics.

THE CONSERVATIVE INTELLECTUAL CULTURE

The characteristic figures of conservative intellectual culture are no longer professors and intellectuals. The characteristic figures are lawyers and journalists. This, as much as anything, is an indication of how far conservatism has come.

Making the law and reporting on how the law is or isn't getting made: In some ways, these seem the principal activities of idea-minded conservatives nowadays. Once again, this may be a product of the success of the intellectual endeavor, over the years, in asking and answering the basic questions. But there are no more basic questions to ask and answer, or so it seems, and so it seems neither inappropriate nor terribly significant that for those interested in the life of the mind these days, at least outside the academy, action consists of either a seat at the table where the big decisions are being made; or a place at the peephole into the room with the table, in order to describe it for others (and second-guess it).

The conservative intellectual culture reflects the broader media culture around us. That broader culture now worships two principal deities: Much and Quick. Our culture produces an extraordinary volume of information for anyone interested in consuming information. Never have so many had so much access to so much, nor so quickly. What is a media culture to do in the age of the Internet and 24-hour cable programming on politics? The answer has been: Go along with it. In addition to a new breed of on-line "magazines" whose content changes from hour to hour, we have seen biweekly, weekly, and daily publications break out of their traditional "news cycle" to give us the benefit of their reporting and analysis as soon as they can post it on their web sites. Conservatism, for its part, is now propagated as much by simultaneous e-mail transmission as by any other medium. To be au courant is to answer a liberal argument made on a morning cable show by early afternoon. It may, however, be an indication of how well-formed conservative thought is that it can propagate answers so quickly.

THE QUESTIONS TO THE ANSWERS

Is anything wrong with this? On one hand, no. In the first place, there is no undoing the profusion of cable or the availability of the Internet. We live in our time. It would be the height of folly to cede such powerful tools as the Internet and cable to people out to do in the conservative project. As long as these media are available, it only makes sense to seize them and use them the best one can. In the second place, the sometimes-rote quality of the propagation of conservatism and conservative positions is hardly the product of imposition of intellectual orthodoxy by some central committee taking as its charge the enforcement of discipline among the cadres. There is no such committee. Instead, the familiar quality of conservatism is a product of widespread agreement among thoughtful people. Its completed character is testimony to the sway of reason among reasonable people.

But is a swift and certain conservatism, even if such a conservatism is essential, actually sufficient? Here, there is reason to pause.

The long-term success of conservative ideology depends on how well that ideology understands and describes the world and predicts outcomes in it. If, in point of fact, conservative ideology is perfectly formed at present, then there is no particular risk in the current state of conservative intellectual culture. But if not, then what? And how will conservatives know?

The liberal experience should send a cautionary signal to conservatives. Liberalism as an ideology proved remarkably disinclined to engage in self-examination. The intellectual energy of liberalism was largely taken up in a decades-long argument between the go-fast liberals and the one-step-at-a-time liberals. Liberalism had no particular response to external pressure, either in the form of the failure of the world to act in accordance with its expectations or in the form of the conservative intellectual critique of liberalism during the heyday of the formation of conservative ideology. Liberalism, comfortable in the wielding of political power, simply did so—until there came the point at which it lost political power as a result of the bankruptcy, insufficiency, and stubborn wrong-headedness of its ideas.

Liberalism would surely have been better off had some substantial number of its most talented adherents been able or willing to take a step back from their ideological certainty and re-examine their premises in the light of real-world results. (One could say that some liberals did take this road, only to become conservatives; on the other hand, it is hardly obvious that the only alternative to liberalism is ideological conservatism.)

Conservatives should profit from this error. Some of them ought to take it as a project of some urgency to step back from the now hurly-burly world of conservative political and intellectual culture and take a long, hard, detailed look at conservatism. The alternative is merely the assumption that all is well. That is a dangerous assumption. Even if all is well, it is better to say so on the basis of serious self-scrutiny than on a whim, or worse, out of the ideological conviction that all must be well. And suppose all is not well. Suppose one or another problem becomes apparent. There is at least a possibility that such problems as arise can be addressed and corrected before their steady accretion threatens the totality of the project of conservative governance.

If ideological conservatism now is relatively self-confident in the con-viction that it has the right answers to the important questions, the time has come for the right questions about the answers.

TIME TO THINK

One thing is certain. No serious conservative self-scrutiny will arise spontaneously from the current media culture. Rather, such scrutiny can only be a product of a deliberate decision on the part of some number of serious people to take the time to think about some pretty serious things. And the product of their deliberations will not be the least suited to delivery via sound bite or e-mail.

They will write essays. These essays will be published in a magazine that has made a deliberate decision to make its stand outside the news cycle. In a culture increasingly given to Much and Quick and more and faster, this magazine will take the radically contrarian view that serious-ness necessitates deliberation, and that an article that can be read with profit and enjoyment a year or two or a dozen after it first appears is potentially at least as valuable a thing as all the e-mail traffic in between.

This magazine, in turn, will be read by people who appreciate the limitations of the media culture of Much and Quick—and the perhaps-hidden dangers this culture poses to conservatism. This magazine and its audience will, in short, constitute the dynamic element of modern con-servative thinking.

CONSERVATIVISM AT CENTURY'S END: A PROSPECTUS

CONSEQUENCE

The creation of modern conservative ideology was an exercise in ideas—in many cases, ideas about the consequences of an older set of ideas, those of liberalism. But conservatism is no longer merely about ideas, because conservative ideas are having consequences of their own. The success or failure of conservatism, in the long run, will depend on how well conservatism understands those consequences and adapts to them.

THE PROJECT OF THIS MAGAZINE

To serve as the preeminent vehicle for new conservative thinking and new and serious thinking about conservatism.

To monitor the progress of conservative ideology as it moves from the realm of theory to the world of practice, the political world.

To reexamine as necessary the premises, logic and conclusions of conservative thinking in order to ensure that conservatism remains intellectually rigorous and vital.

To create or re-create a community of conservative thinkers and writers capable of bringing to the challenges of the present the same clarity, conviction, and conscience their intellectual elders brought to bear on the problems of a different time.

In a world of ephemera, it is time for some number of people to devote their energies and attention to matters of lasting consequence.

★ A LOVELY WAR: HOW ★ CLINTON & BLAIR DREAM

John O'Sullivan

From *National Review*, June 14, 1999

Oh, oh, oh it's a lovely war, begins the old verse. Ever since the Kosovo intervention started, commentators have noted that this is a liberal war. Its methods, for instance, are those pioneered by Presidents Kennedy and Johnson in Vietnam—"graduated escalation" and all that. It also has a liberal aim—to protect the Kosovar Albanians from "ethnic cleansing"—that is quite untainted by any selfish U.S. or Western interest. And, finally and conclusively, its methods have completely undermined its aims, since graduated escalation has allowed Serbian forces ample time to empty Kosovo of ethnic Albanians. Q.E.D.

NATO's intervention certainly did not have to follow this course. Since Milosevic had already sent forces against Slovenia, Croatia, and Bosnia, the West might reasonably have decided that curbing his capacity to cause trouble at NATO's backdoor was a legitimate strategic aim. Acting on that logic, it would then have recognized Kosovo as a state that had been entitled to claim its independence when the former Yugoslavia broke up but had been forcibly prevented from doing so by Serbia. That in turn would have provided a basis in international law to recruit, train, equip, and purge an effective Kosovo Liberation Army (as American mercenaries, with official U.S. backing, trained the Croatian

Army) and, when the time came, to support these local ground troops with purposive NATO air support. The likely outcome cannot be foretold with precision—as Hitler said, he who starts a war enters a dark room—but the policy would at least have had a desirable and achievable war aim: namely, a new and more stable Balkan balance of power in which a weaker and chastened Serbia is surrounded by militarily defensible states allied to NATO.

But this conservative strategic vision—though advocated by some, notably Lady Thatcher and Noel Malcolm, the historian of the Balkans—was never really considered, let alone followed. This is in part because, although the policy is moral in the traditional sense of seeking to achieve a legitimate aim by prudent and proportionate means, it nonetheless has the flavor of 19th-century realpolitik about it, rather than the windy, high-minded moralizing that liberals like Bill Clinton and Tony Blair mistake for an ethical foreign policy.

There was also, however, a specific reason of policy why the conservative strategy was rejected: Although it was opposed to Serbia's aggressive nationalism, it was not opposed to ethnic nationalism in principle. Indeed, it would have enlisted the ethnic nationalism of Croatia and Kosovo (as well as the multiethnic patriotism of Bosnia) to check the Serbian variety.

As for the underlying theoretical question of whether ethnic nationalism is a legitimate basis for statehood, the conservative strategy (like conservative political theory in general) gives no single answer. Sometimes ethnic nationalism will ameliorate popular discontent with the least upheaval—for instance, granting the Slovaks independence peacefully; sometimes it will make matters worse, as in multiethnic Bosnia disrupted by the national claims of Bosnian Serbs; and sometimes it is an irresistible force even though its first effects will be to make matters worse, as is perhaps the case with Albanian nationalism in Kosovo. The conservative theory of statehood is that circumstances alter cases.

But Bill Clinton has a much grander theory of statehood than that platitude. His vision is opposed to ethnic nationalism as the basis for statehood in principle; it favors a new international order in which ethnic groups enjoy limited cultural autonomy in large, new, multi-ethnic, multicultural federations like, er, the good old U.S.A.; and it sees the Kosovo war as the first battle in the realization of this benign future. Here are two excerpts from a recent speech by the Hot Springs Metternich:

> (1) "If we were to choose this course [either independence or partition for Kosovo], we would see the continuous fissioning of smaller and smaller ethnically based, inviable [*sic*] states, creating pressures for more war, more ethnic cleansing, more of the politics of repression and revenge."
>
> (2) "Finally, we must remember the principle we and our allies have been fighting for in the Balkans is the principle of multi-ethnic, tolerant, inclusive democracy. We have been fighting against the idea that statehood must be based entirely on ethnicity." This is a sort of upside-down Wilsonianism. Where Wilson pushed national self-determination, Clinton pushes a liberal, multicultural empire in which ethnic groups are limited to cultural self-expression.

But there are a number of narrow and unvisionary problems with this vision. In the first place, many—perhaps most—existing states are based on ethnic nationalist foundations, including such American allies as Japan, Germany, Spain, Israel, Ireland, France, and almost all of central and eastern Europe. Are they all illegitimate? All doomed to be subsumed into new multicultural entities? And if so, are they aware of the fact—or that America's (and NATO's) new policy is their national euthanasia?

Second, far from fading from the scene, ethnic nationalism is advancing. The collapse of Communism liberated a host of ancient nations in Europe and Eurasia from the prisonhouse of multiculturalism that was the Soviet empire. Now, the USSR really was a polity in which ethnic nationalism was limited to cultural expression, so that, in Anthony Daniels's mordant description, "under Communism, all minorities dance." But the peoples concerned found that unsatisfactory. And having so recently gained their political independence, they cherish it. Clinton's new policy is thus a victim of spectacularly bad timing.

Third, the new multiethnic, multicultural democracies that the president sees as the hope of the future do not actually exist as yet. The European Union, which he cites, has the ambition to become a multicultural federation, but as yet it is still a colloquy of national governments. And the multiethnic federations that used to exist—principally the Soviet Union and Yugoslavia—have perished, leaving behind them nations in which ethnic nationalism is all the fiercer for having been suppressed for 50 years.

These states were not, of course, democracies—but the unfortunate fact from Clinton's standpoint is that there are no examples of successful, long-running, multiethnic, multicultural democracies. (The apparent but misleading exceptions, India and Switzerland, raise questions larger than can be dealt with in a brief article.) Democracy seems to require the kind of fellow feeling of which nationalism, whether of an ethnic or a cultural kind, is the main modern expression.

Finally, Clinton's international vision has spawned an incoherent policy towards Kosovo. Because he is opposed to ethnic nationalism tout court, he has had to oppose independence for Kosovo or any real aid to the KLA. NATO's policy, still in place though widely derided as absurd, is to compel Serbs and Kosovar Albanians to live together in a multicultural federation ruled by Milosevic. Naturally, that would require the more or less permanent presence of U.S. and other NATO ground troops to ensure that the inhabitants of the Clinton-Blair "Third Way" utopia did not all murder one another. But are there enough American soldiers to sustain this vision everywhere? Hardly. Indeed, there may not be enough to sustain it here at home in balkanizing America.

★ A KENNEDY APART ★

Peter Collier

From *National Review,* August 9, 1999

Once again the endless stream of images of the family—windswept, winsome, so extraordinary in appearance. Once more the summoning of all the old ghosts—Joe Jr., the doomed aviator; Kick, who also died by air; JFK in the motorcade in Dallas; RFK making the last speech in Los Angeles; and finally, in sad parodies of the tragic eloquence of these deaths, the silly recklessness of David and Michael and now the handsome young man with his mother's air of mystery, who fell out of the sky on his way to a wedding.

In some ways, John Jr., born at the family's high-water mark, was the most Kennedy of them all—America's Child from the moment his father smuggled the photographer into the Oval Office, and America's Orphan from the moment his mother got him to salute the coffin pulled by the riderless horse. Yet among his relatives, John Jr. was a stranger, an un-Kennedy with a threatening power he had not yet fully possessed to show what a soulless machine the Kennedys have become.

There was always a facade of solidarity, but from the beginning he was the family's exotic. His early experiences resembled those of a hemophiliac prince growing up in protective isolation, particularly in comparison with his cousins' struggles for primacy in the rough-and-tumble of the Compound. Standing at their fence offering to sell "Kennedy sand" to passersby for a dollar a bag, they grew up in a sort of boot camp in which they learned how to mock those who worshipped them. They knew from the outset what they were, if not who—executives in training for the family business.

By contrast, John Jr. was a Kennedy without an agenda, discovering himself as he went along. The loss he had suffered was no greater than that of his RFK cousins, but he did not mend so quickly. In the sequestered apartment in New York, he tried to make Secret Service men into surrogate fathers, and he shyly asked his mother's friends if they wanted to hear his "real father," then took them to his room to listen to records of JFK's speeches.

After Bobby's death, Jackie, saying that she feared America had declared "open season on Kennedys," took her children and left. In their irritation over her decision to become a modern Cleopatra using the world as her Nile, her countrymen missed one of the crucial factors in her decision: After 1968, she saw that Hyannisport, a place where there were no adults left, would become a toxic site for young people. She was right. Soon RFK's brood and the cousins they controlled were playing a generational version of *Lord of the Flies* there, while her own son preserved his relative innocence in unlikely venues—the island of Skorpios or the yacht Christina, with its El Grecos and its barstools covered in the skin of whale testicles.

While the others grew up Kennedy, as that concept was being reinterpreted in the seventiess and eighties, John Jr. grew up Bouvier. On his infrequent visits to the Compound, they called him a "mama's boy" and, even more cruelly, from their point of view, taunted him for not being a "real Kennedy."

He was indeed an observer rather than a participant. He watched as his cousins engaged in the heavy drug use and casual self-destruction that became events in their postmodern Kennedy Olympiad. These other Kennedys—real Kennedys—became as much an object lesson for him as for everyone else. They had no one teaching them, as Jackie taught him and Caroline, how to control their imagery or to normalize a taste for the grandiose. Nabbed in heroin buys, shown paralyzing strangers in their vehicles, revealed to have exploited fourteen-year-old baby-sitters—while he merely rollerbladed in Central Park—the cousins were a godsend in that they made him, an awesomely unique figure, seem a regular guy.

Almost without willing it, he had the ability to shine a light on the dreary, airless place the Kennedy Legacy had become. It was said that he studied his father's life. As he did, it must have occurred to him how little the new Kennedy construct had to do with JFK. In 1979, when John Jr. spoke at the dedication of the Kennedy Library, he heard of the outrage expressed by Bobby's eldest son, Joe, over the fact that, while there had been a 30-minute film about JFK, the one about RFK was only five minutes long. But the apparent discrepancy in the two brothers' relative importance was a mirage. The Kennedy Legacy was clearly dominated by Bobby and the changes he was said to have undergone in his last, intense years.

Composed after Dallas and bearing the indelible imprint of the sixties, the Legacy turned engagement, moral passion, and social concern into family shtick. It became a family ideology implicating every male Kennedy and allowing them only one posture—that of Tribune to the Underclass. It was so powerful that it scooped up the personality of JFK and included him too, when in fact he was something else altogether—cool, detached, remote, a creature of irony who distrusted commitment. (In one famous moment, when his brother was brooding in the Oval Office, Jack told a friend who noticed it, "Oh, don't worry about Bobby: He's probably all choked up over Martin Luther King and the Negroes today.")

As they fetishized themselves, the Kennedys proposed that the Legacy was based on martyrs who offered themselves as ritual sacrifices to enliven and ennoble our democracy. This was believable until Chappaquiddick. The day Mary Jo Kopechne died, things began to change. The accident and the clumsy attempt to cover it up began to drain the Kennedys' accumulated capital. It brought into the foreground the nihilism present in the family's rise from the Irish-Catholic ghetto: Rules are the way they keep us down; rules are for suckers. After this, the Legacy was no longer just idealism and compassion. It was also ruthlessness and heedless appetite, which ignored the collateral damage and, when caught, protested that this was merely the cosmic whimsy of the "Kennedy curse."

Staggering under the weight of Bobby's Legacy, Teddy made that contribution. He also took all the moral passion and sense of discovery characteristic of RFK's last days and homogenized it into party-line liberalism, making sure that every Kennedy male who came after was a man in its iron mask. It was a commitment so petrified that it could not change even as the liberalism it supposedly embodied changed. Gradually, the Democratic party withdrew from the family, leaving them members only of the Kennedy party.

John Jr. escaped all this. He maintained at least a tincture of the promise that Ted and the others had leeched out of the Legacy. He was a beefcake narcissist who was oddly selfless, with a charisma that was genuine in spite of himself; a symbol who was able to offer himself for the consumption of popular culture without getting eaten up. He showed a glimpse of the personal while remaining aloof—an icon with a human face.

Politics was in his blood too. But unlike his cousins, who began that grim death march toward power even when they were teenagers, he came to the subject on his own terms—as editor of a gossipy magazine that regarded politics as a contact sport, but not as Mortal Kombat. (Perhaps this was in homage to his father and the left-out part of the Legacy, since JFK sometimes said that he might have been a journalist if his elder brother hadn't died, causing the old man to use him as a prosthetic for his own ambition.)

As his cousins sweated and grunted, managing only to look like little boys clomping around in Daddy's shoes, John Jr. seemed not only more mature but ever more Kennedy as well. He could lend them the authority of his name as in 1994, when he went to Massachusetts to help rescue his Uncle Ted from his sinking Senate race. But while he dabbled in the family, he also didn't hesitate to create a great schism three years later, when he wrote in his magazine that his cousins Joe and Michael were "poster boys for bad behavior."

It was as close as any Kennedy has come to issuing a moral condemnation of a blood relative, although it was still a half-gesture. "Perhaps they deserved it," he proceeded to write of the public disapproval of their misdeeds. "Perhaps they knew better. To whom much is given, much will be required, right?" The repetition of "perhaps" and that last "right" captured it all and showed him to be his father's son: casual, irreverent, launching a serious critique while appearing to disown it, using irony as squid's ink to create a stir and then make his getaway.

Joe accused him of exploiting the situation to give *George* a boost: "Ask not what you can do for your cousin, but what he can do for your magazine." And there was no doubt some truth in that. But there was also no mistaking the generational challenge John Jr. had issued. "I am not you," he was saying. "I'm not bound by that Kennedy Legacy you have shrunken and diminished in returning it to the ward-heeling barroom politics of our great-grandfathers' day."

The sense of possibility that John F. Kennedy Jr. embodied had less to do with America than with the Kennedy family itself. He was warning about what a dreadful and dreary burden the Legacy had become, and was offering the Kennedys one last chance to escape from themselves. In the unbearable lightness of his dying, he has sealed the family's fate.

★ UNMANNING STRUNK ★ & WHITE: A NEW ELEMENTS OF STYLE

Andrew Ferguson

From The WEEKLY STANDARD, October 4, 1999

It's hard to imagine a book more misconstrued than *The Elements of Style*, or a writer more misjudged than E.B. White, who co-wrote "the little book" with William Strunk Jr. This year is the centenary of White's birth, and looking through the handful of news articles that have marked the occasion I see he's sometimes referred to, by newspaper editorialists, Op-Ed writers, and other enthusiasts, as "America's foremost man of letters" or even "the greatest essayist of the century." A humorous man with a high but realistic estimation of his gifts, White would have enjoyed the extravagance of the claim, coming at the end of a century that produced George Orwell, G. K. Chesterton, Rebecca West, Edmund Wilson—essayists who swung the heavy lumber and hit the long ball, as White, a miniaturist by inclination, did not and did not try to do. All the same, White was an amiable and disarming writer, the kind whose influence, if you discover it at a certain age, is almost always wholesome and hard to shake off. He was just a journalist but a superior one. His legacy, as the legacy of deadline writers tends to be, consists not of any one or two great works but of the desultory leavings that survive a fifty-year career in the trade: perhaps a half-dozen enduring essays, a few memorable scraps of light verse, a long and enjoyable volume of letters, and three well-loved children's books, including *Charlotte's Web*. It's a pretty fair basket of goods. And of course it includes *The Elements of Style*, which has just been revised for the first time since White's death in 1985.

This is the fourth edition of *The Elements of Style*. Since its commercial debut in 1959, it has sold more than 10 million copies, at an average clip of a quarter-million a year, making it easily the most successful American textbook ever published. This spring, Random House's Modern Library, in yet another gimmicky millennial list, placed *The Elements* at number twenty-one on its selection of the hundred best nonfiction books of the century; not to be outdone, a few months later a team of New York City librarians chose it as one of their "twenty-one classics for the twenty-first century."

For durability and popular appeal, *The Elements of Style* has to be reckoned more than a textbook. But why this should be so is not at all clear. The little book is often praised for reasons that seem suspect. In an afterword to the new edition, the CBS news personality Charles Osgood boasts of carrying the book in his pocket at all times. (Osgood is one of those TV commentators who is known among his peers as a "writer's writer"; and like other great TV stylists he employs a ghostwriter. Maybe he means he pockets the ghostwriter, who carries *The Elements* for him.) The implication of such boasts—Osgood is not the first to make it—is that a careful writer must have the book constantly at the ready, to settle a dispute about, say, the use of the conditional in the subjunctive mood.

The only problem is that, as a comprehensive guide to grammar and usage, *The Elements* is nearly useless. Running fewer than a hundred pages in most editions, it is not a sweeping survey of the scene, and was never intended to be. Its design consists of eleven "Elementary Rules of Usage," eleven "Elementary Principles of Composition," a chapter on "Matters of Form," another on "Words and Expressions Commonly Misused," a closing essay on the act of writing—and that's it. (The new edition adds a glossary, which makes the book more serviceable than its predecessors, but only slightly.) The "rules" and "principles" are maddeningly spotty; vast areas of grammar go unmentioned altogether. If

Osgood really wants to settle those heated arguments about syntax that must erupt routinely among the craftsmen in the CBS news-room—or, for that matter, if a student just wants to know what the hell an appositive is—he will be better off leaving *The Elements* in his pocket and buying a copy of the *MLA Style Manual* or any one of a dozen others that actually treat the subject with encyclopedic breadth and detail.

No, Charles Osgood notwithstanding, *The Elements of Style* is something else entirely—something much less than many of its partisans pretend, and something much greater, too.

The eccentric design of the book makes sense in light of its origins. *The Elements of Style* was first published in 1918 by its author, a Cornell professor named Will Strunk. Strunk himself was the one who tagged *The Elements* "the little book." He printed it privately for classroom use by students in his composition course, among whom was E.B. White. Nearly forty years later, in the spring of 1957, White received a surviving copy in the mail from an old college friend. Charmed, he set down an appreciation of the book and its author for the *New Yorker*.

" 'The little book' has long since passed into disuse," he wrote. "Will died in 1946, and he had retired from teaching several years before that. Longer, lower textbooks are in use in English classes nowadays, I dare say—books with upswept tail fins and automatic verbs. I hope some of them manage to compress as much wisdom into as small a space, manage to come to the point as quickly and amusingly."

The day after White's essay appeared an editor at Macmillan took the hint—if a hint is what White intended—and wrote him asking to see a copy of Strunk's book and wondering whether White's piece might be used as an introduction to a new edition. White sent along his copy, with a note expressing some reservations. "Whether the book has virtues that would recommend it to teachers of English, I don't feel qualified to say. . . . Sometimes the book, like the man, seems needlessly compressed, and it is undeniably notional." He mentioned its lack of comprehensiveness, the large gaps in its survey of grammar and usage. White had a theory to explain this odd construction. "I think [Strunk] felt the need for a labor-saving device in correcting papers. With the 'little book' in the hands of his students, he could simply write in the margin of a theme: 'See Rule Two.' "

Despite his doubts, White offered his help if Macmillan wanted to reissue the book. He had two conditions. First, though Strunk's copyright had lapsed, Macmillan would have to get permission from his heirs and pay them royalties. (To this day royalties are split equally between the White and Strunk families—a handsome annuity that must amount to several hundred thousand dollars.) And second, he wanted the chance to comb through the book, bring it up to date, and offer some of his own thoughts on the subject of rhetoric.

Though always a slow worker, he thought the project would take him a month. It took nearly two years.

"I discovered," he wrote many years later, "that for all my fine talk I was no match for the parts of speech—was, in fact, over my depth and in trouble. Not only that, I felt uneasy at posing as an expert on rhetoric, when the truth is I write by ear, always with difficulty and seldom with any exact notion of what is taking place under the hood."

There were other problems. As White dug into the book its inadequacies became more apparent. "Omit needless words," Strunk had written in Rule Seventeen, and the professor had followed his own advice so rigorously that he often omitted essential words, too. Some of his entries were not merely concise but incomprehensible. Others, conversely, were written with a bagginess unbecoming a book on rhetoric. White recast them, put them in his own voice, and in so doing gave the sharp, uncompromising rules a surprisingly light and agreeable tone. He went at the text with a free hand—always careful, he said, to preserve "the spirit of Strunk."

In *E.B. White: A Biography,* Scott Elledge offers several examples of White's recastings. All are improvements. For instance, under Rule Twelve, "Use definite, specific, concrete language," Strunk had been inappropriately verbose: *Critics have pointed out how much of the effectiveness of the greatest writers, Homer, Dante, Shakespeare, results from their constant definiteness and concreteness.* In White's hands, the rule becomes concrete and the sentence snaps: *The greatest writers—Homer,*

Dante, Shakespeare—are effective largely because they deal in particulars and report the details that matter.

White greatly expanded Strunk's chapter on "Words and Expressions Commonly Misused," dropped a chapter on spelling, and added a funny, inspiriting essay on style. And so Will Strunk's book became an E.B. White book—or better, it became Strunk-and-White, as it's known today, a blend of the professor and the practitioner, the prickly old pedagogue and his most talented student.

There was one other element to *The Elements* that White refused to tamper with—the sternness that White himself most admired about the original and its author. Much of *The Elements* is a *rule* book; it is prescriptive, a study in right and wrong. As White prepared his revision, the new *Webster's International Dictionary* hit the bookstores in a burst of publicity. It was the first great dictionary organized according to the "descriptivist" principle: the notion that, in the chaotic swirl of an ever-changing language, lexicographers "should have no traffic with artificial notions of correctness or superiority. [They] should be descriptive and not prescriptive." Descriptivists imported relativism into the study and teaching of English; and having seized the new *Webster's*, they threatened to carry every other guide to grammar and usage with them.

The editors at Macmillan got jittery. They farmed the manuscript out to several professional grammarians, who unanimously denounced the book's unyielding ethic—its insistence, for example, on such "lost causes" as the difference between *like* and *as*, or *will* and *shall*. White's editor passed along their objections, with hints that the revised *Elements of Style* should conform more closely to "modern educational theory." White's reply is worth quoting at length. Forty years on, it still has the power to invigorate a failing prescriptivist heart.

> I was saddened by your letter—the flagging spirit, the moistened finger in the wind, the examination of entrails, and the fear of little men. I don't know whether Macmillan is running scared or not, but I do know that this book is the work of a dead precisionist and a half-dead disciple of his, and that it

has got to stay that way. I have been sympathetic all along with your qualms about "The Elements of Style," but I know that I cannot, and will-shall not, adjust the unadjustable Mr. Strunk to the modern liberal of the English Department, the anything-goes fellow. I am against him, temperamentally and because I have seen the work of *his* disciples, and I say the hell with him. . . . Either Macmillan takes Strunk and me in our bare skins, or I want out.

To me no cause is lost, no level the right level, no smooth ride as valuable as a rough ride, no *like* interchangeable with *as*, and no ball game anything but chaotic if it lacks a mound, a box, bases, and foul lines. That's what Strunk was about, that's what I am about, and that (I hope) is what the book is about. Any attempt to tamper with this prickly design will get nobody nowhere fast.

White won the argument, and the book was published in 1959 as he revised it, "in the spirit of Strunk." The trade edition quickly perched atop the bestseller list and stayed for several months. Its college edition sold half a million copies in the first three years. White made two subsequent revisions, in 1972 and in 1979; he left the design intact but added substantially to the section on "Words Commonly Misused," piling up expressions that had come to annoy him in the intervening years.

Every book on words and how to use them is, to one degree or another, a grab bag of its author's crotchets and punctilios, and this is doubly true for *The Elements of Style*, which assembles the prejudices of not one irascible language maven but two. White's disdain fell particularly hard on words he thought carried the odor of the pompous, the inexact, or the trendy. The 1959 edition damned the then-new coinage *personalize* ("a pretentious word, often carrying bad advice"). The 1972 edition did the same to *finalize* ("a peculiarly fuzzy and silly word. . . . One can't be sure what it means, and one gets the impression that the person using it doesn't know, either, and doesn't want to know"). By the

1979 edition, things had gotten so out of hand—with the invention of *prioritize, customize,* and the rest—that White composed a brief essay excommunicating all freshly made verbs ending in *ize:* "Never tack *ize* onto a noun to create a verb. Usually you will discover that a useful verb already exists. Why use *moisturize* when there is the simple, unpretentious word *moisten?*"

White was a master of what the professors call the American plain style, consisting mainly of straight-flowing sentences unimpeded by secondary clauses, with the subject, verb, and object bound closely together. It is hard to dissemble in the plain style, hard to show off. White's taste, if *taste* can describe something so essential to a man's character, is for the simple and unaffected; and it is stamped on every page of *The Elements.* About the overworked word *insightful,* he wrote: "Usually, it crops up merely to inflate the commonplace." The objection is telling.

Unlike many precisionists, he was not against neologisms as a matter of principle—in the little book there are passages about the "organic" and "dynamic" nature of language that would please any descriptivist. But if the language is constantly renewing itself, as the descriptivists say, White wanted it to do so in the direction of clarity and precision, away from airiness and abstraction: Let new words illuminate meaning, not obscure it. He was against neologisms only of a certain kind. Consider *finalize*—what moves a man to coin the word, in place of "conclude" or "settle" or "complete"? Does it convey some subtlety of meaning these more commonplace synonyms do not? Unlikely. Instead, the fellow who *finalizes* is merely reaching for the word nearest at hand regardless of its sense, in which case he is lazy, or, alternatively, he is trying to sound official and authoritative, in which case he is just strutting. In neither case is he worthy of emulation.

In the same way, White counseled against such gassy nouns as "feature," "factor," and "dimension." They are tools of obfuscation rather than expression; a sentence that relies heavily upon them may sound impressive at first hearing but is liable not to mean much of anything, which becomes apparent when you try to recast it into concrete words.

White objected to the use of *hopefully* (standard meaning: "with hope") for "it is to be hoped," and *presently* (standard meaning: "soon") for "currently." A descriptivist will defend the new usages in the name of enriching our dynamic language. In fact, though, they diminish it. When, through constant misuse, *fortuitous* becomes synonymous with *fortunate, imply* with *infer, comprise* with *constitute,* the language shrinks and distinctions become harder to draw.

Many of these cavils are windmill-tilting, of course. *Finalize* is probably here to stay, along with the new senses of *hopefully* and *presently.* Writerly crotchets, even those as sound as White's, are often doomed, as he understood. But one of the intentions of *Elements* is to enliven the writer, to make him alert and self-conscious as he expresses himself, to induce him to assemble his own grab bag of phrases and words that he can't abide for their pretentiousness, their cloudy meaning, or their confused purpose. And since White's last revision in 1979, the list of such words has only grown. He would be disinclined to *reach out* to *communicators* whose *writing skills* lead them to tag every group a *community,* even when it is *faith-based* or *meaningful.* The state of the language today would plunge him into the grieving process.

Which only heightens the anticipation for the new revision of *The Elements of Style.* Over the last twenty years the book has grown whiskers—and not merely in its hidebound prejudices or its hardy prescriptivism. Students who bought the book last year, still in its 1979 incarnation, would have found Strunk and White railing against the old advertising slogan "Winston tastes good like a cigarette should," which no one under the age of thirty has ever heard of. They would learn to leave plenty of space on the first page of a manuscript, so the editor will have room to make notations for the "compositor." (Mommy, what's a compositor?) And when they needed to revise a draft by transposing paragraphs, *Elements* advised them to cut the manuscript with scissors and physically rearrange the order of the material. The world of Strunk and White is a world of typewriters and pencils, not word processors.

Notwithstanding these antiquarian references, sales remained brisk. In 1994, the mergers and recombinations roiling the publishing industry kicked ownership of the book to Allyn and Bacon, a firm specializing in textbooks. "Here we had this wonderful title," the company's president, Bill Barke, told me the other day, "but it didn't have A & B's editorial imprint, if you see what I mean. There was a lot of datedness. I thought maybe we could provide our editorial input to updating it, combine it with our marketing clout, and really improve the performance of this product."

Written by a pair of mossbacks, *The Elements* is a book beloved by mossbacks, and Barke was alert to the dangers of tampering with the text. "With a classic like this," he said, "the real problem you get is that people think every word is kind of sacred." He fished around among White's surviving friends and colleagues for a new reviser—John Updike was approached, and so was White's stepson, the great *New Yorker* writer Roger Angell—but they demurred. ("We could never finalize anything," Barke said of the negotiations.)

In the end, the task of revising the little book was given over to a team of freelance copy editors, working with Allyn and Bacon's own in-house editors. This is the bad news. (I'll get to the good news in a moment.) Freelance copy editors are the curse of the publishing business. With publishers lopping off staff by the fistful, freelancers have acquired terrific power. As many writers have discovered, they tend to be of a type: working alone, over-schooled and undereducated, usually armed with degrees from the further reaches of the liberal arts curriculum—sociology, for example, or women's studies. As a rule they are exquisitely sensitive to the marginal and the beside-the-point; they can spot an instance of gender or ethnic insensitivity at a hundred paces, even as typos, grammatical errors, factual misstatements, and egregious misspellings glide by them unnoticed.

They have made their mark on the fourth edition of *The Elements of Style*. In setting examples of correct and incorrect usage side by side, the format of the book has always been to put a poorly constructed sentence on the left and a corrected version on the right. And so it is in the new edition, with the exception of Rule Twenty ("Keep related words together"), where the correct and incorrect examples have been mistakenly, and rather obviously, transposed.

The error will doubtless cause some puzzlement in American class-rooms; then again, maybe not. In any case it's hard to see how this little glitch could have escaped the notice of professionals, until you look else-where under Rule Twenty and find the revision that must have truly concerned them. In the earlier editions, one of the good examples reads: "In the fifth book of *The Excursion*, Wordsworth gives a minute descrip-tion of this church." The revisers have dumped this, replacing it with an example of their own. In the fourth edition we now read: "In *Beloved*, Toni Morrison writes about characters who have escaped from slavery but are haunted by its heritage."

"If people still read Wordsworth," Barke told me, "we would have left him in. But they don't. So we took him out."

He's got a point (Mommy, what's a Wordsworth?), and the same rea-soning probably forced the substitution of Sylvia Plath for Keats and of Sappho for Pliny the Younger in other examples. Even so, mossbacks sniffing through the new text in hopes of finding further evidence of political correctness will be largely disappointed. The new edition shows signs of only one overarching principle of revision, which is this: Almost every use of the male pronoun to encompass both men and women has been meticulously excised. Strunk and White, in their fourth edition, have been unmanned.

Sometimes the pronoun simply vanishes, leaving the original sen-tence otherwise intact. Where once we read "A writer may err by making his sentences too compact and periodic," we now read: "A writer may err by making sentences too compact and periodic."

On other occasions the sentence is purified through the use of par-ticiples. Where once we read "The unskilled writer often violates this principle, from a mistaken belief that he should constantly vary the form of his expression," now we read: "The unskilled writer often violates this principle, mistakenly believing in the value of constantly varying the form of expression." Sentence by sentence, line by line, "the writer" assumes a ghostly form.

The revisions aren't as good as the originals, of course; there's a loss of vigor and cadence in the loss of specificity. My own guess, though, is that most members of the mossback community will not find the changes particularly troublesome. The use of *he* for *he and she* will presently (by which I mean soon) be a lost cause. And if nothing else, this neutered edition will forestall many pointless, not to say insane, classroom arguments launched by feminist undergraduates who would have been appalled at the masculine tone of earlier editions (and who would later become freelance copy editors to get even).

But White, who as we've seen didn't allow for lost causes, would probably have objected to the change. One of the last pieces he submitted to the *New Yorker*, where he had worked for fifty years, was a lampoon of the same unisex principle that has now altered his book. This was in the mid-1970s, and the piece was rejected. "To me," he wrote an editor at the magazine, "any woman's (or man's) attempt to remove the gender from the language is both funny and futile." Funny, maybe, but not at all futile.

For the 1979 edition of *The Elements of Style*, he wrote a little sermon on the subject:

> The use of *he* as a pronoun for nouns embracing both genders is a simple, practical convention rooted in the beginnings of the English language. *He* has lost all suggestion of maleness in these circumstances. . . . It has no pejorative connotation; it is never incorrect. Substituting *he or she* in its place is the logical thing to do if it works. But it often doesn't work, if only because repetition makes it sound boring or silly. . . . Alternatively, put all the controversial nouns in the plural and avoid the choice of sex altogether, and you may find your prose sounding general and diffuse as a result.

And that, of course, is precisely what the new editors have often done—put the nouns in plural form, to de-sex them. And sure enough, the prose sounds general and diffuse as a result. What is truly remarkable, however, is that almost all of White's antineutering sermon, as quoted above, stands unaltered in the new edition. The new editors have inserted a single sentence in the middle of it, as a hedge: "Currently, however, many writers find the use of the generic *he* or *his* to rename indefinite antecedents limiting or offensive." Otherwise the passage is as White wrote it. His sentiment is still there, but now he sounds confused.

The same holds true throughout the new edition. The hoary disapprobations survive, no matter how out-of-step with the times: Don't begin a sentence with *however;* abjure *finalize, personalize,* and *prioritize;* use the serial comma; avoid *offputting* and *ongoing;* don't use *people* as a plural for *person, nauseous* as a synonym for *nauseated,* or *like* for *as.* Every one of the lost causes is still there. The compositor is still there! All that has really changed—aside from the defenestration of poor Wordsworth, Keats, and Pliny—is the de-sexing of the pronouns. This is odd, to say the least, in a text that is otherwise so thoroughly reactionary. But it is a tribute to the monomania of contemporary editors that the discordance is allowed to stand. As we say these days: Whatever. Just as long as you get the pronouns right.

So this is the good news: The little book endures, its strength only slightly diminished. Most important, White's last chapter has been left largely untouched; for it is here, in the essay called "An Approach to Style," that you come upon the book's beating heart, the source of much of its power. Here, at the end, is where you glimpse what Strunk and White have been up to all along.

The essay appends to the body of the book twenty-one additional rules—though here, in contrast to the earlier sections, they are gently called "reminders." "The preceding chapters," White writes, "contain instructions drawn from established English usage; this one contains advice drawn from a writer's experience of writing." The tone is more relaxed, less formal, not at all censorious. The persnickety pedagogue has slipped offstage, and the reader finds himself in the pleasing company of the man who wrote *Charlotte's Web.*

E.B. White was not notably a man of ideas. In politics, in fact, he was a bit of a booby. On those few occasions when he aspired to the pundit's role, as the *New Yorker's* editorial writer, it was to advance the woolly idea of "world government" after World War II. Wilfred Sheed once wrote that White embodied the spirit of the early *New Yorker,* "the spiritual home of the graceful writer with nothing to say." (Of course, Sheed was writing of the period, blessed in memory, when *New Yorker* writers did have nothing to say.) "White," he continued, "must be the archetype and all-time champion [of such writers]."

This isn't entirely fair; if nothing else White was a writer who knew enough to stay away from words like *archetype.* He had things to say, but they were small things, seemingly. "He was quite wonderful," wrote Joseph Epstein, in an otherwise dismissive essay on White, "at describing buildings at dusk, snow in the bright sun, a lake in the rain." Small things, perhaps; but the smallness is deceptive. His work is cherished today (by those who cherish it) because what he offered in his writing was himself, sui generis, E.B. White and no other—a man genial, tolerant, humorous, without artifice or pretense, and always with a half-moon of melancholy rising up against the backdrop. To fashion a style that allowed this self to show through so consistently and so indelibly, and over so long a span of years, must have been a difficult labor, an achievement attained at great cost: no small thing.

"An Approach to Style" is, oddly enough, an extended brief against style, as style is generally understood. "Young writers," he wrote,

> often suppose that style is a garnish for the meat of prose, a sauce by which a dull dish is made palatable. Style has no such separate entity; it is nondetachable, unfilterable. The beginner should approach style warily . . . by turning resolutely away from all devices that are popularly believed to indicate style—all mannerisms, tricks, adornments. The approach to style is by way of plainness, simplicity, orderliness, sincerity.

Each of White's twenty-one reminders nudges aspiring writers in this healthy direction, with advice they almost certainly don't want to hear. "Place yourself in the background." "Write with nouns and verbs." "Do not overwrite." "Do not affect a breezy manner." "Use orthodox spelling." And finally, and most painfully for the young person aflame with the desire for self-expression: "Prefer the standard to the offbeat."

There is a single consideration underlying all these reminders: concern for the other, for the reader. "Most readers," White says, "are in trouble about half the time." To neglect this fundamental fact—to indulge in obscurity for obscurity's sake, to choose words carelessly, to ignore the rules of usage—is a kind of moral transgression. Concern for the reader is what moves White to counsel clarity, simplicity, the avoidance of pomp and pretense.

Two things strike you as you dwell on White's reminders. First, he has touched on the very tendencies that lead a writer astray when he is bursting to express himself. And second, these are temptations that are not limited to the act of writing.

He closes the book with this advice:

> Do not forget that what may seem like pioneering may be merely evasion, or laziness—the disinclination to submit to discipline. . . . In choosing between the formal and the informal, the regular and the off-beat, the general and the special, the orthodox and the heretical, the beginner [should] err on the side of conservatism, on the side of established usage. No idiom is taboo; no accent forbidden; there is simply a better chance of doing well if the writer holds a steady course, enters the stream of English quietly, and does not thrash about.

The Elements of Style is undeniably a great book—whether it ranks among the century's twenty-one best is open to debate—and like many great books it pretends to be about one thing when in truth it is about another. It masquerades as a guide to usage but it is really a book about life—about the value of custom, the necessity of rules, the corruptions of vanity, the primacy of good taste, and the transcendent importance of always taking your fellows into account. This is what the book was about in the first edition, and it's what it is about in the fourth; and it will be so—hopefully!—in the fifth and sixth and seventh editions, for as long as the little book survives.

★ A REVOLUTION TO ★ SAVE THE WORLD

Thomas Fleming

FROM *CHRONICLES*, JULY 2000

"Beyond Left and Right" was the title of the *Antiwar.com* conference which brought together Pat Buchanan and Alexander Cockburn, Justin Raimondo and Lenora Fulani (to say nothing of two *Chronicles* editors) in the same room (if not all at the same time) for a broad critique of the aggressive New World Order launched by the Bush and Clinton administrations. It was a cordial exchange, in which left and right did not pass each other like ships in the night but crossed at a 90-degree angle after exchanging salutes. However, before quartering the hammer-and-sickle with the *fleur-de-lis*, opponents of U.S./NATO imperialism might ask what the two sides have in common.

To answer that question, most of the radicals and reactionaries in San Mateo, California, would agree in opposing the U.S. policy of imperialism and in condemning last year's aggression against Yugoslavia. Beyond that point, agreement becomes more difficult, partly because so many different political perspectives are represented, partly because some of us—even most of us—are unclear about what we do believe or about how the United States turned into what it is today. If there is to be not a coalition but some sort of joint operation, both parties had better be clear about the limits of what they agree upon.

The only ideological coalition worth talking about will be the union of reactionary Christians when they find the will to resist the Jacobin governments that have destroyed their world, but even a popular front alliance should have its rules. At a bare minimum, it could not include sentimental pacifists who oppose the use of violence, civil disobedients who believe in doing evil that good may come of it, or nostalgic leftists who cannot believe that Stalin, Mao, Pol Pot, and Tito have let them down.

One part of the problem lies in the Cold War America to which so many conservatives look back as a Golden Age. In America today, nearly all of us are children of the Cold War. Some of the speakers at the conference opposed the U.S. policy of containment, opposed the undeclared war in Vietnam that cost so many Vietnamese and American lives, and resisted the demonization of the Russian people as our natural enemy. Others thought that communism was a nightmare menace that had to be kept in its box and still believe that Ronald Reagan's buildup of the American war machine brought down the Berlin Wall and saved the world from an Evil Empire.

I understood both positions, because I had opposed both the war in Vietnam and despised the American left's manifest attraction to communism. Where were the isolationist reactionaries in the sixties? Russell Kirk, I know, disliked America's Southeast Asian adventure, but he kept his peace. What else was he to do? He was part of a coalition defined by aggressive anticommunism. Other isolationists drifted toward the left and found a home there. I do not know what would have happened if conservatives like Kirk could have joined forces with Eugene McCarthy and William Appleman Williams. Certainly, a different sort of coalition would have been the result. But after the death of Robert Taft, conservatives had little choice but to identify themselves with resistance to godless communism in what they regarded as a struggle for the world.

Near the end of the Cold War, Jean-François Revel published an influential book under the title, *How Democracies Perish*. Revel's thesis, like the thesis of earlier Cold Warriors such as James Burnham, was a variation on the old story of Lenin and the rope: The greedy West, incapable of understanding the ideological force of communism, was collaborating with the very powers that would destroy it, and if communists lacked the money to buy the rope from the West, well, the West would always lend it to them.

On a deeper level, however, the West's failure to combat its enemies can be traced to the very socioeconomic system it seeks to protect. In theory, the Cold Warriors were protecting the peoples of Britain, France, and the United States against the expansion of an evil empire, but nations can only be successfully defended by people who believe in nationhood, which is anathema to the liberal assumptions that are the foundation of most Western states.

At the heart of liberal democracy lies the conviction that all nations are the same or ought to be; and just as all individuals are, in principle, equal and should be able to compete in the marketplace for success, so all nations, cultures, and religions are basically equal, so long as they are willing to enter into the marketplace of ideological competition. Liberal nation-states cannot control immigration, restrict citizenship, or protect trade, precisely because the nation-state is only a temporary stop on the train line that leads to a globally integrated marketplace in which we are all—or ought to be—citizens of the world, not citizens of the United States.

In this quest for a global utopia is based on the principle of equality, modern states have undermined the family, made war upon the church, and ridiculed every principle of morality and common sense. As a substitute for divine law and the wisdom that comes from human experience, they have offered us a nonsensical philosophy of human rights, and to enforce these rights, they have broken every moral law known to civilized people while at the same time celebrating their moral superiority over the tribal cultures of the Balkans.

If anyone resists the conversion process, he and his people are labeled genocidal criminals; CNN will obligingly show doctored photos of concentration camps and mass graves; international tribunals will declare him guilty of crimes against human rights; and the U.S. government will put a price on his head—as if that were not in itself a crime.

During the Cold War, the diverse political and economic systems of the West were lumped together under the rubric of Western Democratic Capitalism. This was part of an effort to create a Western ideology with which to oppose the ideology of Marxist communism, but—and it is time to speak plainly—the democratic capitalism extolled by Cold War liberals (most of whom called themselves conservatives) and unreconstructed Trotskyists (who called themselves neoconservatives) has very little in common with the democracies of Switzerland and ancient Athens or, for that matter, with the old American republic.

Greek and Swiss democracy worked in small-scale communities and was actually based on the will of the people, and it has virtually nothing in common with the vast bureaucracies that govern the United States and the nations of the European Union. In fact these systems are the very opposite: For the Greeks, the family and the little community was almost everything; today, Western governments make war on the family and on every little community, whether ethnic or religious. The attempt to create a New World Order translates this principle of national and anti-human bureaucracy to the global level.

It is time to set aside the popular misconception that democracies do not wage aggressive war or establish empires. Who were the most democratic peoples in history? The Athenians who, as soon as they established a democracy, created an empire; the Florentines, who subjugated most of central Italy; the liberal British monarchy of the 19th century that controlled India and much of Africa. Who were more democratic than the 19th-century Americans who annihilated the Indians, kicked the Spanish out of Florida, and grabbed a large part of the continent from Mexico before going on to subjugate the southern third of the republic?

The triumphant democrats went on to conquer Cuba and Puerto Rico and wage a genocidal war against the people of the Philippines. Democracies, both actual (like 19th-century America) and phony (like America today), are by their nature expansionist because they cater to the appetites of the masses and are enthralled by the rich and powerful. If you have any doubts, consider only the history of the United States in this century or even in the past ten years.

In our time, however, "democratic capitalism" is far from democratic, and if capitalism has anything to do with the free market, it is not capitalist, either. America is fast becoming a plutocracy, and terms like "capitalism" and "free enterprise" are used loosely to mean a system of transnational corporations that seek to control the world's business.

Any attempt to suppress economic freedom, as took place in the former Soviet Union and in the former Yugoslavia, has disastrous consequences both for a national economy and for human social life. Even the mixed economic systems of Scandinavia and Britain have tended to undermine creativity and initiative and to destroy social institutions. This is what so many of our potential allies on the left refuse to understand. They look at businessmen and see the enemy, but when the same corporate executive goes to work for the Department of Health and Human Services, he is working for the good of mankind.

Economic freedom is an essential quality of human dignity, and when governments attempt to repress that freedom—as they do in communist and socialist countries—they are destroying human dignity. In the West, however, which is supposedly devoted to economic liberty, governments regulate small businessmen in order to benefit the giant corporations and under misnamed free trade agreements and the World Trade Organization, a small coterie of multinational executives is attempting to eliminate competition, destroy small economic communities (such as nations), and to replace free enterprise with a global economic bureaucracy that will act as a NATO without weapons, though they will always be able to call in the NATO troops whenever their usual methods of bribery and intimidation fail.

Free trade, in fact, nearly always spells empire. Who have been the greatest free-traders of the past two centuries? British imperialists and the bipartisan free-trade imperialists of the Bush-Clinton administrations. Libertarians and classical liberals have to decide whether they are going to be free-trade imperialists or patriotic isolationists.

True democracy, in the spirit of Thomas Jefferson, means that the government leaves people alone—not simply as individuals, but as families and members of communities. A truly democratic state may not attempt to engineer an artificial unity of diverse regions and peoples, as the Italian fascists did; or suppress religion and shift populations, as Stalin did; or manipulate internal boundaries and laws to benefit one group at the expense of another, which is done in the United States today in the name of minority rights and in the old Yugoslavia. All these tricks, whatever pretty names they are called by, should be seen for what they are: parts of a political system that aims at total control over human social life.

In the United States, this revolutionary project began to take shape about the same time as Marxist revolution in Russia, but it was not until the 1930's that American political leaders began to impose a national-socialist regime that paralleled developments in Italy, Germany, and the Soviet Union. The American ideological state, however, is distinguished from the others in one important respect: Instead of relying on coercive force, on jackboots and lager, gulags and *Pravda*, the new American state employed the art of seduction. Consumerism, sexual immorality, pre-scription tranquilizers, and commercial TV more effectively under-mined the old American character than any of the devices employed by the hard totalitarian states.

Fifteen years ago in *Chronicles*, we began to point out that Americans were no longer citizens of a republic but subjects of an empire, and that this imperial system has been erected on the ruins of our old republic. The new American religion of false democracy, rigged markets, and multicultural mass culture can only complete the destruction of Europe that was begun in Serbia by American bombs.

For our leaders, the ongoing task is to find ethnic brush wars in Chechnya or Kosovo that demand a graduated response of concern, alarm, condemnation, and intervention. The evidence of Bosnia and Kosovo suggests that this degraded Western elite will not be satisfied until the entire world is a Disneyland replica of San Diego. For them, nations do not exist except as local administrative units of the global marketplace; this attitude was revealed recently when a top Clinton administration official asked for an expanded role for the United Nations High Commissioner for Refugees to protect refugees within a state—in other words, to give the UNHCR the implicit right to intervene in internal struggles.

What is the American left's public response to the economic wing of the New World Order? Riots staged by androgynous hooligans who have watched one too many PBS documentaries on the sixties. "You say you want a revolution . . ."—but they do not. A revolution requires courage and discipline.

We have seen these faces before, chaotic, resentful, stupefied. They danced in the streets at the Festival of Reason; they drank and fornicated behind the Paris barricades in 1848; and they greeted the Bolsheviks as the liberators of the human spirit from God, morality, mathematics, and hygiene.

The cultural left defines itself by its hatred of Christendom, but there are remnants of a more humane, almost Chestertonian left that sees the New World Order as the realization of the Rockefeller dream of one market/one state/*ein Reich/ein Führer*. They can see the mark of the beast on the faces of Madeleine Albright and George Soros, and—who knows?—in struggling against these devils, they may join the side of the angels.

★ READING ELIAN ★

Charles Paul Freund

FROM *REASON,* JULY 2000

On the morning of April 22, Attorney General Janet Reno and other Justice Department officials woke to a very big problem: a series of seven pictures, snapped by Associated Press photographer Alan Diaz, of Federal agents seizing the country's most celebrated six-year-old, Elian Gonzalez. Television and the Internet displayed images of a terrified child confronted by a heavily armed, helmeted, goggled, body-armored commando whose weapon was clearly pointed in the boy's direction.

Behind this figure was a second commando, implying visually that a significant armed force had entered the home. (According to the home's residents, this second raider is aiming his weapon at a group of persons that includes a five-year-old boy.) In two of the AP photos, the armed figure in the foreground is reaching for Elian as the boy recoils in horror. If that didn't look very good Saturday morning, it looked no better by Easter Sunday, when one or the other of the "reaching" images was on the world's front pages.

A plain reading of these images is that they reveal an extraordinary exertion of armed Federal force in an otherwise peaceful domestic setting in which no one is offering resistance. Chris Matthews, the newspaper columnist and host of CNBC's political talk show, *Hardball*, suggested in an interview that the images lent credibility to those "black helicopter" conspiracists who are always warning of an imminent military crackdown. Early polls taken that weekend indicated that a plurality of Americans were troubled by the raid's brutality, as implied by the AP stills (and as fully illustrated by video footage taken outside the Miami site of the invasion).

Many people, in other words, understood the images as illustrating a disturbing level of Federal force. Department of Justice officials immediately embarked on a remarkable campaign intended to change the meaning of those pictures. Rather than having the images perceived in *political* terms, a succession of Federal spokespersons—foremost among them Reno herself—worked assiduously to turn the pictures into *moral* images. That is, they sought to have the photos illustrate not an invasion, but a rescue; not an attack on the Miami family with whom Gonzalez was living, but an effort to reunite the boy with his Cuban father; not brute Federal force at all, but Federal compassion.

How can anyone change the meaning of a picture? The camera may not lie, but it will confess to just about anything. That is, the meaning of photographic images is remarkably elastic. Changing—even reversing—their apparent meaning by recontextualizing them has become a familiar process. It happens repeatedly in court; the Rodney King tape, in which a man being beaten by police was redefined as cops defending themselves from attack, is the most publicized such example. It happens often in news footage; "packed train" images from Kosovo last year were presented as pictures of genocide rather than of brutal expulsion. Indeed, some of the best-known pictures ever taken have been quietly recategorized as doubts about their content have grown: A world-famous Robert Capa image from the Spanish Civil War, known for decades as "Moment of Death," is now called simply "Man Falling." For all their apparent concreteness, photographs have a remarkable capacity to change before our eyes.

Janet Reno and her allies used a variety of approaches in their attempt to change the meaning of the raid imagery and mitigate its impact. In fact, they may have broken new strategic ground in this field. Here's a quick rundown of their major efforts.

"IMMINENT DANGER"

The administration repeatedly justified the armed seizure of the boy on the grounds that he was in grave danger. Indeed, if one believed the government's claims, not a moment could be spared. Thus, the armed commando seen reaching for Elian was engaged in a courageous rescue of the boy from harm.

Was there evidence for this dramatic claim of danger? That depends on what the meaning of "evidence" is. What the government had was a letter to the Immigration and Naturalization Service written on April 18 by a New York pediatrician named Irwin Redlener. Dr. Redlener had watched a homemade video of Elian released by the Miami family earlier that week, and had concluded that the boy was "in a state of imminent danger to his physical and emotional well being in a home that I consider to be psychologically abusive."

Redlener had never visited the home, had never spoken to the boy, and knew nothing firsthand of Elian's physical or emotional well being. It is unlikely that any pediatrician who habitually relied on videotape alone for the purposes of diagnosis would be able to maintain his license to practice. In fact, doctors who had spent time with the boy in Miami had come to quite different conclusions: that the boy would suffer psychologically if he were returned to Cuba. But Redlener had one credential that the Miami doctors lacked: He had served on Hillary Clinton's task force during her ill-fated efforts to reform the nation's health care system. Noting the connection, the Association of American Physicians and Surgeons, an Arizona-based professional group, termed Redlener an "administration operative." (Another government doctor was later to suggest that the Miami relatives should receive counseling.)

Perhaps the government's use of Redlener's "diagnosis" should be understood as part of Elian Gonzalez's transition back to a Cuban environment (if that is what ultimately occurs); the perversion of therapeutics for political ends is, after all, a totalitarian tradition. In any event, there has been no further information about the supposed abuse of Elian by his Miami family since the raid, with a single bizarre exception. That was an early report that the boy might have developed a crush on his cousin Marisleysis, a story briefly floated as apparent evidence that the Miami environment was unhealthy. Mercifully, the government soon abandoned the absurd implication.

"The Gun Was Pointed to the Side"

It is arguable that the only time that Elian Gonzalez was ever in demonstrable danger while in the home of his Miami relatives was when that home was invaded by armed Border Control commandos. That is the source of the inherent drama in the famous pictures showing an MP-5 machine gun pointed toward him. Among Janet Reno's first comments in the wake of the raid was a denial of endangerment.

Reno insisted that the AP photos show that "the gun was pointed to the side," away from the boy, and that the commando's "finger was not on the trigger." But the terror-stricken child seems not to be aware of these details, and in fact they are entirely beside the point. In concentrating on trigger fingers, Reno is changing the focus of the images. In other words, she is engaging in misdirection.

An argument about the location of the trigger finger might be appropriate if the INS were being charged with intending to shoot the boy. But assassination is not the issue: extreme and reckless federal measures are.

A number of weapons and security experts have taken public issue with Reno's characterization of the raid imagery, and what it reveals about the handling of the gun. Among them is Stephen Hunter, a member of the *Washington Post* Style staff. Hunter is the author of a series of successful novels in which guns play a major role, and he is highly regarded for his technical expertise. ("Hunter must have been a gun in a former life" is a typical sample of the praise he has elicited from his gun-culture readers.) Here's what he wrote in the *Post* about the safety issues raised by the image.

"What struck me most about the photograph isn't the gun

itself, but the way in which it's held. It's very close to being out of control. These are not one-handed weapons, and except for emergency circumstances, they are not even two-handed weapons. They recoil so persuasively they must be secured at three points: They must be moored against the shoulder or the center of the chest; the firing hand grips the pistol grip and controls the trigger; and, finally, the other hand must secure the muzzle via the foregrip or a front vertical grip. The officer doesn't even have the weapon secured against his shoulder, as police are taught to do." Although the INS claims that the gun's safety is on, Hunter states categorically, "It is also true from the photograph that the safety is off."

Hunter's reading of the dangers of the raid was supported by a number of security experts. "I think that the risk here was very, very high," Gary Stubblefield, a former Navy SEAL who is now a security consultant, told the *Boston Herald* on April 23. Tom Mann of Guardian International, a security firm, saw the raid the same way. "When the government is going to use that kind of force," he told the *Herald*, "usually it's when someone's life is in danger." According to Stubblefield, "You only use these kind of tactics to get the bad guy and save the good guy and there was no saving necessary here. The risk was almost unconscionable."

"AGGRESSIVE, PHYSICAL RESISTANCE"

In the wake of the raid and the dissemination of the disturbing images of force, INS officials attempted to change the public perception of the pictures by shifting the point of view from which they should be seen. According to these officials, there was indeed violence at the scene of the raid, but it came from Elian's relatives and their supporters, not from the INS. Thus, though the images indicate that the gun-wielding Border Patrol commandos are in control of the situation and are terrifying the child, that is a misperception. Understood from the point of view of the commandos themselves, the images presumably reveal a group of dedicated public servants attempting to protect themselves from a level of resistance that they had never before faced.

Agents who invaded the Miami home filed post-action reports with their supervisors. These reports were described to the press a few days after the raid, and were reported in the *Orlando Sentinel* on April 26. According to those reports, the agents were "jostled, screamed at, and their orders disobeyed." As Maria Cardona of the INS characterized the gist of these reports to the press, "The agents met an aggressive, physical resistance." Indeed, one veteran INS agent reportedly told his supervisors, "I have never encountered this much resistance." Similarly, the *Washington Post* quoted James Goldman, who led the raid, as saying, "In 22 years in Federal law enforcement, the intensity level, the effort to stop us, I've never seen anything like it before."

Requests by the press to examine these reports were denied, but the only incident of "aggressive, physical resistance" attributed by Cardona to those inside the target house was an attempt to block the front door with a couch. All the other aggressive resistance cited occurred in the street, and included some persons linking arms in a human chain to prevent or slow the agents' entry. INS agent Betty Mills, who carried Elian Gonzalez to a waiting van, claimed to have been pushed into some bushes, but it is unclear from the video footage who—if anyone—pushed her; she may have been jostled accidentally by a fellow agent. Agents also claimed that allies of the Miami family threw objects at them, and in fact they can be seen doing so in the video footage as the INS agents are leaving the scene of the raid.

In attempting to portray the agents as the victims of unprecedented violent resistance, government officials were in effect "recasting" the drama implied by the photographs, and reassigning the motivation for the Federal agents' behavior. The government was thus taking a page from the Rodney King defense. In the first trial of the police officers involved, defense attorneys persuaded a Simi Valley, California, jury that it was the pummeled King who was motivating the appalling action, because he continued to move while being beaten with batons. Had he only lain still, these lawyers argued, the beating would have ended.

Jose Garcia Pedrosa, a lawyer for the Miami family, rejects the INS version of motivation. "Any violence that occurred at the house," he told the *Orlando Sentinel*, "was brought there by Janet Reno."

"RENO ALLOWED PHOTOS"

On April 25, the *Washington Post* carried a remarkable story headlined "Reno Allowed Photos During Elian Siege." According to this account, which was attributed only to "sources," Reno "personally decided not to prevent photographers from taking pictures" of the raid. Reno, said these sources, was "seeking to avoid allegations of a government coverup" of the kind that has haunted her since the Branch Davidian siege ended in more than 80 deaths by burning seven years before. Indeed, she foresaw that Alan Diaz himself would be present inside the house and taking photographs, said the sources, but liberally decided not to have him ejected. Her reported openness was also motivated by the fact that both her parents were journalists, according to the account.

Thus, while the content of the Diaz photographs may be unattractive, the very existence of the pictures is a supposed tribute to the government's policy of honesty, and to Reno's commitment to democracy, the First Amendment, and freedom of the press.

"It was a gutsy decision," Carl Stern told the *Post*. Stern is a former reporter who was also a Reno spokesman early in the administration. Roger Pilon of the Cato Institute saw things differently. According to him, removing the AP photographer when he was already in the house "would have been even greater police-state measures."

Attempting to limit the impact of damaging images by taking credit for those images is unusual, and may in fact be unprecedented. If the military had thought of this stratagem during the Vietnam War, for example, it could have tried to mitigate the damage of all that embarrassing footage of soldiers setting fire to villages by claiming that such images represented the very freedom that the military was fighting for. Certainly the most striking element of the story is its implication that Reno deserves extra credit for "allowing" the news media to do its job.

In fact, the *Post* account was one of several narratives that encouraged the public to see the pictures from Reno's pained and empathetic point of view. In the *Miami Herald*, for instance, the attorney general is quoted as asking herself, "How would [Elian] feel, suddenly being put in the arms of a stranger? What would he think? How frightened would he be? And I kept thinking, I wish I could see him when his daddy gets on the plane." In an extraordinary bit of sharing, Deputy Attorney General Eric Holder informed the press that after Reno had ordered the raid to begin, "She put her head on my shoulder and wept."

The day after the *Post* printed the account of Reno's liberal press policies, Tony Zumbado was taken to the hospital. Who's he? He was the NBC cameraman on location the night of the raid, and the designated broadcast and cable pool cameraman. He and his soundman were alerted to the approach of the INS raiders moments before their arrival. Zumbado told the *New York Times* what happened when he attempted to cover the raid from inside the home. "We got Maced, we got kicked, we got roughed up."

NBC reporter Kerry Sanders, who was also outside the Gonzalez house on the night of the raid, described what happened to the right-wing Web site Newsmax.com, which has published the most detailed account.

According to Sanders, Zumbado encountered INS agents already in the house when he entered. Zumbado's soundman, still outside, was hit in the head with a rifle butt and fell to the ground bleeding. Zumbado, the camera perched on his shoulder, fell backward when someone yanked the heavy video and audio cables that were attached to it.

"At that point," says Sanders, "somebody smacks him in the stomach. Tony is hit in the stomach and goes down. And then the agent puts his foot on Tony's back and puts a gun to him and says, 'Don't move or I'll shoot.'

"Tony tells me that as he looks up around, he sees the family there and he sees these little red dots on Lazaro's [Elian's great uncle's] fore-head, on Marisleysis' [Elian's cousin's] forehead. Which of course are the laser sights from the machine guns. He sees them all trained there and then he hears what's going on in the back room. But he's not in that back bedroom because he's now down on the floor with a foot in his back and [someone is pointing] a gun to his head [and] saying, 'Don't move.'"

Zumbado had a pre-existing back condition that was apparently exacerbated when a Federal commando planted a boot on his spine. The Wednesday after the raid, Zumbado, unable to move without pain, was removed from his home by stretcher and taken to a Miami hospital. While there, he would have been able to read about Janet Reno's liberal press-coverage policies at his leisure.

"Father and Son"

By the afternoon of April 22, the day of the raid, those defending the decision took their most effective action in limiting raid-imagery damage: They offered counter images. Photographs of a happy Elian in his father's arms at Andrews Air Force Base, and of the boy playing with his half-brother, were released to the press. The shot featuring the father was to accompany the raid pictures in much of the press coverage, and to dominate coverage in such major agenda-setting papers as the *New York Times*. Indeed, it was the cover shot of the next issue of *Time* magazine, which captioned it "Papa!" The photo was played with an air of denouement, of happy resolution. All's well that ends well.

"Happy resolution" was precisely the narrative pushed by the Justice Department. "Earlier this morning," Janet Reno told reporters at an April 22 press conference, "federal agents began to reunite Elian Gonzalez with his father and uphold the rule of law." These were the first on-the-record words out of the attorney general's mouth the day of the raid, and they established the themes that Federal spokespersons were to pursue relentlessly in the weeks afterward. The raid, according to this story, was a necessary prelude to a heartwarming family reunion. No administration figure was to address the raid issue without at least once formulating a sentence referring to the benevolent reunion of a boy and his father.

The most florid of these father-son formulations came from Reno herself, during a bizarre May 1 appearance on *The Oprah Winfrey Show*. Sinking in an ocean of warm fuzzy rhetoric, Reno managed to evoke the Gonzalez reunion as a model for a great American joining of hearts. "I think it is time for us all to come together," the attorney general told the popular daytime hostess, "father and son, community, people who care about each other to make democracy work."

Who took the pictures of a happy Elian and his father? The father's $850-per-hour lawyer, Greg Craig. (Craig had written to the major news media, calling on them not to cover the raid at all in the name of "decency.") Notwithstanding the attorney general's embrace of openness and the free press, no reporter would be allowed to photograph the pair. The Air Force base, outside Washington, was closed to everyone—including, somehow, U.S. senators—in the interests of family privacy and healing.

Elian's Miami relatives were to argue that the "reunion" images were fakes, a desperate and ill-considered charge that was quickly proved false. The pictures are real enough—why shouldn't the boy be glad to see his father, especially given the violence with which he had been snatched from his Miami home? The question is, is the story that these pictures tell a false one?

The "reunion" pictures imply a resolution. Certainly, that is how the administration has used them, and how they have been treated by leading periodicals. But there is no reason to assume that the reunited Gonzalez family will now live happily ever after. If Elian returns to Cuba, he apparently will be housed in a state school for at least three months by a regime that considers children its property. Fidel Castro has promised as much. Thus, the Elian narrative may be far from completed: Lying ahead may be precisely the ugly possibilities that were all along at the heart of the Miami custody battle. Of course, if Reno had told the press or even Oprah Winfrey that "Federal agents have begun the process that will end in a Castro reeducation facility," that wouldn't have sounded so good. Better to pretend that a story has ended happily, than to admit that an unhappy story may be beginning, one that featured the armed connivance of the American government.

The "reunion" pictures also imply familial intimacy. Certainly, Janet Reno has cited exactly this excuse in keeping the press and everyone else away from the family. That wouldn't be an unreasonable act, if it were true. But it is not true. (One notable exception occurred in May, when Elian was on display at a political dinner in Georgetown.) More important, perhaps, the family has been surrounded by a gaggle of Castro "diplomats" since the moment the boy arrived at Andrews, and this same extended "family" all moved in together at the Wye Plantation, a government-owned property across the Chesapeake Bay from Washington. In other words, Juan Miguel Gonzalez has almost never been out of sight of his Cuban overseers since his arrival in the United States, a circumstance that continues to raise questions about his free agency. Yet, the attorney general of the United States defines this situation as one of "privacy."

Cuba's "diplomats" in Washington—they staff an "interests section," and not an embassy—are a notably thuggish lot. A few days before the Miami raid, a dozen of them emerged from their building to beat up anti-Castro protesters, men and women, who were demonstrating on a public sidewalk. Federal police who were guarding the building actually had to intervene. In the two centuries Washington has been the seat of government, foreign diplomats have used their immunity for a great many nefarious purposes, from stiffing the city on parking tickets to espionage. But the crude criminality of this attack may be a first. The administration has expressed its "concern."

Finally, the "reunion" images portray a happy little boy. Elian may in fact be very happy, but not everyone is satisfied to take Greg Craig's or Fidel Castro's word for the matter. On April 29, the Association of American Physicians and Surgeons released a letter to the INS expressing its concern that the boy's medical treatment may have been politicized. It asked the INS "to disclose the names and backgrounds of all U.S. government-appointed medical personnel involved in the treatment or evaluation of the boy." The AAPS added that it was "not confident that the glowing reports from anonymous government doctors of the boy's easy adjustment following a traumatic seizure at gunpoint are indeed, unbiased, or for that matter, firsthand." The government has since identified a social worker and a psychiatrist who have tended to Elian.

On April 27, Customs officials in Washington searched the bags of Elian's Cuban pediatrician, who was en route to Wye Plantation, and found such sedatives as Miltown and phenobarbital. This discovery has fueled persistent claims that Elian may have been sedated following his seizure. In fact, there is no evidence that the boy has been mistreated in this way, but the AAPS's point remains perfectly valid: There was no independent information about the boy during this crucial period, and neither the U.S. nor Cuba had any credibility on the subject.

The administration's response to the raid imagery reflects the media strategy it has employed through two terms of scandal. It had on its hands a narrative it didn't like, so it attempted to create a counter-narrative. That new story demonized Elian Gonzalez's Miami family as disturbed and violent, celebrated government commandos as victims, subsumed inconvenient emotions within the person of an empathetic attorney general, and even appropriated the problematic imagery itself. Tacked on was a useful but false fairy-tale ending in which Little Elian lives happily ever after. But his story has not really ended at all. If Elian sails off into the sunset, he'll land in Cuba. A lot of good Janet Reno's empathy will do him there.

★ HOW CIVILIZATIONS ★ FALL

Kenneth Minogue

FROM *THE NEW CRITERION,* APRIL 2001

How do civilizations fall? Islamic thinkers had an image for it. Consider a civilization based upon a court in a thriving city—Baghdad, for example. Arts and the intellect flourish. But over several generations, as the great Islamic philosopher of the fourteenth century Ibn Khaldun put it, the civilized become decadent with luxury. They lose their sharpness and think only of the good and the beautiful. And then some tribe of fierce Bedouin, smelling out weakness, come thundering in from the desert and storm the city. As barbarians, they do not understand the usages of civilization. They stable their horses in the libraries and use sculptures as doorstops, pictures for target practice. Given a pillow, Ibn Khaldun tells us contemptuously, they suppose it to be a bundle of rags. In time, however, the power of a superior culture is felt, and these people adopt and sometimes extend the ways of civilization, until they too are overthrown in their turn.

This is the way the world goes. Sometimes it happens in one lifetime, as with those barbarian soldiers who rose to become Roman emperors, sometimes in slow motion, as with the fall of the Roman Empire, in which many centuries were to elapse before the new civilization emerged from the disorders of the barbarian invasions. With us, the decor is quite different, but the realities may be closer than we suppose.

One reason we may not realize this is that the very distinction between barbarism and civilization has been suppressed by the current relativism, which asserts the equality of all cultures. Nobody, of course, seriously believes this. Quite apart from technology, the moral inequality of cultures is conspicuous in the position of women in different cultures. It was only the West that abolished slavery. But it is a mark of current decorum—perhaps avoidance of the dreaded "triumphalism"—that we should not proclaim any superiority in European civilization, even though it is the one place the millions want to get into. Instead, we must make do with a rationalist doctrine which transposes the usages of European civilization into a rather unsatisfactory set of abstractions about universal rights. By this device, all cultures (including the Western) can equally be found guilty of moral violation in one way or another.

In the past, civilization was a sensibility shared by a class of people, while barbarism would be found not only in tribes beyond the frontier, but also in the slaves and the servile within the realms of civilization itself. In modern liberal democracies, this clear relation between a culture and a class has disappeared. Everyone is touched by the higher forms of culture. Schooling, museums, and the media are available to all. But barbarism remains an active force in modern societies, partly in gracelessness and ignorance, and partly in a loss of cultural coherence found among those who mistake a few years at an institution of higher learning for education itself.

In modern Europe, we don't quite have Bedouin storming in from the desert (merely millions of depressed migrants trying to slip through the gates), but the tendency towards barbarism is an active force all around us. Hence the formula for overthrowing a Western society must be not "storm the walls" but "organize your own barbarians" within the walls. Those who hate European civilization know that it cannot be taken by direct assault. It must thus be captured from within. This was the plan adopted by many revolutionaries, most notably, of course, by Marx who constructed a new and hostile tribe within the West called "the proletariat." They could be made into a revolutionary tribe by equipping suitable people (industrial workers for example) with a unified consciousness, so that in every transaction they understood themselves as a collective. They were being victimized by the oppressive bourgeois. Like the guardians in Plato's Republic, these revolutionary insurgents had to be taught to be docile within the movement while snarling at those without.

Marx provided the model for all subsequent movements aiming to take power. His "make your own tribe" kit was found useful by nationalists, anarchists, and many brands of socialist. Hitler made the most creative use of it by playing down victimization and representing every Aryan as a superior type of person. It took the world in arms to get rid of him. But before long, revolutionaries discovered that a revolution based on the proletarian tribe only really worked if you were dealing with pretty unsophisticated peoples—preferably non-Europeans who lacked all experience of freedom and genuine political life. In socially mobile European states, the workers mostly found better things to do with their time than waste it on revolutionary committees and the baby talk of political demonstrations. Something new was needed.

It was provided by such socialists as Mussolini and Lenin who adopted the principle of the Praetorian Guard: a tightly knit vanguard party, which could use the masses as ventriloquial dummies and seek power on its own terms. This development was part of a wider tendency towards the emergence of oligarchies ruling through democratic slogans.

In the course of the 1960s, a new tribe was established that also sought to overthrow the Western citadel from within and had notably greater success. This was Betty Friedan's radical feminists. It was a tribe constructed out of women who had taken some sort of degree and were living domestic lives. Technology had largely liberated them from the rigors of beating, sweeping, and cleaning, while pharmacology had released them from excessive procreation. In tactical terms, radical feminists made one innovation that has turned out to be crucial to the destiny of the West over the last half century. They suppressed almost completely the idea that their project involved a transfer of power and operated entirely on the moralistic principle that their demands corresponded to justice.

What lay behind this momentous development? It is a complicated question, but I think that Diana Schaub understood the essence of it in her essay "On the Character of Generation X":

> [Betty] Friedan was right that the malaise these privileged women were experiencing was a result of "a slow death of the mind and spirit." But she was wrong in saying that the problem had no name—its name was boredom. Feminism was born of boredom, not oppression. And what was the solution to this quandary? Feminists clamored to become wage-slaves; they resolutely fled the challenge of leisure.

And by "leisure," Professor Schaub means something classically Greek: the higher employment of the mind once the necessities of life have been dealt with.

The first task of this new movement was to create the shared consciousness necessary for tribal functioning. Like all forms of psychic collectivism, "consciousness raising" (as it is known) exploits indignation and cultivates righteousness. It operated in this case with the basic liberatory image of the prison and, identifying happiness with being in the labor force, argued that only male oppression over the centuries had "confined" women to the domestic sphere. What radical feminism essentially did was to deny complementarity between the sexes and set men and women up as competing teams playing exactly the same game, but a game in which all the rules were stacked against the women. It was only on this eccentric assumption—i.e., that women had identical talents and inclinations to men—that they could support the conclusion that there had been foul play. As with Hitler's appeal to the Aryan race, the basic principle was one of flattery: women, it revealed, are a marvelously talented set of people who have been iniquitously suppressed by males running a patriarchal system.

This message entrenched identity politics, an emerging form of fundamentalism in which every judgment must begin from a supposedly essential self-identity as female. One implication (as with Marxism) was that a class of experts understood social reality better than any particular woman could, and any woman failing to agree needed the falsity of her consciousness corrected. Joined together, these judgments constituted the new doctrine now simply called "feminism." This was a massive psychic transformation in the life of European peoples. Back in the Second World War, Rosie the riveter was certainly a woman, but she was also a wife, a patriotic American involved in a struggle against fascism, and many other things besides. Most fundamentally of all, radical feminism attacked the very conception of the feminine as something that had been imposed upon women by superior force and had been reinforced by a culture of romance found in European art and literature.

All of this might be construed (as it was by radical feminists themselves) as a massive access of confidence among women, but it might also signify a complete collapse of the feminine in the face of a wider and more ambiguous project using women to create a totally androgynous (and manipulable) world. In such a world, men and women would become virtually indistinguishable.

Here then was nothing less than an attempt to destroy not merely an existing structure of power, but also the civilization that it sustained. In Ibn Khaldun's terms, it was an attempt to conquer the West from within, not by directly attacking its power (for no one doubted that the men had all the power needed to repel such an attack), but by exploiting certain features in its culture. And in order to understand the significance of this movement, we need to characterize the European civilization that was the object of their attack.

The most obvious fact about it is one that we can hardly mention, now that the revolution has succeeded, without embarrassment or derision, because it is a fact which powerful contemporary forces make recessive. It is simply that this civilization is, in the crude terms of creative hits, the achievement of white males. The history of Western civilization is a succession of clever men developing the set of traditions or inventing the benefits which, intertwined, constitute the West. And from Thales and Euclid to Einstein and George Gershwin, nearly all of them were male. They constitute the set of "dead white males" whom the radical revolutionaries in the sub-academic culture have denigrated and vowed to remove from their pedestals. I once heard a feminist put it this way: "There's no such thing as a great mind." This doctrine is so powerful that the simple factual statement that it has been men who have created what is commonly meant by Western (and for that matter, any other) civilization seems like an insensitive affront to the equality of mankind. And the next step in my argument must be to deal with this as a problem.

To say that men created all these things is true, and significant, but it is rather like stranding a lot of fish on a barren shore. It leaves out the medium of social and political life without which none of this could have happened. Like all social life, Europe was a world of sexual complementarity, and there is no reliable way of sifting out what was contributory from what was not. But of women we may say what Falstaff said of himself—namely that he not only had wit but also was a cause of wit in others. But by seeming to set women up as a weak team in relation to inventive men, I am merely pointing to the mistake radical feminists, who have accepted the abstract idea that the one thing that counts is who invented this or created that, themselves make. It is in pursuit of this mistake that they have attempted to set up a competing canon of writers, philosophers, painters, and so on whose talents were suppressed by the patriarchy. These resuscitated figures are often worth looking at in their own terms, but they cannot serve as a new canon. Camille Paglia famously said that if we had waited for women to invent civilization we should still be living in grass huts. It is also true that if we had waited for men to make life comfortable we should still be living in pigsties. For centuries women have determined the way we live. Radical feminist doctrine is that this is not enough: women can only be recognized as equal, and enjoy equality of esteem with men, if they are recognized as excelling in exactly the same activities as men. Women must, as a team, be able to point to a scoreboard of artistic and technological achievements on the same scale as men. Feminist tribal consciousness depends upon absorbing this and similar beliefs. But the whole rigmarole depends upon assuming that women are the same as men, that their happiness is found in exactly the same areas as that of men. But this is quite untrue, and it is a mistake that could only have occurred to a set of women whose minds had been deranged by a superficial contact with education in the humanities.

The point can be put another way: Western civilization is distinguished by an unusual curiosity about both nature and the lives of other societies. Europeans have appropriated many of their ideas and inventions from other civilizations. Partly for this reason, it has been extraordinarily open to others who wish to engage in its activities. Its religion, its languages, and its knowledge have been widely diffused, and by the twentieth century people from all over the world had become scientists, historians, novelists, artists, etc., in the Western manner, many of them indeed coming to live in the West. Some people from customary societies abroad have found Westerners cold and remote, but many more have experienced the West as a liberation.

The same is true for women. At various times in the past many women have had access to education, and, from the eighteenth century onwards, some women developed an increasing taste for taking up professions previously restricted to men. By the late nineteenth century they were making their way into universities. In doing so, they often suffered a certain derision from the more brutish among their male confrères. Other men were always on their side, however, and during the first half of the twentieth century women broke into many fields previously restricted by convention. Radical feminism as a tribal consciousness needs to tell this story as a struggle against oppression, and so in some ways it was. But we ought not to get this out of proportion. We are not talking of slavery or war.

The beneficiaries of this new development were for the most part middle-class white women, and they were merely experiencing the resistance common to any form of upward mobility. They were unmistakably following a rising wave created by the increasing flexibility of Western societies. It was in any case a Christian civilization, which meant that individual character counted as much as customary status. In most civilizations, human beings fit into a customary schema as warriors, wives, priests, scholars, artisans, merchants, and so on. The West became, as Ernest Gellner used to put it, "modular" in that individuals have multiple talents and skills and can fit together with others in flexible ways responding to new situations. Like furniture that can be rearranged at need, Europeans have the versatility to fit into many possible arrangements of work or pleasure. As women began to develop a taste for education and had opportunities to participate in a world beyond the domestic (previously available only to the rich), they soon succeeded (as they usually do) in getting what they wanted. Liberal feminism was thus a natural development from within the civilization. Suddenly in the 1960s, this development was overridden by the new radical doctrine that women could and should do everything men did. Liberal feminism emerged from the Western tradition, and traditions are flexible. It had no problem in admitting women to new professions without dramatically altering the wider relations between the sexes. But, radical feminism was doctrinaire and demanded that all women should live in the one true manner. A melodrama of oppression was needed to fire up the new tribe. Just as Buddhist priests must meditate on a human skull so that they will develop the right consciousness of human mortality, so feminist doctrine thrives on horror stories of women not allowed to take degrees at Oxbridge until this century. By contrast with the horrors of the twentieth century (or indeed the situation of women elsewhere in the world), we may diagnose a certain lack of proportion.

The openness of Western cultures is shown by the way in which, during the first half of the twentieth century, Western women were enjoying higher education and finding distinction in professional and academic fields. The numbers of women who largely devoted their lives to these fields was relatively small, and some people thought this was a problem, but it was only a problem for those who took their bearings from statistics rather than from the responses of actual people. The false assumption of male and female isomorphism is, however, the reason why at frequent intervals feminists in journalism become lobbyists and set up, as a defect in society, any difference in average wages between men and women or in the relative percentages of women in top jobs.

This was the continual drip of the movement against patriarchy, and it is a well-known principle of propaganda that a proposition repeated enough will crush opposition. But these figures and this argument make no rational sense, and the fact that they appear regularly in newspapers as if they did make sense is why they must be challenged.

The key to modern Western civilization is its openness to talent wherever found. The feminist demand for collective quotas has overturned this basic feature of our civilization. The crucial point is that the character of a civilization is revealed by its understanding of achievement. European civilization responded to achievement wherever it could be found. To replace achievement by quota entitlements is to destroy one civilization from within and to replace it with another. We are no longer what we were. The problem is to explain how the West collapsed.

It did not result from warriors storming the walls of a decadent civilization, but by a fifth column exploiting weakness from within. And the weapon of attack was not the sword, but a moral rhetoric demanding justice. Economic and political implications (such as that able men would be denied jobs now having to be filled by quota) seldom featured in discussion. The defenders of the status quo found themselves profoundly confused, partly because they had earlier acquiesced in regarding moral and religious ideas as merely subjective. They could not agree on a line of defense, and the attack often came from within their own families. The objective of the attack was to get women with degrees into the higher ranks of the labor force. Of the more profound implications of this structural collapse, I am not concerned here. I must concentrate on the more pressing question of why the defenders so easily capitulated.

In earlier centuries, the project of getting women into the labor force would have been visionary, partly no doubt because no one thought in terms of a labor force. For one thing, women were necessary to keep the home fires burning. In any case, the world of work outside the hearth was hardly inviting. Ploughing the land required relentless physical input beyond the strength of most women; nor were they keen to exercise the broadsword. And, during a longish stretch of life, women would have their hands full with bearing and nurturing children.

In the modern world, however, getting women out of the home and into work was not at all visionary, since the thing called "work" was now largely done in centrally heated offices in front of a computer. In the push-button world men had created, physical strength was hardly ever needed, especially in the more attractive jobs. Work had been the curse of Adam, parallel with childbirth as the curse of Eve, but work now turned out to be a rather agreeable shuffling of symbols in an office full of friendship and event. It was not difficult to present this kind of work—the kind that interested the humanities graduates who largely fuelled the radical movement—as a liberation from the confinement of family life and the tedious babble of the toddler. And it fitted into a wider socialist notion that a person's value was the contribution made to the welfare of others. It had been an old dream of Zionist socialists and Bolsheviks (among others) to absorb the family into society with everyone living communally, restaurants and daycare centers replacing family arrangements, and women working each day alongside the men. Here this dream was reborn, no longer as an aspect of utopia, but as the final achievement of justice against an oppressive world.

Let us now turn to the nub of this question: why did the insurrection succeed? There was no question of the insurgents disposing of superior firepower or warrior virtues, though the tribe of radical feminists certainly displayed intrepidity of the first order. Indeed, the key point is that it was their very weakness that was the condition of their success. Even the fact that, intellectually speaking, radical feminism had nothing to say that had not been said by earlier forms of social perfectionism merely meant that the opposition had already been softened up for victimological attack. And for all the indignation about oppression, radical feminists were less a moral force than a naked interest, demanding jobs for their members, jobs carrying the same salaries and status as men. It was even commonly admitted that outstanding women had not in recent times had much trouble making their way in the academic and workaday world. The issue was to get women of merely average abilities into these positions.

In principle, the men held all the cards. They were the managers, the rulers, the professors, and the directors of enterprises. And they were the trustees of the one thing on which their civilization depended: namely, the career open to talent. No doubt there were times where prejudice prevented women from getting such and such a job, but hiring able women was something managers had long been doing. For in the early twentieth century, women resembled Jews: some people might not want to hire them but the failure to recognize ability would soon be punished by competitors stealing an advantage. These considerations soon ceased to apply once radical feminism has established the basic idea (always denied) that the program was to establish a 50 percent quota for women in all desirable jobs.

We may understand what happened by considering a similar assault on tradition mounted about the same time as the radical feminist challenge. In the 1960s the universities of the Western world were shaken by enemies who turned academic self-understanding against itself. Universities were commonly recognized as communities of scholars and students. "Well," said the radicals, "if it's a community, why are we students left out in the cold, with no power on university committees? Why are we not consulted about the content of our curricula? Why are we subject to god-professors imposing on us courses of study irrelevant to our needs?" Dazed and confused by these questions, which were often expressed (as is the technique) with almost samurai displays of fearsome aggression, the dons yielded. They betrayed their trust in the scholarly vocation partly from confusion and partly in order to avoid unpleasantness.

This example not only illuminates the success of radical feminism, but also reveals something of the long-term significance of these massive shifts of power. For the real threat to universities came not from students but from government. Students were a minor irritant in academic life, but governments were now bent on destroying the autonomy of the institutions of civil society. Students merely functioned as their fifth column. They had the effect of forcing universities even more into a public domain. Students wanted the academic to become the political and that was the effect they had. Before 1960 universities largely ran their own affairs. By the beginning of the twenty-first century, they had all succumbed to the state subsidies that destroyed their autonomy.

The success of the radical feminist assault on European civilization operated in a parallel fashion. "You say you believe in equal opportunities for women, but why are there no women in management, or as bishops, or as professors, or heads of big corporations?" "Why are women paid on average only x percent of what men get paid?" The real answers to these questions would take one deep into the role and structure of the traditional family, the difference between the things that make men and women happy, and the different relative suitability of men and women for different tasks. And such real answers would obviously have to dissolve the rather gross distinction between "men" and "women" in order to recognize that, over a wide range of activities, especially activities such as those of management, it was the individual that counted, not what in technical femspeak is called "gender."

Any recognition of these complexities dissolved before the fact that the questions being asked were rhetorical. In fact, as with student radicals, they were not questions at all, but slogans masquerading as questions. These pseudo-questions set the agenda, and the only admissible answers would be the dogmas of the doctrine: Only patriarchal oppression prevented men and women being equally represented in "positions of power."

The politics of this assault were clear enough, and they illustrate what Mancur Olsen diagnosed as the Achilles heel of democracy: that a small group passionately campaigning for specific benefits will always prevail against a large majority whose direct interests are but marginally affected. Radical feminists were a relatively small group, but their message was plausible at some level to most women, and in families men had wives and daughters whose good they wished to promote. No political party would take up all of this program, but it did electoral prospects no harm to convey a general sympathy for the cause, and once in government enthusiasts would advance legislation under the motherhood slogan of equal opportunity. Very soon a network of powerful bureaucracies was bringing radical doctrine to bear on all areas of government. The courts could be relied upon to extend their power by regulating contract and by extending the law of tort. Within a generation, the revolution had not only succeeded but also created throughout Western nations an occupying army of equal opportunity officers entrenched in personnel departments up and down the country.

And why not? It might well be demanded. Many women have great abilities and a modern society ought not to abide by conventions which may have been necessary in the past but which progress had made unnecessary. The most successful societies have been those in which women have been freest to participate widely. All of that is true and was already recognized in the advance of liberal feminism before the 1960s. The problem only arises with female quotas throughout the world of work.

In a few significant areas, however, no such demands are made. These areas are either where women graduates have no wish to go (rough outdoor work) or where lack of ability could lead to instant disaster, such as brain surgery or piloting commercial aircraft. Women are to be found in both, but only on the basis of ability. Universities are obviously a soft touch because the consequences of educational betrayal take decades to emerge. The effect of university quotas for "gender diversity" for example has often been to fill humanities departments with women in order to equalize numbers "distorted" (one might say) by technology and the hard sciences where even passably able women are hard to come by. Many women in the humanities departments are indeed very able, but many are not, and they have often prospered by setting up fanciful ideological courses (especially in women's studies), which can hardly pretend to be academic at all.

What, however, of areas where women are patently unsuited—such as the army, the police force, or firefighting? They have in fact all been under attack because although women are unsuited to the rough work at the bottom, these areas have enviable managerial opportunities higher up. They are one more irresistible gravy train. The firefighting case was dramatized by the New York judicial decision that a test of fitness for the force that nearly all women failed must be discriminatory, and therefore illegal, an extension of the idea of "the rule of law" far beyond any serious meaning. This was the doctrine called "disparate impact." Similar considerations have affected women in the armed forces. Standards of entry have been lowered in order that women may qualify. One argument for so doing is that the rejected tests looked for qualities only rarely needed in the field, and that may indeed be true. Yet, the idea that soldiers are heroic figures doing something that women generally cannot do has forever been part of the self-understanding of men, even those who have never heard a shot fired in anger. A small boy inclined to cry out at the sting of iodine or the prick of an injection might be told "be a soldier." Today according to the feminist doctrine he is more likely to be told to express his feelings.

The assault of women on areas such as the church raises similar issues. In principle there is not the slightest reason why women should not take on a priestly role, and one might indeed suspect that feminists may be right in diagnosing resistance in part to an unhealthy attitude to women on the part of some of the clergy. In a pastoral role, women might well be better than men, as some women are in politics. The problem is that women priests raise very awkward questions of Christian theology. Jesus selected only male disciples. Was the son of God then merely a creature of his own culture? Here most conspicuously the entry of women changes entirely the conception of the activity and not for the better. Female clergy have done little to reverse the current decline of the church. Indeed while women as individuals have often enhanced what they have joined, the entry of women in general has seldom done much for any area previously dominated by men—except, significantly, bureaucracy.

It is the military case that is the most telling. No one doubts the inferiority of women in physical strength and sport. No football team would think of fielding women against a first-class team of men. Yet the governments of Western countries, currently feeling unthreatened by any major military power, are prepared to gamble their security on female warriors. It would not be so serious if female battalions had been formed whose performance in action could over time be tested in real situations without endangering the security of Western countries. But the feminist program is to make the army, like the rest of society, conform to an idea, and the women want to go where the men are, to be fully integrated so that when dirty and unfeminine jobs must be done, there are men to do them. Liberal feminists took the risk of setting up academic colleges of their own, but radical feminists needed to have men around. They wanted to be integrated. And all of this happened not because political wisdom declared it necessary for the defence of the country, nor because the electorates pushed for it, but as the result of agencies setting up legal and bureaucratic strings.

Let us now return to the teasing question of why the male custodians of our civilization sold the pass. Some element of cowardice must certainly be recognized, because the radicals were tribal warriors making ferocious faces and stamping their feet. The defenders were white, male, and middle class, and the radicals had long been engaged in a campaign to erode the morale of each of these abstract categories. They denoted racism, sexism, and elitism respectively. Caricatured in terms of these abstractions, men found it difficult not to be written off as oppressors of women. Again, the defenders were not united. Many had been longstanding advocates of liberal feminism and from confusion believed that radical feminism was merely a rather hysterical version of classical liberalism. Retreat is a notoriously difficult maneuver to control. Each concession could be used to demand further concessions in the name of consistency. Hence the appearance in all English-speaking countries of legislation mandating equal opportunities—and who could possibly be against that? Before long, the movement had taken over the universities, many public bodies, industrial firms and, above all, the media. Quite rapidly, hiring for status-giving jobs requiring degrees had become closely circumscribed by a set of rules. The dogma was that 50 percent of all jobs belonged to women, though the reality of quotas was long denied.

There are, of course, deeper currents. One of them is that men tended to react to radical feminism with a high-minded feeling that nothing but justice, a notoriously fluid idea, should determine public policy. The balancing of justice with power, which constitutes the art of prudence, was being lost. This was a collapse of practical wisdom not difficult to explain. It is a consequence, we may guess, of the collapse of religion in the West. Christianity requires individuals to sacrifice everything for the nicest points of perfection, but it does not require that worldly institutions should do the same. But cocooned as prosperous Westerners so often are from the immediate consequences of folly, and increasingly detached from any profound understanding of the culture that had produced them, the trustees of our civilization have indulged in the most exquisite forms of self-abnegation. They were soon believing, for example, that language itself had rendered women invisible and that justice required the corrective use of the generic feminine. They were no doubt able to indulge such fancies because they had long ago picked up the idea that political correctness was really a bit of a joke, something of no practical significance in the real world. Hardly a week could pass without some piece of politically correct absurdity surfacing and being laughed over and forgotten by the men who had now lost both the will and the capacity to resist.

But beyond lie far deeper currents in Western societies. Just as the ferment in universities led rapidly to the state taking them over, so the ferment of radical feminism carries out the old Bolshevik program of creating a community of homogeneous creatures animated by some single project—in fact, the totalitarianism which, as an external assault on the walls of the West, we thought we had vanquished in battle with external enemies.

My view is, then, that the radical feminist revolution is nothing less than a destruction of our civilization. It has all happened in such a way that people have not yet realized what has happened. And there are some who might say, well, at least it has improved the condition of women. But this, I think, is a mistake. Such a view would accept the initial dichotomy, so fatal to European civilization, that men and women have separate destinies. In fact, of course, they do not. Still, it is no easy business to give an account of quite how they fit together. Indeed, no comprehensive theory of this relationship can be given. But many things we can confidently say. One is that women have specifically feminine qualities of their own which prevent them, as a general rule, from fitting entirely successfully into the structures men have created. No problem, say the radical feminists: let us change the structures! That can indeed be done, but something is lost. The point is that "men" put "women" (if we may generalize wildly) on a pedestal, and also despise them as weak; love and adore them in chivalrous terms, but also tend to oppress them and use them. A parallel ambivalence will be found in the way women treat men. A whole world of games and conventions has grown up around these attitudes, and they look different viewed from the barracks and from the bedroom, in the sitting room or in the shop. Radical feminism is essentially a humorless rationalism which seeks a single right attitude to be imposed on men and women alike.

There is a further point, and a more complex one. European civilization, we might say, has only stayed ahead of the game of world power because it is so remarkably innovative. It lives off ideas. Sometimes academics attempt the paradoxical business of trying to theorize innovation and creativity, but the results are inevitably banal. Creativity is essentially mysterious. Yet every so often, some movement gets into its head the idea that it has cracked the innovation code and found the formula for progress. This is what I am inclined to call the Bolshevik fallacy, because Lenin and his associates actually believed it, and the Soviet Union showed us what happens as a result of such hubris.

But the problem is wider. The whole world is now involved in the business of modernization, which means copying the mode of life constantly being transformed in Europe, and now in America—by white males, now often joined by clever individuals (both men and women) from other parts of the world. Globalization and the computer are the latest of the marvels with which our civilization has astonished the world. The point is that so far, no other civilization has been able to pick up the torch of innovative leadership. It may even be that Europeans themselves have lost the trick, or gone as far as they can go; or it may not. We simply cannot know.

What does seem to be clear, from the record so far, is that women do not have this capacity to innovate. They bring great talents to developing what Thomas Kuhn called "normal science," but they have no record of creating the "paradigm shifts" that lead in new directions. It may be, of course, that as the feminists sometimes claim, this is because they were never encouraged to engage in these activities. But to need encouragement, to depend on models to follow, is precisely not to have a capacity to innovate. It has been men who have invented things and found challenges in nature, such as climbing high mountains or sailing alone around the world. And once men have done it, women will also do it. These remain highly notable enterprises, well beyond the reach of all but a few men, but they also exemplify the fact that innovation remains largely the specialization of white males. Women can do marvellous things with a house, but they do need the house to be there in the first place.

My argument is, then, that European civilization has been attacked and conquered from within, without anyone quite realizing what has happened. We may laugh at political correctness—some people even deny that it exists—but it is a manacle around our hands. It binds us quite tightly, though some freedom must be left, because without the contribution of subjugated males, things would very rapidly decline. What political correctness amounts to in reality is a treaty of accommodation reached between the conquerors and the conquered. Women have forced their way into money and status, sometimes beyond their merits, but they have also lost a freedom (Professor Schaub calls it "leisure") that might have saved them from being formularized in terms of contemporary Western styles of work. Had this not happened, we might well have been saved from some of the discontents that currently afflict us. To be "socially included," as women have been in the workforce, has many practical advantages, but it involves a spiritual loss. So far the conquerors have not destroyed the geese that lay the golden eggs, so the surface of our civilization does not reveal how profound the change has been. But underneath that surface, there are currents which no one understands.

There has been a revolution, then, but a silent one. It has taken place with such stealth, and so gradually, that people have become accustomed to it little by little. I am reminded of the famous Chinese executioner whose ambition it was to be able to cut off a head so that the victim would not realize what had happened. For years he worked on his skill, and one day he cut off a head so perfectly that the victim said: "Well, when are you going to do it?" The executioner gave a beatific smile and said: "Just kindly nod."

ABOUT THE CONTRIBUTORS

CHRISTOPHER CALDWELL is a senior editor at the *Weekly Standard*. He writes a weekly Washington column for the *New York Press*. His articles appear in the *Atlantic Monthly, National Review*, the *New York Observer, Slate*, the *Spectator* (London), the *Wall Street Journal*, and other publications.

CHRISTOPHER HITCHENS is a contributing editor for *Vanity Fair* and a columnist for the *Nation*. He has also contributed to dozens of international periodicals, including *Harper's*, the *New York Review of Books*, and the *Guardian* (UK). He has written several books, including *The Trial of Henry Kissinger* and most recently, *Why Orwell Matters*.

KENNETH ANDERSON is professor of law at American University's Washington College of Law. He frequently writes for the *Times Literary Supplement*, and has published numerous articles in scholarly journals and other periodicals. He wrote several human rights reports during his tenure as Director of the Human Rights Watch Arms Division, and acted as the legal editor for the book *Crimes of War*.

MARSHALL BERMAN teaches at CUNY in New York, is on the editorial board of Dissent, and contributes to the *Nation*. He is the author of *All That Is Solid Melts Into Air* and *Adventures in Marxism*.

DAVID BROOKS is the author of *Bobos in Paradise*. He is a senior editor for the *Weekly Standard* and a correspondent for the *Atlantic Monthly*.

PATRICK H. CADDELL served as a pollster and strategist in the presidential campaigns of George McGovern, Jimmy Carter, Gary Hart and Walter Mondale.

TUCKER CARLSON is a political analyst for CNN and a co-host of *Cross-

fire. He also writes the national affairs column for New York and is a contributing editor to the *Weekly Standard.*

ANDREW COHEN has written for the *Guardian, Village Voice,* the *Nation,* and other publications.

PETER COLLIER is the Publisher of Encounter Books. He has jointly written several books with David Horowitz, including *The Kennedy's: An American Dream and Destructive Generation.*

MARC COOPER is a contributing editor of the *Nation* and a columnist for *LA Weekly.*

RUTH CONNIFF is the Washington Editor for the *Progressive.* Her articles have also appeared in the *New York Times,* the *Washington Post* and other major newspapers.

CHRISTOPHER D. COOK is an award-winning investigative journalist who writes widely on agribusiness, labor, and welfare among other issues. He has written for *Harper's Magazine, The Nation, Mother Jones,* the *Progressive,* the *Economist* and *The Christian Science Monitor.* He has also worked as new editor for the San Francisco Bay *Guardian.*

ANNE-MARIE CUSAC is Managing Editor of the *Progressive.* She has won a George Polk Award and a Project Censored Award for her investigative reportage on prison conditions.

BENJAMIN DEMOTT is Emeritus Professor of English at Amherst College and most recently published *Killer Woman Blues: Why Americans Can't Think Straight about Gender and Power.*

ERICH EICHMAN is the books editor for the *Wall Street Journal.*

ANDREW FERGUSON is a national affairs columnist for *Bloomberg News.*

Thomas Fleming is President of The Rockford Institute and Editor of its publication, *Chronicles: A Magazine of American Culture,* for which he writes a regular column called "Hard Right."

Thomas Frank, a founding editor of *The Baffler,* is the author of *The Conquest of Cool* and *One Market Under God.*

Charles Paul Freund is a senior editor of *Reason,* and has written extensively on the political manipulation of culture. His has written for several major periodicals, including the *Washington Post, Film Comment, The Columbia Journalism Review,* and the *New York Times.*

Thomas Geoghegan, a labor lawyer, is the author of *Which Side Are You On?,* and most recently, *In America's Court: How a Civil Lawyer Who Likes to Settle Stumbled into a Criminal Trial.*

Philip Green is on the editorial board of the *Nation* and has written for the *New York Times Magazine, Dissent,* and the *American Political Science Review,* among others. He is a visiting professor of graduate political science at The New School.

Nat Hentoff, a weekly columnist for the *Village Voice* for over 30 years, has written scores of articles on politics, focusing on the First Amendment and other areas of the constitution. He is the author of over a dozen books, including most recently *The Nat Hentoff Reader.*

Bill Kauffman is associate editor for the *American Enterprise Magazine.* He has written for several magazines and newspapers, and has published four books, including *America First!: Its History, Culture and Politics,* and *With Good Intentions?: Reflections on the Myth of Progress in America.*

Tony Kushner is a playwright. His work, *Angels in America,* earned him a Pulitzer Prize and two Tony Awards.

MARK LILLA is Professor at the Committee on Social Thought at the University of Chicago. He is the author of *G.B. Vico: The Making of an Anti-Modern*, *The Reckless Mind: Intellectuals in Politics*, and the editor of *New French Thought: Political Philosophy*.

TOD LINDBERG is research fellow at the Hoover Institution and editor of *Policy Review*. His work as also appeared in Commentary, *National Review* and the *Wall Street Journal*, among others.

KENNETH MINOGUE is Emeritus Professor of political science at the London School of Economics, and author of *A Very Short Introduction to Politics* and *Alien Powers: The Pure Theory of Ideology*.

JOHN O'SULLIVAN is editor-in-chief of *United Press International* and Editor-at-Large for the *National Review*. He has written for several major international publications, including the *New York Times*, the *National Interest*, and the *Washington Post*. He previously served as special advisor to Margaret Thatcher.

JONATHAN RAUCH, a senior writer for the *National Journal* and correspondent for the *Atlantic Monthly*, is the author of *Kindly Inquisitors: The New Attacks on Free Thought* and *Demosclerosis: The Silent Killer of American Government*.

ADOLPH REED JR., an expert of race and the construction of racial identities, has written several books, including *Stirrings in the Jug: Black Politics in the Post-Segregation Era* and *W.E.B. Du Bois and American Political Thought: Fabianism and the Color Line*. He is currently a professor of Political Science at New School University.

DAVID RIEFF is the author of several books, including, *Slaughterhouse: Bosnia and the Failure of the West*, and most recently, *A Bed for the Night: Humanitarianism in Crisis*.

ARUNDHATI ROY was trained as an architect. Her first novel, *The God of Small Things,* won the Booker Prize.

JONATHAN SCHELL teaches at Wesleyan University and the New School University. A Fellow at the Nation Institute, and co-founder of a recently formed citizen's initiative to negotiate the abolition of nuclear weapons, he is the author of nine books including *Fate of the Earth,* which was published in twenty countries.

SUSAN SONTAG has written novels, stories, essays, and plays; directed films; and worked as a theater director in the United States and Europe. In 2001 she was awarded the Jerusalem Prize. Her most recent books are the novel *In America,* which won the 2000 National Book Award for Fiction, and a collection of essays, *Where the Stress Falls.*

ANDREW SULLIVAN, currently a columnist for the *Sunday Times* (London), has written extensively on politics and homosexuality. He was the editor of the *New Republic* for five years, and has written frequently for numerous magazines and newspapers, including the *New York Times Magazine,* and his own website, *andrewsullivan.com.* He is the author of two books, *Virtually Normal* and *Love Undetectable.*

DAVID TELL is the opinion editor for the *Weekly Standard.*

JAMES WEINSTEIN is the author of *The Decline of Socialism in America, 1912-1925* and the founding editor of *In These Times.* His latest book, *The Long Detour,* will be published in 2003 by Westview Press.

RUTH R. WISSE is professor of Yiddish and comparative literature at Harvard University, and the author of *The Modern Jewish Canon* and *If I am Not Myself. . . . : The Liberal Betrayal of the Jews.*

PERMISSIONS

We gratefully acknowledge all those who gave permission for written material to appear in this book. We have made every effort to trace and contact copyright holders. If an error or omission is brought to our notice we will be pleased to remedy the situation in future editions of this book. For further information, please contact the publisher.

Left Hooks
Nat Hentoff, "Hurt Feelings and Free Speech", reprinted by permission of the author © 1992 Nat Hentoff; Ruth Conniff, "Colombia's Dirty War, Washington's Dirty Hands" reprinted by permission of *The Progressive,* © 1992 *The Progressive;* Philip Green, "A Few Kind Words For Liberalism", reprinted by permission of *The Nation,* © 1992 *The Nation;* Andrew Cohen, "Me and My Zeitgeist", reprinted by permission of *The Nation* © 1993 *The Nation;* Tony Kushner, "A Socialism of the Skin", reprinted by permission of *The Nation* © 1994 *The Nation;* Adolph Reed Jr., "Looking Backward", reprinted by permission of *The Nation* © 1994 *The Nation;* Adolph Reed Jr., "Martyrs and False Prophets", reprinted with permission of *The Progressive* © 1995 *The Progressive;* Thomas Frank, "Dark Age", reprinted with the permission of the publisher © 1995 *The Baffler;* Susan Sontag "A Lament for Bosnia", © 1995 by Susan Sontag. Reprinted with permission of The Wylie Agency, Inc. Anne-Marie Cusac, "Life in Prison", reprinted by permission of *The Progressive* © 1996 *The Progressive;* Thomas Geoghegan, "Child Labor in the 1990s", © 1996 by the New York Times Co. Reprinted by permission; Benjamin DeMott, "Seduced by Civility", reprinted by permission of *The Nation* © 1996 *The Nation;* Marshall Berman, "Unchained Melody", reprinted by permission of *The Nation* © 1998 *The Nation;* Christopher D. Cook, "Plucking Workers", reprinted by permission of the author © 1998 Christopher D. Cook; Arundhati Roy, "The End of Imagination", from *The Cost of Living* © 1999 by Arundhati Roy. Used by permission of Random House Inc. Patrick H. Caddell & Marc Cooper, "The Death of Liberal Outrage",